John Donne: Life, Mind and Art

John Donne
Life, Mind and Art

JOHN CAREY

New York
OXFORD UNIVERSITY PRESS
1981

Printed in the United States of America

to Gill
Leo and
Thomas

Contents

Author's Note

I should like to record my gratitude to Dame Helen Gardner, with whom, some years ago, I studied Donne as a graduate student, and from whose generosity and guidance I have inestimably benefited; to Robert Ellrodt, whose *Les Poètes métaphysiques anglais* has been an inspiration to me; and to Elsie Duncan-Jones, who put her formidable knowledge of seventeenth-century literature at my disposal by kindly reading through the typescript of this book, and offering useful suggestions.

The notes will be found at the end of the book, and are identified by key numbers in the text.

J.C.

Merton College, Oxford
February 1980

Introduction

Donne's contemporaries recognized him as a totally original and matchless poet. He was 'Copernicus in Poetrie': greater than Virgil, Lucan and Tasso put together.[1] Even embittered traditionalists, who found Donne upsetting, acknowledged his revolutionary impetus. William Drummond, the Scots poet, evidently had Donne in mind when he complained about 'transformers of everything' who had destroyed the 'ornaments' of poetry and replaced them with 'metaphysical ideas'.[2] Donne's uniqueness has, it's true, been sometimes questioned. Dr. Johnson alleged that he had borrowed from Marino, and some modern critics, improving on this hint, have striven to confuse his poetry with baroque architecture, mannerist painting, *gongorismo*, *preciosité*, Euphuism, and other late-Renaissance developments. Such theories depend for their credibility on vagueness and muddle, and they quickly evaporate under analysis. Marino's poetry, for instance, examined alongside Donne's, has been shown to differ from it in every important respect.[3] But if, like his contemporaries, we accept that Donne was unique, we still need to explore, before we can understand him, the structure of his imagination and see what makes it individual. That is the aim of this book.

It will not do to ignore Donne's limitations, for they are part of his peculiar excellence. Ben Jonson thought him 'the first poet in the World in some things',[4] and the things he is by no means first in have often been accusingly listed. His poems lack colour and music. We don't go to him for flowers, pastoral, myth, warm humour or serene joy. He is not tranquil and sustaining like, say, Matthew Arnold, nor does he love the English countryside. He complained, on the contrary, of its 'barbarousness and insipid dulness'.[5] These shortcomings, together with the suspicion that his love poetry would have embarrassed Juliet or Perdita, have earned him the disapproval of C. S. Lewis,[6] among others.

In some respects, Donne isn't a love poet at all. The physical characteristics of the girl he's supposed to be talking to don't concern him. Nor does her personality: it is completely obliterated by Donne's. He doesn't even seem to feel sexually excited. As sensualists the Victorian poets far outclass him. Take Browning, for instance:

> There you stand,
> Warm too, and white too: would this wine
> Had washed all over that body of yours
> Ere I drank it.[7]

Donne never rises to single-minded lust like that, though other poets in his day managed it. Barnabe Barnes wished he could turn into the wine trickling down his girl's throat.[8] Campion jocularly retorted that he'd come out at the other end as her urine,[9] but as Barnes's poem shows he'd already thought of that, and found it a ravishingly intimate prospect. He makes us feel, like Browning, what it means to ache for female flesh. Donne does not.

The unusualness of Donne's poetry was quite apparent to Donne. He admitted he was 'startling',[10] but stuck defiantly to his own rhythms and perspectives. 'I sing not, Siren-like, to tempt; for I / Am harsh',[11] he informed his friend Samuel Brooke. He took a disdainful view of what other poets were doing, criticizing their hackneyed nature imagery in a verse letter to the Countess of Salisbury. Their metaphors, he reports, have made the very sun stale:

> . . . his disshevel'd beames and scatter'd fires
> Serve but for Ladies Periwigs and Tyres
> In lovers Sonnets.[12]

Typically, Donne renovates the tired poeticism even as he throws it aside. His word 'disshevel'd' creates a confusion of fiery tresses, and it was three centuries before Yeats awakened the image again with his 'dishevelled wandering stars'.[13] Surveying current literature, Donne evidently felt, too, that the Elizabethan fashion for chivalric romance, which engendered Spenser's *Faerie Queene*, was absurd. In his 'Essay of Valour' he makes comic capital out of an imaginary era 'before this age of wit' when there was no known way of winning a lady 'but by Tylting, Turnying, and riding through Forrests'.[14]

In tracing the distinctive structure of Donne's imagination, I shall use the sermons and other prose works as well as the poems. It's often assumed that early and late Donne, poet and preacher, were different people. Donne, as he grew older, wanted to believe this, and talked as if he did, which is how the illusion got about. Sending *Biathanatos* to Sir Robert Ker, for instance, he stressed that it was 'Jack Donne' not 'Dr. Donne' who wrote it.[15] But there weren't two people. The more we read the poems and sermons the more we can see them as fabrics of the same mind, controlled by similar imaginative needs.

That's not to deny that Donne changed. At the level of opinions and social attitudes he clearly changed a great deal. He grew repressive, as people generally do with age and success. 'Lascivious discourses' and satires, such as he had written when young, were, he came to believe, instruments of the devil.[16] The poet of 'Going to Bed', having entered the pulpit, became a devout advocate of virginity. Sexual intercourse, even in marriage, is, he admonishes, gravely suspect.[17] The poet of Satire III, who had pleaded the individual's need and right to search for the true religion irrespective of kings and governments, insists after taking orders that every subject must remain in the church in which he has been baptized, and that kings and governments are perfectly justified in compelling him to do so by 'pecuniary and bloudy Laws'.[18]

But to express this new opinion Donne, significantly enough, uses the image he had used to express its contrary. Satire III imagines Truth standing eminent 'On a huge hill',[19] and in a sermon of 1622 Donne maintains that the Church of England stands on 'such a Hill, as may be seene every where'.[20] The implications Donne draws from his two hills are contradictory. In the satire he argued that, since Truth was on a hill, it was necessary to take a circuitous route, investigating the claims of different churches, before reaching it. In the sermon his point is that the true church's hill site allows it to be seen unmistakably from all sides, so there is no need to investigate the claims of different churches. Donne's argument is a reversible coating, but the imaginative kernel remains constant: the simplified, surreal landscape, void except for one looming feature. This landscape is recurrent in Donne. Its starkest appearance comes in that weirdly lit nightmare which the waking girl describes to her nurse in 'On his Mistris':

> oh, oh,
> Nurse, oh my love is slaine; I saw him goe
> Ore the white Alpes, alone.[21]

If, reading Donne, we watch the shaping imagination instead of the transient opinions, we shall find this appearance of the same lonely crag in different settings quite unsurprising. His grasp of the world did not basically change, so his master-images had to be adapted to meet the new subject matter which his career threw in

their way. In 'Loves Progress', for instance, Donne is a celestial
sphere floating up the 'empty and etheriall way' between a girl's legs.
In 'Goodfriday, 1613. Riding Westward' he is a sphere again, but his
orbit takes him past Christ on the cross.[22] Sphere-motion—superior,
mathematical and angelic—satisfied some of his deepest apprehensions, so he found pretexts for writing about it whatever his topic.
The same goes for gold and wombs, which he could seldom stop
thinking about for long. 'Loves Progress' depicts the womb and
'Centrique part' of the girl whom Donne is about to delve into as a
gold mine.[23] A sermon of 1624 shows the Almighty taking the girl's
place. 'Centricall Gold, viscerall Gold, gremiall Gold', Donne
informs his congregation, is 'in the Matrice and womb of God'.[24]
The same sermon makes God into the 'Eastern Hemispheare' of
spices as well as the 'Western Hemispheare' of gold—'both the
India's of spice and Myne',[25] in fact, as Donne's sweet golden girl
had been in 'The Sunne Rising'. The bringing together of east and
west—an idea Donne endlessly nags at—is, we see, like mountains,
spheres, gold and wombs, adaptable to God or girls indiscrimi-
nately.

Perhaps it was awareness of this imaginative continuity in himself
which made Donne notice it in others. He observes in an early
sermon how the prophets and other biblical writers have retained
the metaphors and turns of phrase appropriate to their worldly
jobs.[26] When he preaches, phrases from his love poems keep escaping
from him. The 'midnights startings' of the nightmare-shocked girl
reappear as the 'midnight startlings' of the atheist in God's presence.
The 'rags of time' from 'The Sunne Rising' turn up in contrast with
God's eternity. The transplanted flower which 'Redoubles still, and
multiplies' in 'The Extasie' becomes Lady Danvers who, in Donne's
commemoration sermon for her, 'doubles and multiplies by transplantation' like a flower. The famous compasses of 'A Valediction:
forbidding Mourning', with a firm foot which 'makes me end,
where I begunne', are placed in God's hand in the sermons as the
instrument of his providence: he 'carries his Compasse round, and
shuts up where he began'. In 'Loves Growth' gentle love deeds, like
blossoming trees, 'do bud out now'; in a sermon the trees 'do bud
out' as a symbol of the virgin birth. 'Call not these wrinkles, graves,'
Donne protests in 'The Autumnall'; but from his pulpit he chides
women who fill 'the wrinkles, and graves of their face' with cosmetics.[27] And so on.

Just chance repetitions, of course: the reflex actions of a mind
which spent its whole life making phrases. But they are symptomatic

of continuity in the imaginative processes from which phrases grow. Occasionally in the sermons Donne seems to be reliving a whole poem from his early days:

> God . . . hath often looked upon me in my foulest uncleannesse, and when I had shut out the eye of the day, the Sunne, and the eye of the night, the Taper and the eyes of all the world, with curtaines and windowes and doores, did yet see me, and see me in mercy, by making me see that he saw me.[28]

The God who looks, there, through 'curtaines and windowes' is a more respectful version of the busy old fool who looked 'Through windowes, and through curtaines' at the lovers in 'The Sunne Rising'.

Tracing the reappearance of words and images throughout Donne's work is, the reader will gather, one method this book will adopt in mapping his imagination. Like many writers and artists, he had his obsessive side, so recurrence is common in him, and critics have noted it, though not always intelligently. C. S. Lewis, for instance, takes it as a sign of Donne's limited erudition. 'Some scraps of learning', he comments, 'such as that of angelic consciousness, or of the three souls in man, come rather too often—like soldiers in a stage army'.[29] Crowing over Donne's educational shortcomings would not, however, serve much purpose, even if it were justified. It seems a wiser course to enquire what light his fanatical attachment to certain ideas can throw on his artistic individuality.

The ideas to which he is attached are, like the two Lewis cites, generally of a theological type, which naturally puts some critics off. It's tempting to assume that the worthwhile element in Donne comprises the poems and a few rousing bits from the sermons, and that the rest of his *œuvre* can safely be consigned to the rubbish tip of history. Evelyn Simpson, for instance, who admires Donne as a 'maker of verbal spells', regrets that so much of his time was taken up with 'outworn controversies, and lumber inherited from the Fathers and Schoolmen'.[30] The fact remains, however, that the imagination which wove the spells was identical with the one which found the lumber intriguing. If we can discover why—if we can locate in the lumber the shapes which fascinated Donne, and connect them with his poetic enthusiasms—then we may come to see that the spells weren't random magical happenings but outgrowths of an integrated consciousness.

This critical procedure will, admittedly, entail regarding the doctrines to which Donne attaches himself not as elements of religious truth but, rather, as imaginative choices. But then, that is what religious doctrines are. For their ultimate truth or falsehood cannot be tested, and all the available evidence—such as that of Scripture—is so diversely interpretable that individual decisions in the matter are bound, in the end, to rest on the psychological preferences of the believer (or unbeliever): that is to say, on the structure of his personality and imagination. Viewed in this way, a writer's religious beliefs provide an invaluable guide to the workings of his fancy (as, of course, do his political and moral views, which are based on similarly arbitrary preferences).

All this is perhaps no more than a rephrasing of what T. S. Eliot meant when he said that Donne picked out ideas because he was 'interested in the feeling they give'[31]—only I would argue that what Eliot observes is not an individual aberration on Donne's part but, however we may disguise it from ourselves, the universal practice.

This study will try to show, then, that Donne's opinions upon such furiously controverted issues as original sin, election, resurrection and the state of the soul after death, were generated by recognizably the same imagination as the poems about love and women. They are not dull side-tracks but members of an animated whole in which every part illuminates and is illuminated by every other.

In order to have a sympathetic feeling for Donne's mentality we must learn something about his life and the society he found himself in. My early chapters will supply the basic biographical facts (in so far as they're known), while examining the effects of the two vital factors in his career, his desertion of the Roman Catholic Church and his ambition, on his poetry. Later chapters will look at Donne's response to the physical and organic world, to change, to death, and to human reason. These subjects are chosen because around them his imagination and intellect were at their most active. The last chapter concentrates on Donne's passion for fusion or interpenetration. It comes last because if there is a single, essential quality which makes Donne Donne, this is it.

❧ 1 ❧

Apostasy

The first thing to remember about Donne is that he was a Catholic; the second, that he betrayed his Faith. He was born in 1572. His father was a successful London businessman who rose to be one of the wardens of the Ironmongers' Company.[1] He died when Donne was four, and his widow remarried within six months, taking as her second husband Dr. John Syminges, a wealthy Catholic medical practitioner and President of the Royal College of Physicians.[2] Donne's mother was not only, like his father, a Catholic, but a member of one of the most celebrated Catholic families in the land. She was the youngest daughter of the poet and playwright John Heywood; and Heywood's wife—Donne's grandmother—was Joan Rastell, the niece of Sir Thomas More. So on his mother's side Donne was descended from the More circle, the foremost group of intellectuals in early sixteenth-century England, internationally famous, and devout Catholics. Donne was profoundly aware of this ancestry. When he mentions Sir Thomas More and his 'firmnesse to the integrity of the Romane faith',[3] it is with evident pride.

The disadvantages of being a Catholic in Elizabethan England are difficult to generalize about. On the one hand, as the careers of Donne's father and stepfather suggest, it was possible, if you were sufficiently circumspect or well-connected, to prosper. On the other hand, you might end up having your intestines torn out. Developments in international politics could make your situation suddenly more dangerous, without your taking any step in the matter. You could not, if you remained faithful to your religion, hope to play any part in public life, and you were debarred from taking a university degree by the requirement that graduates should subscribe to the Thirty-nine Articles.

The financial incentives to join the Church of England were strong. By a statute of 1585, Catholics who refused to attend Anglican services were liable to a fine of £20 a month. An average parish schoolmaster's salary at the time, it's worth reminding ourselves, was £20 a year.[4] Offenders who found themselves unable to pay were to have all their goods and two-thirds of their land confiscated. This law, Catholics complained, was so strictly enforced that small farmers and husbandmen who possessed only one cow for the sustenance of themselves and their children had it taken from them, and where there was no livestock to appropriate recusant houses were stripped of bed linen, blankets, provisions and window glass. Cecil, it was rumoured, had boasted that he would reduce the Catholics to such destitution that, like swine, they'd be glad to find a husk to feed on.[5]

The anti-Catholic legislation also made it high treason for any Jesuit or seminary priest to be within the Queen's dominions, and felony for any lay person to relieve or receive him. In effect, this meant that it was felony to practise the Catholic religion, because it was necessary to receive a priest in order to hear mass or make confession. Spies, some of them renegade priests and Catholics, gave the authorities advance warning about where masses were to be celebrated. Catholic households were commonly raided, and in the search for priests' hiding places walls were knocked down, rooms ransacked and floors torn up. The householder had not only to defray the cost of this damage, but also to pay the searchers for their trouble. In their private life, Catholics were inevitably a prey to blackmail and intimidation. They could not claim redress for personal injuries, or retrieve money owed to them. If they attempted to, they found themselves threatened with exposure.

Among the victims of this persecution scares spread rapidly. A report would go round that the Queen's Council had passed a decree for the massacre of all Catholics on a certain night, whereupon terrified families would abandon their homes and pass the night in the fields. Others would hire boats and drift up and down the river. These alarms first occurred in 1585, and persisted until the defeat of the Armada, so they were a feature of Donne's early adolescence. At the same time, new prisons were established at Wisbech, Ely and Reading, and filled with Catholics. A separate prison for women recusants was opened at Hull. In the common prisons, Catholic prisoners were victimized. The felons incarcerated with them were encouraged to abuse them, and deprive them of their share of alms and bread. John Gerard, the English Jesuit, reports that when his manservant was captured and shut up in Bridewell he was given barely sufficient food to keep body and soul together. His cell was tiny, bedless, and crawling with vermin, so that he had to sleep perched on the window ledge. The gaolers left his excrement in the cell in an uncovered pail, and the stink was suffocating. In these conditions he waited to be called out and examined under torture. The poet and martyr Robert Southwell also testifies to the systematic starvation of Catholic prisoners: 'some for famine have licked the very moisture of the walls'.

Some of the tortures employed on Catholic suspects were so vile that Southwell cannot bring himself to speak of them, but the ones he does describe are fearful enough. Prisoners were deprived of sleep, until they lost the use of their reason; they were disjointed on the rack; they were rolled up into balls by machinery 'and soe Crushed, that the bloud sprowted out at divers parts of their bodies'. As the dislocations caused by the rack occasioned some revulsion among the public, Topcliffe, Elizabeth's chief torturer, introduced the refinement known as the manacles. These were iron gauntlets, fitted high up on a pillar. The prisoner who was to be interrogated had his wrists inserted into them, and was left hanging, sometimes for several hours. Gerard, who underwent this torture, includes an account of the procedure in his autobiography, which conveys how oddly decorous the arrangements were. 'We went to the torture room in a kind of solemn procession,' he recalls, 'the attendants walking ahead with lighted candles.' The commission of five who were to question him included Francis Bacon. When Gerard had been suspended from the pillar,

> a gripping pain came over me. It was worst in my chest and belly, my hands and arms. All the blood in my body seemed to rush up into my arms and hands and I thought that blood was oozing out from the ends of my fingers and the pores of my skin. . . . The pain was so intense that I thought I could not possibly endure it.

Gerard endured it, in fact, for five hours, during which period he fainted eight or nine times, and each time was supported until he recovered, and then left to hang again. Since he persistently refused to betray his fellow Catholics, the commissioners grew restless. 'Then hang there until you rot off the pillar,' shouted William Wade, the diplomatist, later knighted by James I. Gerard was suspended the following day also, but after that they realized he wouldn't talk, and gave up. His arms were so swollen he could not get his clothes on, and it was three weeks before he could hold a knife.

The number of Catholics actually executed was, by the standards of twentieth-century atrocities, quite small. Between the passing of the new anti-Catholic legislation in 1585 and the end of Elizabeth's reign, a hundred priests and fifty-three lay persons, including two women, were put to death. The method used to dispatch the victims amounted, however, in many cases to makeshift vivisection, so it atoned in terms of spectator interest for its relative rarity. When the Babington Plot, which had been known about and fomented almost from the first by government agents, was 'discovered' in 1586, instructions, to which the Queen was a party, were given to the hangman that 'for more terror' the young men responsible should be disembowelled alive. This operation apparently upset some of the onlookers, so the government published an official statement saying that the Queen was disgusted too, and had given orders for a more merciful slaughtering of the second batch of conspirators.[6]

It's clear, though, from eye-witness accounts, that vivisection continued to be used as a remedy against Catholics. The fate of John Rigby, killed in 1600 under the Act of Persuasions, which made it high treason to embrace the Roman religion, exemplifies this.[7] After he had been hanged, Rigby was cut down so quickly that he stood upright 'like a man a little amazed' till the executioners threw him to the ground. He was heard to pronounce distinctly, 'God forgive you. Jesus receive my soul', whereupon a bystander put his foot on his throat to prevent him speaking any more. Other bystanders held his arms and legs while an executioner cut off his genitals and took out his bowels. When he reached up inside Rigby to extract his heart, his victim was 'yet so strong that he thrust the men from him who held his arms'.

Confronted with judicial proceedings of this kind, English Catholics felt not only pity and terror, but isolation. Their fellow countrymen were not simply indifferent, they rejoiced at the Catholics' discomfiture. 'In the midst of our calamaties,' the English Jesuit William Weston recalls, writing of the Babington executions, 'the bells were rung throughout the city, sermons and festivals held, fireworks set off, bonfires lit in the public street'. The beleaguered minority could be excused for feeling that they were among not human beings but some species of jubilant demon.

Some readers may ask what all this has to do with Donne's poetry, but I imagine they will be few. It would be as reasonable to demand what the Nazi persecution of the Jews had to do with a young Jewish writer in Germany in the 1930s. Donne was born into a terror, and formed by it. It determined, among other things, his reading matter, which wasn't that of an Englishman but of a European intellectual. He remained aloof from the flood of patriotic English literature which was being loosed on the market in the 1590s. On the other hand, he was one of the few Englishmen of his day to know Dante in the original; he had read Rabelais; and when a correspondent asked him about Aretino—a writer of scandalous repute, scarcely whispered about in conservative English circles—Donne was able to give him an expert run-down of Aretino's works.[8] As for the English people, Donne's account of them in his earliest poems, the *Satires* and *Elegies*, quivers with disgust. They are coarse-grained, narrow-minded materialists: smug burghers with stinking feet and breath and swollen bellies, who stuff themselves with rich foodstuffs and then snore their evenings away crammed into armchairs. Donne, in the *Elegies*, defiantly cheats and cuckolds these lumbering freaks.[9] He survives on the fringes of society, a master of back stairs and side alleys, hard-up, outcast, victorious. It was a fantasy life which had magnetic appeal for a young man who could see that English society had closed its ranks against those of his Faith. Donne's fastidious withdrawal from the great mass of English people is reflected, too, in the style of his poems. Superior, difficult, designed for circulation among a few kindred spirits, they make no concessions to the barbarous clods and half-wits he had the ill luck to be living among. Most clearly of all, Donne's intractable egotism and his determination to succeed (factors which, as we shall see, mark the poems indelibly, and which some critics have censured) were a perfectly natural reaction to his early experience of injustice and victimization.

Because of his family connections, Donne was dragged into the very centre of the storm, and was forced to watch its bloody course with the closest attention. The victims were among the most gifted and intrepid of England's youth: young men like Edmund Campion, executed in 1581, who had been sent to the Catholic colleges abroad for their education, and who returned on their suicidal missions, joyfully embracing martyrdom to save their motherland from Antichrist. We know that Donne attended such executions. He records that he has seen Catholic bystanders, oblivious of their own danger, praying to the priest's mangled body, in hope that the new martyr would take their petitions to heaven with him.[10]

Possibly young Donne witnessed these sights while in the care of the Catholic tutors whom his mother employed to educate him. Their purpose would be to arouse in the boy a spirit of emulation, for martyrdom was in his family and it might justifiably be hoped that, with careful indoctrination and God's grace, he would join the glorious company himself. Nor were their efforts vain. The martyr's crown shone before their pupil's eyes. He dwelt tirelessly upon it, and came to regard it almost as part of his inheritance. 'I have beene ever kept awake', Donne tells us, in a meditation of Martyrdome, by being derived from such a stocke and race, as, I beleeve, no family, (which is not of farre larger extent, and greater branches,) hath endured and suffered more in their persons and fortunes, for obeying the Teachers of Romane Doctrine, then it hath done.

Donne's account of his family's sufferings is scarcely exaggerated. John Heywood, his grandfather, fled abroad in 1564 rather than accept Anglicanism. Ten years later, on Palm Sunday 1574, when Donne was two, government searchers descended upon Lady Brown's house in Cow Lane, near the Donne home, and made a catch: Thomas Heywood, formerly a monk of St. Osyth's and Mrs. Donne's uncle, was arrested. On 14 June he was put to death in the usual obscene manner.[11] Two of Donne's uncles, Ellis and Jasper Heywood, became Jesuits.[12] For Jasper it meant throwing up a promising career. He had been a page to the then Princess Elizabeth, and a fellow of Merton and All Souls. Like other members of his family, he venerated the memory of Sir Thomas More. Apparently Ellis and Jasper possessed a precious relic, one of More's teeth, which miraculously parted in two so that each of them could have half. After taking Jesuit vows in Rome, Jasper illegally re-entered England and became head of the Jesuit mission. It seems likely that he took refuge in the Donne house for a while. Certainly he made contact with his sister, Donne's mother. So the children found themselves in the middle of a real-life adventure story. It was no game. In 1583 Jasper was hunted down. He had been trying to escape across the Channel, but his boat ran into a storm. He was rapidly put on trail with five other priests, found guilty of high treason, and condemned to be hanged, drawn and quartered. While Jasper was in the Tower, Donne's mother visited and nursed him, secretly carrying messages between him and his fellow Jesuit, William Weston, who had come over to carry on the fight. Eventually Weston took the immense risk of going into the Tower with her on one of her visits, so that he could consult with the prisoner. Donne, though only twelve, was selected to play a part in this escapade, and taken along too. Perhaps Mrs. Donne calculated that having a boy there would allay the warders' suspicions. The disguised Weston might even be passed off as the lad's father. Anyway, it seems clear that Donne went, because he later recalls being present at 'a Consultation of Jesuites in the Tower, in the late Queenes time',[13] and no other plausible occasion for this is known.[14]

What must he have felt? Weston, in his autobiography, remembers his own trepidation 'as I saw the vast battlements, and was led by the warder past the gates with the iron fastenings, which were closed behind me'. To a twelve-year-old the gloomy precincts would have been even more daunting. He was entering the very lair of the great beast. No wonder the sense of perilous trespass, and the memory of a 'grim eight-foot-high iron-bound' man, striding like a colossus in front of a gate, lingered so vividly when Donne came to write his youthful love poems.[15] And was there, mingled with his fear, resentment? Did the boy grudge the hold which these stern, devoted men—his uncle and the furtive stranger—had over his mother's love and allegiance: a hold so strong that she was prepared, it seemed, to lay down her life for them? Perhaps: for he was later to let loose his rancour against the Jesuits with a pertinacity that seems to reflect a personal grudge. He could not forgive them for their intransigence. In the end he came to feel that they alone were to blame for all the slaughter and suffering. For they would not allow English Catholics to compromise. They demanded total loyalty to the Faith, and total opposition to the English crown; and so they attracted to themselves the hatred which unswerving probity always earns.

To young Donne, compromise must have seemed increasingly the most attractive course. His tutors were 'men of a suppressed and afflicted Religion, accustomed to the despite of death, and hungry of imagin'd Martyrdome';[16] but they did not find him so hungry. He was not sent abroad to be educated at one of the Catholic colleges, but went up, instead, with his brother Henry, to Hart Hall, Oxford, a favourite resort of Catholics because it lacked a chapel, and so made avoidance of public worship easier.

Terrible stories were circulated, by priests and Jesuits, about what happened to Catholics who attended Anglican services to evade the fines for recusancy. A certain Francis Wodehouse of Breccles in Norfolk, it was related, had found, as soon as he entered the polluted sanctuary, that his stomach became a raging furnace. He drank eight gallons of beer to put out the fire, but only when a priest was brought to shrive him did the heat abate. He never wavered again. Donne would certainly know of such cases, for one had occurred at his own college shortly before he arrived there. An undergraduate called Francis Marsh had succumbed to the temptation to enter an Anglican church, but immediately afterwards remorse unhinged his reason. He stripped himself naked, made his way out of college, and began to run through Oxford, heading for the market square. He was apprehended, forcibly restrained and put to bed, and friends tried to pacify him. But he would not be comforted, and within two days he was dead. He 'wasted away', a contemporary reported, 'in sheer agony of mind'.[17] Such examples would keep before Donne the supernatural risks incurred by backsliders.

When John and Henry Donne matriculated they gave their ages as eleven and ten respectively. Actually they were a year older than this, but the law required students, on reaching the age of sixteen, to subscribe to the Thirty-nine Articles. For a Catholic, that was out of the question, so to evade the regulations Catholics frequently went up to university very young, or lied about their ages—or both, as the Donne boys did.

We now come to the most obscure period of Donne's life. He matriculated at Oxford in October 1584, and he was admitted to Lincoln's Inn from Thavies Inn, where he would have had to spend at least a year in preliminary study, in May 1592. Nothing certain can be said about his movements between those two dates. We don't know, in the first place, how long he stayed at Oxford. As a Catholic he was of course debarred from proceeding to a degree, since he could not take the required Oath of Supremacy. Walton, his first biographer, who knew him only in later life and so may be unreliable about the young Donne, says that he transferred from Oxford to Cambridge in 'about' his fourteenth year, and that he moved from there to London and was admitted to Lincoln's Inn in 'about' his seventeenth. There are no records of Donne having been at Cambridge, but that doesn't disprove Walton's statement, since Cambridge records are incomplete. Walton has clearly got his dates wrong, for according to his timetable Donne entered Lincoln's Inn in 1588 or 1589 (his seventeenth year), whereas documentary evidence shows that 1592 is the correct date. But otherwise Walton may be quite reliable: Donne may have spent his teens studying at Oxford and Cambridge, and then gone immediately to the Inns of Court.

However, Walton also says that Donne travelled for 'some years' in his youth, first in Italy, then in Spain, studying the cultures and learning the languages of those countries.[18] From Walton's account it appears that Donne's travels began in 1597. That can't be so, because in 1597 or early 1598 he started work in London. Still, he may have travelled earlier, and there's some evidence which suggests that he did. For one thing, he seems to have had a reputation among his contemporaries as a traveller. For another, Walton is remarkably circumstantial about the travels. He says that Donne originally intended to go on from Italy to the Holy Land, to see Jerusalem and 'the Sepulchre of our Saviour', but that he was prevented from doing this, so went to Spain instead. In later years, Walton adds, Donne often mentioned 'with a deploration' that he had missed seeing the Holy Places. That sounds authentic. Another bit of evidence that may be relevant is the earliest extant portrait of Donne. It survives in an engraving by William Marshall, bears the date 1591, and gives the sitter's age as eighteen. Donne has long curly hair, an incipient moustache, ear-rings in the shape of a cross and a fashionably wide-shouldered doublet. He carries a sword, the ornate hilt of which he is rather awkwardly holding up so as to get it into the picture. The portrait is surmounted by a Spanish motto: 'Antes muerto que mudado' (Sooner dead than changed).

Now it's true that the authorities at Oxford and Cambridge in the late sixteenth century were complaining that the new-style under-graduates looked more like courtiers than scholars and were sporting fancy hose and rapiers.[19] If Donne's portrait is that of a youth just down from Cambridge it merely bears out their grumbles. Natur-ally enough, though, the Spanish motto and the picture's obtrusively experienced air have suggested to some that it depicts a young blood recently returned from the Continental travels Walton speaks of. Quite possibly Donne's stay at Cambridge was shorter than Walton believed, and the years spent abroad were 1589–91. Whatever the exact period, the cultures Donne chose to submerge himself in were, of course, Catholic. He escaped from persecution and insular bigotry to visit the home of his Faith. From this angle, the portrait's defiant motto, the crosses Donne wears, and the militant stance may take on a further meaning. They may be a flamboyant assertion of his loyalty to the old religion. The very language of the motto could be seen as an arrogant gesture: rather, as William Empson has remarked, as if a modern American were to display a motto in Russian.[20] For to ordinary English people Spain was still the great enemy.

If this guess about the meaning of Donne's portrait is right, he was soon given a chance to see whether he would really rather be dead than changed. The Inns of Court, to which he and his brother Henry went, were not the mere lawyer factories of modern times. Contem-poraries hailed them as 'the Third Universitie of England', though even that gives the wrong impression, for there was practically no organized tuition. Really they operated like residential clubs or hotels, accommodating well-off young men who wished to acquire some metropolitan polish. At least three-quarters of the students were from the gentry or nobility. Most of them had no intention of

taking up the law as a career. They despised the poorer students who
were in search of a professional qualification, and adopted aggres-
sively cultivated and aristocratic manners to distinguish themselves
from these career lawyers. They were great dabblers in poetry, and
they enjoyed organizing revels and masques, which gave them the
feeling that they were in touch with court life.[21] Among these bright
sparks, Donne was soon an acknowledged leader. Since so many
scions of the ruling class were gathered in the Inns, they were a target
for Catholic missionaries. The authorities viewed them with distrust. Lincoln's Inn Fields were notorious as a haunt of priests who, it
was said, would blow a special trumpet to summon the Inns of Court
men to mass. The Donne boys, Walton's account makes clear, were
still being educated by Catholics. Their mother appointed tutors to
instruct them in mathematics and 'other Liberal Sciences', and also to
instil into them 'particular Principles of the Romish Church'. To
the Catholic proselytizers the brothers must have seemed useful
contacts.

It was this aspect of life at the Inns which brought Donne up
against the reality of his position. In May 1593 a young man called
William Harrington was arrested in Henry Donne's rooms on suspicion of being a priest.[22] Henry, of course, was taken into custody too.
When charged, Harrington denied that he was a priest, but poor
Henry, faced with torture, betrayed him. He admitted that Harrington had shriven him while he was staying in his rooms. Harrington
had, in fact, received his calling as a boy of fifteen in his father's house
in Yorkshire, where he had met and been inspired by Edmund
Campion. He had been educated in the Catholic colleges at Douai
and Rheims, and had trained to become a Jesuit in the novitiate at
Tournay. Like other Catholic martyrs, he refused to be tried by a
jury because he did not wish to implicate more men than necessary in
the guilt of his destruction. He was condemned and, on 18 February
1594, taken out to die. In the cart, with the rope round his neck, he
began to address his 'loving countrymen', only to be interrupted
with insults by Topcliffe. But his courage did not fail, and he
denounced Topcliffe from the scaffold as a 'tyrant and blood-sucker'.
Like the Babington conspirators, he was disembowelled alive. Stow
records that, after he had been hanged and cut down, he 'struggled'
with the executioner who was about to use the knife on him.

Henry Donne, having knowingly harboured a priest, was guilty
of felony. But he did not live long enough to come to trial. Imprisoned at first in the Clink, he was moved to Newgate, where the
plague was raging, and died within a few days. To Donne his death

brought not only grief but peril. Because of his kinship with Henry, his own religious activities were now likely to attract scrutiny. Plainly the time had come for serious thought. Besides, he was now twenty-one, and had collected his share of his father's estate—a sum large enough to make him independent of his mother and her Catholic advisers. The dilemma that faced him was acute. If he remained true to his Faith, his chances of preferment and success in the world would be curtailed. Further, the efforts of the Jesuits, with whom his family were inextricably connected, would make it difficult to remain neutral. Pressure would be brought on him to assist in the mission, and if he complied how long would it be before he shared Henry's fate?

If, on the other hand, he became an apostate, the result confidently predicted by the Church was so hideous that most people have, since Donne's day, simply refused to believe in it any more. But for his generation eternal damnation was no myth. They were like men walking over a furnace, separated from it by a thin crust which might at any moment part and drop them into the flames. There would be, as Donne later put it, 'a sodain flash of horror'[23] as you fell in, and then unending fire. Even Satan, Donne believed, might decline to change places with a damned soul in these circumstances, for its torments would be fiercer than his.[24]

Many other young Catholics had, of course, been forced to cope with the situation now confronting Donne, and had outlined the alternatives with dismaying clarity. Either you remained loyal to God and his truth, or you sent your forsworn soul 'headlong to hell fire'. This choice was that 'dreadfull moment', wrote Robert Southwell, 'whereupon dependeth a whole eternity'.[25] Donne had probably met Southwell and read his *Humble Supplication* in which this statement is made. His words, fearful in their import, seem to have stuck in Donne's mind, and years later, trying to startle his congregation towards the end of a sermon, he echoes them, reminding his hearers of the endless pain of the cursed soul, and of the instant of decision that led to it: 'upon this minute dependeth that eternity.'

Perhaps we are merely fancying that echo. But there can be no mistake about the agony of Donne's choice. And he chose hell. That is to say, he deserted the Catholic God, and there are still Catholics, four centuries later, who believe that in doing so he damned himself. He was an apostate, their spokesman declares, of a 'quite specially shameless' kind. 'The near kinsman of martyrs, whom he reviled for hire.' In full knowledge, he committed a mortal sin against the Faith, and though, we are told, it may be hoped that the prayers of his martyred relations won for him the grace of death-bed contrition, 'so far as we know, he died an apostate and made no sign'.[26] If we are inclined to dismiss this sort of thing as primitive superstition we shall be far from understanding how it seemed to Donne's family and circle, and how, in his moods of despair, it must have seemed to Donne himself.

His apostasy was not rash or sudden. The points at issue between the Catholic and the reformed churches had been copiously documented by rival divines, and it is typical of Donne's bookishness that he set about reading his way through the whole controversy. Meanwhile he kept, he says, an open mind about religion, and this 'bred some Scandall', for acquaintances came to suspect that he had no religion at all. Still, he persisted, searching for God among the wrangling theologians, and refrained from coming to any decision until he had 'survayed and digested the whole body of Divinity, controverted betweene ours and the Romane Church'. Walton records that, among Donne's papers at his death, there were found excerpts from 1,400 authors, 'most of them abridged and analysed with his own hand'.

The poetic evidence of this crisis is Satire III—the great, crucial poem of Donne's early manhood.[27] For most of its length it is not a satire at all, but a self-lacerating record of that moment which comes in the lives of almost all thinking people, when the beliefs of youth, unquestioningly assimilated and bound up with our closest personal attachments, come into conflict with the scepticism of the mature intellect. The poem begins in a flurry of anguish and derision, fighting back tears and choking down scornful laughter at the same instant:

> Kinde pitty chokes my spleene; brave scorn forbids
> Those teares to issue which swell my eye-lids;
> I must not laugh, nor weepe. . . .

Donne seeks relief in anger, denouncing the pastimes (sex, squabbling, adventure) on which young men like himself fritter away their energies. It is a characteristic outburst: he was always, as we shall see, dismayed by what he felt to be his lack of concentration and purpose. This initial tirade over, the poem settles down to the one subject which, Donne asseverates, it is worth settling down to: 'Seeke true religion.' So far as he can see, the normal reasons for espousing Catholicism or Protestantism are pathetically inadequate. People display a senseless preference for antiquity or novelty, or they accept what their godparents tell them, or they give up trying to choose and become apathetic. Instead of thinking things out for themselves, they submit to the authority either of the Pope or, if they are Protestants, of the English monarch:

> Foole and wretch, wilt thou let thy Soule be ty'd
> To mans lawes, by which she shall not be try'd
> At the last day? Will it then boot thee
> To say a Philip, or a Gregory,
> A Harry, or a Martin taught thee this?
> Is not this excuse for mere contraries,
> Equally strong? cannot both sides say so?

No one before Donne had written English verse in which the pressures of passionate speech could be retained with such unhindered power. What agitates the lines, and the whole poem, is terror of hell. 'The foule Devill', Donne warns, waits to snatch your soul. Your only chance of escape is hard thinking:

> On a huge hill,
> Cragged, and steep, Truth stands, and hee that will
> Reach her, about must, and about must goe;
> And what th'hills suddennes resists, winne so;
> Yet strive so, that before age, deaths twilight,
> Thy Soule rest, for none can worke in that night.
> To will, implyes delay, therefore now doe:
> Hard deeds, the bodies paines; hard knowledge too
> The mindes indeavours reach.

These famous lines, in which Donne transposes the traditional image of the hill of Truth into his own strenuously mimetic rhythms, have rightly attained classic status. But their rather awkward relationship with what Donne says elsewhere in the poem has not been remarked on. When reprimanding youthful irresponsibility at the start, he laid the emphasis on obedience to parental example. Those who ignored it, he cautioned, might find themselves worse off than the virtuous heathen who died before Christ's coming:

> and shall thy fathers spirit
> Meete blinde Philosophers in heaven, whose merit
> Of strict life may be'imputed faith, and heare
> Thee, whom hee taught so easie wayes and neare
> To follow, damn'd?

It is true that Donne is chiefly concerned in this part of the poem with moral conduct rather than the choice of true religion. Nevertheless, the lack of consistency between the assumption that there are 'easie wayes' to salvation available from one's father, and the insistence (in the hill of Truth passage) that salvation depends on 'hard knowledge' which the individual must win for himself, is glaring. Put side by side, the excerpts reveal the conflict between adult independence and fidelity to inherited beliefs, from which all the heat and impatience of the poem evolve.

The phrase 'thy fathers spirit' has a particular resonance because we associate it with the Ghost's speech in *Hamlet* ('I am thy father's spirit'), which it's hard to keep out of our heads. Perhaps we shouldn't try to, for an early version of *Hamlet* had been acted by 1589,[28] and Donne may be echoing it. Was he also thinking of his own father (dead, like old Hamlet, and speedily replaced by a step-father)? As he had been barely four when his father died, his memory of him must have been hazy at best. But that would not necessarily make it less poignant. Much later in life he recalled, in a letter to his mother, 'the love and care of my most dear and provident Father, whose soul, I hope, hath long since enjoyed the sight of our blessed Saviour'.[29] During the spiritual crisis which produced the 'Holy Sonnets' the thought of his father's spirit watching his struggle certainly came into his mind:

> If faithfull soules be alike glorifi'd
> As Angels, then my fathers soule doth see,
> And adds this even to full felicitie,
> That valiantly I hels wide mouth o'rstride.[30]

Reading that, it's hard to believe that in Satire III, when Donne writes about religion and fathers, he does so without any thought of his own father, whose religion he is about to abandon. His father had been a Catholic, and the 'easie wayes and near' he taught were those of Rome. Since he assumes that his father is in heaven, and since Satire III is adamant that there is only one true religion which leads to heaven, the argument of the poem would appear to be over before it has begun. There is no need to start labouring up Truth's hill; Catholicism must be right. Viewed in this way, the contrast between the part of the poem which springs from Donne's deeper emotional loyalties, and the part directed by his brave new investigative spirit, becomes sharper. In a prose account written some fifteen years later, Donne was to describe in cooler terms the strife of heart against head that he had to undergo before he could break free of Catholicism:

I had a longer worke to doe then many other men; for I was first to
blot out certaine impressions of the Romane religion, and to
wrastle both against the examples and against the reasons, by
which some hold was taken; and some anticipations early layde
upon my conscience, both by Persons who by nature had a power
and superiority over my will, and others who by their learning
and good life, seem'd to me iustly to claime an interest for the
guiding, and rectifying of mine understanding in these matters.[31]

Here, time has distanced Donne's apostasy, and he is able to sound
objective. He can now talk openly about the personal bonds which
he had to sunder, and about his consciousness of disappointing
people whose lives and minds he admired. In the Satire, written
during the crisis, these aspects were too painful to mention, and had
to be suppressed. Only in the oblique and uncertain allusion to his
dead father do we get any hint of the kind of inner attachment Donne
found himself struggling against. There is no other mention of
family or friends. The poem's effort is to make out that choosing a
religion is a purely intellectual business, as unemotional as moun-
taineering. Donne needed to convince himself of this, in order to
allay his personal turmoil. So the Satire is not an account of a crisis
but an operative part of one. It was, for its author, a necessary
poem, and its inconsistency and misrepresentation are part of its
vigorous life.

Though Donne eventually came to accept Anglicanism, he could
never believe that he had found in the Church of England the one
true church outside which salvation was impossible. To have
thought that would have meant consigning his own family to damnation. Instead he persuaded himself that the saved would come
from all churches: 'from the Eastern Church, and from the Western
Church too, from the Greek Church, and from the Latine too, and,
(by Gods grace) from them that pray not in Latine too'.[32] This is an
opinion he often repeats in his letters and sermons; but the fierce
young poet of Satire III would have found it intolerably tolerant.
Indeed, it is one of his chosen targets:

> Graccus loves all as one, and thinkes that so
> As women do in divers countries goe
> In divers habits, yet are still one kinde,
> So doth, so is Religion; and this blind-
> nesse too much light breeds; but unmoved thou
> Of force must one, and forc'd but one allow;
> And the right.[33]

There speaks the Catholic. For though Donne, in this Satire, is busily shuffling off his Faith, the conviction that there is one 'right' church which alone certifies salvation is part of his Catholic upbringing. No church would ever mean so much to him again, and consequently when he abandoned Catholicism he lost an irreplaceable absolute. A Catholic could not have written, as Donne was to write when he had already been three years in Anglican orders, 'Show me deare Christ, thy spouse, so bright and cleare.'[34] The important thing about this much-disputed sonnet, in which Donne asks that he may be granted a vision of the true church, is not that it implies any 'disloyalty' to Anglicanism but that it reveals the lasting disorientation his apostasy entailed. A Catholic would not have needed to ask; he would have known.

   Although Donne, as an Anglican, consciously gave up the belief in one 'right' church, part of him, preconditioned by his Catholic childhood, still clung to it. This leads to almost comic contradictions in his sermons, in which a saintly mildness towards those of other religious persuasions coexists with diatribes against Catholics and schismatics. We should beware, he tells his congregation, of imagining that no opinion but our own can be true on such matters as the sacrament. Yet within a few paragraphs he is denouncing transubstantiation as a 'heretical Riddle' and 'Satans sophistry'.[35] The proneness of Roman Catholics to homosexuality is another subject he is fond of touching upon when incensed.[36] And though, as we have seen, he declares that the saved may come from all churches, he can be found describing religious toleration as 'a new spiritual disease'.[37]

   These muddles show us two elements in Donne's personality colliding. On the one side is the desire for a single, all-eclipsing viewpoint, together with the need to vilify those who dissent from it. This part of him is prominent in his satires, of course, and in some of his love poems—witness 'The Comparison', where his own girl's perfections are contrasted with the filthy deformities of another's. But on the other side, beside family sympathies, there is an urge towards unity and assimilation which we shall often meet in Donne's imaginative world, and which inclines him to restraint. Accordingly he see-saws between the two attitudes.

   When Donne renounced Catholicism isn't known, and it would be foolish to hope to pinpoint some particular day or week. Satire III shows, as we've seen, that he has been able to prise his intellect away from the old Faith, otherwise there'd be no need to set out on a search for truth. He must have been ready to pass himself off as an Anglican when he became secretary to the Lord Keeper, Egerton, in 1597.

Egerton was himself an apostate, who had joined sides with the
persecutors of Catholics, conducting the prosecution of several martyrs, Edmund Campion among them.[38] He would naturally sym-
pathize with Donne's defection.

Why did Donne become an apostate? To answer that we should have
to be confident that we could plumb the springs of human motivation. But three possible reasons suggest themselves: he was ambitious, he was an intellectual, and he was reacting, in a not uncommon
way, against the love and admiration he had felt as a child for his
elders and teachers. To take these in turn: first, his ambition. This
will be the subject of our third chapter, but we need to touch on it
here because it prompted him not only to desert the Roman Church
but to attack those of its members who were still wavering in their
loyalty between the Pope and the English king. He took steps to
present himself to the great of the land as a militant Anglican, fit and
willing to abuse, in public, those valiant Catholics who had gone to
the scaffold for their Faith.

   In 1610 he published a work called *Pseudo-Martyr*, which was a
contribution to the controversy about whether English Catholics
should or shouldn't take the Oath of Allegiance to King James. Since
the Oath merely required from the person concerned an assurance
that he would not commit murder, it was a fairly reasonable docu-
ment. The Catholic had to swear that he did 'from his heart abhor,
detest, and abjure, as impious and heretical, this damnable doctrine
and position, that princes which be excommunicated or deprived by
the Pope may be deposed or murdered by their subjects'.[39] The
Gunpowder Plot had recently shown, however, that some Catholics
were of an altogether different persuasion, and even the more peace-
able English recusants found the Oath's language offensive. James
himself took a lively interest in the matter, and had published in 1607
An Apologie for the Oath of Allegiance, over which his Jesuit opponents
made merry. Stung by this public ridicule, the King set aside other
business during the winter of 1608–9 in order to reissue the *Apologie*
with corrections and a lengthy new preface. James's advisers found
this literary activity tiresome, especially as important affairs were
being neglected, and the Venetian ambassador reported that their
devotion to his royal person was becoming strained.[40] Donne's
Pseudo-Martyr argues that Catholics should and must take the Oath,
and as soon as his work was printed he hurried down to Royston,
where the King was staying, expressly to present him with a copy. It
was a shrewd move, for Donne was able to appear as a skilful

controversialist, upholding the official policy of the state and helping his sovereign out of a tight corner. The book received considerable limelight, and boosted Donne's reputation enormously. He got an honorary M. A. from Oxford, and the Dean of Canterbury, in a fit of enthusiasm, mentioned Donne and Bacon side by side as modern thinkers.[41] The Catholics were furious, charging Donne with 'venemous malignity' and deploring his 'blasphemous, and Atheistical jests against Gods Saints and Servants'.[42]

Did Donne, in the interests of self-advancement, suppress what he really thought when he wrote *Pseudo-Martyr?* Did he covertly adjust his opinions to concur with the government's? Perhaps: though in one respect the case which he argued was close to his heart. As we've noted, he was genuinely exasperated by the hard-liners in the Roman camp, notably the Jesuits, who insisted that it was impossible to be a loyal Englishman and a good Catholic. Their intransigence had virtually enforced his own apostasy, by denying him any outlet for his worldly talents and ambitions while he remained faithful to his God. So he was out for their blood. Besides, he'd seen too much heartache and distraction among members of his own family and co-religionists not to feel that the extremists had a lot to answer for. Pity, as well as resentment, prevailed with him when he urged English Catholics to forsake the Jesuits and secure their own lives by taking the Oath.

But if *Pseudo-Martyr* accurately represents Donne's views in this respect, in others it shows signs of temporizing. For only the previous year he had written a thoughtful letter to his friend Goodyer about the Oath of Allegiance, in which he says that, so far as he can see, there is right on both sides. Obviously, he concedes, the English government can't feel safe without the Oath. But, on the other hand, the supremacy which the Roman Church claims would patently be diminished if it allowed the Oath to be taken. What's more, the Church's assertion of supremacy seems to him, he says, to have just as much basis as the similar assertion made by kings like James I, since both are, in fact, quite arbitrary.[43] There's no sign in this private letter of the robust championship of royal supremacy which Donne was to exhibit, some months later, in *Pseudo-Martyr*.

Pseudo-Martyr claims that royal authority has been imposed on men by God. 'God inanimates every state with one power, as every man with one soule.' To refuse to take the Oath of Allegiance is therefore not just a political matter but contrary to the 'Law of Nature'. It's also perverse; those who refuse must know, in their hearts, that it would be reasonable to comply, for 'God hath Imme-

diately imprinted in mans Nature and Reason, to be subject to a power immediately infus'd from him'. As for Catholics who court martyrdom by remaining true to their faith, they also abrogate the Law of Nature, because 'no man by law of nature may deliver himselfe into a danger which he might avoide'.[44] They are not martyrs but pseudo-martyrs.

When Donne put forward this medley of superstition and assertion, which tallied so conveniently with James I's theory of the divine right of kings, he was using, at best, only half his mind. For in private his opinion of the Law of Nature was considerably more sceptical, as we may gather from his treatise on suicide, *Biathanatos*, probably written within a year or two of *Pseudo-Martyr*. 'This terme the law of Nature', he there writes, 'is so variously and unconstantly deliver'd, as I confesse I read it a hundred times before I understand it once.' 'Nature', Donne perceives, is simply a word people use to embrace everything which happens in the world; so it's absurd to suggest that anything which has actually happened can be contrary to the Law of Nature. So far is Donne from believing that it's 'unnatural' to deliver oneself into an avoidable danger, like the martyrs, that he maintains, in *Biathanatos*, the naturalness of choosing to kill oneself.[45] *Pseudo-Martyr* reads, then, like a compromise, and a dishonest one. Donne's wish to curry favour with James, and his genuine sympathy with ordinary English Catholics, made him simplify issues which he knew to be complex.

So much for ambition as a motive for his apostasy. Secondly, as I have said, Donne was unrelentingly intellectual, and that too seems to have contributed to his disenchantment with Catholicism. The superstitions of the Roman Church, and the tales of miracles in which the writers of saints' lives specialized, struck Donne as beneath the dignity of a rational human being. To the fury of his Catholic antagonists he filled *Pseudo-Martyr* with ludicrous instances of these, sedulously culled from approved Catholic authorities, and complete with scholarly annotation: how St. Anthony had preached to some fish, which put their heads above the water to listen, and how at the end of the sermon some of the fish had spoken and others bowed; how the same saint, when a penitent confessed to him that he had kicked his mother, replied 'If thy foot offend thee, cut it off', whereupon the man amputated his own foot, but St. Anthony considerately did a miracle to fix it on again. How a certain Friar Andrew, to correct his appetite for poultry, made the sign of the cross and commanded the birds to fly away, though they were roasted.[46]

Also offensive to Donne's intellect was the blind obedience which Catholicism exacted from its votaries. This was something the Jesuits were particularly keen on. 'We ought always', St. Ignatius wrote, 'to hold that we believe what seems to us white to be black, if the Hierarchical Church so defines it.'[47] Outstanding examples of obedience, cited with reverence by accredited Catholic authors, are bundled together, in *Pseudo-Martyr*, into an uproarious saga of sanctified buffoonery. One of St. Francis's novices, we learn, set plants in the ground upside-down, because the saint had advised him that was the correct procedure; another, reminded that only those who became like little children could enter the kindgom of heaven, started tumbling around like a toddler; a particularly zealous believer planted a withered stick and, at his abbot's command, fetched water from two miles off, twice a day for a whole year, to water it.[48]

But what Donne aims to sweep away with his derisive laughter isn't always, if we take a second look, exactly contemptible. He lists among his instances of ludicrous presumption the action of Gonzaga who, on hearing of an outbreak of the plague, made a vow to visit those who were infected.[49] Donne's ridicule here tells us something about himself rather than about Catholicism. He makes us realize how alien to his combative, critical nature were not only the simple faith, but also the selflessness which the Catholic authorities whom he ransacked for his jokes were striving to nourish. He had the limitations, as well as the strengths, of the intellectual.

As for the third of the motives that arguably severed Donne from Catholicism—reaction against those he had been taught as a boy to reverence—this can be most readily detected in the book he published the year after *Pseudo-Martyr*, entitled *Ignatius his Conclave*. A satire against the Jesuits of the most scabrous kind, it was written in Latin so as to set not only England but Europe laughing at the pious terrorists who had embroiled Donne's family in disaster. It takes the form of a debate in Hell in which St. Ignatius Loyola, the founder of the Jesuit order, defends his right to pre-eminence in the infernal regions against a number of counter-claimants—including Copernicus, Paracelsus, Machiavelli and Christopher Columbus—who, though they lay claim to earth-shattering innovation and wickedness, are out-argued by the warrior saint. He and his Jesuits, he successfully maintains, have done more to convulse the world with evil than any other created being except Satan himself. And in fact the Devil is so appalled by Ignatius's revelations that he fears the Jesuit leader would soon take over as monarch of Hell should he

remain there. Accordingly he dispatches Ignatius and the Jesuits to
make a new Hell in the moon.

The multiple charges laid against the Jesuits by Donne range from
genocide to sodomy. It was solely on Jesuit advice, Donne claims,
that the Spaniards slaughtered the native inhabitants of the New
World, reducing their numbers from 200,000 to 150. As for sexual
morality, the aim of papal legislation in this sphere is, he avers, to
reserve buggery for the princes of the Church, whose appetites have
become so inordinate that one cardinal, the son of Pope Paul III,
actually raped a bishop. 'His stomacke', Donne reports with glee,

> was not towardes young beardlesse boyes, nor such greene fruit:
> for he did not thinke, that hee went farre inough from the right
> Sex, except hee had a manly, a reverend, and a bearded Venus.
> Neither staied he there; but his witty lust proceeded yet
> further . . . that his Venus might bee the more monstrous, he
> would have her in a Mitre.[50]

Though the story wasn't, it seems, true, Donne did not invent it. It
was one of several pungent morsels he picked out, for his satire, from
the common effluent of anti-Catholic slander. His sermons keep up
the campaign of hate against the Jesuit order, manifesting what
certainly sounds, at times, like bitter family feeling. 'As a Father, as a
Master; I can preserve my Family from attempts of Jesuits,' he
proclaims: to let a Jesuit escape is like sparing a fox or a wolf.[51]

It is time to look at Donne's poems and the way they reflect his
apostasy. But, briefly, we may note that though he forsook the
Roman Church he never, in a sense, escaped its grasp. It remained
close to his mind as a reproach or a threat, or as an adversary with
which he hoped he might finally be reconciled. He knew that his
Catholic upbringing had marked him indelibly, and that his spirit
could not grow straight in any other direction. He often, in later
years, warned Christians against changing from one church to
another. It was needless, he said, for 'in all Christian professions
there is a way to salvation', and it was damaging. A man who
changes his church, he told Goodyer, is like a coin from which the
features are filed away. Even though this may be done to stamp the
coin with a better impression, it will always look 'awry and squint'
afterwards. So do 'minds which have received divers impressions'.[52]
He had reason to know. Further, his sympathies remained with the
persecuted Catholics, though he had joined their persecutors. The
thought of government spies and butchers like Topcliffe and Philips
never failed to turn his stomach. They are still among his targets in

The Courtier's Library, which probably received its final form as late as 1611.[53] This bitter little satire, spraying its fire about like a rusty Sten gun, and disguised as a catalogue of rare Latin books, was, needless to say, never published in Donne's lifetime, and it is remarkably anti-Protestant in tone. Finally, it's no surprise to learn that Donne was an eager advocate of schemes to reunite the churches of Christendom. He hoped for much from the dispute between Venice and the Papacy in 1606, and warmly admired Paolo Sarpi, the Venetian champion, whose *History of the Council of Trent* suggested that the Church as a whole needed to be reformed along something resembling Anglican lines.[54] Nothing came of it, of course. But Donne's enthusiasm is entirely understandable: by healing the rift in the Church, he could heal himself.

ℰ 2 ℰ

The Art of Apostasy

The griefs of English Catholics in the late sixteenth century have passed into oblivion. By one of time's heartless tricks, practically all that students of literature glean from that communal agony are the poems of a young man who did not choose to share the suffering of his co-religionists. His apostasy no longer matters, except in the realm of art: we wonder whether it touched his poems, and listen for its tremors in their depths. How *were* they affected by his betrayal of Catholicism and the anxieties that it bred? When we approach the *Songs and Sonnets* with that question in mind, a feature that cannot fail to impress us is their perpetual worry about fidelity and falseness.

The other young poets of the 1590s generally complain, in their sonnet sequences, about the frigidity or the cruelty which they find in girls. They are fatally prone to fall for icy-breasted tigresses. Once or twice Donne adopts this popular pose himself, but mostly the torment he chooses to imagine is quite different. His difficulty lies, we gather, not so much in getting the girl into bed as in ensuring her fidelity afterwards. Sometimes he's jaunty about this, proclaiming self-defensively that he's just as false as women and doesn't want fidelity. Sometimes he's tearful and piteous, assimilating himself to a tiny, fragile object which brutal female treachery would shatter. 'She that, Oh, broke her faith, would soon breake thee', he croons protectively to the little black bauble on his finger in 'A Jeat Ring Sent'.[1] Often he reassures the girl: their love will last; their souls are one. But fear lingers, and is what makes the reassurance needful. Behind the rapture is the suspicion that nowhere 'Lives a woman true, and faire'.[2] Donne's entire output as a love poet could be seen as a way of surviving and surmounting this bitter knowledge. Whether he flaunts it with cynical nonchalance, or writhes in exasperation, or celebrates the blissful release from his phantom which he finds in a girl's arms, the shadow of separation and loss is the seed of his restless sexuality.

The love poems display, in this matter, a profound anxiety about the permanence of human relationships, and especially about his own ability to attract or merit stable affection. They do so with a persistence which, even if we did not know about his apostasy, we should be tempted to ascribe to some major rift in his personal life. What seems to happen is that Donne, in the fantasy world of the poems, rids himself of his disloyalty by transferring it to women, and directing against them the execrations which he could be seen as meriting. He avails himself, in this way, of that healing distortion of the truth with which fiction always rewards its creators. It is an additional part of the manœuvre that he should, in the poems, remove the subject of treachery from the religious sphere, where in real life it belonged, and transfer it to the relatively innocuous department of sexual ethics.

There are moments in the love poems when this mask drops, and the religious preoccupation shows through. Sometimes it's so fleeting that we're not quite sure whether it has happened at all. The song 'Goe, and catche a falling starre', for instance, which rejects the possibility of a 'true, and faire' woman, catches briefly at hope:

> If thou findst one, let mee know,
> Such a Pilgrimage were sweet.[3]

There's no mistaking the poetic effect of the word 'Pilgrimage'. It floods the line with relief, like a sob of joy. And though it could be used quite neutrally in the late sixteenth century, it was also fraught with Catholic potential. Has Donne's mind relapsed, for an instant, to his childhood world of faith and certainties, and does that account for the word's emotive charge? At all events, we observe that, when Donne allows himself to imagine a state beyond betrayal, he chooses a word which relates to sanctity, not sex; and this suggests that the love poems are a veil for religious perturbations.

At times they are scarcely even a veil. We find Donne brandishing, as if in defiance, religious language which is scaldingly appropriate to his own state:

> Although thy hand and faith, and good workes too,
> Have seal'd thy love which nothing should undoe,
> Yea though thou fall backe, that apostasie
> Confirme thy love; yet much, much I feare thee.[4]

Donne's bravado, in these lines from 'Change', takes the form of defusing, by ribaldry, words which bristle with painful connotations. 'Faith' and 'good workes' were the key terms in the arguments about justification waged between Catholics and Protestants. The 'good workes' Donne refers to, however, are sexual, and the faith is

secular. His girl is prepared to 'fall backe' in the uncomplicatedly
physical sense of lying down and opening her legs. Her 'apostasie'
will prove her fidelity. By juggling with the word until it means its
opposite, the apostate poet disarms it.

'Change' is one of the Elegies and, though our dating of Donne's
poems is for the most part guesswork, we can at least be sure that
these were written early: that is, they belong to the same part of his
life as his decision to renounce Catholicism. It's not surprising that
we should find him striving to neutralize in them unpleasantly
significant words. His elegy 'The Bracelet' supplies other instances.[5]
In this poem Donne has lost a gold chain belonging to his girl, and
agrees to supply twelve gold coins so that the goldsmith can melt
them down for a new chain. By choosing the coins known to the
Elizabethans as 'angels', Donne lets into his poem a level of punning
religious allusion, unjustified by the main subject but quickly
dominant. It is on this sensitive level that the poem's flippant inten-
sities occur:

> Shall these twelve innocents, by thy severe
> Sentence (dread Judge) my sins great burden beare?
> Shall they be damn'd, and in the furnace throwne,
> And punisht for offences not their owne? . . .
>   But thou art resolute; Thy will be done.
> Yet with such anguish as her only sonne
> The mother in the hungry grave doth lay,
> Unto the fire these Martyrs I betray.

Damnation, hell fire, the betrayal of martyrs, and the 'great burden'
of the poet's sin are not subjects we should normally expect in a love
elegy. But our knowledge of Donne's predicament at the time he
was writing gives them an almost confessional relevance. The feeling that he is the cause of innocent suffering, and the apparently
arbitrary introduction of a mother and a dead son in the context of
martyrdom, are also factors which, given Donne's family history
and his brother Henry's fate, we readily recognize as appropriate.
Donne's mind is running on subjects close to his conscience, and the
wit of the poem may be seen not just as a dazzling excursion but as
the answer to a spiritual need.

Whereas in 'The Bracelet' and in an elegy like 'Recusancy',[6] with
its joke about excommunication, the religious content is bold and
obvious, we occasionally find in other elegies seemingly chance
references which, against the background of Donne's apostasy,
acquire heightened significance. An instance occurs in 'The

Perfume' where Donne describes his stealthy entrance into the
girl's house:

> Even my opprest shoes, dumbe and speechlesse were,
> Onely, thou bitter sweet, whom I had laid
> Next mee, mee traiterously hast betraid.[7]

Here it is less the paranoia about betrayal, extending even to scent,
which arouses interest than the detail of the 'opprest shoes'. For
Donne is glancing, as his annotators inform us, at one of the ghastlier
penalties of his day—the *peine forte et dure*, which was inflicted on
those arraigned for felony who stood mute and refused to plead. It
was a matter about which he retained, even in later life, curiously
intense opinions. We find him declaiming in a sermon of 1629
against 'distempered wretches' who defy the courts by refusing to
answer when charged. He would not, he announces, administer the
Sacrament to such an offender, 'how earnestly soever he desired it at
his death, how penitently soever he confessed all his other sins'.[8]

Generally prisoners who refused to plead were simply trying to
save their dependants from destitution. For if the trial went forward,
and they were found guilty of felony, their property would be
confiscated by the state; but if they died under the *peine forte et dure* it
would not. Why should their forlorn courage have rankled so with
Donne? What was there about this offence that always made him
touchy, and motivated the callous joke, in 'The Perfume', about the
prescribed punishment? His unhappy revulsion from Catholicism
holds, perhaps, the key. For standing mute when charged was not
only a ruse to save property. It was also a common practice among
Catholics who wished to save the jury from staining their consciences with innocent blood by returning a verdict of guilty. When
Donne was a lad the *peine forte et dure* attained a sanctified notoriety in
Catholic circles, for it was the fate of Margaret Clitherow, the first
woman martyr of the Elizabethan age.

Margaret Clitherow, the wife of a York butcher, had become a
Catholic in 1574, and was charged in 1586 with harbouring Jesuit and
seminary priests. Refusing to plead, she was sentenced to be pressed
to death. Her fortitude and gentleness during this ordeal are
described in the brief biography written by her confessor John
Mush, which spread her fame through England. She was stripped
and laid on the ground, with her hands bound to posts. A sharp stone
was put under her back, and a door placed on top of her, upon which
weights were piled 'to the quantity of seven or eight hundred weight
at the least, which, breaking her ribs, caused them to burst forth of

the skin'. The official sentence had stipulated that she should be pressed for three days, and kept alive, during that time, with 'a little barley bread and puddle water'. But a gentlewoman of York, won over by her holiness, persuaded the executioners to dispatch her quickly, and she took only a quarter of an hour to die. At the time of her death she was about thirty years old, and pregnant.[9]

Donne's jest about his 'opprest shoes' may not, then, be as pointless as it at first seems. Like his jocular treatment of martyrdom in 'The Bracelet', it could toughen him against thoughts and feelings which he no longer dared to entertain. He handles holy things so as to cauterize himself. Elaborate blasphemies are also incorporated into the love poems, as if it were not merely Catholicism but Christianity that Donne had to cure himself of. When he proclaims that his love can be expressed only by negatives, or compares the naked girl in 'Going to Bed' with 'soules unbodied', he is ingeniously perverting what St. Thomas in the *Summa Theologica* had written about God's nature and the joys of the blessed. The debate between Catholics and Protestants over Christ's 'imputed' grace is likewise turned to indecent account.[10] It's odd, we may think, that a student who was working his way through a programme of theological reading in order to discover the true religion should have put the fruits of his reading to such irreligious use. But Donne's devotion was always fitful, crossed by reckless or despairing moods—'This intermitting aguish Pietie', he called it.[11] His blasphemies suggest that his struggle to free himself from Catholicism led him, at times, into cynicism and disbelief.

Donne's learned profanities allowed him to make something totally new out of the love elegy. We can appreciate this if we compare his poems with Ovid's *Amores*, or with the tame repetitions of Ovid's formulas which sixteenth-century poets turned out in Latin and the vernaculars. Ovid's forays into the *demi-monde* of Rome were activated by nothing stronger than urbane indecency. Donne's elegies by contrast are extravagant and fantastic in their language and demeanour. More was going on in their creator's brain than Ovid dreamed of: they are the record of a soul trying to coarsen itself.

But Donne's immersion in theology had a more generous and spiritualizing contribution to make to his love poems than this. If we turn to 'Aire and Angels', which also borrows from St. Thomas, we find that all ridicule has been refined away from the theological allusions:

Twice or thrice had I lov'd thee,
  Before I knew thy face or name;
So in a voice, so in a shapelesse flame,
Angells affect us oft, and worship'd bee;
  Still when, to where thou wert, I came,
Some lovely glorious nothing I did see.[12]

And at the end, when Donne has explained how he tried to love her
body, but found its beauty too overwhelming, the angel returns to
the poem:

Then as an Angell, face, and wings
Of aire, not pure as it, yet pure doth weare,
  So thy love may be my loves spheare.

Donne was always passionately interested in angels, as we shall see.
No subject in his theological reading touched his imagination more,
and he derived his angelology almost wholly from Aquinas. But
here he is not pondering the angels for their own sake. He uses their
divine mysteriousness to adumbrate mysteries in human love which
are common and baffling. Why should a particular girl, the moment
we set eyes on her, seem exactly right? We talk about 'meeting the
girl of our dreams', and that turn of phrase assumes, as Donne does,
that somehow we knew and loved her before meeting her. Donne's
previous visions of the girl, though, are not dreamy but holy. They
are given the fleeting purity of fire or disembodied voices; they
evoke worship, not desire. And when he eventually sees her she
remains ethereal, still a part of his spiritual life, too bright for his
eyes—a 'lovely glorious nothing'. That too corresponds to, though
it transfigures, something in our ordinary experience of love. For
when we fall in love, the girl does not seem at first like the earth-
bound objects and people around her. She has a radiant separateness,
like a being from another sphere, so that we tremble or grow
breathless at the thought of touching her. Donne's use of Aquinas
here enhances the seriousness of the poem and of Aquinas, rather
than lessening both as the elegies do. The comparison of girl to angel
is never at risk of being a compliment, as it would be in standard
Elizabethan poetic usage. It communicates a wonder. Research into
the divine enlightens Donne's vision of the human.

This deepening effect of religion on the love poetry is most
apparent in 'The Canonization', 'The Relique' and 'The Funerall'. In
the first of these we can positively feel the holiness welling up as the
poem goes on. The religious content starts on a blustering level,

roughly that of the love elegies. Donne carries on like a disappointed careerist who has flung the world away for love, as he did when he married, and is maddened by the thought of what he has lost. He is hysterical and desperate—'Wee can dye by it, if not live by love'— and the worn Elizabethan pun on 'die' (which could mean 'have an orgasm') gives him the chance to fortify his rage with blasphemy:

> Wee dye and rise the same, and prove
> Mysterious by this love.[13]

The poem achieves this petulant triumph at the expense of Christ's resurrection, which becomes a riddling weapon in the invective: bedmates can 'dye and rise' as well as the Saviour of mankind. But the poem sloughs off its smut in its last two stanzas. The thought of death remains in Donne's mind, and brings its sepulchral comfort. There will be rest in the grave, and something more—official re-instatement: a place in the establishment at last. Donne imagines himself and the girl being invoked as saints in future ages. 'The Canonization' is usually reckoned to be much later than Donne's apostasy, but his habits of thought remain Catholic when he feels himself threatened. The intercession of saints was Catholic doctrine, disowned by Anglicans. It calms Donne, however, at the end of his stormy poem, to think of future worshippers praying to him to intercede with God on their behalf.

The comfort comes partly from being received back, through make-believe, into the Catholic Church: 'Canoniz'd for Love'. It is apostasy, as well as a ruined career, that the poem's end magically cancels. The limpid tones of the worshippers' prayer render mock-religion authentic, surmounting the earlier blasphemy:

> You whom reverend love
> Made one anothers hermitage;
> You, to whom love was peace, that now is rage. . .

The word 'hermitage', with its Catholic resonance, invests their love with purity. As with 'Aire and Angels', we recognize that the accent of religious wonder has redeemed the poem. Of pathos, too. For those future worshippers are, after all, wrong. Donne's furious tirade in the poem shows us that love is not 'peace' to him at all. He reaches peace only by believing that someone, after his death, will account him peaceful.

> Remember me when I am dead
> and simplify me when I'm dead.[14]

Donne, like Keith Douglas, wants that. Simplifying will wipe away
the hurts and betrayals.

'The Relique' and 'The Funerall' are both death-wish poems too.
They covet the authority of death, and in order to secure it 'The
Relique' ends with a message intoned from beyond the grave. Like
'The Canonization' this poem gets more sacred as it goes on. At first
Donne's intellectual contempt for Catholicism dominates. When his
skeleton and its hairy bracelet are hauled from the grave they will, he
prophesies, be added to the Church's grisly bric-à-brac and adored
by silly women. Donne confounds these misguided worshippers by
launching into a defiant humanist manifesto, which segregates himself and the girl he loves from their pious follies:

> . . . since at such times, miracles are sought,
> I would that age were by this paper taught
> What miracles wee harmlesse lovers wrought.

> First, we lov'd well and faithfully,
> Yet knew not what wee lov'd, nor why,
> Difference of sex no more wee knew,
> Then our Guardian Angells doe; . . .
> These miracles wee did; but now alas,
> All measure, and all language, I should passe,
> Should I tell what a miracle shee was.[15]

Humanist? It seems so, until we get to the 'Guardian Angells', and
their inclusion comes with an etherealizing surprise after the dismissal of religion's mumbo-jumbo earlier. Belief in guardian angels was
always attractive to Donne. Even if you do not believe in them, he
warned, 'yet know, that you do all that you doe, in the presence of
Gods Angels'.[16] The confidence that there was a special heavenly
being, commissioned to watch over him, which had been instilled
into him as a child, couldn't, it seems, be relinquished. That childish
article of faith shines out here, and bathes the lovers in its light. They
were not just chaste, we learn, but innocent: untarnished by sex, like
angels. Donne desires the purity as well as the authority of the grave.
To say what he wants to say about love, he has to imagine himself
dead, and the girl shrivelled and cleansed to a glittering relic. The
poem is religious because it strives to find a home for those instincts
of worship and sanctity which we identify as the religious emotions;
and it finds that home in the girl's chastity. In this respect it is a
humanist poem as well. The seriousness of religion's mysteries
transfigures the girl, and it does so because Donne is claiming that

she is *more* serious than religion's mysteries: a human wonder. If we were to try and explain the poem in terms of Donne's psychology we might say that his rejection of Catholic superstition (relics, miracles) had left his hunger for holiness without a focus, so he invents a version of human love elevated enough to satisfy it. Love fills the crater left by apostasy. 'The Relique' cannot be reduced to such formulas, but they are a part of its life.

So, too, with 'The Funerall' which, like 'The Relique', glances slightingly at Catholic superstition, only to replace it with something which is both Catholic and superstitious. Donne asks that the twist of hair around his arm should be buried with him:

> For since I am
> Loves martyr, it might breed idolatrie,
> If into others hands these Reliques came.[17]

That worship of relics among the Catholics constituted idolatry was a common Protestant charge. But despite this sceptical touch, the poem is far from depriving its relic of supernatural power. Donne steeps himself in religious fantasy, and dies, in that twilit world, the martyr's death which real life robbed him of. His feelings flow again along the channels worn in boyhood. The first stanza is hushed with awe as he dwells upon his sacred object:

> Who ever comes to shroud me, do not harme
>   Nor question much
> That subtile wreath of haire, which crowns mine arme;
> The mystery, the signe you must not touch,
>   For 'tis my outward Soule. . .

We are reminded, reading the lines, that they were written by the nephew of a man who possessed half of one of St. Thomas More's miraculous teeth. With each of these three poems Donne's responsiveness to the mystery of saints and relics is unmistakably the harvest of his upbringing in the Roman Church.

What complicates the poems, and saves them, by its complication, from the usual mistress-worshipping paeans of Elizabethan poetry, is that they are simultaneously and indecisively sacred and secular, religious and anti-religious. They bear the marks of a religious crisis, and one that has not yet sunk exhaustedly into the stock of past experience, but is active upon the turns and conflicts of thought. Like many of Donne's poems, they are, because of these cross-currents, virtually impossible to see clearly: they will not stay still. From our standpoint that is a condition of their greatness: it keeps them alive.

And from Donne's standpoint, we may surmise, it was what initially brought the poems into being. They offered a private theatre in which unresolvable oppositions could be entertained as they could not in the decisive business of life. That is why emotions of holiness fraught with Catholic implications inhabit the poems; and it is why they never inhabit them securely, but always encounter subversive elements—are, indeed, subversive themselves from the start, because they have been isolated from their rightful religious function, and transferred to human love.

Donne's 'Holy Sonnets', like his love poems, are torn by conflicts. They are full of sound and fury, and hang together by the makeshift expedients of passionate argument. Critics who fancy that religion is a sedate affair have found them unsatisfactory. Wilbur Sanders, for instance, complains of their 'blustering sophistry'[18]—quite a good description of the element that saves these great poems from the perfection of the merely devotional. The dates of the religious poems are rather more certain than those of the secular. 'La Corona' belongs to 1607; 'A Litanie' to 1608; and the 'Holy Sonnets', or several of them, to 1609 and 1610. If the turmoil in love poems like 'The Canonization' came from the effort to dispel religion, and absorb its sanctities for secular use, the heat of the 'Holy Sonnets' is generated by Donne's painful re-entry into religion's atmosphere. Though he had never ceased, in any formal sense, to be a Christian, he had come to feel, it seems, that he had lost God. We may gather this from the sonnet which he wrote, some years later, on the death of his wife, where he says that her example had prompted him to seek God again. His soul's new effort aroused the old torments. As we have seen, his mind turned, at this period of his life, to his Catholic father, whom he imagines in heaven watching his son's inner struggles. Not only was Donne's consciousness of his apostasy renewed by his renewed religious quest; the shameful waste of the years between also festered. The idolatrous effort to transfer his instinct for worship from God to women, which he had recorded in the love poems, confounds him, but he cannot rid his mind of it.

We can see this—and see the awkward eruption which memory of his profane love causes—in a sonnet which would plainly attract the attention of anyone on the lookout for blustering sophistry:

> What if this present were the worlds last night?
> Marke in my heart, O Soule, where thou dost dwell,
> The picture of Christ crucified, and tell

Whether that countenance can thee affright,
Teares in his eyes quench the amasing light,
Blood fills his frownes, which from his pierc'd head fell,
And can that tongue adjudge thee unto hell,
Which pray'd forgivenesse for his foes fierce spight?
No, no; but as in my idolatrie
I said to all my profane mistresses,
Beauty, of pitty, foulnesse onely is
A signe of rigour: so I say to thee,
To wicked spirits are horrid shapes assign'd,
This beauteous forme assures a pitious minde.[19]

Donne's logic is patently worthless here. The argument he recalls
using for getting girls into bed (that only ugly girls are unyielding)
was always fatuous, and applied to Christ on the cross it is gruesome.
We cringe from the blasphemy. No poet who wanted his sonnet to
develop with smooth and decorous power could possibly have
allowed the last six lines to stand: they would have been erased and
replaced by some continuation of the octave's resplendent serenity.
The result would have been lovely, but inert. As it is, the poem owes
its dramatic upheaval to its grotesque erotic argument, which tilts it
towards hysteria. How could anyone believe that, we wonder, as we
read the sestet? And as we wonder, Donne's desperation is brought
home to us. He contemplates the Saviour's bloody face, and searches
for some argument that will assure him of salvation. But all he can
find among the dazed, licentious thoughts that have become habitual
to him is the hideous piffle about pity and pretty faces which the last
six lines throw up.

The poem's argumentative collapse gives us a glimpse of a mind
humiliatingly aware of its limits, when faced with the divine. Donne
does not, of course, comment on the collapse of his argument. The
sonnet has no coda, pointing out that something has gone wrong
with its line of thought. In this it resembles many of the *Songs and
Sonnets* which, as we shall see, similarly depend on our detecting
lapses or contradictions in their reasoning, which they draw no
explicit attention to. But we can tell that he felt, and continued to
feel, how soiled his brain and tongue were, when he thought of
Christ's eyes and their 'amasing light'. 'I would say something of the
beauty and glory of those eyes,' he wrote later in a sermon, 'and can
finde no words, but such as I my selfe have mis-used in lower
things.'[20] The sermon confesses what the last six lines of the sonnet do
not confess but simply show: the incompetence of the polluted mind.

The unfitness of what he can find to say to God repeatedly afflicts Donne in the 'Holy Sonnets'. Even when he manages to pray, he sneers at his own efforts: 'In prayers, and flattering speaches I court God.'[21] Nor is it just that he feels unworthy—that would be quite proper. What worries him is that he can't feel unworthy enough. Something inside him is numb or crippled. He has dissipated himself in chasing after women; now he wants his sighs and tears back again, but there's nothing left:

> O might those sighes and teares returne againe
> Into my breast and eyes, which I have spent,
> That I might in this holy discontent
> Mourne with some fruit.[22]

The feel of not to feel it lies like a lump in his heart. He implores God to smash or melt him—'Batter my heart . . . breake, blowe, burn and make me new'[23]—but the desperation of the 'Holy Sonnets' depends on that prayer not being answered. If it were, he would be able to feel the saving pangs of pain. As it is, the pain which tears the sonnets is the pain of painlessness, of spiritual paralysis, which signals God's desertion. The hunger for pain is clamorously explicit:

> Spit in my face yee Jewes, and pierce my side,
> Buffet, and scoffe, scourge, and crucifie mee.[24]

It is envy of the crucified Jesus, rather than pity for him, that thrills in that cry. Donne flings himself on the nails and the sword; hugs the cross; lifts his face, revelling, for the spittle; tastes, in delicious anticipation, the whips. But nothing happens. He is not fit, he realizes, for those bloody joys. Unlike Christ's, his death could do no good. After the ecstatic masochism of the poem's start, he huddles back into his old feelings of uselessness and sin.

It is not difficult to understand Donne's need for suffering. That his soul's deadness should plague him could seem odd only to a soul already dead. But, familiar as his feelings are, they were also the outcome of his peculiar spiritual history. In renouncing Catholicism he had evaded persecution and the mortifying disabilities which English law imposed. Unlike his brother, and other prominent members of his family, he had forfeited martyrdom. It was, we recall, a goal that had shone before him from his childhood on. 'I have beene ever kept awake', he declared, at the very time when he was composing the 'Holy Sonnets', 'in a meditation of Martyrdome.'[25] He could not help comparing the agonies of the English Catholics with his own relative ease. He desires pain, in the sonnets, competitively: there seems to him something feeble and deprived about his immunity. As if to quiet a lingering guilt or disappointment about his escape from persecution, Donne continued throughout life to remind himself, in the sermons and elsewhere, that duller and less valiant types of endurance might, in the end, be as meritorious as martyrdom. God, he assures his congregation, will accept 'our tears of repentance and contrition' as if they were a martyrdom in themselves. All martyrdom is not 'a Smithfield Martyrdome'. To undergo setbacks in our lives and careers 'entitles us to the reward of Martyrdome'. Even in bereavement, he grasps at the bitter satisfaction of feeling martyred, as we see from the sermon which he preached after his daughter's death. His grief, he reminds himself, will improve his status in heaven; for all grief is 'a degree of Martyrdome, and so a degree of improving, and bettering our Resurrection'.[26] The wish to be a martyr was one of Donne's strongest impulses, and his denial, in *Pseudo-Martyr*, that the Catholics who had died for their faith were true martyrs may be seen as a way of reducing their advantage over him. Going on living, he maintains, is the real martyrdom, precisely because it involves resisting the allure of the scaffold. For ardent spirits, 'Not to be Martyrd, is a martyrdom.'[27]

Donne's need for a God who would make him suffer, voiced so stridently in the 'Holy Sonnets', can be related to this sensitivity about missed martyrdom, as well as to the feeling of inner coldness which is part of the same dissatisfied complex. To rouse his soul from its torpor he had recourse, it seems, to the programme of Spiritual Exercises which had been devised by St. Ignatius Loyola, and which were frequently prescribed to Catholics by their confessors. The full course of Exercises was designed to take four weeks, and comprised meditation upon one's sins, and upon the life, Passion and resurrection of Christ.[28] The aim was to simulate emotion. The exercitant was advised, for instance, in the third week, not to admit any joyful thoughts at all, even holy ones, but to excite himself to pain and anguish by incessantly recalling the sorrows of Christ. Catholic spiritual advisers testified to the success of the regime. John Gerard relates that one of his charges, a leading gentleman in the county, got as far as the last day but one in the second week without any visible emotion, but 'then suddenly the south wind (so to speak) blew over the garden of his soul', and he wept for three or four days without stopping. Even when business forced him to go out he could speak only in a voice broken by sobs; and he followed Gerard everywhere 'like a one-year-old'.[29]

Whether Donne took the whole of this affecting course, or even approached it in a systematic way, we don't know. But the wording of the Spiritual Exercises can be traced so clearly in the 'Holy Sonnets' that their presence in Donne's mind when he was writing is beyond doubt.[30] This was noticed by T. S. Eliot as long ago as 1930, though he refers rather strangely to the 'stock of images' which Ignatius and Donne have in common.[31] Images, in the normal sense of the word, are generally absent from the Spiritual Exercises. What rather strikes the comparing reader is the obedience to, and modification of, Ignatius's specific instructions which the 'Holy Sonnets' reflect. Ignatius, for instance, advises those who are contemplating Christ's passion to 'ask for grief, tears, and pain in union with Christ in torment'.[32] We can discover this petition for tears in Donne, but it does not sound, when we find it, self-abasing or lachrymose. It has become a vast gesture of despair at his own aridity and unresponsiveness:

> You which beyond that heaven which was most high
> Have found new sphears, and of new lands can write,
> Powre new seas in mine eyes, that so I might
> Drowne my world with my weeping earnestly.[33]

In the meditation on one's sins, occupying the second exercise of the first week, Ignatius calls for 'an exclamation of wonder, with intense affection, running through all creatures in my mind, how they have suffered me to live'.[34] Donne follows this direction also, but we miss, in his outcry, the intense affection Ignatius expects. Instead there is irritation at his own failure to deserve the life-supporting ministrations of the universe:

> Why are wee by all creatures waited on?
> Why doe the prodigall elements supply
> Life and food to mee, being more pure than I,
> Simple, and further from corruption?[35]

And instead of the long, rapt catalogue of natural wonders which the Ignatian worshipper was expected to embark on, Donne's list of the world's contents—horse, bull, boar—is impatiently curtailed. Despite these divergences, the initial Ignatian impulse is unmistakable, and more general resemblances between the arrangement of Donne's thoughts in the 'Holy Sonnets' and the Ignatian practice have been observed by several critics. He used the *compositio loci*—the vivid imagination of a scene or situation, such as his own death—and he follows it with prayer or colloquy as the Exercises prescribe.

So at the very time when Donne was preparing his ribald attack on Loyola and the Jesuits in *Ignatius his Conclave*, his spiritual life—preserved for us in the 'Holy Sonnets'—was shaping and nourishing itself on what they had taught him. This may help us to understand the sonnets' inner turmoil. Nor are the vestiges of Catholic devotion limited to this reliance on the Exercises. '*La Corona*', Helen Gardner has shown, incorporates, in its first sonnet, ideas and phrasing from the Advent Offices in the Roman breviary, and recalls, in its second and third sonnets, the Hours of the Blessed Virgin which formed part of the 'Primer', the prayer book of the Catholic laity inherited from the Middle Ages.[36] The prominence which '*La Corona*' and 'A Litanie' give to the Virgin would have been suspect to many Protestants. In 'A Litanie' she is credited with a share in mankind's redemption. She is:

> That she-Cherubin,
> Which unlock'd Paradise.[37]

After he took Anglican orders, Donne was to reprehend any such papistical notion. 'Nothing that she did', he insists, speaking of the Blessed Virgin in an early sermon, 'entered into that treasure, that ransom that redeemed us.'[38] The sanctified resonance which Catholic words like 'hermitage' and 'pilgrimage' retain for Donne in the love poems can be picked up again in the metaphor he employs for Mary's womb in '*La Corona*':

> Thou . . . shutst in little roome,
> *Immensity cloysterd in thy deare wombe.*[39]

The cloister image derives from a matins hymn used in the Roman Church for feasts of the Blessed Virgin. Donne's rendering of it inevitably reminds us of the love in 'The Good-morrow' which 'makes one little roome, an every where',[40] and the link-up suggests how closely Donne's early religious training influenced his love poetry, though a different 'deare wombe' was involved.

At all events, the Catholic notes in Donne's religious poems are remarkably clear and full. They are the work of a man who has renounced a religion to some manifestations of which he is still, at a profound level, attached. It would, of course, be an exaggeration to present him as a crypto-Catholic, furtively resorting to religious practices that he would, in public, have abjured. His situation was less simple. On the one hand, certain aspects of Catholic devotion were second nature to him. On the other, though he had become a

part of the Anglican propaganda machine, he was keenly aware of
shortcomings in each of the existing churches. Writing to Goodyer
about the Catholic and the reformed religions, he described them as
'sister teats' of God's graces, but added that both were 'diseased and
infected'.[41] One corollary of this critical awareness was a sense of his
own isolation from the company of God's elect: he was outcast, a
part of no whole.

The fear of damnation gripped Donne, though he knew it was
sinful to feel it. 'A sinfull, and a rebellious melancholy', he calls it in a
sermon, but adds in the next sentence that it is 'the hardest humour to
be purged' from the soul.[42] This 'sinne of feare' remained with him
long after he had taken orders, as 'A Hymne to God the Father'
shows.[43] It disrupts the 'Holy Sonnets'. The anticipation of divine
judgement is a horror:

> . . . my'ever-waking part shall see that face,
> Whose feare already shakes my every joynt.[44]

It has been suggested that, knowing this to be his besetting sin,
Donne artificially stimulated it in himself in order to combat it. 'In
Holy Sonnet I,' Louis Martz writes, 'we watch the speaker, in the
octave of the poem, deliberately arouse sensations of "despaire" and
"terrour" at the thought of sin and death and hell, and then, in the
sestet, firmly repel them by confidence in God's grace.'[45] But is this
what we watch? Here is the sonnet:

> Thou hast made me, And shall thy worke decay?
> Repaire me now, for now mine end doth haste,
> I runne to death, and death meets me as fast,
> And all my pleasures are like yesterday,
> I dare not move my dimme eyes any way,
> Despaire behind, and death before doth cast
> Such terrour, and my feebled flesh doth waste
> By sinne in it, which it t'wards hell doth weigh;
> Onely thou art above, and when towards thee
> By thy leave I can looke, I rise againe;
> But our old subtle foe so tempteth me,
> That not one houre I can my selfe sustaine;
> Thy Grace may wing me to prevent his art
> And thou like Adamant draw mine iron heart.[46]

Donne declares himself unable to combat, by his own efforts, the
temptation to despair. When he looks up to God, he can rise above it.
But the efforts of the 'subtle foe' of mankind, Satan, ensure that this

relief is temporary. That God's grace 'may' give him power to surmount the devil's wiles, Donne is sure. He is sure, too, that God 'may', if he wishes, draw his heart to him, though it is still, when the poem ends, 'iron'—locked, unrepentant, irresponsive. God may turn himself into a magnet ('Adamant') to redeem this unpromising waste metal—but will he? The initiative must come from God: without his 'leave' Donne cannot even look up for a moment. But that God will take this initiative, Donne is not sure. His present state, as expressed in the sestet, is one of despairing inadequacy: he cannot sustain himself for a single hour. He is a drowning man, earnestly informing an inscrutable bystander on the bank that if only he tosses in the life belt all will be well. But no life belt is forthcoming, and, what is worse, the man in the water knows that he does not deserve to be saved. Martz's assurance that we watch Donne 'firmly repel' despair by confidence in God's grace hustles us over the conditional nature of the poem's ending, and so misreads doubt as confidence, drowning as rescue.

The same need for unilateral action on God's part, and the same certainty that God has not taken the necessary action yet, are expressed in 'Batter my heart'. At least, here, his heart is no longer 'iron': he loves God, but it does no good. He feels no reciprocal love from God: the devil has him:

> . . . dearely'I love you, and would be lov'd faine,
> But am betroth'd unto your enemie,
> Divorce mee,'untie, or breake that knot againe,
> Take mee to you, imprison mee, for I
> Except you'enthrall mee, never shall be free,
> Nor ever chast, except you ravish mee.[47]

God's failure to make any move exasperates Donne. It is not only fear but indignation that we can hear behind the vehemence of the 'Holy Sonnets'. He flares into reproachful questions:

> Why doth the devill then usurpe in mee?
> Why doth he steale, nay ravish that's thy right?
> Except thou rise and for thine owne worke fight,
> Oh I shall soone despaire, when I doe see
> That thou lov'st mankind well, yet wilt'not chuse me,
> And Satan hates mee, yet is loth to lose mee.[48]

The last three lines are a warning to God: he may go too far, may look away too long. Implicit in them is that frantic attempt to blackmail God with promises or threats which we are all tempted to

resort to, in moments of unbearable stress, whether we believe in
him or not. Save my child, and I'll believe in you, we say. Save me,
says Donne, or I'll stop believing you ever will: then you'll have lost
me for good. And I'll stop 'soone': you haven't much time. Absurd,
of course. But the petulant challenge, hedged about with self-
justification (aren't I 'thine owne worke'?), and with wheedling
pathos (after all, 'thou lov'st mankind well', why not me?), and with
insinuated unflattering comparisons (Satan bothers about me more
than you, though I'm yours by 'right'), is wholly real. The voice
lives. The temptation to tell God outright that it's all his fault, which
we observe among the mixed-up feelings, is a measure of the
extreme to which Donne feels himself pushed by God's infuriating
nonchalance. If, as Louis Martz suggests, these sonnets began as
calmly plotted devotional exercises, intended to extirpate fear and
despair, we can only say that they failed as exercises, and so succeed
as poems.

Donne's fear that he belongs to the devil was not a nebulous fancy.
Belief in the physical reality of Satan was practically universal at the
beginning of the seventeenth century. Sightings of him walking the
earth in various shapes are frequently reported in contemporary
memoirs and pamphlets. Those suffering from religious despair
were especially prone to his visitations. Robert Burton testifies that
such people habitually 'smell brimstone' and 'talk familiarly with
devils'. In the casebooks of a seventeenth-century doctor we find
several patients who are convinced that they have seen the devil, in
human or animal form. John Bunyan used to feel Satan plucking at
his clothes as he knelt in prayer.[49] There had been an occurrence of
this kind quite recently in Donne's own family. Shortly before his
uncle, Jasper Heywood, died at Naples in January 1598, the devil had
appeared to him and told him that he was going to Hell because of his
unorthodox teaching. Luckily Heywood had more confidence than
his nephew: 'Liar,' he shouted, and the devil left discomfited.[50] We
cannot share the terror of the 'Holy Sonnets' unless we feel the devil
Donne speaks of as a living creature, a family acquaintance, close
at hand.

In Donne's day the natural outcome of religious despair was
suicide. It was the devil's masterpiece. When he found a soul which
felt itself to be cast out from God, and drowning in sin, he tempted it
with thoughts of self-slaughter, so as to make it securely his own.
This was the standard explanation of suicide, endlessly repeated in
the writings of divines, and dramatized in the morality plays.[51]
Donne, with his 'iron heart', his cowering terror ('I durst not view

heaven'), his frantic but frustrated desire for repentance ('Teach mee
how to repent'), and his feeling that he belongs contractually to the
devil ('betroth'd unto your enemie'), approaches the despairing condition of Marlowe's Faustus after he has made his pact with Satan:

> My heart is harden'd, I cannot repent.
> Scarce can I name salvation, faith, or heaven,
> But fearful echoes thunder in mine ears,
> 'Faustus, thou art damn'd!' Then guns and knives,
> Swords, poison, halters, and envenom'd steel
> Are laid before me to dispatch myself.[52]

Donne knew these fatal apparitions well. He was often seized, he tells
us, with the desire to kill himself. And since he could not cure himself
of this 'sickly inclination', he struggled to believe that it did not
come from the devil after all. We can't be sure, he contends, that 'all
which kill themselves, have done it out of a despair of Gods mercy'.
So vital did this point seem to him, that he wrote a whole treatise to
prove it. Yet all along he knew, as he admits, that his preoccupation
with the subject might come from Satan. It could be that 'the
common Enemie' found 'that doore worse locked against him
in mee'.[53]

Other symptoms of religious despair in Donne's 'Holy Sonnets'
resemble, it has been noted, those observable in the spiritual auto-
biographies of extreme seventeenth-century Protestants. He envies
the animals, because they cannot be damned, as he can:

> If lecherous goats, if serpents envious
> Cannot be damn'd Alas; why should I bee?[54]

He suspects that his wickedness outweighs that of all the rest of
creation. Against the sins of all the souls that ever were, he balances
his own. 'Above all these, my sinnes abound.' Both these morbid
obsessions can be paralleled in John Bunyan's record of his spiritual
crisis, Grace Abounding. Bunyan, too, envied the beasts: 'gladly
would I have been in the condition of a dog or horse, for I knew they
had no soul to perish under the everlasting weights of hell for sin, as
mine was like to do'. Bunyan, too, believed his sins unequalled
among mankind: 'I thought none but the devil himself could equalise
me for inward wickedness and pollution of mind. I fell, therefore, at
the sight of my own vileness, deeply into despair.'[55]

These similarities are natural. For Donne's renunciation of Catholicism left him writhing in the trap which was always set to catch the
Protestant soul. He explains the predicament clearly, in one of the

'Holy Sonnets'. If only he could repent, he would secure grace and be saved ('grace, if thou repent, thou canst not lacke'); but where can he get the grace to repent, if he needs to repent before he gets grace ('who shall give thee that grace to beginne?')?[56] Donne's question throws into prominence the central difference between Catholic and Protestant theology. Catholics believed—and believe—that man's fallen soul is saved by an infusion of grace, received in the first instance through the sacrament of baptism, and developed by the other sacraments which the Church administers. From birth to death, the Catholic reposes in the loving care of a grace-dispensing organization. Moreover, he can take effective steps to earn salvation for himself by the performance of good deeds, which God's grace makes meritorious.

The early seventeenth-century Protestant was, by comparison, isolated and helpless. He did not believe that the Church or the sacraments could confer grace. He discarded, as superstition, the notion of a wonder-working clergy. The mass, in which Christ's sacrifice was re-enacted in order to impart to the worshippers the saving benefits of that sacrifice, appeared to Protestants a piece of blasphemous play-acting. The basis of Protestant theology was the doctrine of justification by faith alone. Faith, in this context, did not mean mere belief in God's existence, as in more modern usage: even the devils in Hell, it was agreed, had that sort of faith. They knew, to their cost, that God existed. Faith meant belief in your own salvation. It necessitated a psychological act by which you accepted Christ consciously as your personal saviour. But this psychological act could not come about through your own effort. Faith, the Protestant theologians believed, was wholly in God's gift. Man could do nothing to attain it. Nor was there any point in his trying to qualify for it by virtuous behaviour. God selected those whom He would save according to an inscrutable process, known only to Him. Man's 'good works', as the Catholics envisaged them, simply did not exist in the Protestant scheme of things, for Protestants believed that man, as a hopelessly depraved and fallen creature, was incapable of good works. Nothing he did could merit salvation.

The opportunities for self-torment inherent in these Protestant doctrines were, it will be appreciated, almost limitless. For that very reason many Protestants were already moving, in the early years of the seventeenth century, to a more moderate and hopeful position. They laid greater stress on sacraments, and discouraged the terrified self-searching which Puritanism prompted. Donne's sonnets show that he was, however, far from this sort of benign Anglican compromise. What he found himself in was the Puritan dilemma. To be saved, you must believe you are saved. But how can you believe you are saved, unless you are already saved? How can you assure yourself that you have taken the necessary psychological step, and attained faith? And if you need to assure yourself, must that not indicate that you have not yet taken it? Since God alone can give you faith, and nothing whatsoever you do can deserve it, it follows that you can do nothing to escape damnation. You may, of course, pray to God to save you; but the damned may do that too. We are not saved by prayer.[57]

Protestantism, so conceived, was a recipe for anguish. That was the price of independence. The Protestant would brook no priestly interference between himself and his God, so he rejected the Church's sacred ministrations. Accordingly the burden of his eternal welfare descended upon him alone. Justification by faith meant, in effect, justification by state of mind. Ceaseless, agonized introspection almost inevitably resulted—at least in those of intense and questing temper; for how could you resist looking at your mind to see if it was in the right state? Donne, in abandoning the Catholic for the Protestant church, had entered the realm of doubt, and had he not made this move the 'Holy Sonnets' could never have been written. They are the fruit of his apostasy. For all their vestiges of Catholic practice, they belong among the documents of Protestant religious pain, and their suffering is the greater because they are the work of a man nurtured in a more sustaining creed. The determination to win salvation by personal endeavour, which we saw in Satire III, was a Catholic trait. Now, in the 'Holy Sonnets', Donne acknowledges that God must act first, and that his own efforts are futile:

> Batter my heart, three person'd God; for, you
> As yet but knocke, breathe, shine, and seeke to mend; . . .
> I, like an usurpt towne, to'another due,
> Labour to'admit you, but Oh, to no end.[58]

Assurance must come from outside. Yet, as a Protestant, Donne has cut himself off from that outside assurance which, for the Catholic, the Church and the sacraments supplied.

Donne's apostasy, then, may be seen as a necessary condition of some of his greatest love poems, as well as of his 'Holy Sonnets'. Further, if we are right about the psychological consequences of his apostasy, it allows us to see that his religious poems and his love poems are not as remote from each other as they might appear. We have suggested that the love poems display, in their obsession with woman's inconstancy, a profound anxiety about his own ability to attract or merit stable affection. His fear of damnation and of exclusion from God's love in the 'Holy Sonnets' reflects the same anxiety, transposed to the religious sphere. The resentment which Donne had directed against his fickle mistresses is redirected to strike at his own inconstancy ('I change in vowes, and in devotione') and at God, who appears negligent and inattentive. Awareness of his own unlovable nature—his 'blacke Soule' and 'iron heart'[59]—combines with exasperation at God's failure to cherish him enough.

We may appropriately end this chapter by looking at the sonnet Donne wrote on the death of his wife in 1617, for he makes his own unassuageable desire for love—which he both recognizes and puzzles over—the subject of that poem:

> Since she whome I lovd, hath payd her last debt
> To Nature, and to hers and my good is dead,
> And her soule early into heaven ravished,
> Wholy in heavenly things my mind is sett.
> Here the admyring her my mind did whett
> To seeke thee God; so streames do shew the head,
> But though I have found thee, and thou my thirst hast fed,
> A holy thirsty dropsy melts mee yett.
> But why should I begg more love, when as thou
> Dost wooe my soule, for hers offring all thine:
> And dost not only feare least I allow
> My love to saints and Angels, things divine,
> But in thy tender jealosy dost doubt
> Least the World, fleshe, yea Devill putt thee out.[60]

One remarkable thing about this poem is the absence of grief. Donne's high tone suppresses it. In the second line he actually presents his wife's death as a good thing—good for her, and good for him, because she has gained heaven and he is freed from earthly lusts. (She died, aged thirty-three, just after the birth of their twelfth child.) This view of her loss has been described by Donne's editor as 'almost intolerably harsh',[61] but it sounds more like someone making a superhuman effort to put a brave face on things. After the sixth line, the effort collapses, and Donne's disturbed feelings come pouring out. What hurts is the fact that no one loves him as much as he wants. God, he admits, is offering 'all' his love, but it is not enough. He is dissatisfied with himself for being dissatisfied, but that cannot remove the dissatisfaction.

As an approach to bereavement this might be called self-centred. But then, all feelings of loss are self-centred. Donne's inspection of the matter seems outstandingly honest, and poignant in its honesty, as the initial pretence that all is well gives way to undisguised, though apologetic, complaint. The upshot is that God is not a satisfactory lover, since he cannot make Donne feel loved sufficiently. To make matters worse, he has taken away Donne's wife. The meaning of the last four lines seems to be that God has shown his 'tender jealousy' twice in Donne's lifetime: first, by removing him from the Catholic Church, where 'saints and Angels' were worshipped (so Protestants said); second, by killing his wife, so as to curtail his attachment to earthly affections (the world, the flesh and the devil). Actually, as Donne has revealed in lines six and seven, it was his wife who brought him to God. So God's jealousy of her was quite needless. The poem ends on a note of affectionate reproach. How, Donne seems to ask, could God have been so tenderly jealous as to suspect that mere worldly lusts would displace him in Donne's regard?

So ultimately Donne's subject, as in so many of the *Songs and Sonnets,* is disappointment with a lover—though naturally, addressing God, he phrases it very tactfully, and admits that he is himself to blame. The love poem this sonnet is most like is 'Loves Infiniteness'—

> If yet I have not all thy love,
> Deare, I shall never have it all[62]

—where Donne despairs of having total possession of the girl's love, and eventually admits that he doesn't want to have it:

> Yet I would not have all yet,
> Hee that hath all can have no more.

This, like the sonnet on his wife's death, acknowledges that, where love is concerned, his nature is insatiable. He found it impossible to believe that he was loved enough, even by God. If our diagnosis has been correct, one cause at least of this obsession was the early crisis of his apostasy, with the self-doubt, the divided loyalties, the sundering of personal ties, the spiritual estrangement, and the loss of secure inherited trust which it occasioned.

3

Ambition

Our coverage of Donne's biography so far has been rather disjointed. Concentrating on his religious development we have
jumped from the period of his apostasy and of Satire III, roughly
datable in 1595, to the years 1609–11, which saw both his anti-
Catholic propaganda and the spiritual crisis recorded in the 'Holy
Sonnets'. Now we need to go back to the 1590s and fill in the events
in his outer existence which brought him to take Anglican orders in
1615 and embark on his career as a famous preacher which ended
only with his death in 1631.

A thread which runs through the whole and binds it together is
restless desire for work and worldly success. This was so attractive to
him that he came to regard it, eventually, as a religious duty. There is
no theme to which he returns more often in his sermons. 'Be something', is his constant refrain, 'Be sombody.'[1] Inactivity horrified
him. The idle, he proposed, should be sent to the colonies and forced
to work.[2] It grieved him to think that we spend so much of our time
in eating, sleeping, and other trivialities, that none of us can be said to
live more than ten years, properly reckoned.[3] We must, he insists,
put something useful into our hands and our children's hands: 'put a
sword, put a ship, put a plough, put a trade.'[4] If we do not choose a
definite and regular calling, and pursue it unremittingly, we shall be
useless, ephemeral creatures, passing out of life as a hand passes out
of a basin of water, 'which may bee somewhat fouler for thy washing
in it, but retaines no other impression of thy having been there'.[5]

This work ethic was not peculiar to Donne, though he espoused it
with peculiar intensity. It flourished among Protestants, harmoniz-
ing with their faith in progress and utility, and their contempt for
monastic idleness, which Donne shared. 'Any Artificer is a better
part of a state, then any retired or contemplative man,' he maintained. 'Wee are not sent into this world to Suffer, but to Doe.'[6] Nor
did he regard work as an end in itself: the accumulation of wealth was
its proper and legitimate aim. God's command 'Be fruitful and
multiply' means, he argues, that we should strive to enlarge our

possessions and estate, even if we have inherited an ample fortune. 'God gives many men good estates from their parents at first; yet Gods purpose is that they should increase those estates.'[7] Those who do not rejoice in worldly advantages disobey God's command, and so, by consequence, do those 'that employ not their industry, that use not all good means to attaine them'.[8]

Lucre was not the only objective. Behind Donne's discourses upon the ills of idleness lies the belief that only through regular employment can a man relinquish his separate, fragmentary identity and become a part of the world. It is clear that this was something he felt acutely. He wanted to amalgamate. When he speaks of choosing a career, his language does not suggest independent self-advancement but, on the contrary, integration into a greater whole that will swallow up the isolated self. Without a job, he asserts, you are 'no link of Gods Chaine', no 'limbe of the body of this world'; you are an unnecessary incidental—a fingernail, a hair, a 'Mole in the Face'. Even the greatest men are wens or excrescences or 'chippings' unless they are 'incorporated into the body of the world'.[9]

This desire is familiar to us in Donne's love poems, though there it assumes a slightly different guise. The lover wants to escape from his separateness in a self-eclipsing union:

> When love, with one another so
> Interinanimates two soules,
> That abler soule, which thence doth flow,
> Defects of lonelinesse controules.[10]

I have suggested that Donne's abandonment of the Roman Church may have been motivated, in some degree, by ambition. As a Catholic, he could not belong to the body politic. His impulse to be absorbed could not be satisfied. Nor, paradoxically, could it be satisfied by deserting the Roman Church, for that cut him off from the community which had claimed his earliest allegiance. The dilemma was insoluble, and a sense of separation, together with a desire to overcome it, are contending and controlling features in Donne's thought all his life. Their fruitfully divisive influence is evident in the love poems, which alternately celebrate the union of souls (as in 'A Valediction: forbidding Mourning') and deny the possibility of any such union (as in 'Loves Alchymie'). In the religious poems, likewise, disjunction from God and the struggle to end it are, as we have seen, the major subjects.

Donne's worry about personal isolation—'Defects of lonelinesse'—proceeded from his character as well as from his historical circumstances. His powerful sense of singularity prompted and, at the same time, prohibited the total union he dreamed of. After he had become a Christian minister he was, of course, bound to recommend communal virtues, and strive to bring faithful souls into membership of the body of Christ. We find him doing it in one of his most quoted statements, from the *Devotions* of 1623: 'any man's death diminishes me, because I am involved in mankind, and therefore never send to know for whom the bell tolls; it tolls for thee.'[11] Yet even here, it has been shrewdly noted, there is in fact no thought about the man for whom the bell might be tolling, nor any inclination, in the entire meditation, to imagine sympathetically his life and death. On the contrary, the tone and advice are entirely self-regarding: 'any man's death diminishes *me . . . never send to know* for whom the bell tolls.'[12]

Donne's ambitious nature contained within it, then, contradictory seeds: of self-assertion and of self-negation. Both elements—the wish to make his way in the world, and the wish to be integrated into it—inclined him to an active rather than a contemplative life. As an intellectual, however, he inevitably felt torn between thought and action. He told his friend Goodyer that he had been diverted from his practical study of the law at Lincoln's Inn by 'the worst voluptuousnes, which is an Hydroptique immoderate desire of humane learning and languages'. He confesses his studiousness, but sees it as a disease. Intellectual accomplishments are allowable as ornaments to great fortunes, he argues, but what he needs is 'an occupation'.[13]

In his earliest poems, the Satires, this urge for activity is raucously apparent. The first Satire opens with Donne, in his study, berating a tiresome intruder who wants to get him out on to the London streets:

> Away thou fondling motley humorist,
> Leave mee, and in this standing woodden chest,
> Consorted with these few bookes, let me lye
> In prison, and here be coffin'd, when I dye.[14]

The speech contradicts itself. Although Donne professes to want to be left in his study, he calls it a coffin and a prison. Not surprisingly he and the intruder are out among the crowds well before the end of the poem. The very texture of the Satires reflects Donne's active temper. Asked what they are about, we should best reply: agitation. They are remarkable less for their social insight than for their impatient physical movement. This is apparent as much in the vehement, bludgeoning rhythms as in the way the syntax and subject matter are fractured and pushed about. They are hives of energy. In Satire I the verbs describing the actions of the tiresome companion keep the poem mobile. He creeps, skips, grins, smacks, shrugs, stoops, leaps, jogs, drops behind, overtakes, and finally:

> flings from mee
> Violently ravish'd to his lechery.

This frantically animated 'humorist' is a facet of Donne himself, though one which he strives to externalize and condemn. His 'humorous'[15] (i.e. changeable, mercurial) disposition, in love, studies and religion, was something he endlessly and unavailingly deplored, as we shall see.

Apart from restless activity, the main occupation of the Satires is hate. The world observed is corrupt, spurious, lecherous, treacherous and obscene, and the court is the worst part of it. No one, Donne impresses upon us, is as:

> . . . pronc to'all ill, and of good as forget-
> full, as proud, as lustfull, and as much in debt,
> As vaine, as witlesse, and as false as they
> Which dwell at Court.[16]

It might occur to us to ask why, if the world that centres on the court is such an abhorrent place, Donne should have spent the next twenty years straining every nerve to get a foothold in it. Yet that would be a naïve question. Donne's anger is bred from thwarted ambition. His hate is a way of drawing attention to himself:

> Sir; though (I thanke God for it) I do hate
> Perfectly all this towne . . .

While he rips open society's sores, he can project himself as not only more honest and upright than the rest of mankind but as cleverer, full of smart answers, altogether outstandingly able.

Donne was not alone in using satire in this way. Virtually all the English satirists between Gascoigne and Marston were, like Donne, ambitious young men who deliberately gave their satires informal publication, by circulating them in manuscript, in order to bring themselves to notice. Their satirical verses did not reflect serious discontent with the age, but amounted to self-advertisement within the court group, of a kind necessary for those not born into wealthy or influential families.[17] When Donne had managed to attract the interest of his superiors, he quickly dropped satire-writing. It would have been foolhardy to continue, and besides he was too fascinated by the court as a power centre to be concerned with satirizing it. Though James's court was far more obviously corrupt and degenerate than Elizabeth's, Donne never ventured any criticism of it at all. Instead, he did everything in his power to obtain preferment.

The Jacobean age did produce a number of intrepid and committed satirists, but they were of a different breed from Donne and the eye-catching Elizabethan malcontents, being more sincere and less talented. George Wither, for instance, denounced abuses in church and state in his *Abuses Stript and Whipt*, and was imprisoned. Drayton in *The Owle* and Richard Niccols in *The Cuckow* and *The Beggers Ape* contributed fierce attacks on court and administration. Donne had no truck with these writers, and he would probably have agreed with James that they deserved to be 'puld up like stinkinge weeds'.[18] In his sermons he firmly condemns satire.

At the time when Donne was penning his own Satires in the 1590s, all this was years in the future. But it may help to confirm our scepticism about his satires' anti-establishment stance. In 1596 came Donne's chance to satisfy his thirst for action and self-advancement. A fleet was being prepared to attack the Spanish mainland. The land forces were under the command of the Earl of Essex. Those in need of adventure and money flocked to take part—a number of them from the Inns of Court—as gentlemen volunteers: 'three hundred green headed youths, covered with feathers, gold and silver lace', an eyewitness described them. Among these came Donne, who secured a personal introduction to the Earl, probably through his college friend Henry Wotton, who was now Essex's secretary.

If you were an ambitious young man, Essex was the obvious star to follow. He aimed to be the most powerful man in the realm, and looked like succeeding. His gallantry, youth and courage dazzled all eyes, including the Queen's, who loved his company, and would sit with him 'playing at cards or other game until the birds sang in the morning'. As her Master of Horse, he walked beside her, holding her bridle, on state occasions. He was the finest swordsman of the age, and famed for his martial valour. He had been knighted for his bravery in the Netherlands campaign in which Sidney had been killed. The masses adored him. Nor, for all his dash and splendour, was he without political cunning. Intent on commanding the knowledge that would allow him to direct events, he organized an extensive intelligence service, radiating from Gray's Inn, which kept him informed about international affairs. By 1593 he had been promoted to the Privy Council, and it was said that 'all matters of intelligence are wholly in his hands'.[19] Further, he was a warm-hearted dispenser of patronage, and generously rewarded those who followed him.

For Donne, the Spanish expedition must have seemed a matchless opportunity. If he could once earn Essex's notice, there was no knowing what he mightn't aspire to. Writing to Christopher Brooke about his motives for becoming a soldier, Donne mentions prominently his poverty and obscurity: 'a rotten state, and hope of gain'.[20] Another reason, almost certainly, was to get himself known as a loyal Englishman, and so remove any suspicions relating to his Catholic upbringing, which might hinder his public career. By fighting against Spain he would show that his heart was in the right place. This calculation presumably explains the unexpected patriotic effusion ('England to whom we'owe, what we be, and have . . .'[21]) included in his poem about the campaign.

Naturally, there was danger: he might be killed—though even that seemed quite appealing in the abstract. He mentions desire for 'faire death' in his list of motives to Brooke. Thought of hardship excited him too. We may guess at his state of mind from the elegy 'His Picture', which seems to have been written—to some girl, real or imaginary—at this time:

> Here take my Picture, though I bid farewell;
> Thine, in my heart, where my soule dwels, shall dwell.
> 'Tis like me now, but I dead, 'twill be more
> When wee are shadowes both, then 'twas before.
> When weather-beaten I come backe; my hand,
> Perchance with rude oares torne, or Sun beams tann'd,
> My face and brest of hairecloth, and my head
> With cares rash sodaine hoarinesse o'rspread,
> My body'a sack of bones, broken within,
> And powders blew staines scatter'd on my skinne;
> If rivall fooles taxe thee to'have lov'd a man,
> So foule, and course, as, Oh, I may seeme than,
> This shall say what I was . . .[22]

'This', in the last line quoted, is the picture, ostensibly the poem's subject, which he presents to the girl before departure. Presumably it shows him as a silken youth; but we can only surmise. For it is part of the poem's guile that it paints, in rugged strokes, quite another picture than the one it is supposed to be about. It depicts Donne as he wants to imagine himself in the future, after battle or captivity, with a smashed, stained body. And the look of that sturdy veteran is infinitely more compelling, we are made to feel, than the dainty keepsake he is actually handing over, and which the poem does not even deign to describe. Like its author, Donne's elegy is hardily intent on the future.

The poem's ending confirms our feeling that the battered old body is really better than the 'picture', although Donne has all along been pretending the opposite. The girl must tell 'rivall fooles', he advises, that his former 'faire and delicate' appearance was like milk, which feeds love in its 'childish state'; but now her love

> is growne strong enough
> To feed on that, which to'disus'd tasts seemes tough.

Bristles, rough hands, and the other craggy features Donne plans for himself don't only make a man more worthy, but also more appetizing to women. Joining the Cadiz expedition plainly had much in its favour.

The fleet set sail in June, and on the 21st surprised the Spanish ships at anchor in Cadiz harbour. A bombardment, lasting some three hours, was directed at four great galleons anchored at the harbour mouth, among them the enemy flagship the *San Felipe*. Two were set alight by their crews to prevent capture, but the others fell into English hands. In all, thirteen Spanish warships and forty merchant vessels were destroyed, and casualties were heavy. Around the stricken ships the water seethed with horribly burnt men, many of whom fell victim to the fusillades from the English decks as they struggled to keep afloat. Further loss of life ensued when the magazines in the burning galleons exploded. Donne could scarcely have had a more spectacular introduction to warfare.

After the naval victory, Essex rapidly put troops ashore and stormed the city. By nightfall it was in English hands. One of the English captains, Sir John Wingfield, unwisely mounted a horse to enter the town, thus presenting a good target, and was shot through the head. Apart from that the English losses were negligible. Wingfield received a military funeral in Cadiz cathedral, the generals throwing their handkerchiefs, wet with tears, into the grave. Donne, angling for Essex's notice, penned an enthusiastic epigram on Wingfield's heroism and the honour 'our Earle' had done him.[23] Then the victors set about looting Cadiz in a businesslike way, which occupied them for nearly a fortnight. Essex was in favour of staying longer, but the supply problem proved troublesome, so he gave orders that the city, together with its castle and fortifications, should be razed. Churches and religious buildings were alone piously spared. The job was done so thoroughly that the Spaniards had to embark on a complete rebuilding programme.

The English force stopped on its way home to demolish the undefended Portuguese town of Faro. Among the plunder from this raid was the library of Bishop Orosius, a noted Renaissance stylist, which Essex presented to the Bodleian. Donne had evidently got a taste for such activities, and when another expedition was organized the following year, 1597, to attack the Spanish fleet at Ferrol, he again volunteered. This time Essex's fleet had a bad start, since it ran into a storm and had to return to port. Many of the gentlemen volunteers were, Raleigh's captain reported, 'dangerously sicke', and, when they got ashore, 'discharging their high Plumes, and imbroydered Cassockes, they secretly retired themselves home.' Donne was made of sterner stuff. He wrote up the fleet's mishaps in his poem 'The Storme', which cheerfully derides the agonies of seasickness suffered by his comrades, and bristles with callous, witty images:

> And as sin-burd'ned soules from graves will creepe,
> At the last day, some forth their cabbins peepe: . . .
> And from our totterd sailes, ragges drop downe so,
> As from one hang'd in chaines, a yeare agoe.[24]

Then he and the expedition set sail again. This time the ships under Raleigh's command, on one of which Donne was serving, got separated from the main fleet and reached the Azores. These lush, humid little islands in mid-Atlantic had, since the Spaniards had opened up the Americas, become a favourite port of call for their treasure fleets. English privateers regularly lurked among them waiting for prey, and engagements were frequent. Raleigh's flotilla, on this occasion, hit a dead calm off the island of St. George, which lasted two days and produced Donne's companion poem to 'The Storme', 'The Calme'.

These two are his only purely descriptive poems, and they are so packed with sense impressions that you take them in through your skin and body as much as through your mind. The things noticed are casual and disorganized, like reality: sun-seared flesh, sharks, drying washing. In the heat and stillness of 'The Calme' the ships seem to moulder and fall to pieces:

> . . . all our beauty, and our trimme, decayes,
> Like courts removing, or like ended playes.
> The fighting place now seamens ragges supply;
> And all the tackling is a frippery.
> No use of lanthornes; and in one place lay
> Feathers and dust, to day and yesterday.[25]

That was one of the quotations from Donne which Ben Jonson had by heart.

But though Donne was in new and exotic circumstances—becalmed off the Azores—his head, as the quoted lines illustrate, was still full of London life: the court, the playhouse, the second-hand clothes shops ('fripperies'). His powerfully self-absorbed mind imprints itself and its contents on the scene before him, so that we get the effect of a photographic double exposure. The seascape off the Azores is seen through layers of Elizabethan London. As a result the poems, for all their descriptive life, give us a less solid impression of someone venturing into strange climes than do the plain accounts by Elizabethan seamen. Arthur Gorges, for instance, who was on the same voyage, noted approvingly the agriculture of the islands—'pretty little rising hills, and all the fields over full of Melons, Potatoes and other Fruites'—and was much struck by the nocturnal rainbows:

> As we ranged by Gratiosa, on the tenth of September, about twelve a clocke at night, we saw a large and perfect Rainbow by the Moone light, in the bignesse and forme of all other Rainbowes, but in colour much differing, for it was more whitish, but chiefly inclining to the colour of the flame of fire.[26]

That is the stuff which travel books are made of. Donne could never have written one, because his brain so bulged with his habitual preoccupations that it had no time to be interested by a few peasants and foreigners, or by the odd conditions they chose to live in. Typically, we find him writing home from the Continent later in life, when he was staying at Spa, to complain of 'the peremptory barrenness of this place'.[27] Abroad was boring.

After the calm, Essex's and Raleigh's ships found each other, only to become separated again, and if Donne remained with Raleigh's squadron he must have taken part in the dare-devil capture of the fortifications on the island of Fayal. A small English contingent led by Raleigh landed under heavy fire, and after stiff fighting dislodged the Spanish garrison, which fled to the woods. The glory of the exploit was so considerable that Essex, arriving late and jealous on the scene, threatened Raleigh with court martial for undertaking the attack alone. While the commanders bickered, the Spanish West Indian fleet slipped past the English guns, so the Azores voyage was, from a national viewpoint, a failure. However, all was not lost, for on the way home the expedition seized and ransacked three merchant ships sailing from Havana and laden, as an eyewitness reported, 'with Cochynella, and other rich Merchandize, besides the Silver, Gold, Pearle, Civet, Muske, Ambergreece which was amongst the Passengers'.[28] Thievery of this kind was an important element in English maritime policy, though the English seem to have managed to conceal the fact from themselves. The English traveller Fynes Moryson, for instance, was surprised and hurt to find, when visiting Hamburg, that what he had come to regard as the Royal Navy was viewed by foreigners as a pack of pirate ships.[29] Donne plainly had no qualms about plunder, and only regretted that more of it did not come his way.[30]

However, the voyage served Donne's purposes of self-advancement well enough. One of the young warriors knighted by Essex during the expedition was Thomas Egerton, son of the Lord Keeper of the Great Seal. Donne had perhaps known him at Lincoln's Inn: now they had been comrades. Within weeks of the voyagers' return Donne, through young Egerton's good offices, had been appointed secretary to the Lord Keeper, Sir Thomas Egerton, a man of wide power and influence, and one of the key figures in Elizabeth's administration. This was the breakthrough Donne had been waiting for. The Lord Keeper's secretary, it was taken for granted, had a successful career in public service ahead of him. Donne moved into York House, the Egerton London residence, and found himself at the centre of national life. He was employed to investigate malpractice in the legal profession, and Satire V, addressed to Egerton, records his findings.[31] As might be expected, this is a more respectful performance than his previous satires, making it quite clear that Elizabeth—'Greatest and fairest Empresse'—is in no way to blame for the corruption rampant in her realm. Even here, though, he cannot suppress his indignation at the government agents who persecute Catholics. Would it not, he asks, anger the holiest of men,

> yea a Martyr,
> To see a Pursivant come in, and call
> All his cloathes, Copes; Bookes, Primers; and all
> His Plate, Challices; and mistake them away,
> And aske a fee for comming?

It would have been more tactful for Donne to have kept his Catholic resentment out of sight. But as we have seen it was liable to surface whenever he wrote poetry.

This was to be the last of his Satires. Like his love poems, they were a secret, circulated only among friends. Sending some of his

Paradoxes to Wotton, he asks him to promise that he will take no copies of any of his writings: 'to my satires there belongs some fear, and to some elegies, and these perhaps, shame. . . . I am desirous to hide them.'[32] The government was suspicious of satires and love elegies and, by order of the Bishop of London, the public hangman had recently burned a number of printed collections. Egerton's secretary could write such things only furtively: ambition required guile.

Donne is singular among English poets in that he never refers to his poetry except disparagingly. When he sends poems to friends he excuses them as 'light flashes' or 'evaporations' or a 'ragge of verses'. If his correspondent replies admiringly, Donne brushes it aside with the assurance that he does not 'make such trifles for praise'. Even as a young man he expressed dismay that 'love-song weeds' and 'Satyrique thornes' had sprung up in him where the 'seeds of better Arts' were sown, and announced his resolve to give up the 'vanity' of writing poems.[33] No doubt these disclaimers may be ascribed, in part, to defensive shyness. But it is clear that Donne did not even bother to keep copies of some of his poems. When in 1614 he was under pressure from a wealthy patron to make a collection of them, he had to write round to his friends to get his manuscripts back, remarking in typically dismissive fashion that it 'cost me more diligence to seek them than it did to make them'.[34] The image of himself which he wished to encourage was that of a person for whom poetry was no more than a courtly accomplishment. And he became chary of letting even that much be known. When his friend Goodyer encouraged him to address a poem to the Countess of Huntingdon, Donne demurred. 'That knowledge which she hath of me', he explained, 'was in the beginning of a graver course than of a poet, into which (that I may also keep my dignity) I would not seem to relapse.'[35] Naturally in these circumstances the idea of having poetry printed struck him as totally repellent, for it put him on a level with the scum of professional rhymesters. It filled him with shame to think that, for the sake of patronage, he had deigned to publish his Anniversaries in 1611 and 1612. 'I confess I wonder how I declined to it,' he remarked, 'and do not pardon myself.'[36] This contempt for poetry, and for himself in the role of poet, was, it seems, another facet of Donne's ambition. He associated poetry with a volatile element in his personality which he considered it politic to suppress. The urge to write poems was plainly too strong to withstand, but he atoned for it by belittling and neglecting them once they were written. He led a double life, his poetry supplying a covert outlet for impulses which his public self refused to recognize.

Meanwhile, as Egerton's secretary, he was an eye-witness to one of the most celebrated upsets in Elizabethan history. His former commander, Essex—soon to die a traitor's death for attempting an armed rising in the streets of London—had returned from his Irish campaign without Elizabeth's permission, and was made a prisoner at York House, in Egerton's charge. Donne watched the fallen nobleman sympathetically but remotely. He had found alternative support. At court for the Christmas festivities of 1599—festivities that probably included the first performance of *Twelfth Night*—he wrote to a friend describing the 'iollyty and revells', and remarking: 'My lorde of Essex and his trayne are no more mist here then the Aungells which were cast downe from heaven nor (for anything I see) likelyer to retourne.' Donne had no intention of being cast down himself. In 1601 he became M.P. for Brackley, Northants—the seat was in Egerton's control. In the same year he secured a royal grant of a lease of some land in Lincolnshire. Holding land directly from the crown, he was now entitled to write 'Esquire' after his name.[37]

But that was as far as Donne got. Just before Christmas 1601 he contracted a secret marriage with a girl called Ann More. She had been living in York House under Egerton's protection, and was the niece of his second wife, who had died in 1600. Her father, Sir George More, was a wealthy Surrey landowner, and Ann was sixteen or seventeen years old. Donne was twenty-nine. When news of the marriage broke, Sir George exploded in fury, and Donne's world fell about his ears. He was dismissed from Egerton's service, and thrown into prison. Even when Sir George relented, and tried to get Donne's job back for him, Egerton remained adamant. Donne, as he saw it, had betrayed his trust, and so shown himself unfit for confidential employment. Though it took Donne many years to reconcile himself to the fact, his hopes of a public career had vanished beyond recall.

This disaster was scarcely less important than Donne's Catholic upbringing in the effect it had on his view of himself and his world. In some respects, it reopened the scars which that upbringing had left, for it made Donne feel once more estranged and outcast, as if he inhabited a different universe from other people. His letters show that the reactions of his father-in-law and his employer to the marriage shocked him. He had expected nothing of the kind. The self-absorption which rendered him unobservant as a traveller, prevented him from noticing the impression he made on those around him. One reason for Egerton's refusal to reinstate his secretary, apparently, was that he had not much liked Donne's way of improving the wording of letters which he set him to copy.[38] That Donne

remained unaware of the offence he was giving, is what we should
have expected. At a later crisis in his life, when he took holy orders,
he was again amazed by the reaction of someone he thought he knew
well—this time his patron the Countess of Bedford, who gave it as
her opinion that a man with a past life like Donne's had no place in
the Church.[39]

But if the monstrous injustice which overwhelmed Donne when
he married gave him a new awareness of isolation, it also, like the
anti-Catholic persecution of his boyhood, redoubled his determination to succeed, and added stature to his powerful and defiant ego, of
which his runaway marriage was itself an expression. Why, we may
ask, was Sir George so opposed to the match? Part of the answer lay,
no doubt, in Donne's poverty and obscurity. He wrote to his father-
in-law protesting that 'some uncharitable malice hath presented my
debts double at least', but he did not deny that he was in debt. There
was also, apparently, a religious objection. Sir George suspected that
his daughter's seducer was a crypto-Catholic. But the gossip which,
Donne believed, had poisoned Sir George's mind most touched on
his reputation as a libertine. 'That fault', Donne writes, 'was laid to
me of having deceived some gentlewomen before.'[40]

There has been debate among critics about the extent to which
Donne's amorous adventures in the love poems had a basis in real
life. Sir Edmund Gosse's theory that the poems are autobiographical
has been roundly derided—for the most part by persons with literary
gifts infinitely smaller than Gosse's. The evidence is, of course,
scanty. The only first-hand recollection of Donne in his student days
is the often-quoted one of Sir Richard Baker, writing almost half a
century after the event, who recalls that Donne 'leaving Oxford,
lived at the Innes of Court, not dissolute, but very neat; a great visiter
of Ladies, a great frequenter of Playes, a great writer of conceited
Verses'.[41] This need not mean much more than that Donne was
something of a social butterfly, and even if Baker's phrase about
ladies is specifically sexual in intent, it could be mere gossip—
emanating, possibly, from Donne himself. For among his men
friends he preserved, even after marriage, something of a raffish
pose. We find him writing to George Garrard from Paris in 1612,
thanking him for a letter and adding that he loves it 'as my mistress's
face, every line and feature, but best all together'.[42] There is, of
course, no question of Donne having a mistress eleven years after
marrying Ann: it's just the turn of phrase of a man who liked it to be
known that he had a way with the ladies.

But if Baker's testimony doesn't count for much one way or the other, there are two other bits of evidence which seem unexceptionable. Looking back on his marriage in the *Essays in Divinity*, Donne thanks God for rescuing him 'from the Egypt of lust, by confining my affections';[43] and in one of the 'Holy Sonnets' which we have already looked at he tells God what he used to say in his 'idolatrie' to 'all my profane mistresses'.[44] Given these declarations, we can discard the notion that the sexually promiscuous Donne who prowls through the elegies and the more wayward of the lyrics was a figment of his imagination. The Donne who married Ann More may not have 'deceived some gentlewomen', for he may have confined his amours to the lower, and cheaper, social orders. But the tongues which wagged about his philandering to Sir George had something to wag about. Further, we may be sure that Donne's union with Ann put a stop to his loose living. That prayer of thanks in the *Essays in Divinity*, where he says that marriage confined his affections, was addressed, as was the Holy Sonnet, to a God who, Donne believed, knew not only his every action but his every thought. There could be no dissimulation. Donne's fidelity to Ann was absolute: when he had her, he wanted no other woman.

In the early years of their marriage, though, they had to endure poverty and discomfort. They lived, at first, by the charity of his friends and her relations. After a while they moved to a little gabled cottage at Mitcham. Donne disliked it because he felt cut off from the civilized world in the country, and because the house was damp and unhealthy. His study had a cellar underneath it from which there rose noxious vapours, or so he fancied. He became depressed and ill, and was tempted at times to do away with himself. To make matters worse, the family grew rapidly. 'I stand like a tree, which once a year bears, though no fruit, yet this mast of children,' Donne wrote ruefully to a friend. 'Mast' means acorns, beech nuts and suchlike pig food. His estimate of one child per year is scarcely an exaggeration. The Donnes took three children with them to Mitcham in 1606, and during their five years there they had four more. One of the letters which brings us closest to Donne in this period was written on a January night in 1607, in order to keep his mind off the fact that his wife was having their fourth child upstairs. Had she died in labour, he says, he would probably have committed suicide.[45] Since he had no regular employment, simply giving his children enough to eat was at times an acute problem. A death in the family would, in a sense, have been a relief, if it were not for the funeral expenses involved. As Donne grimly remarked, 'if God should ease us with burials, I know not how to perform even that'.[46]

These disgruntled allusions to his family suggest how embittering failure and disgrace were. Exiled from the warmth and splendour of York House, he found himself eking out a wretched existence surrounded by dependants for whose miseries he was all too clearly accountable. He never expresses, in his letters, the natural joy in children or in his wife's love that we might expect from a young father. All that part of his life, it seems, was blighted by want and by the galling consciousness of failure. Even in the most equable letters written from his Mitcham cottage, his dissatisfaction is discernible. 'I write', he tells Goodyer, 'from the fire side in my Parler, and in the noise of three gamesome children; and by the side of her, whom because I have transplanted into a wretched fortune, I must labour to disguise that from her by all such honest devices, as giving her my company, and discourse.'[47] Actually staying in the same room as his wife was, we gather from this, scarcely more than a benign duty. We can glean little, from Donne's letters or any other source, of Ann's personality or interests. Her existence remains almost as shadowy as that of the females in his poems. Sir John Oglander, her brother-in-law, when recording the burial of her stillborn child in 1612, noted that she was 'the best of women',[48] and we have Donne's testimony that

> Here the admyring her my mind did whett
> To seeke thee God.[49]

Around these hints, we may construct our images of womanly patience, fortitude, devotion, gentleness. But all we know for certain about Donne's wife is that she was generally pregnant, and that no one recorded for posterity any clear impression of her character.

That Donne soon grew tired of being cooped up with her seems plain. Not, of course, that there's anything particularly surprising or shameful about that. He was restless and changeable by temperament, and he had an energetic mind which needed to be occupied. To absorb his attention wholly, Ann would have had to be a walking encyclopedia, whereas the chances are that she was virtually uneducated. Donne held firmly conservative views about the inferior status and capacity of women, and he believed that a wife should be chaste, sober, truthful and quiet. Superior accomplishments such as wit, learning, eloquence and music were, he asserted, quite needless.[50] Intelligent conversation and shared cultural interests definitely did not figure among the pleasures he expected to derive from marriage, then, and it's worth noting that in this respect his views were more insulting to women than Milton's, who realized that almost any husband would get bored with sex and submissiveness after a while.

When writing to members of his wife's family Donne, understandably enough, pretended that Ann was everything he could possibly ask for in life. 'We had not one another at so cheap a rate, as that we should ever be weary of one another,'[51] he reproachfully assured his rich brother-in-law. But the situation, as revealed to more intimate acquaintances, was less idyllic. Writing to Goodyer, Donne muses on his need for society and conversation. The presence of his family might, he admits, be expected to banish loneliness, but the sad fact is it does not.[52] In a later letter announcing the birth of yet another child, Donne conveys pretty frankly that, though he would wish his wife no harm, he's glad to be rid of her company for a while: 'I have now two of the best happinesses which could befall me upon me, which are to be a widower and my wife alive.'[53]

Donne was not unfaithful, he was simply clubbable. He liked to be among lively, intelligent males. In London he belonged to two clubs, one of which met at the Mitre Tavern in Fleet Street and the other at the Mermaid. The members included his close friends, like Goodyer and Christopher Brooke, and also courtiers, lawyers and men of letters, among them Lionel Cranfield, who became Earl of Middlesex, Arthur Ingram the financier and civil servant, Sir Henry Neville, Ben Jonson and Inigo Jones.[54] Ann could not compete with the excitement Donne found in this company. The world-obliterating ardour of the love poems ('She'is all States, and all Princes, I, / Nothing else is') does not correspond to the realities of Donne's married life. Or rather, it corresponds to them, if at all, in no simple way. To proclaim the all-sufficiency of the woman for whom he had sacrificed his career may have been the defiant response with which Donne's imagination faced worldly disaster. And it may have been made more defiant by the realization that she did not, after all, mean everything to him.

Even supposing Donne's desire for society had not separated him from Ann, though, his duties as a breadwinner would have done. The kind of employment he wanted lay entirely at the disposal of the court circle. He stood no chance unless he hung around in their vicinity and tried to attract their notice. Accordingly he took lodgings in the Strand. Mitcham was only two hours away on horseback, and he could always return home in an emergency, though he had to be prepared to venture further afield if anyone would pay him to do so. In 1605–6 he was abroad for about twelve months, travelling in France, Italy and perhaps Spain as companion to a young Kentish

knight Sir Walter Chute. He had another prolonged visit to the
Continent, this time for about nine months, in 1611–12, as one of the
suite of Sir Robert Drury. He longed to mix with men of affairs and
be a public success. The need to provide for his family made his
ambition all the keener. In the bad times, when no openings presented themselves, gloom overtook him. He was appalled by his
uselessness; his sense of identity dwindled. Fortune had made him,
he felt, 'rather a sicknesse and disease of the world then any part of it'.
'If I aske my self what I have done in the last watch, or would do in
the next, I can say nothing; if I say that I have passed it without
hurting any, so may the Spider in my window.'[55]

In between these fits of despondency he struggled to get his foot
again on the ladder of success. The fourteen years between his
marriage and his ordination in 1615 are full of frantic attempts to
flatter or cajole persons of elevated social standing into bestirring
themselves on his behalf. These include the recipients of most of the
verse epistles and a sizeable proportion of the surviving letters. The
most regular correspondent was Sir Henry Goodyer, to whom
Donne wrote weekly, on Tuesdays. These letters reveal Donne more
intimately than those to anyone else, and bespeak almost unbounded
love and trust. At first sight Goodyer might appear an odd choice of
friend for an intellectual like Donne. He was a high-spirited,
pleasure-loving Warwickshire squire, a great devotee of hawking,
and a leading figure in the masques and frivolities at court during the
early years of James's reign. Distinctly Donne's inferior as a penman,
Goodyer used to get Donne to compose letters for him. He was also
in the habit of filching phrases and sentences from Donne's correspondence, and working them into his own poems and letters.[56]
However, Goodyer was neither a clod nor a booby. He was cultured
and discriminating. His 'wel-made choise of friends, and bookes'
earned Ben Jonson's praise, and Jonson also said that a few days
hawking with Goodyer had taught him why the sport was so popular with wise men.[57] Goodyer was recklessly generous and hospit-
able, and his gifts and loans helped Donne through the bad years.
Eventually he ran himself into debt.

His friend's spendthrift disposition worried Donne, and he
advised him to travel abroad in order to break his extravagant habits.
This was remarkably unselfish advice, for if followed it would
deprive Donne of a benefactor. But he was always, with Goodyer, a
friend first and a dependant afterwards. His verse letter to him is
outspoken about Goodyer's faults; its lines glow with candour. It is

the noblest of Donne's poems—and in calling it that we do justice to its unusual simplicity as well as to its uprightness. Its opening evokes the lulling rhythms of inactivity—only too well known to Donne—and warns Goodyer against them:

> Who makes the Past, a patterne for next yeare,
> Turnes no new leafe, but still the same things reads,
> Seene things, he sees againe, heard things doth heare,
> And makes his life, but like a paire of beads.[58]

We learn from the last stanza of the poem that Goodyer had, on this occasion, promised to accompany Donne to Mitcham, but had been unable to. Instead, Donne composed his verse letter on his way home, and so kept his friend in his mind as entirely as if he had been travelling by his side:

> But thus I make you keepe your promise Sir,
> Riding I had you, though you still staid there,
> And in these thoughts, although you never stirre,
> You came with mee to Micham, and are here.

The triumphant, impossible affirmation of those last three words is typical. That letters joined the souls of separated friends, in a kind of ecstasy, was one of Donne's favourite theories. Like the Mitre and Mermaid clubs, it provided an escape from 'Defects of lonelinesse'. With no one did he feel this so much as with Goodyer. To see a letter addressed to his friend on his table gave him, he said, 'satisfaction', even if he had no means of sending it.[59] It brought something of Goodyer into the room.

Though Goodyer's open-handedness was invaluable, Donne's love for him was not just mercenary, then. Goodyer's gifts of books made the Mitcham study 'a pretty library', but his intelligence, sympathy and admiration were even greater treasures. His 'natural disposition to mirth'[60] attracted Donne's darker temperament, and the spacious, carefree way of life at Goodyer's country house at Polesworth, in the Forest of Arden, helped Donne to recuperate from Mitcham damps and squalling children. What's more, Goodyer knew the right people. As a gentleman of the privy chamber to James I, he mingled with the dispensers of power, and lobbied them on Donne's behalf whenever opportunity arose. 'I owe you', Donne acknowledged, 'whatever Court friends do for me.'[61] Goodyer was a lifeline.

Through him Donne gained an introduction to another of his patrons, Lucy Countess of Bedford. She was one of the bright young

things of James's court, a prodigy of talent and beauty, if we are to
credit the poets who fawned upon her, and a prominent performer in
the court masques. On one occasion Donne asked Goodyer to pass
on a letter to her 'when the rage of the Mask is past'.[62] Born in 1581,
the daughter of Baron Harington of Exton, she married, at thirteen,
the Earl of Bedford. He became implicated in Essex's rebellion, and
was imprisoned for a while; but Lucy was among the first to greet
James on his accession, and was appointed a Lady of the Queen's
Bedchamber, while her parents undertook the upbringing of the
King's daughter Princess Elizabeth. Lucy's close friendship with the
Queen made her influential. She preened herself on her highbrow
tastes, and encouraged authors to frequent her house. Her portrait at
Woburn Abbey shows her as a thin-faced woman with a long nose,
resting her head on her hand in a self-consciously pensive posture.
Jonson, in one of the poems he addressed to her, says that she had 'a
learned, and a manly soule',[63] so we can be sure that was the kind of
compliment she liked to hear. But it is difficult, when one considers
her stomach for flattery, to take a very generous view of her intelligence. Donne's verse letters refer to her as 'Gods masterpeece' and to
her friends as 'Saints', glorified by her 'election'.[64] The barrage of
pseudo-religious encomium is patently mechanical—a grim, toneless exertion, like mental arithmetic.

How the Countess of Bedford can have received such stuff, and
what sort of relationship it expresses, are puzzling questions. But
Donne's effort to sound both dignified and obsequious suggests that
he wanted to be respected as well as taken on to the payroll, and the
Countess seems to have enjoyed having this daring modern poet,
with his shady past, as her pet laureate. She wrote verses herself and
once, in her garden at Twickenham, showed Donne some. He was full
of admiration, naturally, and begged for copies of them, promising
to keep them secret. From his letter, it appears that the Countess's verses concerned him, or his poems, and were complimen-
tary.[65] We know that she asked Ben Jonson to get hold of copies of
Donne's Satires for her.[66] She seems, then, to have derived gratifica-
tion from mixing with men of genius as if she were their equal or
superior, and having them extol her own efforts.

The one great poem that resulted from Donne's relations with the
Countess was 'Twicknam Garden':

> Blasted with sighs, and surrounded with teares,
>   Hither I come to seeke the spring,
>   And at mine eyes, and at mine eares,

Receive such balmes, as else cure every thing;
    But O, selfe traytor, I do bring
The spider love, which transubstantiates all,
    And can convert Manna to gall,
And that this place may thoroughly be thought
True Paradise, I have the serpent brought.

'Twere wholsomer for mee, that winter did
    Benight the glory of this place,
    And that a grave frost did forbid
These trees to laugh, and mocke mee to my face;
    But that I may not this disgrace
Indure, nor yet leave loving, Love let me
    Some senslesse peece of this place bee;
Make me a mandrake, so I may grow here,
Or a stone fountaine weeping out my yeare.

Hither with christall vyals, lovers come,
    And take my teares, which are loves wine,
    And try your mistresse Teares at home,
For all are false, that tast not just like mine;
    Alas, hearts do not in eyes shine,
Nor can you more judge womans thoughts by teares,
    Then by her shadow, what she weares.
O perverse sexe, where none is true but shee,
Who's therefore true, because her truth kills mee.[67]

Significantly, there is nothing in this poem which suggests that it
relates to the Countess of Bedford, except its title. (That also, as it
happens, gives us a clue to its date, for the Countess did not acquire
Twickenham Park till 1607, so the poem must be later than that: it
belongs to Donne's early middle age.) In every other respect the
poem outgrows the situation that gave rise to it. Its sombre, baffled
yearning does not sound remotely like the tribute of a lap-dog poet.
The stream of compliment which Donne judged appropriate for his
verse letters to the Countess has mercifully dried up. Instead,
Donne's ego has taken over. He has become the centre of his own
poem, and dropped his subservient role. He strides like a shade
through the garden, carrying venom and death. He establishes himself at the garden's sad heart, an eternal weeper, visited by pilgrims.
The Countess, and everything that appertains to her, have been set
aside. Donne was not really in love with her (as we've seen, he

thanked God for confining his affections to his wife), and even if he had been the suggestion that her fidelity to the Earl of Bedford was an inconvenience to him would, given the difference in their social rank, have been a ludicrous impertinence. But he transforms himself, in the poem, into a lover, in order to surmount the humiliating fact that he is no more than a beggarly dependant. His importunity and distress, his shame and self-loathing and sense of being laughed at, become marks of a heroic though unavailing love, rather than elements in the common lot of all who go cap in hand after greatness. In this respect, the poem is a triumph of untruth. It redeems reality, as art must, and makes it tolerable. Through its fiction, Donne regains his manhood.

Did Lady Bedford ever see 'Twicknam Garden'? It seems unlikely; but Donne certainly did incur her displeasure on one occasion, and from the way he talks of it we may deduce that he did not keep his poetic role as despairing lover sufficiently hidden when in her company. He writes to a friend in 1612 to say that he is out of favour with his patroness: 'But I have been heretofore too immodest towards her, and I suffer this purgatory for it.'[68] Lady Bedford could not be expected to tolerate familiarity, especially if it would make her look ridiculous. Besides, as age drew on she became increasingly prim. She fell seriously ill in 1612 and was attended on her sickbed by a Puritan divine, Dr. John Burgess, whose spiritual counsel deeply affected her. She was said to have vowed not to attend the court again, and though she didn't keep to this she piously gave up cosmetics, which, it is reported, made her look very strange among all the painted faces.[69]

Donne did not get as much money out of her as he had hoped. When she heard about his plan to enter the Church she promised to pay all his debts, but later thought better of it, and contributed only £30 and—as we have noted—some ungenerous reflections upon his previous way of life. Donne was much put out, and wrote bitterly to Goodyer about the interfering holiness of Burgess who, he suspected, had turned his patroness against him. Prudently he asks Goodyer to burn the letter.[70] He might still touch Lady Bedford for some large sum, and an outspoken letter left lying around could blight her bounty once and for all.

Since Donne's attachment to Lady Bedford was essentially businesslike, it did not preclude his addressing himself with equal ardour to other grand ladies if it seemed worthwhile, and if it was unlikely Lady Bedford would get to know. A female benefactor whom he pursued with loyal persistence was Mrs. Magdalen Herbert, mother of George Herbert the poet and Lord Herbert of Cherbury. Apparently he had met her in Oxford some years before his marriage, but it was not until 1607 that they were reintroduced, and Donne spared no pains to attach himself. By chance four letters to her, written between 11 July and 2 August of that year, survive, recording his wonderment at her supernatural virtues, his appreciation of benefits already received, and his determination not to let her get away. He has decided to write, he announces, 'almost daily'. She is in his estimation 'not only a World alone, but the Monarchy of the World'.

He sent her, too, his first religious poems, the '*La Corona*' sequence, with a humble letter committing them 'to your judgment, and to your protection too, if you think them worthy of it'.[71] The following year he heard that Mrs. Herbert, who had long been widowed, was to remarry (the chosen husband, Sir John Danvers, was only half her age, which caused some gossip). Eager to please, Donne marked the occasion with a fatuous, ogling verse epistle ('To Mrs. M. H.') in which he instructs the paper on which he is writing to spy on Mrs. Herbert and notice whose letters she kisses. He wants to discover her love's identity, he explains, because

> . . . so much I doe love her choyce, that I
> Would faine love him that shall be lov'd of her.[72]

His intention, of course, was to add Sir John to his list of influential friends, and in this he was successful.

His association with Mrs. Herbert produced, apart from her welcome handouts, only one item of value, but that is a unique and wholly Donnean poem, 'The Autumnall'.[73] It relates to the real Magdalen Herbert about as closely as 'Twicknam Garden' relates to the real Countess of Bedford—that is to say, not at all. If Donne's friend Izaak Walton had not left it on record that Mrs. Herbert was the poem's subject, and if one or two contemporary manuscripts of it had not incorporated her name in the title,[74] we should never have guessed that it was about her. Indeed, some scholars still choose to disbelieve Walton and the manuscripts, and point out correctly that Walton has got into a muddle over the poem's date. He says that Donne wrote it when he met Mrs. Herbert at Oxford, where her son Edward was at college, and that at the time Donne was nearly forty and had seven children. Both statements can't be true, because Mrs. Herbert was at Oxford with Edward from 1599 till 1601, and Donne didn't marry till 1601.

Plainly Walton has mixed up two distinct periods in Donne's life: the years before his marriage when he met Mrs. Herbert at Oxford, and the later time, beginning in 1607, when he angled for her patronage. Which period 'The Autumnall' belongs to is anyone's guess, but since it celebrates an ageing woman, the later seems more probable:

> No *Spring*, nor *Summer* Beauty hath such grace,
> As I have seen in one *Autumnall* face.

It dwells affectionately on the woman's wrinkles, and reminds readers that age is a thing we are 'fifty yeares' in attaining. Relate the poem to the real Mrs. Herbert and her feelings, and this must seem grotesquely tactless. Even in 1607 she was only forty. But Donne, as in 'Twicknam Garden', has cut loose from reality. The letters, in verse and prose, which he addressed to the real Mrs. Herbert combine brassy adulation with the adhesiveness of an anxious limpet. The bitter consolations and exhausted cadences of 'The Autumnall' belong to a quite different relationship. Like 'Twicknam Garden' it is poignant, death-struck, and dominated by Donne's ego. The woman disappears beneath his reveries on middle age and cooling passion.

Also, it is a love poem. Donne made no pretence, when writing to the real Mrs. Herbert, that he was in love with her. On the contrary, he told her clearly from the start that his wife was what he loved most in the world. But 'The Autumnall' is a declaration of love, in which devotion, resignation and tenderness somnolently blend:

> I hate extreames; yet I had rather stay
> With Tombs, then Cradles, to weare out a day.
> Since such loves naturall lation is, may still
> My love descend, and journey downe the hill,
> Not panting after growing beauties, so,
> I shall ebbe out with them, who home-ward goe.

It is the sort of poem you might expect a husband to write to a wife after twenty or thirty years of marriage. The jokes about graves and wrinkles could lose their edge only in an atmosphere which had become suffused with mutual trust.

That's true, too, of the '*Autumnall* face' at the poem's start. It teeters on the brink of insult. When Jonson used the same phrase in *The Silent Woman*, he pushed it over the brink: 'A poxe of her autumnall face.'[75] Some critics have read this as a scornful allusion to Donne's odd opening—and maybe it is. But Donne's phrase succeeds precisely because it outbraves ridicule. It gains its peculiar gentleness from our realization that it could not be ventured except where long love and familiarity had made misinterpretation impossible. In Donne's high-flown letters to Mrs. Herbert it would look scandalously out of place. 'You are the Monarchy of the World, and have an Autumnall face.' Unthinkable. Donne's poem stands apart from life. It refashions his relations with Mrs. Herbert into a sleepy idyll, from which all his urgent ambition, and every hint of his financial dependence, have been eliminated. It also, incidentally, bestows upon Mrs. Herbert additional years and wrinkles, so that his love for her may appear generous and selfless.

The noblemen whose assistance Donne solicited during these years are not an entirely attractive bunch. They include James Hay, a handsome Scot who, by virtue of James I's susceptibility to young males, became one of the leading figures at court and was created successively Viscount Doncaster and Earl of Carlisle. Hay was best known for his facility in spending large sums of money, and under his guidance the vulgar excess which characterized Jacobean court entertainment reached a new height. A feast which he gave for the French ambassador at Essex House comprised sixteen hundred dishes, which it took a hundred cooks eight days to prepare. A hundred and forty-four larks went into one dish; twenty-four partridges into another; two whole pigs into a third. There were half a dozen salmon from Russia, each six feet long, and the total bill came to over £3,000. It was Hay who introduced the extravagance known as the antesupper—the most wasteful of the devices for conspicuous consumption perfected by the Jacobean aristocracy. When the guests came in they found a table piled 'as high as a tall man could well reach' with costly viands. But before they could touch the food it was removed by servants and thrown away, and a second banquet, equally colossal, set before them.[76] It's odd to imagine a figure like Hay showing an interest in Christianity, but in fact he takes the credit, in one of his letters to Donne, for persuading Donne to enter holy orders. However, he makes no bones about admitting that he did so only when Donne had tried everything else, and failed.[77]

Another of Donne's patrons in these worrying years was Sir Robert Drury,[78] a Suffolk landowner noted for his hot temper and inability to hold his tongue. Despite these qualities he coveted a career in the diplomatic service—an aspiration which earned him a good deal of ridicule. He was a daring soldier and, like many of Donne's friends, had served with Essex, being knighted by the Earl under the walls of Rouen. On the Cadiz expedition he commanded a company. Donne's sister Anne lived near the Drurys, and had

married an ex-secret agent called William Lyly who had worked with
Drury's uncle in Paris. Knowing her brother's needs, Anne probably
put Donne in touch with her wealthy and not over-shrewd neigh-
bour, and an opportunity to recommend himself to Drury came in
1610 when Drury's only surviving child, Elizabeth, died within two
months of her fifteenth birthday.

Donne had never met the girl, but he rapidly glorified her memory
in 'A Funerall Elegie', and this evidently found such favour with the
bereaved parents that he followed it up shortly after with the first of
his *Anniversaries*, entitled 'Of the Progres of the Soule'. Wishing to
perpetuate his child in some public monument, Sir Robert urged
Donne to have these poems printed. The request put Donne in a
quandary, for his verses extolled Elizabeth as the acme of the human
race, and it was disturbing to think how Lucy Countess of Bedford
and Magdalen Herbert might react when they read them. However,
Sir Robert was paying handsomely for his funereal satisfaction, and
if Donne refused to publish it might make him look insincere. So the
poems duly appeared in 1611, and were reprinted the following year
along with *The Second Anniversarie*, which Donne had composed in
the meantime.

The Second Anniversarie was written abroad, for in 1611 Sir Robert
persuaded Donne to accompany him on a Continental trip, designed
to improve his own qualifications for diplomatic eminence. Donne's
wife, pregnant as usual, was full of foreboding, and begged him not
to go; but since he was living off Sir Robert he had little choice.
Instead he wrote her (according to Walton) a farewell poem, 'A
Valediction: forbidding Mourning', and left for the Continent with
Sir Robert and Lady Drury, their servants, a pack of hounds and
several hawks. They spent the winter in Amiens and then moved to
Paris. Donne, predictably, was soon complaining in his letters about
the dullness of life abroad, and he was worried to hear, from friends
at home, that his lavish praise of Elizabeth Drury had caused rather
an uproar among the English reading public. He started to compose
an apologetic poem to Lady Bedford, explaining that he didn't really
mean it when he flattered other women, but it was a tricky thing to
pull off and he gave it up.[79]

More profitable employment for his pen presented itself when Sir
Robert Rich passed through Amiens and asked Donne to write a
poem in praise of his sisters, Lady Carey and Miss Essex Rich, the
daughters of Sidney's Stella, a well-known adulteress. Donne had
never set eyes on these ladies, but he obliged gamely, with a totally
worthless set of verses, in which he announces that he has had an

'Extasie And revelation' of them which enables him to acclaim their unparalleled beauty and virtue.[80] The strain of turning out this sort of tribute, which had nothing to do with his inner passions and attachments, is revealed, perhaps, in the story Walton tells about the 'dreadful Vision' Donne saw in Paris during this trip. While he was alone in his room his wife passed through it twice, with her hair about her shoulders, and carrying a dead child in her arms. At her second appearance she stopped, looked him in the face, and vanished. When Donne told Drury of his experience a messenger was dispatched to England, and returned with the news that Mrs. Donne had been delivered of a stillborn child at the very hour when Donne had seen the apparition. It is as if the life which Donne's attendance on the great forced him to suppress had, at this crisis, invaded his consciousness in visible form. He scarcely ever mentions his family in his letters to his grand friends. When he does so, it is with an apology. Writing to Sir Robert Ker, for instance, later Earl of Ancrum and a member of Prince Charles's household, he lets it be known, in passing, that one of his children has just died, and adds: 'Because I loved it well, I make account that I dignifie the memorie of it, by mentioning it to you, else I should not be so homely.' The child, though Donne does not stoop to give details, was Mary, aged three, who died in 1614.

Thanks to Drury Donne was able at last to vacate the damp cottage at Mitcham. On his return from the Continent he moved, with his family, into a house adjoining Sir Robert's own residence in Drury Lane (the site is now occupied by part of the frontage of Bush House). Sir Robert, diplomatic as ever, lost no time in making a fool of himself in official circles. He and Donne, while abroad, had visited Heidelberg, the capital of Frederick, the Elector Palatine, and Sir Robert had taken offence at the somewhat restrained reception he met with there. Back in London he spoke disparagingly of the Elector's court, and received a swift official reprimand. It was a peculiarly crass slip, for Frederick was the destined bridegroom of James I's only daughter, the Princess Elizabeth. They were married amidst lavish festivities on St. Valentine's Day 1613, and Donne, hoping perhaps to dissociate himself from his bungling patron, penned a joyous epithalamion for the occasion.[81] Though willing to take advantage of Sir Robert's generosity, he had, it seems, begun to perceive that he must find a more sagacious friend if his plans for self-advancement were not to founder. As luck would have it, he secured, in the process, the very job which Sir Robert himself dearly wanted.

It happened like this. The most powerful man at court was Robert Carr, Viscount Rochester.[82] In 1603 he had come to England as a page, running beside the royal coach. But he was physically attractive to the King, who used to pinch and stroke him in public, and indulged his desires practically without limit. By 1613 Rochester had fallen in love with Lady Frances Howard, and wanted to marry her. To this there were two obstacles. The first was Lady Frances's husband, the Earl of Essex. However, she sought to divorce him on the grounds that she was still *virgo intacta*—a hypothesis to the falsity of which, it is said, several men about town could testify. The King took a salacious interest in all the physical details, appointed a commission to try the case, and persistently interfered in its deliberations. He even appointed new commissioners, favourable to his viewpoint, in order to force the divorce through.

The other obstacle in Rochester's path was Sir Thomas Overbury, his secretary and confidant, and a friend of Donne's, who was violently opposed to the Howard match. To get Overbury out of the way Rochester persuaded the King to offer him a diplomatic post in France. When Overbury refused he was sent to the Tower for contempt of the King's commands, where he conveniently died. However Rochester was desperate for a replacement to help with the mass of public business which came into his hands, and Sir Robert Drury offered himself for this confidential position. He was turned down, and Donne decided to have a try, making use of Lord Hay to carry his letter to the favourite.

The letter, at once cringing and impudent, survives. Donne intimates that the Spirit of God has inspired him to become a clergyman, and that in that capacity he will be entirely at Rochester's disposal.[83] Surprisingly, the bid was successful. Though he dissuaded Donne from taking holy orders, Rochester took him into his employment. Donne's ensuing missives to his new patron express abject dependence: 'It hath pleased your Lordship to make another title to me, by buying me,' he writes, 'I have lived upon your bread.'[84]

When the Essex divorce was duly granted by the commissioners, the verdict attracted widespread criticism among the devout, and Donne offered to write a defence of it, pointing out to Rochester that since his 'poor study' had been in legal and theological areas his 'weak assistance' might be worth having.[85] It wasn't, however, accepted. Instead Rochester asked for an epithalamion. Given the character of the bride, even Donne seems to have found this ticklish, and the finished poem was not presented until some weeks after the marriage. He does not scruple, though, to allude to the scandal the affair had caused; he praises the bride for defying 'unjust opinion' (she went to the altar with her hair hanging untrimmed to her waist— the mark of a virgin); and he implies that the Archbishop of Canterbury, the Bishop of London, and the three doctors of law among the commissioners who had voted, with them, against the divorce, were vainly attempting to circumvent the will of heaven:

> The Church Triumphant made this match before,
> And now the Militant doth strive no more.[86]

The wedding was celebrated on the day after Christmas, 1613, amid great magnificence. The King sold crown lands worth £10,000 to buy jewellery for the bride, and created Rochester Earl of Somerset, so that Lady Frances might remain a countess.[87]

Donne was quite specific about the posts which he wished his various patrons to secure for him. In 1609 he asked to be given a Secretaryship with the Virginia Company.[88] Later, he asked to be made Venetian ambassador. King James, however, though he admired Donne's talents, maintained adamantly that he had shown himself, by his rash marriage, unfit for confidential employment; and, with what may seem to us rather curious logic, he accordingly urged him to enter the Church. It is plain that Donne resisted this advice not only because he clung to his dream of worldly success, but also because he knew that the clerical profession was despised and considered unfit for gentlemen. He was sensitive to what he called 'Lay-scornings of the Ministry'.[89] He did not want to be thought of as a cassocked pedant but as an alert and resourceful courtier.

It might seem that, having gained so powerful an ally as the Earl of Somerset, he was at last within sight of realizing his ambition; and there is no doubt that Somerset interceded with the King on Donne's behalf. However, he failed; and the year of Donne's dependence on Somerset, 1614, turned out to be one of the blackest in his life. He and his family were ill; his wife had a miscarriage. Little Mary's death in May was followed in November by the death of his son Francis. Expenses had increased with the move to London, for in order to improve his chances of advancement Donne had to keep up appearances, and he had brought a French manservant back with him from the Continent. The begging letters he sent to Somerset and to the Countess of Bedford were urgent and shameless, and must have been humiliating to write.

In April he became a Member of Parliament once more: his court influence secured him the seat for the borough of Taunton. But the

1614 parliament was a fiasco—the only recorded parliament which passed no legislation whatsoever. It occupied itself with violent discussions of the King's imposition of customs duties and his distribution of trading monopolies among favourite courtiers. Christopher Brooke and other former friends of Donne vehemently opposed these abuses of royal power. Donne discreetly held his tongue. When members turned their attention to the King's Scottish favourites and the vast sums of money they consumed, James lost patience, and the parliament was dissolved in June. Donne's tactful demeanour during the session did him no good. When Somerset tried once more to move the King on Donne's behalf, James made it perfectly clear that he would prefer Donne to take holy orders. By December Donne had capitulated, and he was ordained in January 1615.

In part his failure was sheer bad luck, for Somerset was a crumbling giant and he started to crumble soon after Donne had managed to get taken in tow. The favourite was, in fact, a shallow, insolent, obstinate young man, with little beyond his effrontery to recommend him, and during the course of 1614 James, besotted as he was, began to perceive this. Worse, in August he first set eyes on a new and lovely youth called George Villiers, who inflamed his royal feelings even more powerfully than Somerset. The Earl grew jealous, and his open rudeness in James's presence became insufferable.

In 1615, ruin finally overtook Somerset. Word got about that Sir Thomas Overbury, into whose shoes Donne had stepped, had been poisoned while a prisoner in the Tower. Somerset and his Countess were tried for murder: she confessed, he was found guilty. Both were condemned to death, but though their lower-class accomplices were hanged, James reprieved the two aristocrats. They remained in prison until 1622, and were then allowed to live in retirement in the country. No suspicion fell on Donne, and it seems clear that he was innocent of any involvement in the murder plot. When we consider, though, his eagerness to serve Somerset in the matter of the divorce, and the blasphemously elevated terms in which he addressed him, we may deduce that he was not very particular about the path he took to success, or about the moral character of those he received assistance from. But then, it is easier to entertain such reflections if we have never had to depend for our livelihood on the whims of the great, as Donne did.

Taking holy orders did not mean, for Donne, renouncing his ambition or slackening his determination to pursue whatever advantage could be squeezed from his lofty connections. He could not afford to be unworldly, and before taking the irrevocable step of ordination he rode down to Newmarket, where the King was residing, to make sure that James, having propelled him towards a holy calling, would provide for him once he was in it. James gave the necessary assurances, and after ordination Donne returned to Newmarket in some haste, so that the King could keep his word. He was appointed Chaplain-in-Ordinary—a profitable post, for royal chaplains could buy a licence which allowed them to hold two livings at once, and so double their income. James also promised to make Donne a Doctor of Divinity at Cambridge. The University was furious at this piece of royal high-handedness, and refused to confer the degree on Donne. He was regarded, it is clear, as a blatant careerist, who had no right to be in holy orders at all. However, Donne's friends in high places brought pressure to bear, and the Vice-Chancellor was commanded to confer the degree by royal mandate. So Donne got his honour, but amid general bitterness. The Vice-Chancellor and some heads of houses were heard referring to him openly, at the ceremony, as 'a son of night and of darkness'.[90]

The King also gave Donne his first benefice, the rectory of Keyston in Huntingdon, in January 1616, and a few months later his old employer Egerton, now Lord Ellesmere, bestowed on him a second, at Sevenoaks in Kent. The Earl of Kent, to whom Donne had evidently managed to attach himself, contributed a third living, that of Blunham in Bedfordshire, in 1622. It was understood that Donne did not need to reside in these country parishes—they were simply sources of income—but he does seem to have visited Sevenoaks and Blunham annually to preach. According to Blunham oral tradition, he used to go back to London after his visit with a load of cucumbers in his carriage.[91]

The trips to Sevenoaks gave him an opportunity of renewing his acquaintance with another grandee to whom he had long paid court, Richard Sackville, Earl of Dorset, whose seat was at Knole. Donne's instinct for self-preservation seems to have drawn him naturally towards the freer spenders among the aristocracy, and Dorset was notoriously prodigal. He entertained on a sumptuous scale, and was addicted, as his wife ruefully recalled, to the 'noble ways' of the court, such as 'tilting, masqueing, and the like'.[92] His debts provided his heirs with a crippling burden. Before Donne's ordination, Dorset had apparently been rash enough to give him some large assurances of financial aid, which he proved slow in fulfilling. Donne was not the man to let the matter rest. Dorset's honour, he insisted, was involved; there was no backing out, for his promises had been given before witnesses. Despite this importunity, Donne was careful not to offend Dorset, and his courtly skills bore fruit in 1624 when the Earl added the vicarage of St. Dunstan's in the West, which was in his gift, to Donne's tally of church livings.

His main appointment, though, in his early years as a clergyman, was the Divinity readership at Lincoln's Inn, which supplied him with an adequate, regular income and an urbane and sophisticated auditory for his sermons. Then, in 1621, he secured his great prize, the Deanery of St. Paul's (a post which carried with it the further sinecure of Prebendary of Chiswick). This preferment was the result of patiently dancing attendance on the new royal favourite, George Villiers, whom James had created Duke of Buckingham. In pursuit of Buckingham, Donne adopted a servile posture, describing himself as a 'poore worme', and protesting that Buckingham was the only patron from whom he hoped for any advancement. 'All that I mean', Donne explains, 'in usinge thys boldnes, of puttinge myselfe into your Lordship's presence by thys ragge of paper, ys to tell your Lordship that I ly in a corner, as a clodd of clay, attendinge what kinde of vessell yt shall please you to make of Your Lordship's humblest and thankfullest and devotedst servant.'[93] Whether or not Donne also paid Buckingham a bribe to obtain the Deanery is not known. If he did not, it is a considerable tribute to his insinuating arts, for bribes were part of the customary procedure in such transactions.[94] At the time of Donne's appointment the Cathedral buildings had fallen into dangerous disrepair, and he continued his predecessors' policy of neglect. A consignment of Portland stone, which the Bishop of London had purchased to restore the fabric, was 'borrowed', while Donne was Dean, by the Duke of Buckingham for the rebuilding of his town residence, York House.[95] Perhaps Buckingham regarded this as a return for services rendered.

Ambition is, then, a constant element in Donne's life, linking the young soldier and civil servant with the mature divine. His ambitious marriage ruined him, and left him struggling ambitiously to repair the damage. There is no avoiding the fact that he battened on the great unblushingly. To modern readers this may seem degrading and regrettable. Is it not, we may ask, an indictment of Donne's historical period that a genius was forced to abase himself before the rabble of idlers, confidence men and pederasts who ruled the country? Would he not have been an even greater and more prolific poet if he had not squandered his time turning out verse letters, epithalamions and funerary tributes? Might we not have had more *Songs and Sonnets*?

An equally cogent question, perhaps, is whether we should have the *Songs and Sonnets* at all were it not for the thwarted, grasping, parasitic life that Donne was forced to lead. In my next chapter I shall argue that his poetry may be seen as a reaction against the constriction and dependence that actuality imposed. Further, the egotism manifest throughout his career is what impels the poetry. The ambition and the poems are indissolubly linked. To imagine him as a selfless, contented type is impossible, for though that might have given him more time to be a poet it would also have removed the core of his poetic being. The very qualities which made him neglect and belittle poetry were vital to the poems.

Before demonstrating this, it remains to ask when, in the course of the career we have outlined, Donne's poems were written. Unfortunately a complete answer is unavailable. We can be sure that the Satires and the majority of the Elegies belong to the 1590s. The main group of 'Holy Sonnets' has been dated 1609–10. But among the *Songs and Sonnets* there is not a single poem to which a precise date, about which all scholars agree, can be given. However, such evidence as there is suggests that the composition of these poems extended into Donne's frustrated middle age, and it may be that most of them belong to that period. 'A Valediction: forbidding Mourning' is, as we have seen, dated by Walton quite firmly in 1611, just before Donne's trip abroad with Drury, when he was almost forty. He was in his late thirties, we have argued, when he wrote 'Twicknam Garden'. Contemporary allusions to Donne point in the same direction.[96] Though his satires, elegies, epigrams, and early verse letters such as 'The Storme' and 'The Calme' were quite well known in the closing years of the sixteenth century, there is nothing to indicate that he was a lyric poet at this time. On the contrary, even in the early seventeenth century Donne enthusiasts still seem unaware that he has written lyrics. As late as 1614 Thomas Freman congratulates Donne on 'The Storme', 'The Calme' and the satires, but asks him to 'write a bigger booke', evidently believing that this is all he has composed to date. In 1619 Jonson, chatting with Drummond about Donne's poetry, mentions *Metempsychosis (The Progresse of the Soule)*, 'The Calme', the *Anniversaries*, and the elegy 'The Bracelet', but no lyrics.

The first evidence that Donne lyrics were in circulation comes at the end of the first decade of the seventeenth century, when one or two of them begin to appear in books of songs. Ferrabosco's *Book of*

Ayres (1609) has a version of 'The Expiration'; Corkine's *Second Booke of Ayres* (1612) 'Break of Day' and 'The Baite'; Dowland's *A Pilgrimes Solace* (1612) has an adaptation of 'Loves Infiniteness'. The earliest allusion to a manuscript collection of 'Jhone Dones lyriques' occurs in Drummond's reading matter for 1613—which tells us only that a substantial number of the *Songs and Sonnets* were written by the time Donne was forty.

As for internal evidence of date in the *Songs and Sonnets*, it hardly exists at all. 'Loves Usury', if we take it literally, informs us that it was written by a young man, but it is the only poem which does. 'The Canonization' mentions the poet's palsy, gout, grey hairs and ruined fortune, and also refers to the king's face stamped on a coin. This last detail seems a fairly clear indication that it was written after James's accession in 1603 (that is, when Donne was in his thirties), and by the same token 'The Sunne Rising', which includes an apparent allusion to James's love of hunting, and 'The Anniversarie' ('All Kings, and all their favorites') seem post-1603 poems too. Such a test is not infallible, though. Satire II, which is definitely an Elizabethan poem, talks about 'a Kings favorite' and 'a King' quite as naturally as 'The Anniversarie' does, so the opening line of that poem does not conclusively date it.

One or two poems raise special problems. 'The Anniversarie' indicates that the woman addressed was not Donne's wife ('Two graves must hide thine and my coarse'), so who, worried critics have asked, was she? Most people will probably feel that this is rather a wooden way to interrogate poems, though of course if the poem did turn out to have been written after Donne's marriage, then the fact that he needed to imagine himself unmarried might be of interest. Even readers prepared to take lyric poems as works of the imagination have felt that 'A Nocturnall upon S. Lucies Day', which mourns the death of a loved woman, must have some factual basis. To feel so is naïve. Wordsworth, after all, needed no actual death to prompt him to mourn his Lucy. But if Donne's Lucy poem is about a real dead woman, then his wife is the only candidate worth considering. She alone, of the women we know he knew, involved him deeply enough to inspire this desolate utterance. Ann died, worn out by her attempt to bring yet another infant into the world, in August 1617. The stillborn child was buried with her, and her husband proudly recorded on her monument that it was her twelfth baby. The sonnet he wrote about her death, in which resignation gets tangled up with the discovery that no one loves him enough, we have looked at already. Its heavenly yearnings make it, at least on the surface, a more hopeful poem than 'A Nocturnall upon S. Lucies Day', which is bitter, and suicidal. But given the complexity and instability of Donne's mind, we should have no difficulty in believing, if we wish, that both these poems were written for the same occasion, and some of Donne's finest critics have come to that conclusion.[97] If they're right, then Donne was still adding to the *Songs and Sonnets* two years after his ordination.

When we think of Donne as the author of the *Songs and Sonnets*, then, the images which come to mind should include not only the young libertine and apostate but also the disgraced courtier hunched in a damp study at Mitcham; the husband, watching through the night while his dismayingly fertile wife is in labour upstairs; the father harrassed by debts, cramped quarters and playful children; the genteel beggar, pestering friends to place carefully penned flatteries in the hands of noble personages; the unwilling genius, disparaging the poems he found himself writing, which were so different from the versified homage he manufactured for patrons, and which—though he tried later in life to destroy them[98]—were to make him immortal.

৶4৶

The Art of Ambition

Donne's art (both his poems and his sermons) expresses the personality—self-advancing, anxious, unsatisfied—which we have traced in the last chapter. The manner in which it does this is not always apparent, and when it is apparent it may not always strike us as likeable. That is immaterial, of course. What we require in a writer is not amiability but the power to show us alternative ways of experiencing the world. Still, Donne's personality has antagonized some critics, and instead of pretending that it doesn't exist it will be best to confront it at the outset, and show that, far from being a handicap which he was fortunately able to atone for by his poetic skills, it was a needful precondition of the peculiar pressure and complexity of his writing.

A good starting point is afforded by two contrasting accounts of the naval engagement in Cadiz harbour at which, as we have seen, Donne was present in 1596. The first is by Raleigh, who was vice-admiral of the expedition. When the Spanish galleons were surprised by the English fleet, Raleigh recounts, their crews, seeing that capture was otherwise inevitable, slipped their anchors and allowed their vessels to run aground;

tumbling into the sea heaps of souldiers, so thick as if coals had been powred out of a sack in many ports at once, some drowned and some sticking in the mud. The *Philip* and the *St Thomas* burnt themselves: the *St Matthew* and the *St Andrew* were recovered with our boats ere they could get out to fire them. The spectacle was very lamentable on their side; for many drowned themselves; many, half burnt, leapt into the water; very many hanging by the ropes' ends by the ships' side, under the water even to the lips; many swimming with grievous wounds, strucken under water, and put out of their pain; and withal so huge a fire, and such tearing of the ordnance in the great *Philip*, and the rest, when the fire came to them, as, if any man had a desire to see Hell itself, it was there most lively figured.[1]

This scene was also the subject of Donne's epigram 'A Burnt Ship':

Out of a fired ship, which, by no way
But drowning, could be rescu'd from the flame,
Some men leap'd forth, and ever as they came
Neere the foes ships, did by their shot decay;
So all were lost, which in the ship were found,
They in the sea being burnt, they in the burnt ship drown'd.[2]

When we compare Raleigh's account of the death throes of the *San Felipe* with Donne's, we are inevitably struck by the superior humanity of Raleigh's. The soldiers pouring out of the portholes ('ports'), blackened and flaming (in Raleigh's day 'coals' meant glowing or charred embers), are 'lamentable', like souls in Hell. The maimed sailors, shot as they flounder in the water, are 'put out of their pain', and there is compassion in the phrase. Donne treats the slaughter as a joke: the pretext for a smart paradox. There is no pity in his lines.

It would be foolish to adopt a moralistic attitude over this. Donne was a young soldier, seeing action for the first time: he had to toughen himself, and could not afford to feel. Besides, Donne's complicated, ingenious poetry was ill fitted to voice simple compassion. 'It would have been very difficult for him to express something commonplace, if he had to,' said young Isaac Rosenberg, after a friend had lent him a copy of Donne's poems,[3] and the remark is illuminating about both Rosenberg and Donne. But Donne's relative immunity to the sufferings of others is not just a by-product of his poetic technique. We find it throughout his work, in verse and prose. His callousness can startle us. He reproves, for instance, bystanders at executions who hasten the death of the hanged man by pulling his legs. Hanging in the seventeenth century was usually inefficient, and friends of the victim resorted to this measure to prevent prolonged choking. They are misguided, Donne insists: justice has decreed a 'painfull death' and must not be circumvented.[4] Again, it is hard to suppress a shudder when Donne remarks quite casually in a sermon: 'he that travails weary, and late towards a great City, is glad when he comes to a place of execution, becaus he knows that is neer the town.'[5]

The hard, jubilant tone of 'A Burnt Ship' corresponds, in fact, to a pitiless element in Donne's nature, which obtrudes even in his Christian teaching. We find him rhapsodizing, for example, about the 'unexpressible comfort' which those who were saved in the ark must have felt when they saw everyone else drown.[6] Akin to this is his violent dislike of beggars and of the wretched troops of down-and-outs who roamed the seventeenth-century countryside. Even when we take into account the almost universal fear and hatred which these unfortunates inspired in respectable bosoms, the harshness of Donne's onslaught is disquieting. 'Among those herds of vagabonds, and incorrigible rogues, that fill porches, and barnes in the Countrey,' he emphasizes, 'a very great part of them was never baptized.' Consequently it is no part of a Christian's duty to relieve their sufferings, and we shall get no credit for it from God if we do. The mendicant classes produce children without being properly married, and commit other enormities, which make them wickeder, in their poverty, Donne judges, than the most corrupt rich man could ever be. Besides, they could easily obtain employment if they really wanted it: they are idle from choice. As we listen to Donne denouncing the destitute as 'dogs' and 'vermin', we are uncomfortably aware that the brutal penalties with which in his day the law punished homelessness and unemployment, drew their support from just such attitudes.[7]

The self-regard latent in these samples of Donne's Christianity also catches our attention at times when we are piecing together his dealings with friends and family. Writing to Sir Henry Goodyer, to commiserate with him on the death of his wife, Donne compares his own claims to sympathy with Goodyer's: 'If I should comfort you, it were an alms acceptable in no other title than when poor give to poor, for I am more needy of it than you.'[8] It must be one of the oddest statements ever included in a letter of consolation. Donne, when he wrote it, no doubt felt thwarted and miserable, as often, but he had not suffered bereavement. In the circumstances his self-pity seems gauche, not to say unbalanced. Did Goodyer, we wonder, resent his correspondent's mournful effrontery, or was he too used to his egotism to notice?

A similarly unhappy instance of self-absorption occurs in the sermon which Donne preached after the death of his favourite daughter Lucy in 1627. His fatherly grief is, of course, apparent. To make Lucy seem less absent, he clings to the idea—which he never raises elsewhere—that the dead may still be round about us on earth, though unseen. But the sermon's main argument is that Donne, by bearing his misfortune with religious fortitude, will qualify for a 'Better Ressurrection' than the ordinary run-of-the-mill Christian. The climactic paragraphs grope sublimely for words to express the glory of his own risen state. We don't have to be godless, sentimental moderns to find it disquieting that Donne should so smoothly convert his daughter's death into a means of improving his prospects in the next world. The joy of seeing his child in heaven should, we feel, be all that matters. But among the shellbursts of exalted imaginings with which the sermon terminates, that particular aspect of heavenly bliss doesn't, in fact, get mentioned.[9] We call to mind, in this context, Donne's prayer, in another sermon, to the effect that God should punish him 'with losse of parents and children', rather than with anything more damaging to his salvation.[10] It does not, it seems, occur to him that the children and parents concerned might be less keen on the arrangement.

These comments on Donne's egotism are not offered with the aim of belittling him as a human being, which would be futile. The point to be made is that the concentration upon self which, in these social and religious contexts, tempts us to moral indignation, becomes in Donne's poems a major source of individuality and power. His almost unremitting self-involvement as a poet has been finely remarked on by Robert Ellrodt.[11] It is his own name, not the girl's, that Donne engraves on the window. In 'A Valediction: of Weeping' there is no mention of what might happen, during his absence, to the girl—or wife—he is leaving. It is fear of what might happen to him that arouses concern. 'The Funerall' speculates about the fate of his body, but not of the girl's. In the *Songs and Sonnets* generally, the pathetic role is allocated to himself: only one poem, 'A Feaver', shows the girl suffering.

The artistic gain is in self-consciousness, which is so intense that he tends to externalize himself, as if for fuller observation. He becomes a picture, or a skeleton, or a mirror image—as in 'Witchcraft by a Picture':

> I fixe mine eye on thine, and there
> Pitty my picture burning in thine eye,
> My picture drown'd in a transparent teare,
> When I looke lower I espie.[12]

The tiny agonies of the reflections are watched like those of the pitiable, remote selves we watch helplessly in dreams. The same self-absorption inclines Donne to split himself into pieces that can scrutinize and comment on one another. In 'The Blossome' he talks to his heart, which is enslaved by a pitiless mistress:

> Little think'st thou poore heart. . .
> That thou to morrow, ere that Sunne doth wake,
> Must with this Sunne, and mee a journey take.[13]

The news is broken to the heart tenderly, as if it were an ignorant outsider. Donne is so closely aware of the divisions in himself that he can convey how it feels only by dividing into distinct beings. Rather similarly, in 'Loves Growth', he records the effect of springtime on his love as if he were observing the functions of some intricate and separate organism:

> I scarce beleeve my love to be so pure
> As I had thought it was,
> Because it doth endure
> Vicissitude, and season, as the grasse.[14]

Self-inspection was germane to Donne's kind of egotism. He trained himself to be his own psychoanalyst, and believed it the most worthwhile of occupations. The noblest act of the soul, he says in a letter, is 'that which reflects upon the soul itself, and considers and meditates it'.[15] But while recognizing the appeal of self-analysis, he also, self-analytically, recognized its impossibility. You cannot think undistortedly about yourself because you have only yourself to do the thinking with. The poetic externalizations of himself that we have just been looking at were an attempt to get beyond this predicament, but he did not deceive himself about their success. 'Our selves', he blankly asserts in 'Negative Love', are precisely 'What we know not'. 'My selfe' remained 'the hardest object of the sight'.[16] Donne elaborated on the point in a letter to Goodyer: 'Of the diseases of the mind there is no criterion, no canon, no rule, for our taste and apprehension and interpretation should be the judge, and that is the disease itself.' His attempts to experiment with his own mind, and control his moods, have, he reveals, generally failed, because of this inherent obstacle to diagnosis: 'I still mistake my disease.' He perseveres because, though he can't know himself, he feels better placed to try than anyone else: 'If I know it not, nobody can know it.'[17] Besides, to his self-plaguing nature—his 'riddling, perplexed, labyrinthical soule'[18]—the impossibility of self-knowledge made its pursuit irresistible.

His egotism, then, is intimately bound up with his creative processes. By consequence his poems bear the stamp of self more deeply than those of any other English poet. That's not just to say that they are packed with 'I' and 'me'. Donne's 'I' and 'me' are unusually stubborn pronouns, and will not allow the reader to appropriate them. With other poets we accept their lines as part of our inner incantation, and become the 'I' and 'me' they speak of. When we read Wordsworth's

> And I have felt
> A presence that disturbs me with the joy
> Of elevated thoughts. . .

we feel grander and more solemn because we imagine that we are the 'I' speaking. Donne will not allow himself to be requisitioned in this way. His poems remain intransigent blocks of Donne. That is why they arouse the hostility of critics like C. S. Lewis, who want poetry to be promiscuous, amenable and spell-binding, like myth, instead of prickly and individual.

Robert Ellrodt, when characterizing the egotism of the speaker in Donne's love poems, talks of 'le narcissisme de l'amant'.[19] However appropriate in French, the word 'narcissism' in English has an instantly recognizable wrongness when applied to Donne, which may help us to define more closely the kind of egotism his poems stand for. Curiously, though self-absorbed, they are not self-admiring. Their temper is too restless for that. Again, the contrast with Wordsworth is instructive: we cannot imagine Donne informing us that he has 'elevated thoughts'. Complacency could not survive his urgent intricacies. Further, his ego reaches too eagerly after objects beyond itself to be narcissistic: it is goaded by its incompleteness. We can see this, and see the consuming force of Donne's egotism, even in the poem which Robert Ellrodt singles out as being, for Donne, unusually selfless, 'A Feaver':

> Oh doe not die, for I shall hate
> All women so, when thou art gone,
> That thee I shall not celebrate,
> When I remember, thou wast one.[20]

The girl's dying will damage Donne's memory of her, and it is on those grounds that he dissuades her from it. Her predicament is treated as Donne's rather than hers. It is not so much her life as his view of womankind that is, we gather, in danger. Viewed logically, his selfishness, and his neat, impudent way of expressing it, are breathtaking. How insufferable to be told not to die because your lover will not 'celebrate' you if you do! Yet the effect of the lines is, of course, tender, for we can perfectly well see past what Donne says to what he means. His love for her, and his special way of thinking about her, are so important to him that he cannot conceive that they won't be equally important to her. Solicitously, he warns her that they are imperilled. Logic is irrelevant to the muddled, earnest strivings of the ego. The command—'Oh doe not die'—is itself illogical, though natural—for it is hardly to be supposed that the girl is doing it deliberately.

As the poem goes on, Donne becomes engrossed in his private speculations, rummaging among medical, meteorological and astronomical theories so as to bring the girl's plight into some sort of consoling focus. It is a mark of his abstracted musing that he stops, temporarily, addressing her as 'thou' and shifts to 'she':

> And yet she cannot wast by this,
>   Nor long beare this torturing wrong,
> For much corruption needfull is
>   To fuell such a feaver long.
>
> These burning fits but meteors bee,
>   Whose matter in thee is soone spent.
> Thy beauty,'and all parts, which are thee,
>   Are unchangeable firmament.
>
> Yet 'twas of my minde, seising thee,
>   Though it in thee cannot persever.
> For I had rather owner bee
>   Of thee one houre, then all else ever.

The selfishness of love is, in those closing lines, defiantly affirmed. Donne wants to own her; and it is not for her comfort that he wants it. He would want it even if it meant burning and wasting her like a disease. The notion of love as ownership offends our modernism. We are careful to talk, nowadays, as if we believed that the male ought to respect the female's individuality. Donne is above such hypocrisies, and states, with measured resonance, his lethal hunger.

There is another respect in which 'A Feaver' portrays Donne's demanding nature, apart from its blatant selfishness. The loved girl is not addressed simply as a loved girl. She is accorded universal importance. The world, Donne avows, will evaporate when she dies:

> Or if, when thou, the worlds soule, goest,
>   It stay, 'tis but thy carkasse then,
> The fairest woman, but thy ghost,
>   But corrupt wormes, the worthyest men.

This is typically Donnean exorbitance. The upsurge towards the unmatchable is a constant mark of his poetry. His soul felt impelled to reach for peaks and zeniths. It is characteristic, too, that the

woman he is writing about should be superseded. We find that, in the
excitement, she has been transformed into a cosmic principle, or into
a symbol of peerless power and virtue. He balances on the high edge
of language, striving to voice the unsurpassable, and the girl, with all
her personal particulars, is lost to sight thousands of feet below.

We may see this yearning for supremacy as a natural outcome of
Donne's impatience with his own divisiveness and inconstancy, as
well as with the failures and disappointments of his career.[21] What he
craved for was, by its very nature, unattainable. Later, he came to
regard this insatiability of the soul as a special expedient of divine
providence, urging man towards immortality. God, he explained,
has implanted in every man 'an endlesse, and Undeterminable desire
of More then this life can minister unto him'.[22] But long before he
put forward this theory Donne had manifested, through his poetry,
the claims of the transcendent. It was partly this habit of mind which
made the art of flattery less alien to him than it might have been.
Penning versified compliments to the Countess of Bedford or Mrs.
Herbert he could, almost before the poem had begun, leave mere fact
behind and head for the stratosphere. In the *Anniversaries* the uprush
from reality was even easier to manage, for since he had never
known Elizabeth Drury at all he had no chance of giving a truthful
impression of her, and could zoom and spiral freely among the
absolutes.
    What Donne says about Elizabeth in the *Anniversaries* resembles
very closely what he says about the girl in 'A Feaver', though of
course the poems on Elizabeth are much longer. Elizabeth, like the
other girl, is, or was, the world's soul—'the forme, that made it live'.
Now that she is dead, 'the World is but a Carkas'. Man is 'but as a
worme', bred in it; and any virtue that remains on earth must be
Elizabeth's 'Ghost'. Donne works it out, also, that Elizabeth's constitution, like the girl's in 'A Feaver', was too pure for disease to
attack, since it resembled that of the heavenly bodies.[23] The claims
are similar; but there is no question, needless to say, of 'A Feaver'
having anything to do with Elizabeth Drury. It is simply that the
poems he wrote for her express his customary craving for the
superlative, and do so in familiar terms.
    The *Anniversaries*, being more capacious, give extra range to
Donne's imagination. Cut loose from any semblance of sense, the
poems float upwards in aerobatic extravagance. Elizabeth Drury, we
are assured, preserved the created universe from corruption; it was
from her that the actions of all mankind took their worth; she had

read 'all Libraries'; her eyes brought gold to the West Indies, her breast perfumed the East; there were riches enough in her to make 'twenty such worlds as this'. The joyful, absurd claims go on for page after page. At the same time, the gruesome state of the world since Elizabeth's death is eagerly anatomized. Nothing else Donne wrote conveys such liberated inventiveness, or so lavishly gratifies his appetite for excess.

The really surprising thing about the *Anniversaries* is the critical misunderstanding they have occasioned. Jonson began it, observing that they were 'profane and full of Blasphemies', and that if they had been written about the Virgin Mary 'it had been something'.[24] But Jonson no doubt realized that he was being perverse. Pretty clearly he was trying to provoke Donne into discussing his own poetry— which, given Donne's secretiveness, must have been difficult. What's more, Jonson's ruse succeeded. Donne replied 'that he described the Idea of a Woman and not as she was'. That, one would have imagined, was straightforward enough, but critics have contrived to take it amiss. 'I shouldn't have thought that it *is* part of the idea of a woman,' objects William Empson, 'that her death is making the sun fall onto the earth.'[25] But Donne was using the word 'idea' in its common seventeenth-century sense of 'ideal', and for him the ideal had to be utterly beyond the compass of the real. What he told Jonson was that he had in mind, when composing the *Anniversaries*, a supreme perfection—as, obviously, he had. He was writing an essay in exorbitance.

Modern academic expositors, ignoring Donne's frank explanation, have puzzled their heads to discover what he was 'really' writing about in the *Anniversaries*—with bizarre results. Marius Bewley, in an article on 'Religious Cynicism in Donne's Poetry',[26] has put forward the theory that the *Anniversaries* are 'malign jokes' in which Donne secretly celebrates the Roman Catholic Church, under the guise of Elizabeth Drury. D. W. Harding suggests that the subject of the poems is Donne's mother, or rather a vision of perfect motherhood which he cherished as an infant and which, as it faded, left the world a disappointing place.[27] Richard E. Hughes, with firm disregard for the evidence, reckons that the poems are about St. Lucy;[28] and Frank Manley, in his edition of the *Anniversaries*, struggles eruditely to convince his readers that Donne is actually describing the Shekinah—the last sephirath in the cabbalistic system of emanations, representing God's immanence in the world.[29]

The critical thinking in each case is identical: if a poet employs extravagant language, it is assumed that it must be about a subject which the normal person would deem worthy of such language, and the critic accordingly casts around to find one. As an approach to imaginative literature this seems unpromising, and its prevalence among academics gives cause for concern. Barbara K. Lewalski's book on the *Anniversaries* likewise seeks for a decently important subject which the poems might be about, and comes up with the notion that Donne is writing about the image of God, restored by grace in Elizabeth Drury since she is a regenerate soul.[30] The obvious objection to this is that the image of God is restored in all regenerate souls, whereas Donne treats Elizabeth as unique. The failure of her theory to fit the facts of the poems is acknowledged by Mrs. Lewalski, who describes it as a 'paradox'. However, it simply makes the theory untenable.

We return to Donne's own explanation, which is perfectly in tune with what we know of his imaginative habits. He was in pursuit of an ideal—trying to stretch language to make it embody the most exaggerated things that could be thought. It was a voyage into undiscovered spaces of hyperbole. In his letters to friends he wearily reiterated that this was what he was up to. The whole affair had, he stressed, only the most tenuous connection with Elizabeth Drury—'for since I never saw the gentlewoman, I cannot be understood to have bound myself to have spoken just truth.' The plan was to delineate 'the best that I could conceive'[31]—to drive his imagination to its limit.

The one fair criticism that might be made of the *Anniversaries*, given their circumstances, is that they don't express much sorrow. We can appreciate this if we contrast them with the tribute which some unknown poet penned several years earlier for Elizabeth's sister Dorothy, who had died at the age of four:

> She, little, promis'd much,
> Too soone untyed:
> She only dreamt she liv'd,
> And then she dyde.[32]

By comparison, the *Anniversaries* are about as touching as a brass band. But then, it would be unreasonable to expect Donne to sound grief-stricken. Elizabeth's death was, for him, a remarkable piece of luck, since it gave him an opportunity of recommending himself, as we have seen, to a new patron, and, at the same time, of writing dizzy cadenzas of praise which gave relief to his spirit.

He was also able to fit into his poems a zestful account of the contemptible state of the world that Elizabeth had left behind. He

probably got the idea for this from Joseph Hall, the parson at
Hawstead, who was a close friend of Lady Drury, and who had been
noted at university for his 'ingenious maintaining' of the belief that
the world was in decline.[33] Hall supplied prefatory verses for the
Anniversaries, and saw the volumes through the press, so it was
appropriate that Donne should give Hall's pet theory an airing in
them. But in any case the theme suited his own inclinations. He felt
bitter about the way the world had treated him, and his frustration
could find relief in wholesale denunciation of the globe and its inhabitants, as well as in the creation of shining, other-worldly ideals. The
Anniversaries, like 'A Feaver', are able to incorporate both expedients.

The hymns to perfection which Donne wrote for Elizabeth Drury
are the most sustained examples of the art of ambition in his work.
(As bids for Sir Robert Drury's favour they also, of course, represent
the art of ambition in a more prosaic and less interesting sense.) They
are latish and holy poems, and to show how the aspiring temper
observable in them adapted itself, in Donne's early years, to more
mundane subjects we might take his elegy 'To his Mistris Going to
Bed'. This is one of the seven elegies (the others are 'The Bracelet',
'Jealosie', 'The Anagram', 'Change', 'The Perfume' and 'His Picture') which can be dated, on manuscript evidence, before 1599.[34]
Almost certainly it was only the second surviving elegy Donne
wrote (the first being 'The Bracelet'), and belongs, we may deduce,
to his early twenties, when he was a student at Lincoln's Inn. It was
considered too indecent to print, and omitted from the first edition
of Donne's poems which his son got together in 1633. It is a long
poem to quote, but not boring:

> Come, Madame, come, all rest my powers defie,
> Until I labour, I in labour lye.
> The foe oft-times, having the foe in sight,
> Is tir'd with standing, though they never fight.
> Off with that girdle, like heavens zone glistering
> But a farre fairer world encompassing.
> Unpin that spangled brest-plate, which you weare
> That th'eyes of busy fooles may be stopt there:
> Unlace your selfe, for that harmonious chime
> Tells me from you that now 'tis your bed time.
> Off with that happy buske, whom I envye
> That still can be, and still can stand so nigh.
> Your gownes going off such beauteous state reveales
> As when from flowery meades th'hills shadow steales.

Off with your wyrie coronet and showe
The hairy dyadem which on you doth growe.
Off with those shoes: and then safely tread
In this loves hallow'd temple, this soft bed.
In such white robes heavens Angels us'd to bee
Receiv'd by men; Thou Angel bring'st with thee
A heaven like Mahomets Paradise; and though
Ill spirits walk in white, we easily know
By this these Angels from an evill sprite:
They set our haires, but these the flesh upright.
     Licence my roving hands, and let them goe
Behind, before, above, between, below.
Oh my America, my new found lande,
My kingdome, safeliest when with one man man'd,
My myne of precious stones, my Empiree,
How blest am I in this discovering thee.
To enter in these bonds is to be free,
Then where my hand is set my seal shall be.
     Full nakedness, all joyes are due to thee.
As soules unbodied, bodies uncloth'd must bee
To tast whole joyes. Gems which you women use
Are as Atlanta's balls, cast in mens viewes,
That when a fooles eye lighteth on a gem
His earthly soule may covet theirs not them.
Like pictures, or like bookes gay coverings made
For laymen, are all women thus arraid;
Themselves are mystique bookes, which only wee
Whom their imputed grace will dignify
Must see reveal'd. Then since I may knowe,
As liberally as to a midwife showe
Thy selfe; cast all, yea this white linnen hence.
Here is no pennance, much lesse innocence.
     To teach thee, I am naked first: Why than
What need'st thou have more covering than a man.[35]

The despotic lover here, ordering his submissive girl-victim to strip, and drawing attention to his massive erection (the point of Donne's jokes about 'standing'), is of course a perennial dweller in the shadow-land of pornography, particularly attractive as a fantasy role to males who, through shyness or social circumstance, find relations with women difficult. But despite its common pattern, the poem has some more specifically Donnean traits which are worth noting.

The sex exudes a strongly economic flavour. Emphasis is placed on the richness of the woman's clothes. She wears a 'glistering' girdle; her stomacher ('brest-plate') is 'spangled' with precious stones. The 'harmonious chime' striking the hour of bedtime is her chiming watch—a precious bauble in the sixteenth century, which only court ladies or rich citizens' wives could hope to possess. (There are some watches 'to which the very cases are Jewells' Donne was to remark, perhaps reminiscently, years later in a sermon.)[36] The 'wyrie coronet' is particularly suggestive. The word 'coronet' could be used of the gold or silver wreath which might form part of any society woman's elaborate coiffure, but it primarily denoted the small crown worn by men and women of the nobility. The luscious sex-symbol whom Donne puts through her paces may be—or so he hints—an aristocrat. The poet of 'Twicknam Garden' already finds the association of love with rank beguiling. In these respects the situation Donne has concocted gratifies not only his sexual but also his social and financial ambitions. The luxurious accessories of his fantasy seem as important to him as the strip-tease itself.

More important than either is the urge to dominate, and this is not confined to his relations with the woman. His elegy expresses his superiority to other men as well. Although it advertises the expensiveness of the female involved, it disparages people who set store by such considerations. Women, Donne remarks, wear precious stones to catch businessmen ('busy fooles') and other sordid types. He himself belongs to a minority whose values are more exalted. In this way he contrives to sound, provokingly, high-minded and dissolute at the same time. Similarly he exhibits his command of religious language while flaunting his disregard for religion. He alludes to the doctrine that the soul must be separated from the body to experience 'whole joyes', and to the Protestant belief that it was Christ's imputed grace (that is, Christ's righteousness, transferred to man) which made salvation for humankind possible. These theological niceties, thrust into a bawdy poem, typify that defensive and derisive treatment of religion which, as we have seen, Donne's apostasy prompted.

By such tactics the elegy establishes Donne's ascendancy over mammon-worshippers and God-fearing souls alike. He is too refined to associate with the first, and too smart to be taken in by the superstitions of the second. His contempt extends not only to his mesmerized victim but to large sections of the human race. Further, he elevates himself, by his tone and style, above the subject matter he is purportedly occupied with. Just as in 'A Feaver' there was a tendency for the sick girl to be displaced by the alternative subjects which presented themselves to Donne's enquiring mind, so here Donne becomes more and more loftily engaged, as the poem goes on, and his immediate concern with the garment-shedding girl slips into abeyance. The poem's climax is a general eulogy of nakedness, not, as we might have anticipated, an inventory of this particular girl's anatomical assets. Indeed, it comes as something of a surprise, given the elegy's theme, and its general air of lust, to realize that it does not from start to finish mention any part of the girl's body except her hair—not so much as a lip or toenail, let alone a breast or thigh. The salivating survey of female physique which was *de rigueur* in most Elizabethan pornography (see, for instance, Thomas Nashe's enjoyable 'The Choice of Valentines'[37]) has vanished. By comparison Donne is rarefied and abstracted. He hardly seems to see the girl, though his appraising eye dwells on the clothes she takes off.

This lack of purely visual contact may be illustrated by the way Donne employs his delicate and suggestive image of the hill's shadow stealing from 'flowery meades'. The girl's lingering movement as she takes her dress off is provocatively caught by the verb 'steales'. But what the removal of her gown actually leaves her standing in is not something that visually resembles 'flowery meades' at all, but her white shift—as Donne's mention of 'white robes' a few lines later makes clear. The colourful impression created by 'flowery meades' is out of key with this blanched plainness. The image does not, in fact, work at a visual level, but spiritually. The glad excitement, the sense of revelation and dazzling brightness, are what connect the experience of seeing suddenly unclouded countryside with the experience of seeing a girl step out of her dress. It is, incidentally, an indication of the way in which the poem leaves the bedroom level behind, that we cannot tell at the end whether the girl is still wearing her shift or not. The 'white linnen' which Donne is still instructing her to relinquish four lines from the finish may be the shift, but it may be just a sheet from the bed which she is cowering under. The joke about 'pennance' suggests that it is a sheet (because penitents were required to stand in one), but if the girl did take off her shift somewhere along the line, Donne omitted to mention it.

A final element in the elegy's transcendence (and one which, again, reminds us of 'A Feaver', though it could be matched in many Donne poems including the *Anniversaries*), is the inclination to expand the girl into something of universally acknowledged importance—in this case a continental land mass ('Oh my America, my new found lande'). Language of this description enables Donne to enclose the public sphere in the private. He can feel that he has scaled the pinnacle of worldly, as well as erotic, success, and is not lover but ruler. A 'kingdome' and 'Empiree' are at his command, in bed.

In 'The Sunne Rising' Donne's claim to this royal status is placed resplendently at the poem's heart:

> Busie old foole, unruly Sunne,
>   Why dost thou thus,
> Through windowes, and through curtaines call on us?
> Must to thy motions lovers seasons run?
>   Sawcy pedantique wretch, goe chide
>   Late schoole boyes, and sowre prentices,
>   Goe tell Court-huntsmen, that the King will ride,
>   Call countrey ants to harvest offices;
> Love, all alike, no season knowes, nor clyme,
> Nor houres, dayes, months, which are the rags of time.
>
>   Thy beames, so reverend, and strong
>   Why shouldst thou thinke?
> I could eclipse and cloud them with a winke,
> But that I would not lose her sight so long:
>   If her eyes have not blinded thine,
>   Looke, and to morrow late, tell mee,
>   Whether both the'India's of spice and Myne
>   Be where thou leftst them, or lie here with mee.
> Aske for those Kings whom thou saw'st yesterday,
> And thou shalt heare, All here in one bed lay.
>
>   She'is all States, and all Princes, I,
>   Nothing else is.
> Princes doe but play us; compar'd to this,
> All honor's mimique; All wealth alchimie.'
>   Thou sunne art halfe as happy'as wee,
>   In that the world's contracted thus;
>   Thine age askes ease, and since thy duties bee
>   To warme the world, that's done in warming us.
> Shine here to us, and thou art every where;
> This bed thy center is, these walls, thy spheare.[38]

The phrase 'Busie old foole' reminds us of the 'busy fooles' in 'To his

Mistris Going to Bed'; and as the girl in that elegy became America, so this one becomes the East and West Indies. The contempt and arrogance of the elegy persist here; but in commenting on this poem critics have rightly drawn attention to the misgivings which appear, like cracks, in its regal surface. Though emphatic about the all-eclipsing eminence of himself and the girl, Donne seems irascibly conscious of the rest of the world going about its business. What the real court and the real king may be doing stays at the back of his mind, and as if to counteract this the poem evolves its announcement of personal kingship. We remember how ardently Donne wanted, in actual fact, to be 'busie'; how useless he felt in his unemployment, like a spider in a window; how important he thought it to be integrated into the world and the court. The poem's first word has jealousy and resentment in it, as well as contempt.

Donne's vaunting language is, like all vaunting language, an expression of insecurity, and this makes the poem more human. The pretension to kingship that he voices amounts to an acknowledgement of personal insufficiency. That the love of two ordinary, private people might be supremely significant is, we realize, a claim too assured for him to risk. When he tries to formulate it, he finds himself challenging comparison with kings, and to do this is to accept the conventional scale of values, with kings at its top, which he had seemed to be subverting. If lovers can be supreme only by being called kings, then kings are still supreme. The private world is valued only as it apes the public.

When Donne took holy orders he again felt the need to pretend, in his poetry, that the step had made him a king, or super-king. The poem 'To Mr. Tilman after he had taken orders' tells the newly ordained clergyman about the splendour of his, and Donne's, calling:

> What function is so noble, as to bee
> Embassadour to God and destinie?
> To open life, to give kingdomes to more
> Than Kings give dignities . . . ?[39]

We recall, on reading this, that what Donne had really wanted to be was ambassador to Venice, not to God and destiny. The self-aggrandizement of the lines is a form of consolation. In making himself and Mr. Tilman seem noteworthy, the utmost that it occurs to Donne to do is to place them above kings and the dignities they distribute. That would be enough to suggest how preoccupied he was with royalty, even if we didn't know that pursuing the dignities kings distribute had taken up most of his working life.

By comparison with the exhortations of 'To Mr. Tilman', the bid
for royalty in 'The Sunne Rising' sounds vulnerable, and so more
moving. It is noticeable that Donne changes his mind, in the course
of the poem, about what he wants the sun to do. He starts by
commanding it to go away, but when we reach the end we find that
he wants it to stay with him and the girl and warm them. Until he
mentioned it, we hadn't thought of them as needing to be warmed,
and the idea is touching. The transition from dismissal ('goe') to
invitation ('Shine here to us') in Donne's address to the sun is
accompanied by a change of manner. The petulance of the opening
gives place to a conciliatory tone ('Thine age askes ease'). The
speaker does not after all, it seems, want to be left alone with his love.
Nor does he feel that they have, yet, enough pre-eminence. He wants
the sun to shine on them alone. This shift in the poem's demeanour
prevents it from settling into a piece of dead bravado. It has the
instability of a living thing.

In this, and in its anxiety, it resembles another of Donne's greatest
poems, 'The Anniversarie'. But whereas the lover of 'The Sunne
Rising' worries about being left out in the cold, the lover of 'The
Anniversarie' pits himself against the approaching dark:

> All Kings, and all their favorites,
>   All glory'of honors, beauties, wits,
> The Sun it selfe, which makes times, as they passe,
> Is elder by a yeare, now, then it was
> When thou and I first one another saw:
> All other things, to their destruction draw,
>   Only our love hath no decay;
> This, no tomorrow hath, nor yesterday,
> Running it never runs from us away,
> But truly keepes his first, last, everlasting day.

> Two graves must hide thine and my coarse,
>   If one might, death were no divorce.
> Alas, as well as other Princes, wee,
> (Who Prince enough in one another bee,)
> Must leave at last in death, these eyes, and eares,
> Oft fed with true oathes, and with sweet salt teares;
>   But soules where nothing dwells but love
> (All other thoughts being inmates) then shall prove
> This, or a love increased there above,
> When bodies to their graves, soules from their graves remove.

And then wee shall be throughly blest,
But wee no more, then all the rest.
Here upon earth, we'are Kings, and none but wee
Can be such Kings, nor of such subjects bee;
Who is so safe as wee? where none can doe
Treason to us, except one of us two.
True and false feares let us refraine,
Let us love nobly,'and live, and adde againe
Yeares and yeares unto yeares, till we attaine
To write threescore: this is the second of our raigne.[40]

The first three lines of the poem, blending kings and glory with the sun, sound like a fanfare to majesty. But they are a dirge. The gorgeous blaze darkens, and the poet's individual claim springs clear of the dying splendours massed at the start. It is over the wreck of empires and solar systems that the first stanza strides forward.

Despite this brave beginning, anxiety goes deeper here than it did in 'The Sunne Rising', and that poem's perkiness and banter have been stifled. Confidence caves in after the first stanza. As soon as the second begins, we can tell that a more concerned and perplexed voice has taken over, and though this voice tries to argue itself and the girl into putting a brave face on things ('Let us love nobly'), it admits that such courage is a mode of self-deception. There are 'True' as well as false fears, however determinedly one may 'refraine' from thinking about them; and the vision of the sexagenarian lovers in the last line doesn't, when dwelt on, carry much comfort.

The claim to kingship is less confident, too, than in 'The Sunne Rising'. Instead of being flung in the face of the facts—'She'is all States, and all Princes, I'—it is sidled into the poem as a piece of special pleading, while Donne comforts the girl about death. Aren't they, after all, he coaxes her to believe, 'Prince enough in one another'? That qualifying 'enough' betrays the pretence: they are not real princes. And though the third stanza takes a higher tone ('none but wee / Can be such Kings'), the effect is weakened by the need to prop it up with declamation ('Who is so safe as wee?').

But the fact that the poem's confidence gets eaten away doesn't mean that the wish to feel supreme grows less. Quite the contrary: the thought of death is alarming, we must observe, not because death will separate the lovers, or destroy their love, or diminish their happiness. None of these things, Donne persuades himself, will happen. It is alarming because death will end their supremacy. Dead, they will be totally happy ('throughly blest'), but no happier than 'all the rest', and that is unbearable. It is not happiness but superiority that Donne craves, which is why he hustles the afterlife out of his poem, and returns to his royal pre-eminence ('Here upon earth, we're Kings'). He knows that their reign will be only temporary: the time fuse, as the last line tells us, is already burning. But he clings to their earthly reign nevertheless. And that represents a major change of direction in the poem; for at the start it was their disembodied love, free of time, knowing no tomorrow or yesterday, that Donne celebrated. Now it is their monarchy, measured in years.

Donne could, of course, have written a simpler poem if he had assumed that he and the girl would go on being kings after death. Then the need to choose between heavenly blessedness and royal supremacy would have been avoided. Over the centuries other writers have taken this step, either in fantasy or earnest. Shakespeare's Antony sees a royal afterlife for himself and Cleopatra:

> Where souls do couch on flowers, we'll hand in hand,
> And with our sprightly port make the ghosts gaze:
> Dido and her Aeneas shall want troops,
> And all the haunt be ours.[41]

D. H. Lawrence's natural aristocrats, too, tend to assume that they will be on top in the underworld, by virtue of their superior vitality. 'I shall be a king in Hades when I am dead,' Count Dionys assures Daphne in *The Ladybird*, 'And you will be at my side.'[42] Donne was at times prepared to believe that there might be ranks and degrees in heaven. 'That there are degrees of Glory in the Saints in heaven, scarce any ever denied,' he remarked in a sermon of 1626. 'Heaven is a Kingdome and Christ a King, and a popular parity agrees not with that State, with a Monarchy.'[43] He wasn't always so sure. Only three years later, in another sermon, he took a different view: 'all shall rise alike . . . all that rise to the right hand, shall be equally Kings.'[44] Even this egalitarian doctrine, though, would have allowed him to present his lovers, in 'The Anniversarie', as kings in heaven—for he plainly states that they will be among the blessed. But he didn't choose to. He planned his poem so that the frailty, as well as the supremacy, of the kingship it boasts of should be exposed. He pitted love's kings against unkinging death, so that the poem's certitude should be tempered by doubt, its ambition by anxiety.

Although Donne's eagerness to acclaim the sovereignty of himself and his love is, in these two poems, clouded with doubts, it remains unmistakable. He was profoundly excited by the thought of majesty. To readers of liberal views, this might appear a blemish. Donne's equation of his love with kingship, such readers might object, links it with political power and possession. The girl may become the world ('all States'), but she is a world owned and ruled, indeed, rifled and exploited. She is 'both the'India's of spice and Myne'. The same sort of reader would naturally be inclined to dismiss Donne's adulation of the great, and his eagerness for royal favour, as mere opportunism and greed. To understand this part of his mind correctly, however, we must appreciate that veneration for the court and for the grandees who peopled it was so deeply embedded among his imaginative and spiritual impulses that it became an element of his religious belief. If we think of the Renaissance as the epoch in which glorification of the court, and of the prince as earthly God, reached its apogee, then Donne was a Renaissance man in nothing more than this.

From his sermons we can collect testimony of the divine value he attached to worldly pomp which is staggering to anyone brought up in a more severe religious tradition. 'As Princes are Gods', he affirms, 'so their well-govern'd Courts, are Copies, and representations of Heaven.' 'The Kings of the earth', he maintains, 'are faire and glorious resemblances of the King of heaven; they are beames of that Sun, Tapers of that Torch, they are like gods, they are gods.' It is in the courts of princes that Christ, and 'this wisdom which must save our Soules', are 'gloriously and conspicuously to be found'. The Holy Ghost's polished language in Scripture shows that he is a 'good Courtier'.[45]

Donne's opinions coincide closely, of course, with James I's insistence that he ruled by divine right. The divine splendour of majesty should, Donne emphasizes, prompt instant obedience, and silence democratic murmurings. The king, like the sun, is the blazing face of God: 'How glorious is God, as he looks down upon us, through the Sunne? How glorious in that glasse of his? How glorious is God, as he looks out amongst us through *the King*? How glorious in that Image of his?'[46] To argue that the king rules merely by consent of the people is, Donne warns, to disparage God's power. For a private man to censure a king is, whatever the justification, impiety. We have no right to criticize abuses in Church and State, even where they unquestionably exist.[47] It puts our soul in jeopardy if we so much as think ill thoughts about government officials, let alone disobey them: 'we sin against the Father, the roote of power, in conceiving amisse of the power of the Civill Magistrate'.[48]

Donne is far from exempting the Church and its ministers from this obligation of obedience. The interference of the civil magistrate in the private spiritual life of the individual, which has always been anathema to the nonconformist conscience, and which was to stir Milton to righteous fury, seemed wholly proper to Donne. As a churchman, he hated religious schismatics and separatists of all persuasions, and lost no opportunity to vilify them. They fractured the glorious unity of the Christian faith, and should be stamped out by law. God has put our religion, he reminded his congregation, 'into the *hand* of the *Magistrate*'.[49] It is right that we should be compelled by punitive legislation to remain in the Church into which we have been baptized, and to perform its observances.[50] When Dean of St. Paul's he had a member of his congregation committed to Newgate for refusing to kneel when admonished.[51] The Church, like the individual believer, Donne insisted, must humble itself before the king. For ministers of religion to presume to obey their consciences and speak out boldly in the king's presence, as the Old Testament prophets did, is to behave 'perversely, frowardly, dangerously'.[52]

Respect for the grandeur of the court is, like obedience to the king, bound up in Donne's mind with Christian worship. The flamboyant, extravagant costumes assumed by courtiers are not only, we gather, excusable, but an element in religious observance. 'God is said in the Scriptures to apparell himself gloriously,' Donne points out, and he 'weares good cloathes, silk, and soft raiment, in his religious servants in Courts'.[53] So courtiers are actually enhancing God's glory when they cover themselves with expensive textiles. Their desire for wealth, honour and preferment, and their magnificent style of life, may also be seen, in Donne's estimation, as eminently Christian. The Holy Ghost, he reminds us, alludes to God and heaven through the metaphor of riches, and since eternal life is described in this opulent language in the Bible, the way to secure it is by being opulent on earth: 'For, beloved, Salvation it selfe being so often presented to us in the names of Glory, and of Joy, we cannot thinke that the way to that glory is a sordid life affected here, an obscure, a beggarly, a negligent abandoning of all wayes of preferment, or riches, or estimation in this World.'[54] Desire for wealth is, he stresses, perfectly consistent with 'true and heavenly wisdome'.[55] For those who object that Donne's version of Christianity does not seem greatly to resemble Christ's, Donne himself has an answer. 'Every Christian', he observes, 'is not a Christ.' It is true that Christ consorted with publicans and sinners, but if we were to do so, Donne urges, we might be infected by their company. Imitation of Christ is an excess which he cautions his congregation against: 'for it is not alwaies good to go too far'.[56]

The adulation of king and court which streamed from Donne's pulpit might be construed by the cynical as the strategy of a dedicated careerist. But that seems too simple an explanation. As we have seen, his poems, which were not written for the public eye, are comparably entranced by the magic of kingship, and challenge it for themselves. Royalty glowed in the depths of his consciousness. To think himself a king was the furthest reach of his reverie. When he is contemplating the scope of his own spiritual faculties, heightened by love, it is the metaphor of an earthly prince that suggests itself. In 'The Extasie' he instructs the girl that 'pure lovers soules' must not remain in disembodied impotence, but

> descend
> T'affections, and to faculties,
> That sense may reach and apprehend,
> Else a great Prince in prison lies.[57]

In our day, the notion of an incarcerated head of state does not induce any great awe. But for Donne the image evidently expressed a monstrous and supernatural antithesis—a god, locked up; a captive sun. To think of the prurient, owlish James I, with his weakness for pretty boys and his notoriously low standards of personal cleanliness, as a god or a sun must have called for a heroic effort of imaginative detachment on Donne's part. But then, all human ideals, if pursued to an extreme, demand that. Resolute self-deception is the first requirement of any absolutist. In giving his unqualified allegiance to James, Donne answered the need of his imagination. His politics came from his soul. He created the radiant, all-powerful king of the sermons to satisfy the same part of his nature as had turned the girl of 'A Feaver' into the world's soul, or Elizabeth Drury into a divine principle, or himself and his love into all States and all Princes. The urge for an absolute continued to impel him.

The contrast with Milton, which we have already touched on, is in this respect particularly clear. Milton's mind habitually divided the fabric of reality into antagonistic elements: 'L'Allegro' is answered by 'Il Penseroso'; Comus confronts the Lady; Satan wars with God. Donne, equally, if not more, aware of the divisions within himself, aspired towards a wholeness that would surmount and unite them. Markedly different religious and political views flow from this basic antipathy between the two poets. The doctrine of the Trinity, which

seeks to weld separate elements into a transcendent unity, was raptly
celebrated by Donne, but rejected by Milton, who insisted that
Father, Son and Holy Ghost must remain essentially distinct.[58] Milton championed divorce; Donne dwelt, in poems, on the union of
souls and, in sermons, on the mystic union of marriage. The sects
and schisms that fragmented the Christian church were defended by
Milton in *Areopagitica* as a sign of healthy disagreement, and for the
same reason he opposed government censorship, which sought to
suppress conflicting opinions. But Donne, as we have noted,
detested nonconformity, and he supported censorship. When James I
issued his *Directions for Preachers* in 1622, forbidding public discussion of controversial religious and political issues, Donne was chosen
to justify this repressive measure in a sermon at St. Paul's Cross.
James was so pleased with the result that he rushed it into print.[59] On
kingship, Milton and Donne were inevitably and diametrically
opposed. Milton, who wrote the official defence of Charles I's
execution, argued that kings reigned by consent of their people, and
that subjects had a right to call unjust rulers to account. Donne, the
absolutist, was stirred by the image of numinous majesty, scattering
opposition as the sun disperses clouds.

The appeal of this theory of kingship lay, for Donne, not only in its
radiance but also in the unlimited power which it invested in a single
human being. The exercise of power fascinated him, and is a crucial
element in his art. The almost pathological imperiousness of a poem
like 'To his Mistris Going to Bed' is apparent enough. But even
when his early love poems are relatively lyrical and adoring, the urge
to impose power can be observed in them. We might take, as an
instance, his elegy 'On his Mistris' where Donne, about to leave for
foreign parts, exhorts the girl to give up her plan of following him
disguised as his page, and begs her to stay at home and keep their love
secret:

> When I am gone, dreame mee some happinesse,
> Nor let thy lookes our long hid love confesse,
> Nor praise, nor dispraise mee, blesse, nor curse
> Openly loves force; nor in bed fright thy nurse
> With midnights startings, crying out, oh, oh,
> Nurse, oh my love is slaine; I saw him goe
> Ore the white Alpes, alone; I saw him, I,
> Assayl'd, fight, taken, stabb'd, bleede, fall, and dye.[60]

The eerie light which seems to shed itself, from the dream, over the
girl's frightened figure, is not just arresting but an effort of the

dramatic imagination. Donne enters the subconscious mind of another being. In 'To his Mistris Going to Bed' the girl has no mind—only a body and clothes to remove from it. But 'On his Mistris', though a more sympathetic piece, manifests Donne's authority quite as firmly. It is composed, throughout, of instructions. Donne foresees eventualities, calculates risks, chooses one course of action for the girl and vetoes another. Compared to him, she is a child—an impression sustained by the presence of her nurse. She is, too, the poem intimates, almost out of her mind with love for him, so that he fills her dreams, and she has to be warned against her crazy plan of elopement. Thus though it is not, like 'To his Mistris Going to Bed', a punitive poem, it as aggrandizingly establishes Donne's power over the girl's thoughts and actions.

Power is the shaping principle in Donne's verse. It communicates itself through the dictatorial attitudes the poet adopts, through the unrelenting argumentativeness of his manner, and through the manipulation and violent combination of the objects of the sensed world in his imagery. The reader has a sensation of pressure gathered behind the poems, impelling them and subduing their recalcitrant materials. Coleridge, in his lines on Donne, voices this common reaction:

> With Donne, whose muse on dromedary trots,
> Wreathe iron pokers into true-love knots;
> Rhyme's sturdy cripple, fancy's maze and clue,
> Wit's forge and fire-blast, meaning's press and screw.[61]

Donne is envisaged here as a piece of industrial machinery, ruthlessly coercive.

Power—or 'masculine perswasive force', [62] as Donne called it—is also implicit in his syntax and rhythms. Words are packed into the poems like boulders, and the voice clambers over them. Inversions and interjections fracture the run of the lines, necessitating a strenuous advance. These effects can be readily illustrated in lines already quoted from 'The Anniversarie':

> But soules where nothing dwells but love
> (All other thoughts being inmates) then shall prove
> This, or a love increased there above . . .

Interjection (in the second line) and qualification (in the third) give the passage a cramped air, as if the earnest argument had insufficient room. The verse form is made to seem the wrong size. Donne does not float forward on his chosen metre, but grapples with it. Elegance

is an early casualty, but that only convinces us more forcibly of the
resolution behind the whole encumbered enterprise.

Commands and questions also break up the poems, giving them
grip and insistence. The majority of the *Songs and Sonnets* begin with
an imperative, an interrogative, or a superlative, which needs to be
supported and is then often controverted, so that effortful deliberation is conveyed. The poems are more vehement and more heavily
articulated than normal, containing, it has been calculated, roughly
two more verbs per ten lines than is average in English poetry and
between six and twelve more connectives.[63] They are not allowed to
flop into the indicative mood, as descriptive or narrative poems tend
to. Instead, they resemble monodramas, in which the figure of
Donne, cajoling, demanding, enunciating, occupies so much of the
foreground that we only occasionally catch a glimpse, over his
shoulder or under his arm, of some anonymous figure at whom the
flow of language is being directed.

The impression of power is enhanced by the way Donne, as a writer,
apprehends space. Man, in his poems and prose works alike, towers
over the landscape. Donne has a colossus mentality. The immediate
environment, with its local features, shrivels into insignificance as
we listen to him. He sees the earth as a map or globe, and watches the
heavenly bodies flying round it through space. From his eminence he
can survey the mountain ranges and the ocean depths. He sees
Mount Teneriffe, in *The First Anniversarie*, jutting out

> . . . like a Rocke, that one might thinke
> The floating Moone would shipwracke there, and sinke.[64]

He peers down, in the same poem, through the darkening fathoms
which mask the ocean floor, and imagines doomed creatures sinking
through them hour by hour:

> Seas are so deepe, that Whales being strooke to day,
> Perchance to morrow, scarse at middle way
> Of their wish'd journeys end, the bottom, dye.

He is aware of the movement of waters over the earth's surface,
noticing, as he says in 'The Triple Foole', how

> th'earths inward narrow crooked lanes
> Do purge sea waters fretfull salt away.[65]

From the height at which Donne speaks the river systems look like
crinkly paths. We recall Tennyson's 'The Eagle':

He clasps the crag with crooked hands;
Close to the sun in lonely lands . . .
The wrinkled sea beneath him crawls.[66]

But in Tennyson the whole point of the poem is the eagle's exceptional height. Donne reduces rivers to narrow, crooked lanes almost in passing. The giant viewpoint is so much a matter of course that the poem lifts us into the air and stretches the world beneath us before we have noticed what is happening.

Donne's scale of vision is cosmic. The skies are familiar territory. He sees them criss-crossed and partitioned like a cosmographer's chart:

Of Meridians, and Parallels,
Man hath weav'd out a net, and this net throwne
Upon the Heavens, and now they are his owne.[67]

The sun is not imagined as a source of energy, a divine influence nurturing the world, as it seems to other poets. In Donne it is primarily a projectile—an earth satellite with a trajectory and timetable. When he alludes to it, its orbit round the earth is what he notices. He does not see it shining overhead but swimming in the goldfish bowl of space. Because he enjoys this superior position, he can address it as an equal or subordinate: 'Sleep sleep old Sun.'[68] He gives it orders, and threatens to eclipse it with a wink. In the *Essays in Divinity* he squints down at the earth's protuberances and inner recesses as from the vantage point of some X-ray-eyed astronaut:

hills, though they erect their heads beyond the Country of Meteors, and set their foot in one land, and cast their shadow into another, are but warts upon her face: And her vaults, and caverns, the bed of the winds, and the secret streets and passages of al rivers . . . are but as so many wrinkles, and pock-holes.[69]

Out in space, Donne can see the mountains as warts, but he can also see their shadows falling across whole countries. Though diminished, the world remains real and solid.

On Donne's poems, the effect of having this foothold in the stratosphere is drastic. It reshapes their basic design, affecting what is left out as much as what is put in, so that we need to have it pointed out to us what they might otherwise have been like before we can see how outlandish, as treatments of their subject, they are. A convenient poem to demonstrate this is 'Goodfriday, 1613. Riding Westward', because we know a fair amount about the circumstances of its composition. In 1613 Donne was staying at Polesworth, his friend Sir Henry Goodyer's country house in the Forest of Arden. We can gather what Polesworth was like from a poem which Donne and Goodyer wrote in collaboration when Donne was on a visit there, each of them contributing alternate stanzas (Goodyer's here in italics). They addressed it to two unnamed ladies, whom they compare with the springtime delights of the Polesworth countryside:

> *Since ev'ry Tree beginns to blossome now*
> *Perfuminge and enamelinge each bow,*
> *Hartes should as well as they, some fruits allow. . . .*

> *Wee doe consider noe flower that is sweet,*
> *But wee your breath in that exhaling meet,*
> *And as true Types of you, them humbly greet.*

> Heere in our Nightingales, wee heere you singe,
> Who soe doe make the whole yeare through a springe,
> And save us from the feare of Autumns stinge.

> *In Ancors calme face wee your smoothnes see,*
> *Your mindes unmingled, and as cleare as shee*
> *That keepes untoucht her first virginitie.*[70]

This shows us what the conventional poetic advantages of Polesworth were: blossoming trees, flower scents, nightingales, and the river Anker, whose unpolluted waters Goodyer applauds in the last stanza quoted. The Elizabethan poet Michael Drayton, who lived at Polesworth, wrote several sonnets celebrating the Anker's beauties. Donne's visit in 1613 ended on 2 April. He then took horse and rode to Montgomery Castle, which belonged to another friend, Sir Edward Herbert's cousin Philip. On the way he wrote 'Goodfriday, 1613. Riding Westward'. In one manuscript the poem is labelled 'Goodfriday. Made as I was Rideing westward, that daye', which sounds like Donne's own heading for the poem when he later copied it out. Another manuscript reveals that the poem was completed and dispatched to Goodyer for his inspection before Donne had finished his journey. 'Mr. J. Dunne goeinge from Sr H G: on good fryday sent him back this Meditacion, on the waye,' says the manuscript. So, like Wordsworth's *Tintern Abbey*, it was a poem composed in transit, while the poet was actually on the move among the beauty spots.

But it could not be less like *Tintern Abbey* in every other respect. Montgomery lies about sixty-five miles due west of Polesworth, and riding to it Donne traversed what has become one of the most poetically renowned landscapes in the British Isles—the landscape of Housman's *Shropshire Lad*. Wenlock Edge, where Housman saw the wood in trouble, stretches southwards roughly half-way along Donne's route. But when we read Donne's poem we find that, for all he noticed of the countryside he rode across, he might have been travelling on the surface of the moon. His mind is among the planets, ruminating on the irregularities of their orbital motions:

> Let mans Soule be a Spheare, and then, in this,
> The intelligence that moves, devotion is,
> And as the other Spheares, by being growne
> Subject to forraigne motions, lose their owne,
> And being by others hurried every day,
> Scarce in a yeare their natural forme obey:
> Pleasure or businesse, so, our Soules admit
> For their first mover, and are whirld by it.
> Hence is't, that I am carryed towards the West
> This day, when my Soules forme bends toward the East.
> There I should see a Sunne, by rising set,
> And by that setting endlesse day beget;
> But that Christ on this Crosse, did rise and fall,
> Sinne had eternally benighted all.
> Yet dare I'almost be glad, I do not see
> That spectacle of too much weight for mee . . .
> Could I behold those hands which span the Poles,
> And tune all spheares at once, peirc'd with those holes . . .
> Though these things, as I ride, be from mine eye,
> They'are present yet unto my memory,
> For that looks towards them; and thou look'st towards mee,
> O Saviour, as thou hang'st upon the tree.[71]

Warwickshire and Shropshire, with their rivers, birds, trees and sizeable populations, have been obliterated—as, for that matter, has Donne's horse. It is no earthly terrain he passes across. The poem's geography is surreal. He moves like a planet away from a giant crucifix, the landscape's only feature, which he dare not look at, and on which Christ hangs, watching him. In all the two counties, Donne and Christ are the sole figures.

This titanic management of space spreads through Donne's poetry. His eyes are receptacles for oceans: not just our old terrestrial oceans, for he has wept those already, but the oceans that lie upon untrodden worlds among the galaxies:

> You which beyond that heaven which was most high
> Have found new sphears, and of new lands can write,
> Powre new seas in mine eyes, that so I might
> Drowne my world with my weeping.[72]

As for his love, seismic convulsions are not vast enough to figure it. Its turmoils resemble tremors in outer space, wrenchings of the universal framework so remote that their shock waves do not make even a whisper on the earth's surface:

> Moving of th'earth brings harmes and feares,
>   Men reckon what it did and meant
> But trepidation of the spheares,
>   Though greater farre, is innocent.[73]

The girl he bestows his love on is a cosmic force; her gravitational pull controls tides:

>   O more then Moone,
> Draw not up seas to drowne me in thy spheare . . .[74]

When the two of them weep, they engulf the globe. When their love abates, nature returns to pre-Creational havoc:

>   Oft a flood
>   Have we two wept, and so
> Drownd the whole world, us two; oft did we grow
> To be two Chaosses, when we did show
> Care to ought else.[75]

The geography of the poems combines with their other dynamic features to make them the most enduring exhibition of the will to power the English Renaissance produced.

Except, perhaps, for the sermons. For when Donne entered the Church he found in God, and in his own position as God's spokesman, a final and fully adequate expression of his power lust. If we ask what positive quality Donne most consistently reverences in the sermons, the answer is neither beauty, nor life, nor love, but power. His God is a heavenly powerhouse, with all circuits ablaze. He is an explosion of energy. His eye is hotter than the sun, and melts people. He can blast a state with a breath, and moulder a world with a touch. His voice is unimaginably loud. He slaughters children to punish their parents for the 'sinnefull wantonness' in which they were conceived. He breaks backs and necks. He has infinite and fearsome ways of destroying men. His law is martial law. He can choke you with a crumb, or hang you upon the next tree. He can plunge the stage and the players on it, the bed and the lovers on it, through the earth to hell in an instant. He slew '200 thousand *Assyrians* in one night in *Senacheribs Army*'. He has been known to pelt men with great stones from heaven, and smite whole hosts with blindness, and fill mountains with horses and chariots of fire. Earthquakes, plagues and 'putride defluxions' are in his hand. He is, in short, a holy, homicidal terror, endlessly ingenious in the instruments he chooses to torment his creatures with. 'If the Lord be angry, he needs no Trumpets to call in Armies, if he doe but *sibilare muscam*, hisse and whisper for the flye, and the Bee, there is nothing so little in his hand, as cannot discomfort thee, discomfit thee, dissolve and powr out, attenuate and annihilate the very marrow of thy soul.'[76]

God's love and mercy are, in Donne's account, secondary. His power is primary and essential. 'It must be power', Donne explains, that puts God's other attributes into operation: 'It is Power that does all.' As God has spangled the firmament with stars, 'so hath he his Scriptures with names, and metaphors, and denotations of power'.[77]

Further, as the reader will by now have gathered, it is God's destructive power that Donne particularly relishes dwelling on. Of course, his God is the Creator as well as the destroyer. But though the theory of creation—creation as an idea—fascinated Donne, as we shall see, he never set his imagination to flesh it out. Nowhere in his works is there a passage that one could momentarily set beside Milton's entranced and ingenious account of Creation in Book VII of *Paradise Lost*. It is God as killer and pulverizer that Donne celebrates. 'All the evil', he reminds his congregation, 'that is done in the World, God doth.' All plagues, all war, all famine, are from God. God's very name in the Bible, Shaddai, means, Donne points out, 'spoyle, and violence and depredation'. 'Dishonor and Disreputation, force and Depredation, Ruine and Devastation, Error and Illusion, the Devill and his Tentations, are presented to us, in the same word, as the name and power of God is.'[78]

God's agents, the angels, are almost as impressive, as Donne imagines them, in their gift for demolition: 'They are Creatures, that have not so much of Body as flesh is, as froth is, as a vapor is, as a sigh is, and yet with a touch they shall molder a rocke into lesse Atomes, then the sand that it stands upon; and a milstone into smaller flower, then it grinds.'[79] The utility of producing flour which is actually ground-up millstone is not, of course, something we are expected to enquire into. Donne's angels are performing a pure feat of strength, as pointless, in its way, as tearing up telephone directories, only much more colossal. We are to admire them because they possess irresistible force.

Further, Donne was able to feel that, as God's minister, he himself shared this massive potency. He was not simply an ageing man perched in a pulpit; he was an earthquake, or a lion, or a waterfall. His power was not, as it had been in the poems, the indulgence of wishful thinking; his supremacy was no longer a vulnerable fiction. It was a holy truth which his omnipotent master willed him to proclaim. He stands eminent above the unregenerate throng, and daunts them with his awful might. In God's church, he tells his congregation,

> his Ordinance of preaching batters the soule, and by that breach, the Spirit enters; His Ministers are an Earth-quake, and shake an earthly soule; They are the sonnes of thunder, and scatter a cloudy conscience; They are as the fall of waters, and carry with them whole Congregations; 3000 at a Sermon, 5000 at a Sermon, a whole City, such a City as Nineveh at a Sermon; and they are as the roaring of a Lion, where the Lion of the tribe of Juda, cries down the Lion that seekes whom he may devour.[80]

When applying for his present post, we recall, this earthquake and waterfall had recommended himself to the Duke of Buckingham as a 'poore worme' and a 'clodd of clay'. Throughout Donne's life the towering attitudes he adopts, whether in poems or sermons, have to serve as a compensation not only for his persistent sense of worldly failure, but also for the degrading expedients to which, in striving to overcome that failure, he was reduced.

Viewed in this way, the sermons may be seen as the fulfilment of all that the poems yearn towards. We have looked at the desire to dominate in the poems, at the self-aggrandizement which impels Donne to transmute his private love into something of global significance, and at the hunger for an absolute perfection which might transcend his own divisiveness and anxiety. We have looked, too, at Donne's passion for regal supremacy, and at the technical means by which the poems are made to generate power from their very syntax and rhythms. We have observed how in early poems, such as 'To his Mistris Going to Bed', the lust for power takes the form of a wish to insult, humiliate and punish. In all these respects the sermons take over where the poems had left off, and they pursue, under the aegis of religion, the same imperious ends. Even the sadism of 'To his Mistris Going to Bed' finds a natural home in the sermons, for in them Donne's withering rhetoric is turned loose not merely against one wretched, half-naked girl, but against all fleshly beauty. Given this congruence between poems and sermons, it is strange that the early, unregenerate Jack Donne and the grave Dr. Donne of St. Paul's should have been seen, and seen by Donne himself, as dissimilar. They seem, in their different media, to give rein to identical passions. The satires, too, which reveal an inclination to vilify man and society, and to adopt a controlling, superior posture, seem perfectly reconcilable with the sermons. True, Donne disparages satire in the sermons; but by the time he came to compose the sermons he could afford to do so. For he had found something far more corrosive than satire with which to attack mankind, namely Christianity.

Not, of course, that it was only the destructive power inherent in the idea of God that attracted Donne, vital though that was to him. By being eternal as well as omnipotent, God satisfied another of Donne's long-standing requirements. God's eternity provided the perfect focus for Donne's impulse to reach beyond language and thought into wonder. The urge to express the inexpressible, and think the unthinkable, was, of all Donne's ambitious urges, necessarily the most self-defeating. But it was a perennial component of his nature, and is as clearly distinguishable in his love poetry as is his need for power. The rage for supremacy, manifest in the poems, drives Donne beyond not only 'busy fooles' and 'Dull sublunary lovers', but beyond what can be contained in words:

> All measure, and all language, I should passe,
> Should I tell what a miracle shee was.[81]

In the end, his love outgoes not only language but thought. What he loves, he does not know; only what he does not:

> If that be simply perfectest
> Which can by no way be exprest
>   But *Negatives*, my love is so.
>   To All, which all love, I say no.
> If any who deciphers best,
>   What we know not, our selves, can know,
> Let him teach mee that nothing . . .[82]

In this poem, 'Negative Love', Donne's obsession with self-analysis and his ardour for the unreachable merge. They were bound to do so. For whenever he tried to fathom his own mental processes he was brought up, as we have seen, against the impossibility of self-knowledge. Untrodden heights and plumbless depths lay just inside

his head. He strained for a clear gleam in the interior fog, telling
himself that no one else could know his own mind as well as he could
('I still vex myself with this because if I know it not, nobody can
know it'). But the enterprise, he realized, was doomed: the mind
could not read itself ('of the diseases of the mind there is no criterion,
no canon, no rule, for our own taste and apprehension and interpretation should be the judge, and that is the disease itself'[83]). Though
Donne was unusually alive to it, this deadlock in the brain is a part of
our usual experience. Once he has put it into words, we recognize
'Negative Love' as our own love. What we love in a loved person,
and why, are irretrievably beyond knowing—though love itself feels
so natural that we get used to assuming it must be explicable somehow.

Donne liked accelerating towards ever-receding horizons, and
trying to catch his own mind was one way of doing it. It represents
the art of ambition in its purest form. Another way was to invent
unthinkable entities, which he would then try to think about. In the
Songs and Sonnets the entity is usually love, defined in some exorbitant way. 'Loves Infiniteness', for instance, considers the problem of
whether Donne has, or can have, all the girl's love.[84] By the time we
get to the last stanza Donne has typically decided that he does not
want it all, because 'all' is too limited a notion:

> Yet I would not have all yet,
>   Hee that hath all can have no more,
> And since my love doth every day admit
>   New growth, thou shouldst have new rewards in store.

Again, it is not just a private mathematical game Donne is playing.
Lovers do believe, or wish to believe, that their love could not be
greater, and also that it will grow, not stagnate. These are the
conflicts we stumble into once we try to quantify emotions—yet
wanting them quantified is the most natural thing in the world.
'How much do you love me?' is every child's question.

In 'Loves Infiniteness' we can feel the tension between Donne's
effort to quantify love and his impulse to make it exceed all quantity.
In a poem like 'The Computation', the language of quantification is
expressly used to show how inadequate quantity is to love's inten-
sities:

> For the first twenty yeares, since yesterday,
> I scarce beleev'd, thou could'st be gone away,
> For forty more, I fed on favours past,
> And forty'on hopes, that thou would'st, they might last.

Teares drown'd one hundred, and sighes blew out two,
A thousand, I did neither thinke, nor doe,
Or not divide, all being one thought of you;
Or in a thousand more, forgot that too.
Yet call not this long life; But thinke that I
Am, by being dead, Immortall; Can ghosts die?[85]

The years here add up, it has been noted, to 24,000: one thousand for each hour since they parted. But to emphasize that is to distort the poem into something too numerically precise. Its feelings are not mathematical, but measureless. It tosses its vast chronological periods about with wry abandon, to indicate that time and number belong to a different and less serious realm of reality than the experience of loss. At times of parting, we have all felt what Donne means, and have tried to express it in worn phrases about dragging hours or time standing still. Donne does not still time, he speeds it up. He confronts the linguistic problem, original, challenging and ambitious. Number is used to defeat numerability; quantity, to annihilate quantification.

The poems, in these various ways, convert love or a girl into something that cannot be overtaken by speech or thought. In the sermons God and eternity take the place of love and girls, but the urge to outsoar the mind's boundaries remains the same. The technique of numberless numbering, favoured by the lonely lover of 'The Computation', is renovated and adapted to religious purposes. Donne uses it in order to do two contradictory things at once: to fill his congregation's mind with thoughts of eternity, and to impress on them that eternity cannot be brought within the limits of their thoughts. '*Millions* of yeares, multiplied by *Millions*, make not up a *Minute* to this *Eternitie*,' Donne tells them. It will be 'such a Day, as is not of a thousand yeares, which is the longest measure in the *Scriptures*, but of a thousand millions of millions of generations'. After seventy years of life, the damned face 'seventy millions of generations of torments'. God existed 'an infinite, a superinfinite, an unimaginable space, millions of millions of unimaginable spaces in heaven, before the Creation'.[86]

And so on. 'Superinfinite' is Donne's coinage. He liked it, and used it again. Eternity, in his memorial sermon for Lady Danvers, is 'superinfinite evers'.[87] To the art of ambition, 'super-' is an especially appealing prefix, since it cancels and surpasses any chosen word even before that word has been written down. It reinforces the effort to make language reach beyond language which is constantly discernible in Donne's religious paroxysms. The *Oxford English Dictionary* article on the prefix attributes to Donne 'super-canonization', 'super-Catholike', 'super-dying', 'super-edifications', 'super-invested', 'super-Reformation' and 'super-universall'. The list is indicative, but certainly not complete. 'Supermiraculous' and 'superexaltation' can be found on a single page of the sermons alone.[88] 'Superinfinite' does not, needless to say, mean anything. The infinite is incapable of addition. But the word's senselessness makes it better for Donne's purposes, not worse, since it places it beyond the mind's grasp.

Multiplication is also a favourite technique for staggering his listeners, and for suggesting the endlessly reduplicating aeons of space-time. Donne explains that he deals in figures which 'no Millions, multiplied by Millions, can calculate'. Man has been on earth six thousand years, 'but if every minute of his 6000 yeeres, were multipli'd by so many millions of Ages, all would amount to nothing, meerely nothing, in respect of that Eternity, which he is to dwell in.'[89] The poet who in 'Loves Infiniteness' had desired a perpetually multiplying love, now promises a perpetually multiplying bliss: 'for heaven and salvation is not a Creation but a Multiplication; it begins not when wee dye, but it increases and dilates itself infinitely then.'[90]

Like most Elizabethans, Donne had virtually no interest in using numbers for the purpose of serious computation. The general standard of numeracy in his day was extremely low.[91] Arithmetic was unknown in school. The humanists had despised it as a mechanical acquisition: Erasmus said that a smattering of it was sufficient, and Ascham considered mathematics unhealthy because they made people 'unfit to live with others'. Even the more modern-minded seventeenth-century schoolmaster considered that being able to recognize Arabic numerals was as much mathematics as a grammar-school boy needed, and this degree of competence was by no means universal. It was common for boys entering university to be unable to decipher the page and chapter numbers in a book. The general innumeracy did not facilitate national administration. Population estimates in the period reflect little more than the mood of the calculator, and surviving documents show that overseers of the Poor Law were rarely able to tot up a column of figures correctly.

In these circumstances the mere mention of multiplication would be liable to strike Donne's auditors with numb wonder, and the large figures he alludes to would seem even more arcane than they do to us. His own numeracy was probably above average, since he had avoided grammar school and been educated by Catholic tutors. But he seems to have regarded mathematics as, at best, a curiosity, and he was habitually careless with figures. When he cites an authority he is as likely as not to get the page or volume number wrong; and he remarks blithely in the *Essays in Divinity* that the population of the earth may be assumed to have remained constant throughout the ages—without, it seems, suspecting that the statement might benefit from statistical support.[92] The use of numbers to baffle rather than to clarify, which we have noted in the sermons, suited his disposition. The object of mathematics, for him, was not to help thought, but to shock us out of it.

Significantly the one contemporary mathematical calculation which intrigued him was the work of a reactionary German Jesuit astronomer, Christopher Clavius, who published in 1607 an estimate of the number of grains of sand which would be required to fill the whole space between the earth and the stars. (To get the answer you write the figure one and place fifty-one noughts after it.) Clavius was not aiming at accuracy. His concern was to make sure that his number was big enough, and he believed in fact that it would leave a good deal of sand over after the firmament had been filled. To ensure this he had deliberately chosen an undersized grain of sand as his norm when doing the sum, and had attributed larger dimensions to the universe than he believed it had. His model was the *Arenarius* of Archimedes, and like Archimedes he was simply trying to demonstrate the power of numbers. Numbers, he wanted to show, could express even what was normally regarded as infinite.[93]

Donne's objective was precisely the opposite. Accordingly when he refers (as he repeatedly does) to Clavius's calculation, he uses it in contexts which destroy its whole point and reassert, in defiance of Clavius, the inadequacy of numbers. His contemplation of God's eternal curse falling upon sinners, in a sermon of 1627, is typical:

> Men have calculated how many particular graines of sand, would fill up all the vast space between the Earth and Firmament: and we find, that a few lines of cyphers will designe and expresse that number. But if every grain of sand were that number, and multiplied again by that number, yet all that, all that inexpressible, inconsiderable number, made not up one minute of this eternity; neither would this curse be a minute the shorter for having been indured so many Generations, as there were grains of sand in that number.[94]

So much for mathematicians.

We recognize in an outburst of this kind Donne's desire to place himself, and anything he values, beyond the sphere of calculable knowledge—beyond the contamination of the knowable. As we have seen, 'Negative Love' manifests the same desire, and there are poems among the *Songs and Sonnets* which are almost wholly devoted to expressing a refusal to express who or what they are about. 'The Curse', for instance, directs its invective against anyone who so much as speculates about the identity of Donne's girl:

> Who ever guesses, thinks, or dreames he knowes
> Who is my mistris, . . .[95]

and what 'The Undertaking' has to impart is what it is not imparting:

> I have done one braver thing
> Then all the *Worthies* did,
> Yet a braver thence doth spring,
> Which is, to keepe that hid.[96]

The 'lovelinesse within', enjoyed by Donne in this poem, is presented as an immaculate privacy which it would be desecration to speak of. Essentially the poem, like others we have looked at, such as 'The Sunne Rising' and 'The Anniversarie', and like the harangues about the power of God and his ministers in the sermons, is an announcement of Donne's pre-eminence. It meets the need not only to segregate himself from other men, and from their ways of knowing, but also to diminish them by comparison with himself. This need is the basis of what we have called, in this chapter, the art of ambition.

It is also, of course, an index of personal anxiety. At their greatest the poems, we have noted, transmit this anxiety even as they defy it. They do not lie like flawless monuments upon the uncertain feelings beneath them, but allow those feelings voice and movement. In the sermons there is, understandably, a firmer attempt to suppress doubt or uneasiness. Yet the result is far from calm. The violence of Donne's religious rhetoric betokens as unmistakably as do his poems the unappeased, and unappeasable, demands of his nature.

ᦉ5ᦊ

Bodies

We left Donne, in the last chapter, chasing elusive absolutes. Now we must return to the physical world, and consider his response to it. This is a subject upon which critics have had disparaging things to say. 'He never visualizes, or suggests that he has any pleasure in looking at things,' complained Rupert Brooke. 'His poems might all have been written by a blind man in a world of blind men.'[1] The charge has been elaborated by J. E. V. Crofts, in a brilliantly offensive essay, where he asserts that the nature of Donne's rebellion against the literary conventions of his time was determined 'by the extraordinary deficiencies of his equipment as a poet'. Foremost among these deficiencies, Professor Crofts lists Donne's lack of a sense of visual beauty: 'The beauty of the visible world meant nothing to him and yielded him no imagery for serious purposes.'[2]

The most useful way to meet these attacks is not to fish around in Donne's poems for some quotations that might hopefully be pronounced visually beautiful. Nor is it to applaud the critical acumen of Brooke and Crofts, and downgrade Donne accordingly. If Donne seems, much of the time, unconcerned with or immune to visual beauty, then visual beauty becomes an inadequate concept with which to approach his work, and we must set about showing what can take its place. Brooke and Crofts are right, or almost right, so far as they go, but they do not go far enough. The shortage of visual beauties in Donne's poems is not felt as an emptiness, because it is the outcome of other and more intense pressures which have forced visual beauty out. Donne's persistent investigation of inner experience, and his corresponding scorn for 'he who colour loves, and skinne',[3] are only the most obvious of these pressures.

It will be helpful first, though, to accept the Brooke–Crofts viewpoint, and set out the case against Donne. For Donne's aesthetic shortcomings generate their own kind of power, and a survey of them will quickly allow us to appreciate this. Just what Donne lacks can be shown by comparing him with a poet of the same century who was temperamentally his polar opposite, Thomas Traherne.

Traherne feels and celebrates, in poem after poem, an ecstatic joy in
the created world. This stanza from 'The Salutation' is typical:

> New Burnisht Joys!
> Which yellow Gold and Pearl excell!
> Such Sacred Treasures are the Lims in Boys,
> In which a Soul doth Dwell;
> Their Organized Joynts, and Azure Veins
> More Wealth include, then all the World contains.[4]

What Traherne asserts there is, you may say, pretty obvious. Look at
a child and look at a heap of cash, and you instantly see that the child
is infinitely more beautiful and valuable. The idea of sacrificing even
one of its limbs or one of its eyes for money makes the mind reel.
Traherne's apprehension of the child as something wondrously
made ('Organized') is the same as we find in Ben Jonson's epitaph on
his little son:

> Rest in soft peace, and, ask'd, say here doth lye
> Ben Jonson his best piece of poetrie.[5]

But Donne could never have written Traherne's stanza. The intri-
cacy and aliveness of a child's body is, so far as we can tell, something
he never noticed. Likewise, Traherne's exclamatory delight, his
impulse to break into a hymn of praise to the Creator, is something
Donne did not feel, any more than he felt the exhilaration that comes
from the sense of being alive oneself, which Traherne can always
make us share.

Nor is this deficiency in Donne just the result of a wish to write
clever, paradoxical poetry which will gather some of its éclat from
disparaging what other people have conventionally taken pleasure
in. If we turn to the places where he is to be found at his most
intensely serious, the sermons and devotional writings, his almost
total deadness to the world's beauty, abundance and animation is just
as marked. His Christianity is dark and tormented. Traherne, in his
Centuries, remembers the world he saw when he was a child as a
glory, a timeless wonder:

> The Corn was Orient and Immortal Wheat, which never should
> be reaped, nor was ever sown. I thought it had stood from everlast-
> ing to everlasting. The Dust and Stones of the Street were as
> Precious as Gold. The Gates were at first the End of the World,
> The Green Trees when I saw them first through one of the Gates
> Transported and Ravished me; their Sweetness and unusual

Beauty made my Heart to leap, and almost mad with Extasie, they were such strange and Wonderfull Thing.[6]

Donne, by contrast, remarks in a sermon that if we cast our minds back to childhood it is almost certain that the first thing we can remember doing was a sin. Indeed, even before its birth, Donne impresses on us, the human child is a dark and bloody-minded creature, worthy of Hell though it should proceed with its wickedness no further, but die in its mother's womb: 'There in the wombe wee are fitted for workes of darknes, all the while deprived of light: And there in the wombe wee are taught cruelty, by being fed with blood, and may be damned, though we be never borne.' Human flesh is, in Donne's account, 'wet mud', 'dust held together by plaisters'. We are dissolved by putrefaction while we are still alive. We are 'boxes of poyson', and the world we find ourselves in is 'a bed of Adders, a quiver of poysoned arrows'. A 'scurff', a 'leprosie sticks to every thing' in it. Man is 'the Receptacle, the Ocean of all misery', and the odds are three to one, Donne estimates, against anyone being happy, even temporarily. From the day of our birth we are condemned prisoners: 'all our life is but a going out to the place of Execution, to death.'[7]

On this assessment life is, at best, an initiation rite of the most irksome and repellent kind, and the sensible course would be to avoid it: 'If there were any other way to be saved and to get to Heaven, then by being born into this life, I would not wish to have come into this world.' The supposed pleasures of life are systematically devalued by Donne. The beauties of the natural world are, we learn, of little estimation, and of none at all in themselves. They are merely a 'darke and weake way' of acquiring knowledge of God. 'Health, and strength, and stature', though people call them goods, are accidents of dust. Pleasure in food and drink, however refined and elegant, amounts simply to an expensive process for producing 'precious dung, and curious excrements'. Even a seemingly innocuous food like honey is identified by Donne, on Pliny's authority, as 'a sweaty excrement of the heavens . . . the spettle, the fleame of the starres . . . the vomit of the Bee'.[8]

Sexual pleasure is, of course, almost unspeakably foul in this world view, and a man who allows it to enter into his relations with his wife is 'an *adulterer* in his wives bosome'.[9] As for physical beauty, which raises men's lusts, we are to remind ourselves, says Donne, that beauty is less estimable than gold. For to acquire gold 'labour' or 'study' are generally necessary, whereas beauty comes about without the expenditure of any effort. Parents cannot ensure that they will have a beautiful child by working harder or eating special foods. Beauty, wherever it occurs, is simply 'a thing that hapned by chance', and is consequently, Donne concludes, of no real worth.[10] This disparagement of beauty on the ground that it is unconnected with money or hard work, contrasts eloquently with the stanza from Traherne quoted earlier.

Now it may well be countered that, as against this dismal vision of earthly existence that I have assembled from Donne's religious writings, one can find, in the sermons and elsewhere, occasional exhortations to Christians to be joyful. It is also true that, amid the sonorous gloom of the sermons, we catch a glimpse, once or twice, of the speaker's ability to extract pleasure from the simple things of life which his general demeanour would not have led us to suspect. Donne speaks appreciatively, for instance, of the 'cheerful street musick' to be heard on winter mornings in London.[11] Someone who had noticed that, we feel, could not have been so grimly immune to the world's beauties as the sermons pretend. After all, Donne's pursuit of worldly rewards continued almost as vigorously inside the Church as out of it, as we have seen. We begin to suspect that he enjoyed giving his congregation the horrors, and that the negative stress in his sermons is less a sign of temperamental deficiency than an indication of his desire to cow and quell the whey-faced worshippers ranged beneath him. Terror afforded him a histrionic triumph.

Whether or not these suspicions are justified, what we can be sure about is that if we wish to seek out the life in Donne's sermons we shall not find it in the intermittent calls for a little Christian merriment. Indeed, in the putrefying and venomous context that Donne so amply documents, these acquire, at times, a positively sardonic note. Such exhilaration as can be felt comes, rather, from the business of destruction itself. The world is his prey, and he runs it down rapturously. His language responds richly to the task, fabricating abhorrent and coagulated textures for the world's decaying materials. We have only to consider some of the examples we have just cited—the description of the murderous embryo coiled in its mother's womb, for instance, 'fitted for workes of darkness', 'fed with blood'—to appreciate the transforming force of Donne's viewpoint. He glares into the body's innocent depths with sinister delight.

When he imagines the body wounded or rotting, strength at once flows into his pen. He pursues the theme of physical mishap graphi-

cally. Colour, which is almost entirely lacking from his prose,
returns to it as he embarks on the subject of disease—'a green
palenesse', 'a yellow jaundise', 'a blue lividnesse', 'a black morpheu
upon our skin'.[12] The confederates of death take on characters and
voices in the heat of his imagining: 'Here a bullet will aske a man,
where's your arme; and a Wolf' (that is, a cancer) 'wil ask a woman,
where's your breast?'[13] The destructive elements materialize hal-
lucinatedly as nudging companions. Processes of decomposition are
detailed with unmistakable relish. Donne fancies the body 'washed
to slime, in the sea' or stinking and melting in the grave: 'Between
the excremental jelly that thy body is made of at first, and that jelly
which thy body dissolves to at last; there is not so noysome, so putrid
a thing in nature.'[14] The adroitness with which he manages to
suggest here both that decayed flesh is as runny as human sperm, and
that human sperm is as disgusting as decayed flesh, testifies to the
imaginative energy with which he undertakes his task. We sense the
stirrings of a mind in the grip of its subject.

Placed beside this fearsome exuberance, J. E. V. Crofts's request
for visual beauty has a rather plaintive ring. But Crofts was talking
about the poems, not the sermons; and anyway his wish for some
constructive imagining, even in the sermons, seems natural and
healthy enough. Nor, in fact, does Donne disappoint such a wish. The
truly remarkable thing about the sermons, given Donne's spiritual
drift, is their physicality. The human body is densely present in
them, even when it is being disparaged, and even when Donne is
supposed to be talking about something quite unphysical. The soul,
he tells us, 'hath Bones, as well as the body'. It is subject to 'Cramps,
and Coliques, and Convulsions'. Blood pulses in it, and every sin is
'an incision of the soule, a Lancination, a Phlebotomy, a letting of the
soule blood'. The surgical language combines with a sense of the
body's apprehensive, tender parts, though ostensibly the body is not
the subject of Donne's attention at all. Again, he depicts the 'spiritually poore' as 'fretted, galled, exulcerated viscerally, even in the
bowells of their Spirit'.[15] Reading the sermons we are repeatedly
conscious of this need to anchor abstract truths in the human
anatomy. Sin is conceived of not as an action or mental inclination
but as a biological agglomeration of nerves, veins, valves and internal organs. It has a heart, and a liver 'to carry blood and life through
all the body of our sinful actions', and a brain 'which shall send forth
sinews and ligaments, to tye sins together; and pith and marrow to
give a succulencie, and nourishment, even to the bones, to the
strength and obduration of sin'.[16] The rich blend of knowledge and

feeling takes us, there, into the bone marrow, to experience its living softness.

Donne got the idea for importing anatomical density into spiritual contexts from the Church Fathers. The bones of the soul come from St. Basil. Tertullian, Chrysostom and Augustine had all used medical images to discuss the soul and its ailments.[17] But in selecting and developing the topic Donne was following his own inclinations. The structure and functions of the body fascinated him. Allusions in his works show that he was widely read, for a layman, in medical literature, and tried to keep himself abreast of current research.[18] Walton in his verses in memory of Donne picks out his medical knowledge for special mention, and implies that he once considered becoming a physician.[19] Donne's stepfather John Syminges was as we have seen a doctor, and President of the Royal College of Physicians, so Donne would have had the chance to imbibe medical chat from an early age. When he was eleven his stepfather moved the family to a house adjoining St. Bartholomew's Hospital, and this must have made the routines of medication and surgery impinge still more on the boy's consciousness.[20] As a man, Donne found his own ill health a subject of absorbing interest, as his letters testify. During his dangerous illness of 1623 (diagnosed by modern specialists as relapsing fever) he kept a detailed account of his symptoms, and of his doctors' reactions, which he later published. Just as Donne managed, then, to turn his sermons into an outlet for his obsession with power, so he found a way of accommodating in them the excitements of the anatomy theatre and the consulting room.

But there is more to it than that. Donne's way of talking about the body is singular, and singularly arresting, for two reasons. First, he scarcely refers at all to the body in motion. Its potential agility and gracefulness are outside his scope, as, by and large, is its surface appearance. He is attracted, rather, to its organic mass, volume and articulation. His imagination intrudes into its inner structures. His impulse is towards vivisection. Characteristically we find him, in a sermon, framing his enquiry into man's spiritual emptiness in terms of an excursion through the cavities and receptacles of the human anatomy, its 'conduits and cisterns'. 'When I looke into the larders, and cellars, and vaults, into the vessels of our body for drink, for blood, for urine, they are pottles, and gallons; when I looke into the furnaces of our spirits, the ventricles of the heart and of the braine, they are not thimbles.'[21] The sermon has become a physiology lecture, but the lecturer does not remain aloof on his rostrum. He seems to be clambering through the body, as through the levels and recesses of some roomy edifice, pointing out its vaults and furnaces. His sturdy idiomatic language ('pottles') solidifies the structure as he climbs around it.

The second remarkable feature of Donne's anatomical language also appears in this example. The human body is regularly assimilated to, or blended with, inanimate objects ('larders', 'cellars', 'vaults'), and the effect of this is not to deaden it but to intensify its bulk and actuality. This curious but potent technique is one of the distinctive marks of Donne's genius, and we shall be inspecting, in the rest of this chapter, some of the varied ways in which he puts it to work. As a start we might take a passage from the *Devotions*, where we find Donne musing upon the ancient notion of the microcosm—man as a 'little world'—and rejecting it because he feels it does insufficient justice to the complexity of man's body:

> Man consists of more pieces, more parts, than the world. . . . And if those pieces were extended, and stretched out in man as they are in the world, man would be the giant, and the world the dwarf; the world but the map, and the man the world. If all the veins in our bodies were extended to rivers, and all the sinews to veins of mines, and all the muscles that lie upon one another, to hills, and all the bones to quarries of stone, and all the other pieces to the proportion of those which correspond to them in the world, the air would be too little for this orb of man to move in, the firmament would be but enough for this star.[22]

The human body expands beneath Donne's exploring eye, becoming more intricate and manifold. His prose acts like the screwing down of a microscope into focus: familiar bits of body acquire alarming geographical dimensions. By the time he has finished, his gigantic humanoid is craning its neck among the planets. But the effect is not simply one of extension. The bones and stones and rivers and mines and veins and sinews interfuse, so that a more solid creature emerges, complete with humps and pits and cavities. Whereas the 'Azure Veins' in Traherne's poem about boys' bodies suggest no more than a coloured outline, Donne's language blocks the body in and communicates it to our spatial sense. We are aware of a recessed and laminated structure. When he speaks of 'the muscles that lie upon one another', for instance, the wording takes us in through the folded layers of muscle, and lets us feel their depth. Paradoxically the body in the passage impinges on us with greater force because it is likened, throughout, to dead things. We register its separate existence the more definitely, as when we handle a temporarily numbed part of ourselves.

Similar instances in the poems are not hard to find, and they account for some of Donne's most strangely involving effects. Take the lovers in 'The Extasie':

> Our hands were firmly cimented
> With a fast balme, which thence did spring,
> Our eye-beames twisted, and did thred
> Our eyes, upon one double string.[23]

The strung-together, cemented lovers acquire a stony remoteness. The fact that they are inanimate (vacated by their souls) is part of the poem's point, and that deadness allows them to materialize more heavily ('like sepulchrall statues', as Donne says). But the image of the threaded eyes will not stay dead. The notion of a loop of string, with four pierced eyes on it, disturbs. A. S. Brandenburg has declared that we are not supposed to notice the sensuous side of this image, because it would be 'ridiculous and unpleasant'[24] if we did. The critic's alarm is a tribute to the image's efficacy. We wince at the thought of transfixed eyes. By deadening his materials (turning eyes to beads) Donne has made them stick more in our feelings.

The sweat helps too. For it is by sweating palm to palm that the lovers have cemented themselves together. The 'statues' ooze livingly, poised between life and non-life. Sweat, having passed through the skin, has just ceased to be part of a living organism. Like tears, which are in much the same position, it seems to have intrigued Donne by its inanimate animation. He fascinatedly confuses sweat and tears in 'Loves Diet'—'eyes which rowle towards all, weepe not, but sweat.' The sweat of the faithless mistress in 'The Apparition' gleams like metal in the light of her candle:

> And then poore Aspen wretch, neglected thou
> Bath'd in a cold quicksilver sweat wilt lye.[25]

The girl exuding quicksilver, like the lovers exuding cement and string, impresses us by her unusual physicality. Her metal sweat makes her more present. Any eruption from the skin can serve in the same way, for Donne, as a solidifying agent. The husband in 'Jealosie', for instance, is imagined on his death-bed coated in scabs: 'His body with a sere-barke covered'.[26] Inevitably this has prompted comparison with Hamlet's father's description of his poisoned flesh:

> a most instant tetter bark'd about
> Most lazar-like, with vile and loathsome crust,
> All my smooth body.

Both excerpts alert our senses to the diseased surface by amalgamating a dead husk with the living skin. The gain is in immediacy, and the collusion of life and deadness can be used either to repel or to allure the reader. As against the unlovely metal girl of 'The Apparition' we might put the metal girls of Donne's Problem VII. The question investigated in this piece is why the most beautiful women are always the falsest. 'Doth the minde', wonders Donne, 'so follow the temperature of the body, that because those complexions are aptest to change, the mind is therefore so? Or as Bels of the purest metal retain their tinkling and sound largest; so the memory of the last pleasure lasts longer in these, and disposeth them to the next.'[27] Something within the woman, as Donne imagines it, remains quivering and resonant, like a struck bell, after love-making is over. The evocation of a delicately attuned body, with its own memory, independent of the mind, recalls the moment in Lawrence's *The Rainbow* when Tom Brangwen comes courting Lydia Lensky and leaves, on his departure, a bunch of daffodils:

> . . . she went on laying the tray for the vicar. Needing the table, she put the daffodils aside on the dresser without noticing them. Only their coolness, touching her hand, remained echoing there a long while.[28]

The flowers' touch stays in the flesh, like a sound; and in Donne's Problem orgasm fills the body like a musical note setting up its lingering whispers. By likening his girls to pure metal bells Donne suggests the secluded stirrings of their physical life: the metallic image renders them more alive, not less.

Donne's attentiveness to the poetic effects that could be gained when the living and the non-living merged seems to have been accompanied, as we might expect, by a medical interest in those parts of the human anatomy, such as the hair and the bones, where life and sensation have only a dubious and qualified existence. In his survey of current scientific opinion in *The Second Anniversarie* he observed correctly that the hair, like the fingernails, was the subject of much controversy.[29] Experts were unsure whether to classify it as a bodily organ or merely a waste product, an 'excrement'. Fernelius in his *Universa Medicina* of 1610 had placed it uncompromisingly in the excrement class. Donne does not attempt to resolve the scientific problem, but his imagination is drawn to such inert participants in human life. In the discussion among sixteenth and seventeenth-century physicians about whether the bones were sensitive, the general consensus was that they were not, but that they were covered by a sensitive membrane. Donne incorporates a delicate account of this theory into a sermon about good works: 'The Bones themselves have no sense, they feele no paine. . . . But *membranae dolent*; Those little membrans, those filmes, those thin skins, that cover, and that line some bones, are very sensible of paine, and of any vexation.'[30] The point of junction of the feeling with the felt, of the dead with the alive, attracts his scrupulous attention.

In 'The Relique' and 'The Funerall' the junction is refined and complicated. Hair and bones combine, and Donne imagines them retaining, after death, something of their submerged and inscrutable mode of life. When he speaks of the gravedigger unearthing 'A bracelet of bright haire about the bone', the line startles us by its suggestion of death and life coiled together. The hair is dead, but its unnaturally prolonged brightness seems to vouch for some persistent, subterranean vitality. Besides it is, Donne suggests, sensitive to the touch:

> Who ever comes to shroud me, do not harme
>   Nor question much
> That subtile wreath of haire, which crowns mine arme;
> The mystery, the signe you must not touch.[31]

Like the 'little membrans' and 'filmes' that cover live bones, the glowing hair is, or might be, we gather, 'sensible of paine'. It may serve, Donne goes on to conjecture, as a substitute nervous system, giving the bones life and feeling.

These are Donne's most famous bones and hair, but the mysterious living and partly living they participate in is only one manifestation of a wider and permanent interest. The detachment, or semi-detachment, of bones and hair intrigues, and Donne cannot write about them boringly. We find that amid the magic ordeals of 'Goe, and catche a falling starre', hair alights on the head, as if from outside:

> Ride ten thousand daies and nights,
>   Till age snow white haires on thee.[32]

Hair, and its greying, are as distinct from our conscious life, and as unknowable, as the weather. The poet who numbered 'My five gray haires' in 'The Canonization', or reckoned, in 'Loves Usury', 'When with my browne, my gray haires' would 'equall bee', seems to have been an unusually attentive hair-watcher. 'A Monarchy will ruine, as a haire will grow gray, of it selfe,' remarks Donne in a sermon.[33] The might of empire gathers upon a single hair. Bones receive absorbed poetic treatment in 'The Crosse' where, as usual, it is the blend of life and non-life that arrests Donne's attention. Bones, though inert, defend and co-operate with the most vital of living organs:

> . . . thy braine through bony walls doth vent
> By sutures.[34]

It was an Aristotelian notion that the brain had to get rid of excess heat through the joints in the cranial bone, and we can see why it appealed to Donne. It involved, like the theory of bone-covering membranes, an intimate association of the tender and the insentient within the body's confines.

When Donne writes about the act of sex we can find him using the same technique to sensitize his readers. The best instance of this is in his elegy 'The Comparison',[35] which critics have been inclined to dismiss as a bawdy trifle. Wilbur Sanders remarks, for example, that Donne's aim in the poem is 'nothing more than to shock and then to snigger'.[36] The poem systematically compares Donne and his girl with another couple, who are portrayed as exceptionally loathsome. As Donne handles it, though, the poem is not simply a list of insults, but a rich, ingenious and medically informed physical experience—especially the disgusting parts, such as the description of the other woman's sweat:

> Ranke sweaty froth thy Mistresse brow defiles,
> Like spermatique issue of ripe menstruous boiles.

Here we can see Donne pursuing his interest in the body's excremental secretions, and speculatively blending four of them—sweat, pus, sperm and menses—in order to gain something more satisfying than mere sweat. Equally uncomfortable in the result achieved is the description of the woman's private parts:

> Thine's like the dread mouth of a fired gunne,
> Or like hot liquid metals newly runne
> Into clay moulds, or like to that Aetna
> Where round about the grasse is burnt away.

The success of this in gaining its ends depends on the proximity of fire and molten metal to the sexual organs. The implicit notion of copulating with a hot gun barrel employs the conjunction of the tender with the insentient, which we have been inspecting in Donne's work, in a peculiarly alerting way. The witty detail of the pubic hair like burnt grass adds its own scratchy texture to the unpleasantness. This metallic girl is unlike the alluring metal girls of Problem VII in every respect, except that she is metallic. Donne is again experimenting with the conversion of organic to inorganic, though for a different purpose. Throughout the poem his object (a common one for young poets) is to show, by the intensity of his responses, how weak and pale our normal apprehension of the physical world is.

In the elegy's final lines he compares the act of love as the two couples practise it: first, the other couple ('Is not your last act harsh, and violent, / As when a Plough a stony ground doth rent?'), then himself and his girl:

> so devoutly nice
> Are Priests in handling reverent sacrifice,
> And such in searching wounds the Surgeon is
> As wee, when wee embrace, or touch, or kisse.

That last simile, taken from contemporary medicine, is of a physician examining a wound by inserting a probe—a surgical instrument, commonly of silver, with a blunt end, used for exploring the direction and depth of wounds or sinuses. It was a process that continued to interest Donne in his preaching days, though in the sermons the sword of God, piercing the sinner's heart, takes the place of the male sex organ. This sword, Donne tells his auditory, will be 'as a Probe to search the wound'; and he uses the ability to bear 'the searching of a wound without starting' as an instance of fortitude.[37] In the poem the painful connotations of the comparison mingle with a sense of the infinitely gentle and caring penetration which both surgeon and lover are engaged on. As in other instances we have looked at, Donne achieves his enlivening effect by the apposition of life and non-life—in this case, the intrusion of blunt metal among the most shrinkingly sensitive living tissues.

Donne is not, of course, the only poet to use this technique, though he uses it with remarkable persistence and inventiveness. We might compare with the surgical probe in 'The Comparison' the boat's prow in Browning's 'Meeting at Night'. Browning's poem is spoken by a man on his way to visit the girl he loves:

The grey sea and the long black land;
And the yellow half-moon large and low;
And the startled little waves that leap
In fiery ringlets from their sleep,
As I gain the cove with pushing prow,
And quench its speed i' the slushy sand.

The speaker's anticipations colour his language. His expectation of
finding the girl, startled out of sleep with disordered ringlets, affects
the way he sees the waves around his boat; and the prow burying
itself in the slushy sand relates so frankly to the hardness of the male
erection and the soft female wetness which receives it that one is half
surprised to find it in a Victorian poem. The prow's splashy burrow-
ing is a highly sensuous, but limited, version of intercourse because
since both participants are inanimate (prow and sand) we are incited
to concentrate on the physical aspects to the exclusion of the human.
Donne, with his probe and wound, raises the sensitive as well as the
sensuous implications. He reposes his effect firmly in the tenderness
of the human body, as well as encouraging us to apply considerations
which arise from the medical context (the patient's need for the
surgeon; the surgeon's healing efficacy) to the lovers.

Another, and more brutal, image for sexual congress occurs in the
'Epithalamion made at Lincolnes Inne', where the idea of priest and
sacrifice touched on in 'The Comparison' is rounded out. Having
been undressed and put to bed, the bride,

. . . at the Bridegroomes wish'd approach doth lye,
Like an appointed lambe, when tenderly
The priest comes on his knees t'embowell her.[38]

'Embowell' means the same as 'disembowel', the dictionary tells us;
but Donne's line would work much more crudely if he had written
'disembowel', because the form of the word he chooses has the
advantage of sounding as if something is going to be put into the
bowels, and so it fits the context of imminent insertion more naturally. Still, the word's actual meaning is not muffled much by this.
Despite the tenderness of the priest's approach, and the fact that
Donne keeps his knife out of sight, we are inevitably aware that the
lamb's bowels are going to end up in a soft heap on the floor, and that
something comparable in its careful violence is to happen to the
bride. The detail of the priest crawling towards the lamb 'on his
knees' has a curious lifelikeness when applied to the bedroom scene.
We glimpse the bridegroom getting himself into position rather

awkwardly. The whole passage resembles the probe-and-wound simile in its conjunction of love with pain, and, of course, in the way it intensifies the body's vulnerability by bringing it up against something hard and instrumental.

The device of substituting an inanimate object for part of the living situation in a love scene is taken furthest in the 'Epithalamion at the Marriage of the Earl of Somerset', when the bridegroom comes to the bride in bed:

> As he that sees a starre fall, runs apace,
> And findes a gellie in the place,
> So doth the Bridegroome hast as much,
> Being told this starre is falne, and findes her such.[39]

The reference in the first two lines is to a genus of algae called Nostoc which appears as a jelly-like mass on dry soil after rain, and which was supposed, in the seventeenth century, to be the remains of a fallen star or meteor. By turning his bride into jelly Donne conveys, of course, her shivering apprehension: but he does more than that. To find a jelly when looking for a fallen star—let alone for a bride—would inevitably disconcert: there would be an element of perplexity and disappointment. Donne's simile reproduces the bridegroom's feelings complicatedly. Shock mingles with a sense that this is not what he had anticipated, and that the girl, seen naked for the first time, is not the person he thought he knew. There is an alienation effect comparable (as Donne's stanza goes on to explain) to that of meeting friends in new clothes or unfamiliar fashions. The explanation is itself cleverly deadening. Since seeing a girl naked is like seeing someone in odd clothes, nakedness becomes as inert and separate as a garment. Further, by converting his bride into something as lifeless as jelly Donne conveys the bridegroom's fleeting impression that she is, in her nakedness, more wholly composed of flesh than he had quite taken into account.

Donne's feeling for the depth and penetrability of the human body gives him a particular interest in its orifices—the ear, for example. It appears that he was the first to use the word 'labyrinth', with its connotations of spatial complexity, for the semi-circular canals and spiral duct of the inner ear. From the late seventeenth century on, labyrinth became the accepted technical term: the Oxford Dictionary's first record of its usage in anatomy is 1696. Donne has it three times in his poetry, though. Ears are 'labyrinths' in The Second Anniversarie (line 197), in 'A Litanie' (line 218), and, best and earliest, in Satire II:

words, words, which would teare
The tender labyrinth of a soft maids eare.[40]

That nothing sharper than a word would be required to fracture the ear's membranes, confirms for us the delicacy of the structure; and the suggestion of something within the body being torn acts—like the probe-and-wound simile—acutely on our senses.

Intent on establishing the body's inner space, Donne also dwells on the nerves and filaments that hold it together. The lock of hair in 'The Funerall' is drawn out into a hairy network threaded through the body:

> For if the sinewie thread my braine lets fall
>   Through every part,
> Can tye those parts, and make mee one of all;
> These haires which upward grew, and strength and art
>   Have from a better braine,
> Can better do'it.[41]

'Thread' and 'tye' both suggest that the nerves are substantial and handleable, like string, and the idea of inner tying extends our consciousness of the recesses lying under the body's surface. The words 'lets fall' add to this sense of inner space, because they make it sound as if the nerve threads dangle or drop freely through a void. (The remarkably capable hairs, with 'strength and art' of their own, are incidentally further representatives of Donne's hair fixation.)

Interest in anatomical threads appears again in *The Second Anniversarie*, where Donne imagines the soul of Elizabeth Drury speeding up, at her death, through the stars, 'as through the beades, a string'. The notion gives him a chance of bringing into his poem the spinal cartilage. Elizabeth, we are told, threads the stars:

> As doth the Pith, which, least our Bodies slacke,
> Strings fast the little bones of necke, and backe.[42]

We are made to feel her journey with our backbones. 'Pith' sounds soft and pulpy, yet it 'Strings fast' the vertebrae, and so, like 'sinewie thread', it achieves the Donnean blend of toughness and tenderness. Particular hard and soft words like 'slack', 'sinew' and 'hair' clustered together in Donne's brain at an early stage, when he was thinking about bodily strength. Hence the line about 'slacke sinew'd Sampson, his haire off' in 'The Calme'.[43]

Among the most visually engaging of Donne's adventures in anatomy is 'A Valediction: of my Name in the Window',[44] where the spiky little bunch of cuts made when he scratches his signature on glass with a diamond is seen as a tattered skeleton:

> . . . thinke this ragged bony name to bee
> My ruinous Anatomie.

Donne asserts his skeleton's 'firmnesse' and rock-like durability. It is as hard and dead as architecture, representing 'The rafters of my body, bone', stripped of their pliant 'Muscle, Sinew, and Veine'. Thinking of bones as rafters relates to Donne's sense of the body as building, which we came across in the sermons. One sermon actually calls the bones 'Beames, and Timbers, and Rafters' like the poem.[45] But claiming architectural permanence for the scratched glass is, as the poem is always anxiously aware, fanciful. The fragility of claim, name and pane comes upon us when the girl is imagined throwing open the window on some future occasion to talk to a new lover:

> When thy'inconsiderate hand
> Flings out this casement, with my trembling name,
> To looke on one, whose wit or land,
> New battry to thy heart may frame.

The bones are now alive. The small, naked skeleton, quaking on the pane, trapped into overhearing its own betrayal, is an anatomical equivalent of the lover's agitation: an X-ray photograph of his emotional disturbance. And being both firm and tremulous ('bony' as well as 'ragged'), this midget anatomy conveys the body's dual qualities—rigid but vulnerable—as Donne habitually feels them.

The examples looked at so far all portray the human body, but Donne's scope would be unfairly curtailed if we left it at that. He does not write much about animals, but when he does his responsiveness to them is astounding. Take 'The Flea'—a poem which Sir Arthur Quiller-Couch pronounced 'about the most merely disgusting in our language',[46] and which has met with scarcely more sensible comment even from modern critics. Flea poems were, in fact, a smutty old joke. There were scores of them in all the European literatures, going back to an original wrongly ascribed to Ovid.[47] The standard set-up was that a flea found itself on a girl's body, and crawled around, providing a commentary on the bits and pieces it came across. Its remarks on the breasts and genitals were, of course, considered the cream of the jest. Donne shoves all this coy giggling aside, refashions the genre as a toughly argued monologue on sexual union and, dispensing entirely with any mention of the girl's body, concentrates attention on the body of the flea, which has sucked, and so mingled in itself, the blood of himself and the girl:

> This flea is you and I, and this
> Our mariage bed, and mariage temple is;
> Though parents grudge, and you, w'are met,
> And cloysterd in these living walls of Jet.[48]

The delicate intentness of that last line treats a flea as no flea had been treated in English before. The creature's hard black integument is, Donne wonderingly apprises us, alive—'living walls'. The phrase draws on the same awareness as the 'bony walls' of the brain, in 'The Crosse'. Likewise the transformation of the flea to a temple and a cloister, the sacred associations of which accentuate its fragility, reminds us, though the scale has now become microscopic, of Donne in his sermon clambering through the body's vaulted edifice.

From what we have seen of the sermons, it might seem inconceivable that the Donne who wrote those would harbour any feeling for minuscule repositories of life like fleas. But that is not—or not quite—so. 'A Fly', we find him remarking, 'is a nobler creature than the Sunne, because a fly hath life, and the Sunne hath not.' This observation was first made by St. Augustine, and from the frequency with which Donne quotes it in the sermons, it seems to have specially impressed him.[49] The Augustinian fly immediately makes us feel closer to Traherne than Donne's sermons usually do. Come to that it makes us, like Donne's bell-bodied girls, feel nearer to D. H. Lawrence, celebrating life in *Etruscan Places*: 'Brute force crushes many plants. Yet the plants rise again. The pyramids will not last a moment compared with the daisy.'[50] Once or twice in the sermons Donne seems to be trying to match Augustine's Lawrentian paradox. The 'inglorious drop of raine, that falls into the dust', he insists, is as much a child of God, and kin to us, as 'those glorious saints who shall rise from the dust, and fall no more'.[51] And in a later sermon, arguing that God may be seen even in the least dignified creatures, he writes: 'If every gnat that flies were an Arch-angell, all that could but tell me, that there is a God; and the poorest worme that creeps, tells me that.'[52] The gnat almost inevitably flashes into momentary, archangelic brilliance as we read this. Yet the fact remains that Donne is actually saying that gnats are not archangels, and that it would not help if they were. Gnats remain gnats; worms are still poor; drops of rain still 'inglorious'. Donne's sermons, with their darker purposes, cannot make much use of gallant flies or daisies.

Despite the imaginative correspondences between poems and sermons, the religious stance Donne chose in the sermons obliged him
to leave out any mention of fleas with living walls of jet—significant
though they might have seemed to a more cheerful Christian temperament.

But to return to the poems: by far Donne's best biological writing
comes in *The Progresse of the Soule*, a poem which has earned almost
unanimous critical condemnation. Grierson was moved to pronounce that it was not only 'a failure' but that its 'sheer ugliness' and
'wantonly repulsive' details exhibited the most repellent side of
Donne's mind.[53] Evelyn Hardy agreed with Grierson, calling it 'a
curious and repulsive poem', and R. C. Bald considered it the 'most
disappointing' of all Donne's works.[54] Evelyn Simpson has added
her voice to the general obloquy, noting fastidiously that 'De Quincey is the solitary critic of note who has praised this poem'.[55] That
isn't quite true. Browning also praised it, and quoted three lines from
it in his 'The Two Poets of Croisic'. But neither Browning nor De
Quincey prepare one, by their comments, for the extraordinarily
close and subtle responses to life which the poem reveals. De Quincey says that 'massy diamonds compose the very substance' of it, and
that its thoughts and descriptions 'have the fervent and gloomy
sublimity of Ezekiel or Aeschylus'. Browning says (or makes the
character in his poem say) that it is the work of 'revered and
magisterial Donne', and that it 'knolls' from 'the Doctor's bronzed
throat'.[56]

On chronological grounds alone that is rather wide of the mark,
for the poem's preface carries the date 16 August 1601, so we can be
sure that it was written either during or before Donne's employment
as Egerton's secretary. It is far from being the work of revered Dr.
Donne. Its plan is that of a satirical epic, tracing the soul of the apple
which Eve plucked through various bestial and human reincarna-
tions. Where the soul was to end up is disputed. Calvin and Queen
Elizabeth are both candidates. Jonson told William Drummond that
Calvin was to be the soul's eventual repository,[57] but Donne seems
to imply in the poem itself that Queen Elizabeth is the answer. Either
way, of course, it could hardly have failed to make the poem anti-
Protestant, so we may almost certainly take it as further proof of
Donne's lingering Catholic affiliations. But the problem is insoluble,
for Donne did not finish the work. He broke off after stanza 52 of the
first canto, by which time the soul has passed through a mandrake, a
sparrow, several fish, a whale, a mouse, two wolves and an ape, and
has finally reached the girl Themech, sister and wife of Cain, with

whose mother, Adam's fifth daughter Siphatecia, the ape has had
amorous dealings.

From the viewpoint of a grasp of the organic world this poem is
certainly Donne's masterpiece. To put the reader in the right frame
of mind for accepting that claim it will be helpful to quote first its
description of a hatching sparrow. Escaping from the mandrake the
soul insinuates itself

> Into a small blew shell, the which a poore
> Warme bird orespread, and sat still evermore,
>   Till her enclos'd child kickt, and peck'd it self a dore.

> Out crept a sparrow, this soules moving Inne,
> On whose raw armes stiffe feathers now begin,
> As childrens teeth through gummes, to breake with paine,
> His flesh is jelly yet, and his bones threds,
> All a new downy mantle overspreads;
> A mouth he opes, which would as much containe
> As his late house, and the first houre speaks plaine,
> And chirps alowd for meat. Meat fit for men
> His father steales for him, and so feeds then
>   One, that within a month, will beate him from his hen.[58]

For a critic to find a poem which contained those lines—even if it
contained nothing else—'disappointing' calls for dullness of no
common order. Where, among Donne's contemporaries, we may
ask, do we find a newly hatched bird so feelingly documented? The
shell colour, the warmth of the mother bird, and the huge gape of the
nestling combine to induce a sense of fragile but vigorous life.
Despite the human touches (the 'child' kicking as if in the womb; the
'downy mantle') the sparrow remains wholly sparrowish in its
immorality and grossly unfilial behaviour. There is no bid to make
nature endearing. The bones, still 'threds' in a half-transparent jelly,
like that 'ragged bony' name trapped in a piece of glass, or like the
'sinewie thread' the brain lets fall, mingle rigidity and flimsiness in
the peculiarly evocative way which we have been finding so typical
of Donne—and the 'jelly' sets up connections with the 'gellie' the
Countess of Somerset turned into in bed, and with the 'excrementall
jelly' of sperm, and the 'jelly' dead bodies dissolve into, which we
have watched Donne gloating over in the sermons.

What especially takes us, as human readers, inside the sparrow's
skin is the equation between teeth breaking through gums and
feathers growing. We are invited to feel what it would be like to have

a body all gums: to have teeth breaking through our arms. Donne got the idea, I think, from Plato, who writes in the *Phaedrus* about the soul growing feathers: 'Now in this process the whole soul throbs and palpitates, and as in those who are cutting teeth there is an irritation and discomfort in the gums, when the teeth begin to grow, just so the soul suffers when the growth of the feathers begins: it is feverish and is uncomfortable and itches when they begin to grow.'[59] Since Donne was writing a poem about the soul and its doings, the *Phaedrus* would be a likely source for him to consult. But what was metaphysical in Plato, Donne has made physical. The feathers, bursting through the skin like teeth, do not now sprout on a soul but on the 'raw armes' of a fledgling.

Another of the poem's rich, dense and sensitive passages (and it is so great a poem that quotations which would establish the reputation of a lesser writer can be picked out from all over it) is its description of the formation of a human embryo:

> *Adam* and *Eve* had mingled bloods, and now
> Like Chimiques equall fires, her temperate wombe
> Had stew'd and form'd it: and part did become
> A spungie liver, that did richly'allow,
> Like a free conduit, on a high hils brow,
> Life-keeping moisture unto every part;
> Part hardned it selfe to a thicker heart,
>   Whose busie furnaces lifes spirits do impart.
>
> Another part became the well of sense,
> The tender well-arm'd feeling braine, from whence,
> Those sinowie strings which do our bodies tie,
> Are raveld out . . .[60]

The attention to textures is so intense here that it practically deposits the half-formed embryo in our hands, stringy and squashy and seeping fluids. Its heats and pulses and coagulations plug straight into our senses. The nearest thing in everyday experience—and it's not very near—to what Donne has coerced language into doing is the jumpy, touched-to-the-quick feel received from watching films of surgical operations. But whereas that experience is flatly visual, Donne's words bulge with metaphor. Their compacted meanings complicate and enrich. The connotations of 'conduit' and 'furnaces' (like the body's furnaces, vaults and larders in the sermon we looked at earlier) involve us in the embryo's intricate architecture, confirming its technical efficiency and independence. 'Busie', always a fraught word for Donne, makes us aware of vigorous, involuntary processes going forward. The noun 'well', suggestive of cool depth, fuses with 'braine' to give a sense of the mind's plumbless inner abyss. The idiomatic charge of a word like 'stew'd' domesticates scientific observation, and drags physiology out of its technical preserve into the kitchen. Like Donne's flea in its 'living walls', the 'tender well-arm'd feeling braine' is both softly and toughly alive, and the same animating contrast of densities occurs in the switch from the 'spungie' liver to the heart, which materializes out of liquid like a giant blood clot.

The bonded, fibrous consistency of the 'sinowie strings', threading flesh together, is kin to the hair and nerves in 'The Funerall' and 'The Relique', and there are other features of the passage which can be readily related to bits of Donne we have inspected earlier. But when we ask where, outside Donne, we could look for such writing, we are met by a blank prospect. Not until Hughes's *Crow* does anything comparable to *The Progresse of the Soule* happen in English poetry. Hughes, like Donne, steps up the physicality of his words till they land on the page like lumps of raw meat. When Hughes writes:

> Black the blood in its loud tunnel
> Black the bowels packed in furnace

or:

> The blood in Eve's body
> That slid from her womb—
> Knotted on the cross[61]

the knots and furnaces, and the tendency to jam building materials into the body's softness, turn our minds back to Donne rather than anyone else. But Donne is not in danger, as Hughes is, of seeming destructive. He cherishes, at every step, the delicacy of living organisms. Further, the medical aspects of his poem, such as the account of the embryo's growth, correspond closely to the views of contemporary authorities. Technical information and sensory excitement blend and strengthen each other.

The poem is remarkable, too, for its underwater section, in which the life cycle of a fish is traced from the moment of its fishy conception. The emphasis is on the swarming organic forms which the sea holds, and on their unremitting application to killing one another. Within the reckless, lethal abundance, every particle, Donne impresses on us, has its fragile perfection:

> A female fishes sandie Roe
> With the males jelly, newly lev'ned was,
> For they had intertouch'd as they did passe,
> And one of those small bodies, fitted so,
> This soule inform'd, and abled it to rowe
> It selfe with finnie oares, which she did fit:
> Her scales seem'd yet of parchment, and as yet
> Perchance a fish, but by no name you could call it.[62]

Donne gives the processes of spawning and fertilization the enquiring attention we should normally associate with something hatched and pored over in a laboratory tank. But as usual his regard, though clinical, is not simply clinical. His comparisons retail both the flimsiness ('parchment') and the robustness ('oares') of the minuscule creature. Fish life is enjoyed as well as seen. Precision and fancifulness co-operate. Meanwhile the intertouching of 'sandie' roe with male 'jelly' maintains the play of contrasting textures which, we have repeatedly noticed, Donne's physical apprehensions tend to centre upon.

At the other end of the size scale Donne's whale, in which the soul has an eventful stay, combines the force of an artillery barrage with the spaciousness of a floating hotel:

> At every stroake his brazen finnes do take,
> More circles in the broken sea they make
> Then cannons voices, when the aire they teare:
> His ribs are pillars, and his high arch'd roofe
> Of barke that blunts best steele, is thunder-proofe:
> Swimme in him swallow'd Dolphins, without feare,
> And feele no sides, as if his vast wombe were
> Some Inland sea.[63]

The whale's spectacular presentness is achieved by turning it into metal and architecture, after the Donnean fashion, and by solidifying the materials around it. 'Broken sea' (another of those mixed-consistency phrases like 'sinewie thread' or 'ragged bony name') gives the impression that the whale has to fracture its way through a fissile concretion, rather than mere water, and this enhances the beast's actuality. At the same time, as we should by now expect from our experience of Donne's methods, this emphasis on density and extension is counteracted by the whale's vulnerability and by the living secretions it exudes. 'Oyles', we are told, 'outstreat' from it (the verb, with its sense of smooth leakage, was coined for the occasion by Donne, and apparently lay around unused for two centuries until Browning, predictably, used it in 'Ned Bratts'); and it is done to death by a 'flaile-finn'd Thresher' (i.e. a fox shark) and a 'steel-beak'd' swordfish.

When compared with other famous literary fish, Donne's, in this poem, are remarkable for their realism. Milton's fish in *Comus* are luminously beautiful but belong to some other world than our own:

> The sounds, and seas with all their finny drove
> Now to the moon in wavering morris move.[64]

Donne's fish are too busy eating and being eaten to have any time for morris dancing. On the other hand they are not, like Pope's fish in *Windsor Forest*,[65] hampered by layers of Augustan word paint. Their paper-thin scales and sandy roes are naturally poetic, whereas Pope's fish, dyed and gilded, are as ornamental as furniture, and like furniture would last no time at all in water.

But though Donne's creatures in *The Progresse of the Soule* are physically real their realism amalgamates quite happily with exploitation of their imaginary and legendary potential. It is an intensifying not a limiting realism. One animal legend that, given his interest in bodily penetration, understandably appealed to him, was the belief that mice killed elephants by crawling up their trunks and gnawing their brains. To avoid this, it was held, elephants generally put a knot in their trunks before going to sleep. Donne's version brings into prominence, as we have seen him doing elsewhere, the living 'strings' which descend from the brain to the body's regions. His mouse, finding the elephant's trunk unknotted, clambers straight into its interior:

> In which as in a gallery this mouse
> Walk'd, and surveid the roomes of this vast house,
> And to the braine, the soules bedchamber, went,
> And gnaw'd the life cords there; Like a whole towne
> Cleane undermin'd, the slaine beast tumbled down.[66]

As with the lovers' threaded eyes, we sense something tender being horribly pierced, and that increases the tenderness. But Donne's technique of making organisms inorganic ('A *bracelet* of bright haire'; a '*steel*-beak'd Sword-fish'), in order to press them the more starkly upon us, persists too. Under the elephant's skin the mouse finds a 'gallery', a 'house', a 'towne'. In true Donne fashion, the creature is architecture as well as organism. The sensibility that made him interested in the ear's penetrable labyrinth also operates here, though on a grander scale. Equally Donnean is the fact that the elephant's mass is held together by strings ('life cords') which, like the 'sinewie thread' of 'The Funerall', suggest intricate and fibrous cohesiveness. The body in Donne is both a building and a network, and the contrasting textures these metaphors imply require contrasting but complementary physical responses from us.

Vegetable life, as well as the life of fishes and animals, is presented, in *The Progresse of the Soule*, in an extraordinarily involving way. Donne writes, for instance, of the 'gummie blood, which doth in holly grow',[67] and the metaphor, like the feathers breaking through the sparrow's raw arms, tersely induces us to experience the natural world with our own bodies. Vegetation impinges again when the snake, in Eden, plucks the apple. It

> Broke the slight veines, and tender conduit-pipe,
> Through which this soule from the trees root did draw
> Life.[68]

Here, on the enticingly microscopic stage provided by an apple stalk, Donne intrudes into the vegetable world both the human body, with its 'veines', and the fragile building materials ('tender conduit-pipe') which provided the flea's living walls. The stalk's solidity and sensitivity are simultaneously brought before us.

This aliveness to the life of plants carries over into Donne's lyrics, religious poetry and sermons. He expresses the awakening of love in springtime, or the cowing of his spirits which fear or illness occasion, by invoking seasonal greening and dying, the stirring of 'The world's whole sap', and the movements within root and bud. Through these images he relates himself to a realm of being deeper and darker than human intention. So amid the gathering gloom of 'A Hymne to Christ, at the Authors last going into Germany', he feels himself drawn beyond humanity and its superficialities into the primitive communion of trees:

> As the trees sap doth seeke the root below
> In winter, in my winter now I goe,
> Where none but thee, th'Eternall root
> Of true Love I may know.[69]

The kinship with Lawrence, which we have noted once or twice, is here very evident (with the Lawrence, for instance, who writes in *Etruscan Places* of 'the quick powers that run up the roots of plants and establish the great body of the tree, the tree of life, and run up the feet and legs of man, to establish the heart').

The impulse towards the insensate and the primeval which governs Donne's lines contrasts remarkably with the notion of him as a cerebral poet—a purveyor of flashy brainwork, and it is a vital counterpart to the element in his genius which gives that notion currency. The poem 'Loves Growth' has as its major theme the discovery that human love is not human at all, but generated and controlled by biological processes which unite it with the sky and the weather, the sun's 'working vigour' and the growth of the grass. It belongs with the mindless system of nature. Donne makes love as a tree breaks into flower:

> Gentle love deeds, as blossomes on a bough,
> From loves awaken'd root do bud out now.

The delicacy of these lines arises not only from the petal-like unfolding to which the act of sex is likened, but also from the infusion of an obscure phallic consciousness into the budding tree. Nature is aroused. The word 'awaken'd', like the word 'seeke' in the quotation from 'A Hymne to Christ' above, imparts to roots, sap and branches a vestige of sense. So, too, when he speaks in a sermon of the hurt soul which 'as a flowre at the Suns declining, contracts and gathers in, and shuts up her selfe, as though she had received a blow'.[70] He does not tell us what a flower looks like ('visual beauty'), but how it feels. He achieves a fusion, merging the human back into the natural world, and raising the natural world towards the mind's light.

This fusion is, as we have seen, most extensively and triumphantly managed in *The Progresse of the Soule*. The poem is a conglomerate of sensitized zoology and botany: menagerie, aquarium, and maternity ward rolled into one. The humanized plants it contains culminate in a mandrake—the legendary root which shrieked like a human being when unearthed—and of all Donne's mandrakes this is the finest. The soul, the poem tells us, finds it in a 'darke and foggie Plot', and infiltrates through the earth's 'pores' into its vegetable body:

> The plant thus abled, to it self did force
> A place, where no place was; by natures course
> As aire from water, water fleets away
> From thicker bodies, by this root throng'd so
> His spungie confines gave him place to grow:
> Just as in our streets, when the people stay
> To see the Prince, and have so fill'd the way
> That weesels scarce could passe, when she comes nere
> They throng and cleave up, and a passage cleare,
>   As if, for that time, their round bodies flatned were.

His right arme he thrust out towards the East,
West-ward his left; th'ends did themselves digest
Into ten lesser strings, these fingers were:
And as a slumberer stretching on his bed,
This way he this, and that way scattered
His other legge, which feet with toes upbeare.
Grew on his middle parts, the first day, haire,
To show, that in loves businesse hee should still
A dealer bee, and be us'd well, or ill:
   His apples kindle, his leaves, force of conception kill.

A mouth, but dumbe, he hath; blinde eyes, deafe eares,
And to his shoulders dangle subtile haires;
A young *Collossus* there hee stands upright,
And as that ground by him were conquered
A leafie garland weares he on his head
Enchas'd with little fruits, so red and bright
That for them you would call your Loves lips white;
So, of a lone unhaunted place possest,
Did this soules second Inne, built by the guest,
   This living buried man, this quiet mandrake, rest.[71]

Several features of Donne's imagination, which we have been iso-
lating, unite in this prodigious passage. Bulk, pressure and density
loom large. The reader finds himself registering muscular tremors as
the cramped lines unwind. The mandrake shoves itself against our
bodies. Donne gets this effect by likening the earth which the root
squashes to squashed people. The whole elaborate crowd-scene
simile, complete with a personal appearance of Queen Elizabeth, is
introduced for the sole purpose of telling us what it's like to be the
soil round a root vegetable.

Donne's bid to haul our bodies into his descriptive activities
governs the second stanza too. The mandrake groping with its
stringy fingers and upward-pointing toes reaches a part of our mind
where thought and sensation mix. Its indecent hairiness makes it
more sensuously obtrusive, and the syntax jars and jams co-
operatively. The distorted start to the fifth line, for instance ('This
way he this'), makes us feel the sentence being dragged sideways like
the creature's sprawled leg. Further, the threads and filaments that
extend from the mandrake—its pubic hair, the 'subtile haires'
dangling on its shoulders, the 'strings' at the ends of its arms—connect it with the intricate living networks by means of which, as we
have noticed, Donne customarily evokes both the fineness and the

cohesiveness of organisms. Like the skeleton scratched in window glass, it hangs stringily together.

Moreover the mandrake compacts within itself those opposed qualities—numb and quick, dead and vital—which contrive to give bodies, in Donne's writing, substantial existence. It is 'living' but 'buried'. It has mouth, eyes and ears, but they are dumb, blind and deaf. It is protuberantly physical, but 'quiet'. Being both men and vegetables at the same time, mandrakes combined these contrasting qualities in a peculiarly spectacular way, and that partly accounts for the fascination they held for Donne. Almost the only creatures that could vie with them in this respect were paraplegics, and when Donne, in a latish sermon, turns his intrigued attention to a paralysed man, he uses language that instantly recalls his mandrake. 'This living dead man, this dead and buried man' (compare 'This living buried man' in The Progresse of the Soule) has, preaches Donne, 'a soule, but a soule in a sack'.[72] That last phrase vividly enshrines the junction of the feelingful and the unfeeling which Donne found so attractive. At the time he wrote the sermon he had, as a matter of fact, had the phrase lying around in his mind for some twenty years: his elegy 'The Autumnall' already characterizes the body, incapacitated by age, as 'a soules sacke'.[73]

What are we to make, then, of the critical obtuseness which has greeted The Progresse of the Soule? It seems possible that Grierson and the other critics concerned were simply upset by what they took to be the poem's indecency. The description of the coupling of a wolf and a dog (stanzas 41–4), and of the 'toyfull Ape' making love to a young girl (stanzas 46–9), might, one can see, offend the prudish—though the second passage, at any rate, is among Donne's most delicate and tender things, and we shall return to it in another chapter. Whatever the reason for the poem's bad reputation, it is high time that it was reinstated and recognized as the masterpiece of the early Donne. It is tempting to speculate what English literature would have looked like if Donne had finished his poem, and if it, rather than Spenser's Faerie Queene, had come to be recognized as the great Elizabethan epic. In place of Spenser's dreamy conservatism, we should then have had (to inaugurate seventeenth-century poetry, and provide a model for the coming poets) a work which was not only progressive and contentious in its intellectual cast, but also wedded to immediacy and the real world.

The area of experience it opens up for us, with its embryos and organisms, is more usually the province of science than poetry, but Donne never allows it to fade into the monochrome of scientific fact.

He bathes it in feeling. To do this, as we have seen , he constantly relates nature to physical sensation, so that in feeling the world we also come to feel our own bodies. Further, Donne responds with peculiar sharpness, as we have watched him doing in other poems, to situations which emphasize the body's capacity to be felt, as well as to feel. Teeth breaking through gums, the stickiness of blood, the sponginess of liver, the heart's 'busie furnaces'—these, and similar focuses of attention in Donne's fragmentary epic, impress upon us the body's objective existence. The mentality which, in poems and sermons, was drawn towards hair and bones, and enjoyed imagining inert materials lodged in the body's living consciousness, had its training ground in *The Progresse of the Soule*.

Donne's objective view of bodily organs was plainly stimulated by his medical education, and in particular by his interest in the developing science of anatomy. This had made very significant progress in the half-century before his birth, due chiefly to the experiments of Andreas Vesalius, whose work *On the Fabric of the Human Body* appeared in 1543. The imaginative appeal of the subject for Donne is evident. 'Rack't carcasses', he remarks discriminatingly in a love poem, 'make ill Anatomies.'[74] He was trained to regard a body as a specimen you dissect as well as a sensitive envelope you walk around in . What is distinctive in his writing is his fusion of the two aspects. An image such as that of the surgeon's probe inserted into the girl, in 'The Comparison', unites the technical and the tender. Likewise when he writes of a bracelet of bright hair about the bone, or of the scratched skeleton trembling on the window pane, he compounds the body's inanimate structure with its vividly continuing life. Almost invariably when the body, or parts of it, appear in Donne's poems, we can find traces of this dual viewpoint. To take another instance, consider the way the imagined worshippers in 'The Canonization' speak about the lovers' eyes when they address their prayers to them:

> You, to whom love was peace, that now is rage;
> Who did the whole worlds soule extract, and drove
>   Into the glasses of eyes,
>   So made such mirrors, and such spies,
> That they did all to you epitomize,
>   Countries, Townes, Courts: Beg from above
>   A patterne of your love![75]

The metaphors chosen by the worshippers convert the lovers' eyes

into the complex apparatus of an alchemist's laboratory—the tubes
and retorts ('glasses') in which he would distil the 'soule' or essence
of an element such as gold or mercury. But this technical elaboration
coincides with a simple, devotional image of two lovers gazing into
each other's eyes and seeing the whole world gathered in them. The
reader finds himself reacting emotionally as well as scientifically.
This blended response to bodily organs relates, of course, to the
characteristically Donnean mixture of thought and feeling remarked
on by Eliot, but it relates more specifically to the sensitized physiology of which *The Progresse of the Soule* is full. The eyes are glass,
and alive, at the same time.

Another piece of living chemical apparatus occurs in 'The Comparison', when Donne turns his attention to his girl's womb and its
warmth:

> . . . like the Chymicks masculine equall fire,
> Which in the Lymbecks warme wombe doth inspire
> Into th'earths worthlesse durt a soule of gold,
> Such cherishing heat her best lov'd part doth hold.[76]

This reminds us of the 'Chimiques equal fires' which nurtured the
embryo in Eve's womb, and indeed one of the things that attracted
Donne to alchemy was its constant assimilation of scientific processes to human activities like generation and birth. Paracelsus, the
great sixteenth-century quack, magician and scientist, with whose
works Donne was acquainted, habitually talks about metals in terms
of wombs, seeds and conception. In the Paracelsian universe, all the
elements in chemical reactions are living things. 'Metals', he writes,
'can return to quick mercury, can become mercury, and be regener-
ated and clarified by fire, if they remain for forty weeks in perpetual
heat, like a child in its mother's womb.'[77] Such language naturally
fed Donne's desire to see the human body simultaneously as scientific instrument and as organism. He regards his girl's womb both as
a piece of manufactured equipment, stuck together, and as cherishingly alive. Love-nest and laboratory melt together.

Donne's attribution of gender to fire, like his fusion of womb and
alembic, is Paracelsian: 'the natural fire', Paracelsus writes, 'is the
masculine fire or chief agent.'[78] The body's heat, functional and
penetrating, stimulates Donne's chemical imagination. The lovers'
hands 'firmly cimented' by sweat at the start of 'The Extasie' are,
for instance, participating in a scientific reaction. 'Cementation' was
a chemical process, explained by Paracelsus in his treatise *Concerning
the Transmutation of Metals and Cement*,[79] by which one solid is made

to penetrate another at high temperature. Given Donne's interest in bodily excrements, it's understandable, too, that his attention was caught by the alchemists' use of dung to provide the heat for their experiments. Paracelsus believed that gold would increase in weight if buried and 'constantly fertilised with fresh human urine and pigeon's dung'; and to supply the even warmth necessary for the process of extraction, separation and infusion he recommends that the vessel containing the reagents should be 'set in horse dung for a month'.[80] Donne, in a verse letter, notes the method approvingly:

> For when from herbs the pure parts must be wonne
> From grosse, by Stilling, this is better done
> By despis'd dung, then by the fire or Sunne.[81]

The appeal of this for Donne, like the appeal of the anatomy theatre, is that it catches an organic substance—dung, flesh—in the act of turning into a piece of scientific equipment.

The modern writer who has the clearest affinities with this way of imagining is Aldous Huxley. He always enjoys reminding us about the different perspectives from which human bodies can be regarded, and in *Those Barren Leaves* a typical Huxleyan polymath, Calamy, lectures a receptive female on the subject, taking his own hand as specimen. Optically speaking, Calamy observes, his hand is simply a shape which interrupts light. But

> . . . it exists simultaneously in a dozen parallel worlds. It exists as electrical charges; as chemical molecules; as living cells; as part of a moral being, the instrument of good and evil; in the physical world and in the mind. And from this one goes on to ask, inevitably, what relationship exists between these different modes of being. What is there in common between life and chemistry; between good and evil and electrical charges; between a collection of cells and the consciousness of a caress? It's here that the gulfs begin to open. For there isn't any connection—that one can see, at any rate. Universe lies on the top of universe, layer after layer, distinct and separate.[82]

Published in 1925, this excited a generation which was also much drawn to Donne's poetry. The similarities are clear, but so are the differences. When Huxley apprises us of the body's scientific existence it is, more often than not, a despairing joke. There is an instance earlier in the same novel when Irene, a delectable eighteen-year-old, finds herself out of doors on a cold night:

Irene crossed her arms over her chest, hugging herself to keep
warm. Unfortunately this boa of flesh and blood was itself sensitive. Her frock was sleeveless. The warmth of her bare arms
drifted off along the wind; the temperature of the surrounding
atmosphere rose by a hundred-billionth of a degree.[83]

Though Irene is from one viewpoint a beautiful girl, from another
and equally valid one she is an inefficient thermal generator. Huxley
directs our attention to this for no enriching purpose, and in that
respect the contrast with Donne is marked. The 'cherishing heat' of
Donne's girl, radiating from her womb, is enhanced, not demeaned,
by being associated with the temperature necessary for scientific
experiment. His vision is cohesive; Huxley's fragmentary. The universe which for Huxley has split into unrelated layers is still for
Donne, as for Paracelsus, a multitudinous but unified system, full
of vitalizing correspondences and relationships, and sunned by
God's eye.

Donne's profound responsiveness to bodies, instanced throughout
this chapter, raised, for him, one further question, which Huxley's
speculations also precipitated. Are not the mind and the soul merely
functions, or malfunctions, of the body? Dr. Obispo, in Huxley's
After Many a Summer, remarks that Shelley's *Weltschmerz* was the
outcome of chronic tuberculous pleurisy, and that with better medical care all the Romantic poets could have been prevented from
writing as they did.[84] Obispo's cynicism aims to elicit little more
than a squeal of delighted protest. But for Donne, as for other
Renaissance thinkers, the question was real and serious. If the soul
depended on the body, it seemed reasonable to conclude that it was
not immortal but would die when the body died. This was one of the
leading tenets of atheistical thought in the sixteenth century. It was,
for example, the viewpoint adopted by Pietro Pomponazzi, the
dominant figure in the *avant garde* school of Padua until his death in
1525.[85] Pomponazzi's *Tractatus de immortalitate animae* of 1516 dismissed the soul's immortality as a superstition, encouraged by rulers
to keep their subjects docile. Paduan ideas, reaching England partly
through French atheistical thinkers like Jean Fernel, were chiefly
responsible for creating among Englishmen the image of Italy as
atheism's homeland.
    When Donne first formulated the theory of the soul's dependence
on the body, he was sufficiently aware of its dangers to couch it in a
semi-jocular form. His eleventh Paradox argues that 'the Gifts of the

Body are better than those of the Minde', and rests its case on the
body's primacy:

> I say again, that the body makes the minde . . . and this minde
> may be confounded with the soul without any violence or injus-
> tice to Reason or Philosophy: then the soul it seems is enabled by
> our Body, not this by it. . . . Are chastity, temperance, and for-
> titude gifts of the minde? I appeale to Physitians whether the cause
> of these be not in the body.[86]

The appeal to medical evidence is significant. Padua was a medical
centre, much influenced by the thought of the great Arabian physician Averroës, a denier of the soul's immortality. Donne's interest in
the question is intimately connected with his medical knowledge.
The traditional Galenic medicine of his day did, of course, ascribe
differing human temperaments to different mixtures of blood, bile,
black bile and phlegm within the constitution, so it opened the way
for an explanation of spiritual faculties as mere physical symptoms.
Donne again takes the materialist line in his eighth Paradox, arguing
that 'we derive our inclinations, our minds, our souls' from no other
source than our complexions and bodies.[87]

In the Paradoxes Donne defused the subject by pretending he was
fooling. But he was not. The question of the body's primacy continued to perplex him, and it severely affected the version of Christian
dogma which he was eventually able to accept. He found support for
his bodily emphasis in the writings of Tertullian, one of the Church
Fathers, who, like the pagan poet Lucretius, another prime source of
Renaissance atheism, had gone so far as to insist that the soul was not
merely dependent on the body but itself composed of corporal
matter. Tertullian knew a religious lady who had actually seen a soul,
and he taught that the flesh, being conceived and generated along
with the soul from its earliest existence in the womb, is mixed up
with it in all its operations. Thus it is incorrect to suppose that the
senses and the intellect operate separately. To use the senses is to use
the intellect, and vice versa. The sensuous apprehension of thought,
which Eliot and others have found in Donne's poetry, was, for
Tertullian, inevitable.[88]

At one stage in his religious development Donne certainly
believed that the soul died, or slept, with the body, and remained
with it in the grave until the Last Judgement.[89] Even though he seems
to have relinquished this belief, in the interests of orthodoxy, before
he took orders, he continued to assert in his sermons, as he had in his
Paradoxes, that the soul depended on the body and could not exist

properly without it. He quotes Tertullian to drive the point home: 'saies Tertullian, Never go about to separate the thoughts of the heart, from the colledge, from the fellowship of the body. . . . All that the soule does, it does in, and with, and by the body.'[90] Donne can hardly mean what he says here; or rather, the extreme position he voices cannot be reconciled with some of the more orthodox views he was constrained to accept. For if the soul does nothing, except in, with, and by the body, then it cannot survive outside the body at death, or rejoin the body at the resurrection—yet Donne professed that it did both. But he professed it, as we shall see when we discuss his view of death, in a worried and qualified way. His intense responsiveness to the body's material existence, evidenced in poems and devotional writings alike, interfered with his Christianity on this issue, and gave it an individual and deviant slant.

The richest fruit of Donne's tussle with this question is not to be found, though, in his Christian musings, intricate and impassioned though they are, but in the famous lines from *The Second Anniversarie* about young Elizabeth Drury's body:

> we understood
> Her by her sight, her pure and eloquent blood
> Spoke in her cheekes, and so distinctly wrought,
> That one might almost say, her bodie thought.[91]

Elizabeth's thinking flesh is plainly the creation of the Donne who wrote: 'I say again, that the body makes the mind.' But the medico-theological issues have been transcended. There arises from them a vision of a girl's quick colour and sensitive face. Typically, Donne combines this living image with an inanimate one. In the immediately preceding lines, Elizabeth's fluent body had been turned to metal:

> Shee, of whose soule, if we may say, 'twas Gold,
> Her body was th'Electrum, and did hold
> Many degrees of that . . .

Electrum was an amalgam of four parts of gold to one part of silver, which outshone silver in its brightness. Elizabeth's gleaming isolation is arrested in this image. The metaphor makes her, like the bell-bodied girls of Problem VII, refined and remote. The infusion of 'eloquent blood' into the metal animates it without losing its purity. The metal turns to flesh, in which the blood comes and goes as delicately as thought.

So Donne achieves an integration of body and mind. He conceives of Elizabeth's body as an intellectual thing, and he does so in the teeth of deeply entrenched traditions. For centuries Western Christianity had seen the soul as the prisoner of the body—a bird in a cage, an angel trapped on a dunghill. Donne collapses, in an instant, this age-old dualism. That he does so is the more remarkable because the *Anniversaries* vigorously corroborate, elsewhere, the traditional opposition of soul and body. Donne was the least consistent of mortals, and he never felt that an idea had been properly exploited until he had tried it out backwards as well as forwards. But if Elizabeth's thinking flesh is inconsistent with the rest of the poem it occurs in, it is perfectly in key, as we have seen, with the flea's living walls of jet, or the ecstatic lovers' cemented hands.

For that matter it is very close indeed to the way Donne imagines the Countess of Bedford's body in his verse letters to her. It is not, he reports, composed of flesh. Instead, 'walls of tender christall her enfold.'[92] She is made of transparent masonry ('specular stone') of a sort which, according to writers on ancient marvels, the Romans built their temples of. These fantasies are early versions of his account of Elizabeth Drury's body, which likewise combines hard, mineral radiance with softness, and which is similarly transparent, allowing her thoughts to be seen. It would be simple-minded to conclude that the Countess resembled Elizabeth Drury. Donne was not realistically concerned with either female. Obliged to turn out commendatory verses, he takes the opportunity to write about see-through women, as his imagination prompts him to. He does the same in his poem on the death of Cecilia Bulstrode, whom he imagines as a piece of artillery made out of glass ('Christall Ordinance')—too 'cleare' and 'Saphirine' to survive.[93] It was the taste for 'tender christall' that had led him to write about eyes as alchemical glasses in 'The Canonization'.

But Elizabeth's body is an advance on Lady Bedford's and Miss Bulstrode's. Theirs, though both vitreous and vital, are constructed on the old Christian model, in that they are ultimately just cases for their souls. Elizabeth's is different. She does her thinking with it. It is metal, but aware. Accordingly, her pure and eloquent blood is a living assertion of the organism's thoughtfulness, as against the thoughtfulness of the intellect. We are reminded, yet again, of Lawrence. Donne was three centuries ahead of his time. For to eliminate the cold, abstract, mental life, and allow thought to sink back into the sensual body is, with Lawrence, a major aim. *The Woman Who Rode Away*, like many of his fictions, shows the idea in action. Stripped, anointed and massaged by her Indian captors, the woman finds her Europeanized intellect slipping from her:

Their dark hands were incredibly powerful, yet soft with a watery softness she could not understand. . . . Her limbs, her flesh, her very bones at last seemed to be diffusing into a roseate sort of mist, in which her consciousness hovered like some sun-gleam in a flushed cloud.[94]

Lawrence's woman, like Elizabeth, is rarefying—acquiring a conscious body.

In this chapter we have observed Donne observing bodies, and we have noticed that he does so in two contradictory ways. On the one hand he is struck by their material independence, and regards them with the detachment of a trained anatomist. On the other, he feels drawn to their organic sensibility. One view reduces the body to a framework; the other recognizes it as a living presence in all consciousness. Repeatedly and ingeniously, he combines these opposed views, and this is one thing that inclines people to speak of him combining thought and feeling—for thought thinks the body is a dead appendage, and feeling knows it is not. Among the factors that give his love poems their air of self-awareness is his conversion of love to an anatomical model. He disposes of parts of himself as if he were watching himself from a distance. 'Goe, and take my heart from hence'; 'Send home my long strayd eyes to mee'; 'Here I bequeath / Mine eyes to Argus . . . My tongue to Fame'[95]—these formulations, which treat his person as though it were suitable for postal delivery, superimpose organization on emotion, and strive to bring the language of the anatomist into the most involved of human relationships.

When Donne, in other poems, speaks of his heart and the girl's heart as being more black and brittle than jet; or when he rips himself open and finds 'something like a heart' with 'colours' and 'corners'; or when he tells how his heart has been shivered in pieces like glass, we are again aware of the poet's impulse to objectify his experience.[96] What is in fact an integral part of his being and his love becomes a jagged piece of petrified anatomy. The aim is intensity. Only by speaking of his inner self as solid and smashable can he make it sound concentrated and vehement enough. For the same reason he turns himself to metal in the religious poems. He urges God to burn off his 'rusts', and drag his 'iron heart' like a magnet,[97] because nothing but metal could sustain the violence he craves for. Though Donne, in these instances, has other effects in view than when he transmuted girls' bodies to glass or metal, or remarked on the flea's jet walls, the imaginative transference is identical. The same interchange between organic life and the hard, bright world of objects is being pursued.

To end where we began: for Rupert Brooke or Professor Crofts to say that the beauty of the visual world meant nothing to Donne is pregnantly inadequate. The shallowness of mere vision is what his poems struggle to supervene. Whether he is writing about the human body, or animals, or plants, or inanimate objects, his effort is to engage us on other, and deeper, levels than the visual; to sensitize us, rather than to please our eyes; and to enhance our awareness both of organic life and of the solid, intransigent materials in which it inheres.

♔ 6 ♔

Change

Change was a popular subject at the end of the sixteenth century. To many people things seemed to be getting worse. Spenser created the dread figure of Mutability. Shakespeare chronicled Devouring Time. The pastoral; the myth of the Golden Age; the Puritan notion of an uncorrupted, primitive church; the belief in the educational efficacy of Classical literature—these and other imaginings provided relief from a deteriorating present. The world, it was widely believed, was growing old, and might not last much longer. The fact that this notion had been current since the start of the Christian era did not, curiously enough, diminish faith in its reliability. On the contrary, the observations of the world's decay recorded by St. Cyprian in the third century were unhesitatingly quoted in the sixteenth as if they provided evidence for, rather than against, a pessimistic view of the present.

Donne contributed eagerly to the general gloom. In his sermons, as in his *Anniversaries*, he catalogued the world's morbid symptoms, several of them taken directly from St. Cyprian: that modern people were shorter in stature, lived less long, and had paler faces than their ancestors; that summers were not as good as they used to be; that children were born with grey hair.[1] But Donne's interest in change went deeper than these popular fancies, and was more personal. He did not regard mutability just as an implacable external force. He saw, rather, that it was a part of himself, and that to talk about himself (as he repeatedly tried to do in the poems) was to talk about change, and to change as he talked. We have already noticed poems—'The Sunne Rising', 'The Anniversarie'—which end up saying the opposite of what they said at the start, and we shall find other instances of that in this chapter.

Donne seems to have been exceptionally aware of his own changeability. At times he joked about it. The earliest known portrait of him, painted at the age of eighteen, bears, as we have noticed, the Spanish motto 'Antes muerto que mudado' (Sooner dead than changed). This affirmation of changelessness changes itself,

however, as soon as it is placed in context. It is a quotation from
Montemayor's *Diana*, representing the words Diana wrote in the
sand when pledging her love to Sirenus, and the lines which follow
call its dependability into question:

> Mira el amor que ordena
> Que os viene hacer creer
> Cosas dichas por mujer
> Y escritas en el arena.

(Look what love ordains. It makes you believe things said by woman
and written in sand.)[2] The motto's firmness dissolves. We're no
longer sure what to make of it; and Donne stares out enigmatically
from his portrait, watching us flounder.

We find him being equally provocative about his changeable
nature in his 'Defence of Women's Inconstancy', where he asserts
that 'the most ignorant and obtuse men change least often'.[3] But
recognition of his fitfulness could also perturb him. He remembers
his youth, in the *Devotions*, as a period of 'vertiginous giddiness, and
irresolution', when he spent almost all his time trying to decide how
he should spend it.[4] As a student he had been unwilling, he reports, to
'betroth or enthral' himself to any particular subject, so he drifted
shallowly from one to another.[5] His apostasy had been only one
instance of a general unfixedness. His instability riles him because it
placed him beyond his own control. He had to watch helplessly
while his intentions warped and faded:

> Inconstancy unnaturally hath begott
> A constant habit; that when I would not
> I change in vowes, and in devotione.[6]

When he prayed, he could not keep his mind on the prayer. He
would throw himself down in his room, and call upon God and his
angels to be present,

> . . . and when they are there, I neglect God and his Angels, for the
> noise of a Flie, for the ratling of a Coach, for the whining of a
> doore; I talk on, in the same posture of praying; Eyes lifted up,
> knees bowed downe; as though I prayed to God; and, if God, or his
> Angels should aske me, when I thought last of God in that prayer, I
> cannot tell: Sometimes I finde that I had forgot what I was about,
> but when I began to forget it, I cannot tell.[7]

Anything, he found, would suffice to distract him: a straw under his
knee, a fancy in his brain. The chance associations, the sideways

thinking, the quick-mindedness which impel his poems became, when he sought for spiritual quiet, an impediment. Worse, he could not suppress his linguistic alertness, and would keep discovering improper double meanings in the words of his prayers. Memories of his licentious youth would steal into his mind too, however fiercely he strove to exclude them.[8] Doggedly he would make a new effort, kneel down, blot out all worldly ideas, and concentrate on God with every nerve. It was no good: 'suddenly I finde my selfe scattered, melted, fallen into vaine thoughts, into no thoughts; I am upon my knees, and I talke, and think nothing.'[9]

It was the same when he was preaching. While his body stood opening and shutting its mouth dutifully in the pulpit, his mind would dart off on errands of its own. He admitted as much to his congregation:

> I am not all here. I am here now preaching upon this text, and I am at home in my Library considering whether S. Gregory, or S. Hierome, have said best of this text, before. I am here speaking to you, and yet I consider by the way, in the same instant, what it is likely you will say to one another, when I have done.[10]

The inattentiveness is not in itself very remarkable. Everyone has had similar experiences some time or other. What strikes us is Donne's hypersensitivity, and his agitated explicitness about his failing. He is distracted by his own distraction.

Some of his most persistent imaginative habits may be traced to this impatience with a fragmented state of being. It made him hungry for absolutes and totalities—for an imagined woman (like Elizabeth Drury) who would embody 'the best that I could conceive';[11] for a God who would encompass, as Donne put it in a sermon, 'not onely all that is, but all that is not: all that might be'.[12] The eagerness with which he dwelt on eternity, and its power to swallow up thought and calculation, is relevant here too. So, on a more mundane level, is his desire for employment which might bind him to 'the body of the world'.[13] He showed, in these various ways, his need for a focus to absorb the powers of his soul, and bring them to unity. The *Spiritual Exercises* were useful to him for much the same reason: they provided a routine of concentration.

The more fluid and multifarious your mind, the harder it is to feel sure you exist as a definable self. Donne seems to have been disturbed, or at least intrigued, by this sense of absence quite early in life, and to have contemplated what steps he might take to counteract it. Writing to Rowland Woodward in the 1590s, he uses the image of

a burning glass to suggest the self-defining exercise he deems
necessary:

> Seeke wee then our selves in our selves; for as
> Men force the Sunne with much more force to pass,
> By gathering his beames with a christall glasse;
>
> So wee, if wee into our selves will turne,
> Blowing our sparkes of vertue, may outburne
> The straw, which doth about our hearts sojourne.[14]

This simple formula for cultivating real identity didn't satisfy him
for long. In his poems, as we have seen, he acknowledges that the self
is by nature undiscoverable. 'Our selves' are precisely 'what we
know not'.[15] Among the transient and contradictory surges of consciousness, he could isolate no firm personality. His poems are full of
ephemeral beings—ghosts, reflections, shadows, people on the point
of flickering into nothing. Their souls fume out into the air around
them; the sighs of their loved ones consume them. It is as a reaction
to this annihilating tendency that Donne's egocentricity and self-
dramatization operate. His doubts about selfhood made it imperative that he should imprint a firm self on the poems.

There are other indications, outside the poetry, of the same anxious determination: his fondness for having his portrait done in
distinctive and elaborate costumes, for instance. The 1591 miniature
shows a dashing, becurled youth with a sword and ear-rings; the
Lothian portrait is of a melancholy lover, lounging under a big black
hat, with some expensive-looking lace round his collar; in the Isaac
Oliver miniature we find a dapper courtier, with neat ruff and beard;
the 1620 portrait affects a sort of Roman toga and a full-faced stare,
presumably to suggest the sturdy worth of the ancients. The careful
arrangement of these get-ups served the same purpose as Donne's
solicitude about his coat of arms, or his puns on his surname, or his
invention of the two personalities, Jack Donne and Dr. Donne,
which stabilized discordant tendencies in his make-up. Like the
scratching of a signature in a window, they are all subterfuges to
clarify the identity.

Being unusually aware of the diffuse moods and ideas churning
through his brain, Donne was predisposed to recognize a corresponding changefulness in the world outside. One aspect of material
objects which was always curiously attractive to him was the idea
that their very existence had required a change from nothing to

something. This had struck other people before Donne, of course. A standard theological question about the creation of the world was what it had been created out of. There were three possible answers. One, favoured by Aristotle, was that the world had always been here, so did not need to be created at all. The second and neo-Platonic view, deriving from the *Timaeus*, was that eternal matter had existed, separated from God, though caused by him, and that he had used this as the raw material for the world. The third view was that God had made the world out of nothing. This last, being impossible, appealed to Donne most, since it established God's mind-obliterating supremacy. It had also become, by his lifetime, the orthodox Christian theory of creation.

But the very fact of its orthodoxy is what makes Donne's alleluias and ecstasies on the point stand out. He doesn't accept it quietly, and store it away with the other impossibilities Christianity required him to believe. Nor, on the other hand, does he go on to praise the subsequent donkey-work of creation which gave shape to primal matter. God's fashioning of the earth and creatures, pictorialized by Milton in *Paradise Lost*, apparently left him cold. It was the point of transition from nothingness to something that enthralled him. He chose this theme to write on when preparing himself for holy orders in the *Essays in Divinity*, and that alone suggests its importance for him. 'All this Universe,' he muses in the *Essays* when mapping out his subject, 'Earth, Sea, Air, Heaven, and all things were once nothing.'[16] Sermons return to the topic elatedly, perplexedly and often. It should, he points out, arouse your gratitude more than anything else. Certainly you should be grateful to God for making you a man and a Christian. He might, after all, 'have left thee a stone, or a plant, or a beast', or even a Jew. But that he made you at all 'when thou wast no where, nothing',[17] is the ultimate wonder. For, as he pursues the point in a later sermon, 'the disproportion between the least thing, and nothing, is more infinite than between the least thing, and the whole world.'[18] Nothingness is the foe of being: God made it being's cause.

Strictly this cannot, Donne impresses on us, be thought about—though, of course, he thinks around it keenly. It is unthinkable, because once you think of something it is something, not nothing. To make it nothing you have to push it back into the blank that lies on the far side of thought: you have to think an unthought. Donne loved to play among speculations of this kind because they brought him to the brink of non-being. Watching the mind dissolve in the effort to grasp nothing was like watching people dematerialize, as they do in the poems. Both kinds of vanishing trick intensified the precariousness of existence. 'How inintelligible a thing', Donne exclaimed admiringly, 'is this Nothing!'[19] It was a black hole into which everything intelligible slid.

What's more, everything would slide into it, Donne believed, if God ceased to exercise his sustaining power. Created nature did not, in his view, remain in being by itself. It required an unremitting effort on God's part to keep it where it was. If God took his mind off it for a moment, nothingness would engulf it. The sermons frequently raised this contingency, and Donne was already impressed by it when he wrote the *Essays in Divinity*: 'God hath made nothing which needs him not, or which would not instantly return again to nothing without his special conservation: Angels and our Souls are not delivered from this dependancy upon him.'[20] Whether the soul was immortal by nature, or only by virtue of God's preservation, was in fact a matter of dispute, and in choosing between the two hypotheses Donne, significantly, took an unorthodox line. His conviction that the soul would, along with everything else in creation, black out instantly if God didn't keep it going diverged from general Christian teaching.[21] Like any other theological issue, the soul's mode of immortality hinges ultimately on imagination, and so provides a clue to the imaginative make-up of the believer. Donne elected to believe that the soul had an off switch, because if it hadn't it would have been permanent, and permanencies didn't excite him. He wanted, and invented, a universe as changeable as himself, in which all things were continuously on the edge of nothingness.

The appeal of annihilation, which this choice reveals, permeates 'A Nocturnall upon S. Lucies Day', where Donne wills his return to a nothingness even more lost and blank than the original nothing that preceded Creation. He wants to be nothing's quintessence, and says he is so already:

> I am by her death, (which word wrongs her)
> Of the first nothing, the Elixer grown.[22]

The thought, typically, moves in two directions. It is self-affirming as well as self-negating. Though seeking nothingness, Donne prizes himself as a special kind of nothing, not an 'ordinary nothing'. Even among nothings, he is ambitious for distinction. This illogicality strikes us as psychologically true, not just because it sounds so like Donne, but also because it reproduces the mixture of feelings contained in bereavement. The proud scorn with which the bereaved look out on the new, empty, uncaring world is deeply self-valuing, though it is also, in a sense, selfless, since it rejects comfort and renewal and devotes itself wholly to the lost one. Donne voices the perversity of grief, which willingly embraces the darkness and the cold, because they hold the precious dead:

> You lovers, for whose sake, the lesser Sunne
>   At this time to the Goat is runne
>   To fetch new lust, and give it you,
>   Enjoy your summer all;
> Since shee enjoyes her long nights festivall,
> Let mee prepare towards her, and let mee call
> This houre her Vigill, and her Eve, since this
> Both the yeares, and the dayes deep midnight is.

The urge to be an extraordinary kind of nothing contradicts, nevertheless, the urge to be nothing. To be extraordinary is to be something. This confusion in the poem dramatizes yet another theological (and psychological) problem which worried Donne—namely, whether anyone, even the damned in Hell, could actually wish to become nothing. In the sermons he often denies the possibility, but he does so with uneasy vehemence, and with qualifications, which show how much the question perplexed him. While asserting, for instance, that the desire for annihilation is impossible, he acknowledged that people do desire it on the spur of the moment, though they could not, he maintains, if they thought about it:

> Suddenly a man may wish himself nothing, because that seems to deliver him from the sense of his present misery; but deliberately he cannot; because whatsoever a man wishes, must be something better than he hath yet; and whatsoever is better, is not nothing.[23]

Donne derived this piece of reasoning from St. Augustine, who had pondered the question in his treatise on free will. It would be absurd, Augustine decides, to wish not to exist, for non-existence is not something but nothing, and you cannot logically make a choice when the object of your choice does not exist. It does occur to Augustine, in passing, that people commit suicide in the hope of becoming nothing, but he advises his readers not to be unsettled by such illogical behaviour.[24]

Donne, with his suicidal longings, would be unlikely to find this conclusion satisfactory, and the frequency with which he returns to the point indicates his concern. Reading Aquinas probably confirmed his doubts, for Aquinas quotes Augustine in order to disagree with him. The damned in Hell, Aquinas points out, could certainly and reasonably choose to be nothing, for it would be better for them not to be than to be damned.[25] In some of his more depressed musings on the matter, it seemed to Donne that the undamned could just as excusably choose annihilation. After a discourse on the misery of earthly life, in the *Devotions*, he exclaims: 'O who, if before hee had a beeing, he could have sense of this miserie, would buy a being here upon these conditions?'[26] This plainly concedes that the decision to be nothing is so natural that everyone would make it, given the chance.

Of 'A Nocturnall upon S. Lucies Day' Frank Kermode has remarked: 'Donne the poet is claiming what Donne the theologian calls impossible; he constantly recurs to the point that man cannot desire annihilation.'[27] As will be seen, this is wrong on two counts. Donne the theologian does not consistently affirm that man cannot desire annihilation, and Donne the poet does not claim that he can. He presents a speaker who declares that he is a nothing, and declares, contradictorily and self-affirmingly, that he is distinguished among nothings. Poem and theology reflect the same ambivalence, and the same disquieted fascination with non-entity.

For Donne, then, the world was created out of nothing, and always poised to vanish into nothing again. It was unstable, too, because its constituent elements were endlessly changing places with one another. Donne found this cosmic roundabout a congenial subject. 'In the Elements themselves,' he urges in a sermon, 'of which all sub-elementary things are composed, there is no acquiescence, but a vicissitudinary transmutation into one another; Ayre condensed becomes water, a more solid body, And Ayre rarified becomes fire, a body more disputable, and in-apparent.'[28] In the chaos of matter's changing states he saw a counterpart to his own unfixedness. Images of fluidity arise when he allows his mind to dwell on created nature. Men and animals become a downpour of decaying matter, soaking the earth. The 'fluidnesse', Donne calls it, of all temporal things: all 'flowes into putrefaction'.[29] The world, the *Devotions* affirm, continually 'changes and melts in all the parts thereof'. Man 'melts so away, as if he were a statue, not of earth, but of snow'. He is poured out 'like lead, like iron, like brass melted in a furnace'.[30]

With so many creatures melting, the ground, in Donne's vision, practically turns liquid. He sees 'every Church-yard swell with the waves and billows of graves'.[31] People melt with incredible rapidity. 'The sun which goes so many miles in a minute, the stars of the firmament which go so very many more, go not so fast as my body to the earth.'[32] What strikes us is the unreality. True, Donne wrote it when he had a fever, and felt that he was sinking fast. But it is not meant as an accurate account of his symptoms. What he creates is an appalled fantasy about bodies turning, with lightning speed, to fluid; and he does this because the idea of melting irresistibly attracted him. His, and other people's, transactions with God are also related in terms of liquefying flesh. God's judgements cause 'a liquefaction, a colliquation, a melting of the bowels'; the Christian's joy is a 'melting, and colliquation of the inwardest bowels of his soule'; 'a liquefaction, a melting, a pouring out of the heart' is the proper response to God's mercies.[33]

The sermons abound with these rapid thaws, but in the love poetry Donne had to find some different pretext for writing about melting, since neither putrefaction nor the state of a Christian's internal organs would decently fit the context. Sometimes he makes the poem's whole metaphoric level a study in changing states of matter. If we watch what happens to the tears in 'A Valediction: of Weeping', we can see this. Bearing the reflection of the girl's face, the tears become coins. Then their rounded shape, and their enclosure of a midget human being, suggests that they are wombs. Then they become fruits. Then they drop and become water again. Then they harden to terrestrial globes. The indecision about what the tears are is accompanied by a continual change in what they're imagined materially to consist of.

In the context of love, melting also suggested the oozing of the female sexual parts when excited, and Donne introduces this into *The Progresse of the Soule* in the appealing scene where a pet ape falls in love with Adam's fifth daughter, Siphatecia:

> He gazeth on her face with teare-shot eyes,
> And up lifts subtly with his russet pawe
> Her kidskinne apron without feare or awe . . .

> First she was silly'and knew not what he ment:
> That vertue, by his touches, chaft and spent,
> Succeeds an itchie warmth, that melts her quite.[34]

Despite the sportive context, the soft arousal of the lines is a serious achievement, with the word 'russet' finely suggesting the furred gentleness, as well as the colour, of the animal's hand. Melting girls occur also in 'The Indifferent' ('Her whom abundance melts'), where we pick up intonations of a bored, affluent woman luxuriously liquefying; and in 'A Valediction: of my Name in the Window', where the dampness issues from a seduced servant ('thy melted maid'). At the start of 'A Valediction: forbidding Mourning' we have melting lovers:

> As virtuous men passe mildly'away,
>   And whisper to their soules, to goe,
> Whilst some of their sad friends doe say,
>   The breath goes now, and some say, no:

> So let us melt, and make no noise,
>   No teare-floods, nor sigh-tempests move,
> 'Twere prophanation of our joyes
>   To tell the layetie our love.[35]

The queerness of 'melt' here has struck Allen Tate. 'I cannot find in the history of the word,' he reports, 'even as a secondary meaning, the idea of human separation.'[36] In fact, a suitable dictionary meaning is not so hard to find as Tate pretends. Of course, there's no question of 'melt' having anything to do, in these reverent surroundings, with moistening genitals (or, for that matter, with the boring old Elizabethan sexual pun on 'die', which Tate wants to introduce). What is happening is that the lovers' bodies are separating, leaving their souls behind, and Donne asks that the bodies should disappear from the scene (a quite normal seventeenth-century meaning of 'melt') as quietly as if they were dissolving. It's true, though, that 'melt' distils into the stanza connotations of fading warmth and tenderness and soft reluctance which no dictionary equivalent can match, and the word's suffusing richness is an index of its poetic potential for Donne.

Human beings are not the only things that melt. The polar ice caps liquefy too, as in 'Loves Exchange' where the girl's beauty could 'melt both Poles at once', or in the Somerset Epithalamion, where Donne conjectures that if Frances Howard's 'enflaming eyes' or Somerset's 'loving heart' were transported to the frozen North, they would unstop the trans-Arctic trade routes:

> The passage of the West or East would thaw,
> And open wide their easie liquid jawe.[37]

The gargantuan dripping mouth of these lines has come into being not because Donne is really stirred by Frances Howard's eyes or Somerset's amorousness, but because he has found in them a pretext for writing about melting on a global scale. In 'The Calme', the verse letter Donne wrote on the Islands voyage, the ship itself starts to melt:

> As water did in stormes, now pitch runs out,
> As lead, when a fir'd Church becomes one spout.[38]

Donne's simile, applied to the caulking which has oozed from between the ship's planks, is of a church on fire. Its lead roof drips molten around it, turning the whole building into a slow-motion torrent, a tap gushing metal. In what is almost certainly the earliest of Donne's poems to survive, 'The Bracelet', his witty agitation is already centred on the need to melt down twelve gold coins, which are also living beings, in a furnace.[39]

Dropsy, or hydropsy, the morbid condition in which the body becomes swollen with fluid which gathers in the subcutaneous tissues, was of all diseases the most attractive to Donne because it provided a real-life illustration of the body turning to liquid. Hydroptic sufferers appear repeatedly in his poems, and are usually quite arbitrarily dragged in, like the 'spungie hydroptique Dutch' in the elegy 'On his Mistris', or the 'Hydroptique father' in 'The Perfume', or the flooded hold of the ship in 'The Storme', 'With a salt dropsie clog'd'. Like his other imaginative obsessions, hydropsy had to be adapted for spiritual use when Donne went over to religion. The address to God in the sonnet on his wife's death shows us that this adjustment has taken place:

> But though I have found thee, and thou my thirst hast fed,
> A holy thirsty dropsy melts mee yett.[40]

Donne is awash with God, and wants to be more so. Yearning and melting are bonded together in his imagination. God is the ultimate wetness. In *The Second Anniversarie* Donne urges his soul to bloat itself with him until at death it can dive right in:

> Bee thirsty still, and drinke still till thou goe;
> 'Tis th'onely Health, to be Hydroptique so.[41]

Though at a surface level Donne's interests have changed from love to religion, he is still seized by the notion of fluidifying. The liquid images are simply transferred from one context to the other. The gigantic tears which drown the world or overflow farms in the love poems become, by a discreet process of modification, the world-drowning flood of blood and tears in the 'Holy Sonnets'.[42]

Donne's hydroptic fixation also gave him an interest in sponges, since their power to absorb and exude fluid exceeded that of any

other organism. He assimilates parts of the human body to
sponges—'spongie eyes', 'spungie liver'[43]—and is liable to indulge in
imaginative sponge play at the least provocation. In the middle of a
sermon he instructs his congregation to

> . . . take into your memorie, and thoughts, a Spunge that is over-
> filled; If you presse it down with your little finger, the water
> comes out of it; Nay, if you lift it up, there water comes out of it; If
> you remove it out of his place, though to the right hand as well as
> to the left, it poures out water; Nay if it lye still quiet in his place,
> yet it wets the place, and drops out his moisture.[44]

Donne's mind, delightedly dabbling with its oozy toy, is concerned
with religious instruction only in the most tenuous sense, though he
does manage to hitch his sponge to the religion eventually by
explaining that he intended it as an image for a rich man who soaks
up money and 'bleeds' it out when threatened. The connection is
arbitrary: it is sponges Donne wants to talk about, and men don't
have to be rich to give him an excuse for it. 'Every man is but a
spunge,' he announces in another sermon, 'and whether you lay your
right hand or your left upon a full spunge, it will weep.'[45]

Flowing and sucking had, as processes, a similar appeal to melting.
It is noticeable that Donne, though he professes to believe, like other
orthodox Christians, in the immateriality of the soul, habitually talks
about it flowing or being sucked, as if it were liquid. 'Soule into the
soule may flow,' say the souls in 'The Extasie'; and when the soul
leaves the body at death, Donne tells his congregation, God will
'suck it up into glory'. Indeed, the whole created universe will be
'sucked and swallowed into God' in the end.[46] The movement of
water was one of the earliest poetic subjects to claim his attention.
'Recusancy' has an intently detailed account of a stream, and of how
it responds to variations in its channel—flooding over banks in
'flattering eddies', and wrinkling into frowns round branches which
dip to 'kisse' the water surface.[47] It is from the patternings of water
that Donne draws the conclusion, in 'Change', that:

> Change'is the nursery
> Of musicke, joy, life, and eternity.[48]

He was, as we have seen, quite as capable of taking a gloomy view
of change, but the preoccupation with change itself, and with water,
never abated. Rivers and seas figure widely in his writing, not as
geographical locations—he scarcely ever gives them fixed positions
on the globe—but as anonymous masses of fascinatingly amorphous

stuff. He will distinguish discerningly between 'an ebbing back of the main River' and 'a giddy and circular Eddy, in some shallow places of the stream', while conducting a theological debate. He will assert 'The world is a Sea', and then add billowy paragraphs of marine metaphors, full of ebbs and floods and deeps and storms, to justify the idea. Disease, disaster and decrepitude are seen in his sermons as waves and tempests, and the shifts and abysses of our inner consciousness also find watery equivalents. Seas heave and lurch inside man as he walks about: 'a Sea of scruples in his understanding', 'a Sea of transgressions in his conscience', 'a Sea of sinking and swallowing in the sadnesse of spirit'.[49] Seas—vague, unnamed, plumbless—were archetypes of the dissolving and engulfing realities Donne found himself caught among.

Of the moderns, Walter Pater seems closest to Donne on this score—which is odd, for one would hardly expect a Victorian don, living sedately in North Oxford with his sisters and his repressed homosexuality, to have much in common with the Monarch of Wit. But they were both, in their way, deeply frustrated people, and that may have helped them to see reality as something continually being snatched away from them. At all events, the resemblance is unmistakable. Our physical life, Pater affirms, is in perpetual motion—'the passage of the blood, the wasting and repairing of the lenses of the eye, the modification of the tissues of the brain by every ray of light and sound'—and in the inward world of thought and feeling, things look worse still:

> . . . the whirlpool is still more rapid, the flame more eager and devouring. There it is no longer the gradual darkening of the eye and fading of colour from the wall—the movement of the shoreside, where the water flows down indeed, though in apparent rest—but the race of the midstream, a drift of momentary acts of sight and passion and thought. . . . It is with this movement, with the passage and dissolution of impressions, images, sensations, that analysis leaves off—that continual vanishing away, that strange, perpetual weaving and unweaving of ourselves.[50]

Pater alludes, in his epigraph, to Heraclitus, and the Heraclitean doctrine of flux would have been known to Donne, too. But Donne did not need to know Heraclitus in order to feel as he did, any more than Pater needed to know Donne. It is not a question of 'sources' but of kindred visions.

The only proper response to life's destructiveness, Pater argues, is to pursue sensation, and cram as many vital pulsations into our allotted time as we possibly can:

> While all melts under our feet, we may well catch at any exquisite passion, or any contribution to knowledge that seems by a lifted horizon to set the spirit free for a moment, or any stirring of the senses, strange dyes, strange colours, and curious odours, or work of the artist's hands, or the face of one's friend.[51]

This recipe for self-indulgence scandalized Pater's more responsible contemporaries, while earning him the rapturous homage of Oscar Wilde and the aesthetes. Pater himself seems to have been too self-absorbed to foresee the row his doctrine would spark off, and he was shocked and pained by the outcome. The offending passages were omitted from the second edition of *The Renaissance*, lest the book should, as Pater put it, 'mislead some of those young men into whose hands it might fall'.[52] Donne, though, had no one to protect him from the vision of a melting world, or from its consequences, and we can remark in him several of the disturbed symptoms usually associated with Pater's successors in the 1890s. As a young man he became, as we have seen, a dandy and a libertine. Like the aesthetes, he cultivated the art of vivid sensation, and enjoyed outraging the narrow-minded. 'The Comparison' shows both tendencies, as do poems like 'The Indifferent' and 'Loves Usury' which favour sexual promiscuity. The art of epigram, brittle and subversive, appealed to Donne, as it did to Wilde, and he seems to have got a defiant pleasure from being thought unmanly, as the aesthetes often were. He boasts in 'The Perfume' that he is called effeminate because of his habit of wearing scent.

More importantly, we find in both Pater and Donne an emphasis upon the moment, and the need to arrest it. 'Every moment', Pater alerts us, 'some form grows perfect in hand or face'; 'Not to discriminate every moment some passionate attitude in those about us . . . is, on this short day of frost and sun, to sleep before evening.' This impulse to stabilize time by conceiving of it as a series of detachable fragments is a governing factor behind Donne's poetry. He is the poet of momentariness. Unlike other Elizabethans, he does not go in for generalized lyricism. He seizes life in unique instances: 'Now thou hast lov'd me one whole day'; 'And now good morrow to our waking soules'; ''Tis the yeares midnight, and it is the dayes'; 'This is my playes last scene'; 'What if this present were the worlds last night?'.[53] He takes and traps in a poetic line the moment the sun strikes through a curtain, or the moment a tear falls, or the moment

two pairs of lips part—'So, so, breake off this last lamenting kisse.'[54]
The soothing, panting rhythm of the first two words, and the pout of
the lips as one pronounces them, and their incoherence, capture the
smudgy instant when the mind is groping back from passion to
speech.

The wish to stop time becomes explicit in 'A Lecture upon the
Shadow'. Donne makes the wide and dazzling instant of noon an
image for the total openness of fulfilled love. The divergent paths of
lovers, sun, and shadows intersect and lock together. For a moment,
life becomes as clear as a monolith:

> Stand still, and I will read to thee
> A Lecture, Love, in loves philosophy.
> These three houres that we have spent,
> Walking here, two shadowes went
> Along with us, which we our selves produc'd;
> But, now the Sunne is just above our head,
> We doe those shadowes tread;
> And to brave clearnesse all things are reduc'd.
> So whilst our infant loves did grow,
> Disguises did, and shadowes, flow
> From us, and our care; but, now 'tis not so.[55]

The 'flow' of shadows, of dissimulations, pauses. Time holds its
breath. Another instant, and the machine roars into life again. When
the second stanza starts the world disintegrates in doubts and fears.
Unless their love remains at 'this noone', Donne warns the girl, new
shadows will grow around them. Whereas before they strove to hide
their love from the prying world, now they will seek to deceive each
other. When that happens, love will already have died:

> Love is a growing, or full constant light;
> And his first minute, after noone, is night.

But how can she stop it happening? How make the sun stand still, or
immobilize shadows? By casting his poem in these materials, Donne
puts love's collapse beyond question. Love has as much chance of
lasting as twelve o'clock. With the jealous scruples of the second
stanza, 'brave clearnesse' has already vanished. The poem dissolves
itself.

Moments, snatched from time's current, were in this way a source
of fascination and of despair to Donne. When his thoughts turned to
religion, the urgent feeling about particular moments and their
importance persisted. The underlying structure of his imagination

survived the surface shift. While preaching he pounces upon the present instant with pleas and threats and exhortations, as if to cow his congregation and himself into attentiveness. 'Rise now, now *this minute*'; 'this minuute; seek Christ early, now, now.'[56] It was particularly towards the end of a sermon, when the last grains of sand were slipping through the preacher's hour-glass, and bringing time's flight before him, that he would mount these onslaughts, filling his flock with holy terror just as they were about to escape:

> If there be a minute of sand left, (There is not) If there be a minute of patience left, heare me say, This minute that is left, is that eternitie which we speake of; upon this minute dependeth that eternitie; And this minute, God is in this congregation, and puts his eare to every one of your hearts, and hearkens what you will bid him say to your selves: whether he shall blesse you for your acceptation, or curse you for your refusall of him this minute.[57]

The bludgeoning repetitiveness conveys to us not only Donne's desire to intimidate, but also the insecurity from which intimidation springs. The passage's alarmist tactics have, in fact, a quite spurious basis. Christians believe that God knows their thoughts all the time. To tell them that he has his ear to their hearts at some particular moment, is as a piece of news on a level with telling them that their hearts are beating. So there is no crisis. But Donne fabricates one, as he does in his poems, to bring things to a head, and surmount the shapeless drift of day-to-day being.

For all the similarity between Pater's cult of the moment, and Donne's, Donne's attitude to change is more vital than Pater's, and more changeful. Pater's prose envelops change in an atmosphere at once decorous and sombre, like that of a high-class undertaker. He would never have dreamed of laughing at it, as Donne, in the rhymes about woman's inconstancy, often does. Nor could Pater react with any enthusiasm to the endlessly versatile world of matter, which was soon to convert him and his friends to small quantities of calcium and phosphorus. Donne could. Change animated him. When he set his imagination to invent antidotes to change, like eternity, it was as much a product of that animation as when he excited himself about liquefaction and melting.

Nor was conversion to fluid the only material change that interested him. He found transition from fluid to solid, or from either to vapour, equally engaging, and never more so than when he was on the edge of decomposition himself. In the *Devotions* he muses on the vapours which (his doctors tell him) are killing him, and wonders how mere thickened air can be lethal. This leads him to an absorbed passage about extreme material change:

> If this were a violent shaking of the air by thunder or by cannon, in that case the air is condensed above the thickness of water, of water baked into ice, almost petrified, almost made stone, and no wonder that kills.[58]

It's the sort of passage Wordsworth might have remembered when he spoke, in the preface to *Lyrical Ballads*, of poets following the steps of men of science, and carrying sensation into the midst of the objects of science themselves.[59] In fact he obviously doesn't reckon that any English writer has made this breakthrough. But Donne had, and his sentence on the effects of blast is an instance of it. Air clenches into stone; water bakes to ice. Thermal and physical opposites combine. Physics fills with feeling.

Evaporation also intrigued Donne. In 'A Feaver' the whole world vapours with the girl's breath; in 'The Expiration' the lovers' kiss 'suckes two soules, and vapors both away'. Breath and sighs are treated in the poems not as normal pulmonary activities but as types of dissolution—instances of matter flowing into the immaterial. The blood labours to beget spirits; the angel makes its face and wings of air. Both show the same interest in tenuousness and rarefaction. In the sermons Donne speaks of souls which 'evaporate', or which 'breathe and smoak' through the body; or more technically, he remarks on the speed with which mercury evaporates when heated.[60]

The subtle vapours exuded by poisons interested him too. Belief in their potency was encouraged by contemporary drama, where kissing books or skulls, or sniffing nosegays, regularly proves fatal. The 'leprous harlots breath' is imagined in 'The Perfume' as a sort of miasma which kills if inhaled, and Donne's curse in 'The Bracelet' features another of these long-range toxic agents:

> May the next thinge thou stoop'st to reach containe
> Poyson, whose nimble fume rot thy moist braine.[61]

The vapour, threading the nostrils to get at the head's soft centre, has the same uncomfortable intrusiveness as the mouse in *The Progresse of the Soule*, but it is an evaporated mouse, more agile and insidious than a solid one, and so more attractive to Donne's mind. He seems to have kept up-to-date with the literature on poisons, and cites Forestus's *De Venenis* of 1606 in *Pseudo-Martyr*.

Evaporation is also suggested by the shifts between substance and insubstantiality which the poems keep plotting. Souls detach themselves from bodies, and float in the air above them, and return; a 'lovely glorious nothing' takes limbs of flesh; a living girl blends into a dream, or a dream materializes into a living girl. Matter is volatile. This fixation about unfixedness helps to explain why Donne found alchemy so rich as an imaginative idea, despite his suspicion that the whole thing was a cheat. In alchemical thought all matter is permeated with spirit, and interminably transmutable. Melting, rarefying, extracting quintessences and condensing them, were the alchemist's province. These were the experiments his alembic, or retort, was designed for. The alembic's sphere was a mini-world in which the flux of matter which the great world manifested could be trapped. Consequently Donne's imagination couldn't do without it. Further, change inside the alembic was not merely observed but controlled. The agents of devastation became servants; and for Donne, struggling to imprint his ego upon the fluctuating stuff of experience, this made it doubly attractive. The technical language of alchemy emancipated him, too, because it subdued reality, as technical language always does. We find him, in the sermons, rolling the weighty polysyllables over his tongue with alchemical relish, when he is supposed to be talking about such subjects as the forgiveness of sins or the soul's redemption:

> In transmutation of metals, it is not enough to come to a calcination, or a liquefaction of the metall, (that must be done) nor to an Ablution, to sever drosse from pure, nor to a Transmutation, to make it a better metall, but there must be a Fixion, a settling thereof, so that it shall not evaporate into nothing.[62]

On Donne's excursion into alchemy here, Milton Rugoff comments: 'it is curious to find such a passage as this, with its mumbo-jumbo of charlatanism, in a sermon.'[63] But the curious thing is that a critic of Donne should find it curious. Donne's sermons are packed with kindred passages. Nouns ending in -ation are one of his favourite standbys, and generally as here they refer to physical processes ('fluctuation', 'incineration', 'exsiccation', 'inveteration', 'acceleration'), because such words substitute a static, authoritative-sounding formula for a mobile condition. Donne's sermons are just as much concerned with changing states of matter as they are with religion, and that is no surprise, because changing states of matter occupied him all his life, and religion only sometimes.

Allied to his alchemical mania was his curiosity about gold. For many of Donne's contemporaries gold was mysterious and magical stuff, half alive. They believed that it was nurtured and ripened in the earth by the sun, like a vegetable. Paracelsus speaks of the underground veins of metal as 'mineral trees', with their roots in water and their trunks and branches thrusting up towards the surface.[64] All other substances, the alchemists taught, aspire to the condition of gold, which is why base metals turn to gold in the earth through the sun's action. Donne shares this enriching nexus of beliefs. His geology is purely imaginary, but full of feeling. 'The greatest globes of gold', he informs his congregation, 'lye nearest the face and top of the earth, where they have received the best concoction from the heat of the sun.'[65] The less fortunate metals all yearn to achieve this perfection. The subterranean regions seethe with unsatisfied desire. 'Stuffe well dispos'd, and which would faine be gold', fills the earth's 'inward bowels'; but unless it lies near the top where heaven can 'gild it with his eye', it will be perpetually disappointed.[66]

It was not only this vision of the earth's warm, golden entrails that attracted Donne. Gold intrigued him because it was regarded as an indestructible, so infinitely plastic, metal. When it came to shape-changing, nothing was as good as gold. Donne celebrates this aspect in a verse letter to Lady Bedford:

> no fire, nor rust can spend or waste
> One dramme of gold, but what was first shall last,
> Though it bee forc'd in water, earth, salt, aire,
> Expans'd in infinite, none will impaire.[67]

Seen in this way, gold united the maximum of constancy with the maximum of inconstancy. It had an infinitely varied career before it, but would always stay the same. To a man of Donne's imaginative tastes, it was an alluring prospect. Gold, if it knew its luck, could hardly wait to begin. 'If gold could speake, if gold could wish,' he assures us, 'gold would not be content to lie in the darke, in the mine, but would desire to come abroad.'[68] In his poems, he puts gold to work engrossedly: it is immensely important to him as an image source. The property of gold that most stirred him was its expansiveness, as exemplified in the manufacture of gold leaf. A small quantity of gold, he explains in *Biathanatos*, 'by reason of a faithfull tenacity and ductilenesse, will be brought to cover 10,000 times as much as any other Mettall'.[69] The allure of big numbers has, as usual, seduced him, but his exaggeration is scarcely more remarkable than the actual facts about gold–beating, which were already being discussed with interest in antiquity. Pliny, whose estimate Donne would know, reckoned that an ounce of gold would extend to 750 leaves, 3 inches square.[70] Modern commercial practice improves on this, producing 1,200 leaves 3¼ inches square, from an ounce. The minimum thickness attainable depends on variable factors like purity and weather conditions, and isn't certainly known; but an authoritative calculation in Donne's lifetime was that of Mersenne, who put the final area of an ounce of gold at 105 square feet. Donne's phrase, 'Expans'd in infinite', suggests that he liked to feel there was no limit. After two hours' beating gold is already thin enough to let light through—colouring it green or violet, according to the amount of silver present. That Donne found this captivating would be natural enough, even if he weren't predisposed to value versatility in matter. The diffusion of bullion, under the hammer, into a film or mist which a breath could puff away, was an idea his mind kept plunging back to.

In the sermons, perhaps because he felt guilty about the sensuous delight of it, he practically always fits it into a disapproving context. Gold beaten to leaf, he declares, is 'wasted and blown away, and quickly comes to nothing'. It is no good for coining into money. It is associated with sinful inclinations and 'wanton discourses', with 'uselesse and frivolous imaginings' and adultery.[71] For all that, he couldn't stop talking about it. Presumably one of the frivolous imaginings it reminded him of was his own image of the lovers' souls in 'A Valediction: forbidding Mourning':

> Our two soules therefore, which are one,
>   Though I must goe, endure not yet
> A breach, but an expansion,
>   Like gold to ayery thinnesse beate.[72]

The grudging tone of the sermon does not intrude here; the allure of the frail metallic membrane can be undisguisedly indulged. The fact that the gold leaf is likened to souls (Tertullian, incidentally, had also likened the soul's growth to the beating out of gold leaf[73]) involves it and them in tenuous extremes. The leaf threatens to shade off into pure spirit; the souls, no longer quite immaterial, stretch out in a shimmering foil which spans continents. Whether or not this was one of the frivolous imaginings Donne later felt uncomfortable about, he couldn't overcome its basic appeal. The moralistic view of gold-beating his sermons developed was a matter of convenience, and is of passing interest. What remained constant was his need to return, again and again, to this spectacular instance of matter's instability.

Donne's fluid universe, where all matter continually merges into something else, involved a number of casualties, and among these was the concept of human individuality. To suppose that you are the same person two days running is, Donne realizes, scientifically unsound. Further, the notion of love, as a relationship between two individuals, is an illusion, for there are no individuals, only endlessly mobile sequences of temporary states. At times Donne's love poems accept this situation nonchalantly, at times they deplore it, and at times, as in 'The Anniversarie', they defiantly deny it. His fullest poetic working-out of the thesis comes in *The Second Anniversarie*:

> Dost thou love
> Beauty? (And Beauty worthyest is to move)
> Poore couse'ned cose'nor, that she, and that thou,
> Which did begin to love, are neither now.
> You are both fluid, chang'd since yesterday;
> Next day repaires, (but ill) last daies decay.
> Nor are, (although the river keep the name)
> Yesterdaies waters, and to daies the same.
> So flowes her face, and thine eies, neither now
> That saint, nor Pilgrime, which your loving vow
> Concernd, remaines; but whil'st you thinke you bee
> Constant, you'are howrely in inconstancee.[74]

It is calm and rational, but also frightful. The girl with the flowing face, and the man with the flowing eyes, sound like victims of thermal radiation. Montaigne had reached the same conclusion as Donne some years before, pointing out starkly that 'we have no communication with being', because every human nature is in continual alteration and motion, and is apprehendable only as a series of appearances and shadows. 'If perhaps you fix your thought to take its being; it would be even as if one should go about to graspe the water.'[75] Donne would have been naturally drawn to Montaigne. But on the subject of change he could discover in him only what he knew already. Montaigne gives objective formulation to an awareness that permeates all Donne's writing.

Pushed to its limits, the argument Donne pursues would have made *The Second Anniversarie* impossible to write. As a celebration of Elizabeth Drury, it presupposes there was such a person. But if he is right, there wasn't: she vanishes into the universal flux like everyone else. Of course, it might be replied in Donne's defence that his lines in *The Second Anniversarie* refer only to bodies changing, and that a person's spiritual self might be supposed to remain stable. But when he returns to the subject three years later, in the 'Obsequies to the Lord Harrington', he shows that this distinction is untenable, and that spiritual qualities are involved in flux, like the body:

> . . . fluid vertue cannot be look'd on,
> Nor can endure a contemplation.
> As bodies change, and as I do not weare
> Those spirits, humors, blood I did last yeare,
> And, as if on a streame I fixe mine eye,
> That drop, which I look'd on, is presently
> Pusht with more waters from my sight, and gone,
> So in this sea of vertues, can no one
> Bee'insisted on; vertues, as rivers, passe.[76]

True, despite this bewildering state of affairs, Donne does manage to get his Harrington poem written. Indeed, he lamely retracts for the purpose what he has just said about inner flux. Though virtues are as unstable as rivers, yet somehow there 'still remaines that vertuous man there was'—or so Donne conveniently decides. We can hardly blame him. There were sound financial reasons for continuing to write commendatory poems. The deceased Harrington was the brother of Donne's patroness, Lucy Countess of Bedford. Getting his modern theory about the streamy nature of consciousness and the extinction of human identity into a commendatory poem was like getting a jet engine inside a horse. The wonder is that Donne tried it at all; not that, once inside, it blew the poem apart.

Instead of crowing over Donne for his insincerity, we might more usefully consider how his interest in fluid people made him modify the poetic ideas he inherited. The *Songs and Sonnets*, which look like a collection of love lyrics, turn out to be largely about the instability of the self. This appears not only in the mania about inconstancy, but also in the debates about how far love itself accelerates change, causing people to get tangled up in each other and leave bits of themselves behind when they part. It was probably this, as much as his chronic glumness, that prompted Donne to write so often about saying goodbye. The experience of parting from someone you love provides, for the majority of people, the most sudden and convincing proof of the impermanence of what you had taken to be your personality. You have the impression that part of your selfhood has been amputated. Donne's most vivid reproduction of this feeling is 'The Legacie':

When I dyed last, and Deare, I dye
 As often as from thee I goe,
 Though it be an houre agoe,
And Lovers houres be full eternity,
I can remember yet, that I
 Something did say, and something did bestow;
Though I be dead, which sent mee, I should be
Mine owne executor and Legacie.

I heard mee say, Tell her anon,
 That my selfe, that's you, not I,
 Did kill me,'and when I felt mee dye,
I bid mee send my heart, when I was gone;
But I alas could there finde none,
 When I had ripp'd me,' and search'd where hearts should lye;
It kill'd mee'againe that I who still was true,
In life, in my last Will should cozen you.[77]

This is an exasperating poem, of course. It takes ages to sort out the
pronouns: and that's the point. We're made to share the speaker's
disorientation, not just hear about it. The man's puzzlement over his
mislaid personality is mirrored in the puzzling grammar. What
Donne calls 'vertiginous giddiness', and Pater referred to as 'that
strange, perpetual weaving and unweaving of ourselves', is transmit-
ted to us syntactically as we grapple with the sense of the lines. It's
only in relation to Donne's theories about personality that the poem
can be understood. Taken by itself, the claim that a lover dies every
time he leaves his mistress would rightly strike us as footling, but
when we put it in the context of Donne's thought it becomes wholly
serious, indeed undeniable.

   Donne's interest in the fluidity of the self helps to explain his
excitement about reflections, especially reflections in tears. Seeing a
replica of yourself liquefied and coming out of someone else's eye is
an experience likely to readjust your ideas about your stability and
separateness as a person. There's a similar illustration of confused
personality in 'A Valediction: of my Name in the Window', where
Donne tells the girl that when she looks in the pane of glass she will
see her face with his name written across it. The optical mix-up
indicates how love merges people into each other: 'Here you see me,
and I am you.'[78] Love, like time, continually alters the identity, so
lovers can't, strictly, talk about their past experience of love: it
belonged to someone else:

He is starke mad, who ever sayes,
That he hath been in love an houre.[79]

On the other hand, Donne himself announces, in 'The Anniversarie', that he has been in love a year. The contradiction is typical. His
desire for something stable is born of and struggles with his sense of
instability.

Mutual contradictoriness of this type is endemic to the *Songs and
Sonnets*, and has worried some critics. Donne, they protest, changes
his opinions from poem to poem. He argues, for instance, in 'The
Exstasie' that bodily contact is necessary in love, and he argues with
equal force in 'A Valediction: forbidding Mourning' that it is not.
His poems are untrustworthy in tone: flippant one moment, tender
the next. 'Aire and Angels', in which the girl is spoken of with
transfiguring wonder, ends up with a cheap crack about the inferi-
ority of woman's love to man's. 'The Relique', with its miracle
women and 'bracelet of bright haire about the bone', fits in a
grumble about female promiscuity:

graves have learn'd that woman-head
To be to more then one a Bed.[80]

Critics disturbed by such inconsistency have tried to surmount it by
arranging the poems in chronological order, with the 'cynical' ones
coming early and the 'serious' ones later. These arrangements are
fanciful: there is no evidence to show when Donne wrote the majority of his poems. Besides, the assumption that he made a gradual
progression in his attitudes runs counter to what Donne himself
implies about his changeability.

An alternative critical procedure for knocking Donne's poems
into shape has been to deduce from them a general statement about
love, sufficiently vague to encompass the variety of viewpoints they
contain. D. L. Peterson favours this course, and sums up Donne's
philosophy for us:

His own position seems to be that although the appetite for sex
may assume the proportions of lust, and thus deprive man of his
freedom. . . . it need not necessarily do so. For the man who is
able to maintain his sense of proportion, and thus maintain his
freedom, it may remain a source of pleasure.[81]

The shattering banality of this should at least deter future enquirers
from adopting Mr. Peterson's method. If Donne's poems could
really be summarized along the lines he suggests, there would clearly

be no point in reading them. In fact their inner inconsistencies and dubieties of tone make them resistant to summaries of any kind, and that is why they are valuable. They do not take up a 'position'. They refuse to be subsumed. They remain receptive to what is divergent, refractory and uncodifiable in thought and feeling. They show us, as A. J. Smith has put it, that the difference between a man's several experiences of love is part of his understanding of love; and that loving means a variety of things, and none of them exclusively.[82] Their flickering, moody poetic voice, and their brusque changes of tone, transmit to us, through art, those fallibilities in experience which art characteristically subdues. The discordant elements within the same moment of consciousness are admitted, not waived. This achievement is as much rhythmic as verbal. Donne's rhythms give a sense of metrical norms being underscored or overridden, in order to cope with the stresses of the instant. A similar adjustment to the exigencies of circumstance is suggested by his multiple stanza forms—he uses forty-six different forms in all, and only two of them more than once. Every new endeavour required a new shape.

In the poems, as in everyone's everyday life, a common source of instability is the mutually eroding effect of thought and feeling. Sentimental critics dislike the thoughtful component in Donne, and sometimes pretend it isn't there. C. S. Lewis, for instance, says of 'A Feaver' (one of the two Donne poems he finds tolerable), that it is 'a single jet of music and feeling'. In fact, no one could say this who hadn't switched off after reading the poem's first half-line. 'Oh doe not die' does come across as a cry from the heart, but after that, as we have seen, Donne's brain takes over and sets off on its abstruse speculations. By the time he's half-way through, he has become sufficiently abstracted to refer to the girl in the third person ('And yet she cannot wast by this . . .'). This pattern of an initial burst of emotion, which thought breaks down, is frequent. 'The Expiration' is another example. After the achingly tender start ('So, so, breake off this last lamenting kisse'), thought comes to the rescue with its steadying calculations. By the last line, the abyss of feeling has been left safely behind, and the expression has composed itself into neat antithesis ('Being double dead, going, and bidding, goe'). Of course, there's no hard and fast rule about it. We can easily find poems that move the other way. In 'Image and Dream', for instance, feeling overthrows thought. Donne, in the end, chooses heart not head:

> Fill'd with her love, may I be rather grown
> Mad with much heart, then ideott with none.[83]

What all three examples have is mobility. Donne's poems will not
stay still, or stay shut. They open themselves to other ideas and
experiences than the ones they start with, so we get the impression
that they are being worked on while we read them. They have a
recent, experimental feel, like a stretch of new road, where you have
to edge past tar boilers and gravel lorries and men leaning on spades.
Effort is still in the air, and the surface is half fluid.

To the generation of English writers and critics after the First
World War, it was this unfixedness of Donne's poems that seemed
appealing. The young Eliot selected for praise Donne's 'fidelity to
emotion as he finds it; his recognition of the complexity of feeling
and its rapid alterations and antitheses'.[84] Aldous Huxley likewise
found psychological realism the 'important and original quality' of
Donne's work;[85] and Virginia Woolf admired Donne's 'determination to record not the likenesses which go to compose a rounded and
seemly whole, but the inconsistencies that break up semblances, the
power to make us feel the different emotions of love and hate and
laughter at the same time'.[86] This critical emphasis did not carry with
it a realization of the extent to which mobility was important in
Donne's thought about the world and himself. But it was right and
perceptive for all that. Donne's own way of talking about his poetry,
on the rare occasions when he talked about it at all, also suggests that
he regarded it as a quick, untrustworthy thing reflecting the passing
moment. He refers to poems which he encloses in letters, as 'rags' or
'flashes' or 'evaporations'.[87] Even when, in a sermon, he discusses
metrical composition more generally, he retains a view of poems as
unstable processes. 'The whole frame of the Poem', he asserts, 'is a
beating out of a piece of gold, but the last clause is as the impression
of the stamp, and that is it that makes it currant.'[88] The emphasis on
the ending looks a bit exaggerated here, especially if applied
wholesale to poetry, but it fits in well enough with Donne's own
insistent modification and development of his material throughout a
poem, and with the sense he gives us that it would be unwise to
conclude anything about it until it's concluded.

Or when it's concluded, come to that. For the conflicts of attitude
within Donne's poems relate to irresolvable confusions within the
human personality, and though we can often recognize vividly
enough the tangle Donne is in, we cannot simplify matters (as we
sometimes can in George Herbert) by identifying one side of the
poem as the voice of error and the other as the voice of truth. As an
instance of these immitigably crossed cross-purposes in Donne we
might take 'The Apparition':

When by thy scorne, O murdresse, I am dead,
And that thou thinkst thee free
From all solicitation from mee,
Then shall my ghost come to thy bed,
And thee, fain'd vestall, in worse armes shall see;
Then thy sicke taper will begin to winke,
And he, whose thou art then, being ty'rd before,
Will, if thou stirre, or pinch to wake him, thinke
    Thou call'st for more,
And in false sleepe will from thee shrinke,
And then poore Aspen wretch, neglected thou
Bath'd in a cold quicksilver sweat wilt lye
    A veryer ghost then I;
What I will say, I will not tell thee now,
Lest that preserve thee;'and since my love is spent,
I'had rather thou shouldst painfully repent,
Then by my threatnings rest still innocent.[89]

This has been nominated as one of Donne's more 'Petrarchan' poems, on the grounds that the scorned lover calling his lady a murderess and threatening revenge was a role which imitators of Petrarch liked to adopt. Serafino even has a poem in which he warns the lady that he will haunt her when dead, and make her curse the day she refused to love him.[90] 'The Apparition' is wholly different though, not only because of its drama and wit, but also because of its inconsistency. At the start Donne is professedly dying of unrequited love; yet at the end he tells the girl that he is out of love, and would rather she suffered, after his death, than that she should grant him her love and save his life. How can he be dying of love, and out of love? Does he love her, or doesn't he? Does he pretend he's still in love, and dying of it, to make her ashamed? Or to justify his hatred, which he can do only by making out that she has damaged him irreparably? Or is he really still in love with her; and does he say he's not because he's in a rage and wants to pay her out? Or because, being the cruellest thing he can say, it might just frighten her into loving him in return? These different possibilities don't exhaust the alternatives that the poem suggests, but they're enough to indicate the confused motives underlying it.

Further, the poem doesn't sort them out into alternatives. It implies them all at once, reminding us that only in a simplified account of the human psyche do contradictory feelings like love and hate have to be regarded as contradictory. Hawthorne pertinently ventures in *The Scarlet Letter*:

It is a curious subject of observation and enquiry, whether hatred and love be not the same thing at bottom. Each, in its utmost development, supposes a high degree of intimacy and heart-knowledge; each renders one individual dependent for the food of his affections and spiritual life upon another; each leaves the passionate lover, or the no less passionate hater, forlorn and desolate by the withdrawal of his object. Philosophically considered, therefore, the two passions seem essentially the same.[91]

Though more pedestrian, this breaks the same ground as 'The Apparition'. Even in death, Donne can't imagine not pursuing the girl. There's no telling whether the poem's scabrous, clever tone is adopted as a weapon to hurt her, or as a shield to hide his own incoherent feelings. Sarcasm and jocularity serve either purpose, or both, in life, and our not being able to guess which is uppermost is no more than we should expect from our daily observation.

Though 'The Apparition' is an extreme example, it is not singular. Complexity of attitude is the usual thing in Donne, and usually arises from changes or contradictions within the poem. The complexities are not riddles to be solved, but natural and unresolvable, like living. They keep us at bay, as people do, and, as with people, there is no chance of cracking them open to find clear meanings inside. We have to surmise, and have nothing to go on but our own experience. Trying to understand them, we're obliged to think our way down into our own divisive impulses, and that makes the poems educative, as 'The Apparition' is, or (to take a similar instance) as 'Twicknam Garden' is, where the speaker calls himself a 'selfe traytor' for bringing love into the garden, yet prays that he shall not 'leave loving'.[92]

These self-contradictions seemingly go unnoticed by the speaker, but there are others where he ostentatiously rejects (or seems to) all that he has been saying. Take 'Womans Constancy':

> Now thou hast lov'd me one whole day,
> To morrow when thou leav'st, what wilt thou say?
> Wilt thou then Antedate some new made vow?
>   Or say that now
> We are not just those persons, which we were?
> Or, that oathes made in reverentiall feare
> Of Love, and his wrath, any may forsweare?
> Or, as true deaths, true maryages untie,
> So lovers contracts, images of those,
> Binde but till sleep, deaths image, them unloose?
>   Or, your owne end to Justifie,

> For having purpos'd change, and falsehood; you
> Can have no way but falsehood to be true?
> Vaine lunatique, against these scapes I could
>   Dispute, and conquer, if I would,
>   Which I abstaine to doe,
> For by to morrow, I may thinke so too.[93]

Commenting on this poem, Wilbur Sanders says flatly that the girl is a 'whore',[94] but it is not a poem that will permit flatness. Is she, even, unfaithful? The accusation that she will leave him on the morrow may be quite groundless—just a product of the speaker's own feelings of insecurity and antagonism. His warning that he may leave her may come down to insecurity, too. He cautions her that he can't be taken for granted, because he's afraid to let her see how deeply involved he is. Or, to take it another way, the speaker's whole outburst may be a cover for his own infidelity. He, not the girl, may intend to leave on the morrow. It is after all he, not the girl, who makes up the arguments for inconstancy. His attack on the girl may simply be a way of getting rid of her, and appearing self-righteous at the same time. Not only don't we need to choose between these readings, we can't. To decide, we'd need to know more about the man and the girl, and neither exists. All we have is a voice, speaking a poem, in which insecurity and inconstancy insecurely and inconstantly mingle. It is unresolved and alive, not dead and settled. The peculiar vacillation the poem exhibits is, incidentally, quite natural to Donne. As we have seen, he subscribed to the belief in personal flux ('We are not just those persons, which we were'), but also strove, in poems like 'The Anniversarie', to deny it. These impulses could only be reconciled in a poem which simultaneously accepted and denounced the belief, as 'Womans Constancy' does.

The change we come to at the end of 'A Valediction: of my Name in the Window' is different again, for it suddenly shrugs off the poem we have been reading, disowning it as mere pretence. The little skeleton cut in the glass, and the idea that it will have to defend Donne's interests against rivals while he is away—in fact, the whole fabric of the poem—is, the speaker submits, nonsense:

>   But glasse, and lines must bee,
> No meanes our firme substantiall love to keepe;
>   Neere death inflicts this lethargie,
>   And this I murmure in my sleepe;
> Impute this idle talke, to that I goe,
>   For dying men talke often so.[95]

Donne manages dramatic tone sensitizingly here. The stanza returns us to reality and firm substantial love. The brusque recantation surmounts fears. Yet fears have been voiced and will not go away. Trying to ignore them only makes their menace clearer. As the final stanza counteracts the rest of the poem, so the rest of the poem counteracts the final stanza, making its briskness seem blustering. And the speaker limps out on a note of apology which does nothing to increase our confidence in his confidence. Insecurity, Donne shows, is not the opposite of security but its shadow.

The aim of this chapter has been to show that change was an idea fraught with imaginative and intellectual potential for Donne. Though, like other men of his age, he was liable to register gloom or exasperation when confronted with change, its true role was that of an ally. It facilitated his interpretation of the world and himself, and stimulated his creativity. It supplied him with a ruling interest broad and multiform enough to embrace and unite all the areas of reality in which his mind operated. It helped to determine the theological issues that would occupy him, and the dogmatic stand he would take up on them, just as it determined the themes and manner of the *Songs and Sonnets* and the diversity of attitudes which the collection contains. In devious but understandable ways it also affected his moral and social concerns. His insistence, for example, that everyone should get a job relates to his passion for fixedness, which stems directly from his obsession about change, and both relate, in turn, to his own aimlessness and inconsistency, and to his excitement about the idea that God changed nothing into something when he created the world. This last idea does not, admittedly, connect in any obvious way with the need for full employment, but Donne spells out the connection repeatedly, arguing that to change yourself into something, by getting a job, is the only fit recompense to God for changing you into something when you were nothing. The argument illustrates the irrational but tenacious way in which moral convictions find support in imaginative fancies.

Change, it seems probable, would not have been so central to Donne's thinking if he had not been intrigued by his own changeability. The motto on the miniature, painted at eighteen, indicates that this was already the element he singled out when he contemplated himself, and the careful ambiguity of the motto suggests the complexity of his reaction to it. It continued to be the focus of his self-scrutiny throughout his life. The Donne who confessed to his congregation 'I am not all here' was the same as the Donne who wrote the *Songs and Sonnets*, and was giving evidence of the same redeeming ability to remain unabsorbed by any one thought or attitude that we find in the poems. Their changeable, contradictory voice was ultimately a function of his personal character. It does not belong to the poetic surface, or to the manipulation of rhetorical figures, but to the man.

7

Death

Nor dread nor hope attend
A dying animal;
A man awaits his end
Dreading and hoping all . . .
Man has created death.[1]

Being man-made, death is infinitely various. Each individual invents
his own idea of it, and the shapes he invests it in reveal the scope and
structure of his imagination. It is a creative exercise which no one
escapes, except infants who die before they can talk or think, like
animals. Donne was notoriously, along with Webster and other
Jacobeans, 'much possessed by death',[2] but his tastes in death were
specialized, and many of the more popular deaths available in his day
made little or no appeal to him. He did not warm, for instance, to
Death as World Champion, though the figure had good Classical
antecedents and was celebrated by Sir Walter Raleigh in a famous
passage from the *History of the World*:

> O eloquent, just and mighty Death! whom none could advise,
> thou hast persuaded; what none hath dared, thou has done; and
> whom all the world hath flattered, thou only hast cast out of the
> world and despised: thou hast drawn together all the far stretched
> greatness, all the pride, cruelty and ambition of man, and covered
> it over with these two narrow words, Hic iacet.[3]

This splendid encomium is, of course, irrational, for the figure
addressed does not exist. But human beings naturally like to feel that
those more successful than themselves are going to be punished, and
in the grip of this desire they will seize on anything, even death, as a
popular hero. Raleigh's attitude was widely fancied in the seventeeth
century, and still has adherents.

Donne, on the other hand, preferred to think of ways in which
death could be minimized. His sonnet to death might almost be a
reply to Raleigh:

Death be not proud, though some have called thee
Mighty and dreadfull, for, thou art no soe,
For, those, whom thou think'st, thou dost overthrow,
Die not, poore death, nor yet canst thou kill mee;
From rest and sleepe, which but thy pictures bee,
Much pleasure, then from thee, much more must flow,
And soonest our best men with thee doe goe,
Rest of their bones, and soules deliverie.
Thou art slave to Fate, chance, kings, and desperate men,
And dost with poyson, warre, and sicknesse dwell,
And poppie, or charmes can make us sleepe as well,
And better then thy stroake; why swell'st thou then?
One short sleepe past, wee wake eternally,
And death shall be no more, Death thou shalt die.[4]

It is part of the strength of this poem that its argument is so weak. Its
ill-assorted reasons tumble out in no recognizable order, reflecting
inner disarray. The speaker is plainly trying to convince himself, and
failing so badly that he cannot even decide whether he wants to say
sleep is better than death or vice versa. At first, on the flimsiest
grounds, he says death 'must' be better than sleep; then he decides
that sleep is better than death. The last four words of the sonnet,
which are meant to crown the edifice, actually topple it. After
insisting from the start that death is nothing to be afraid of, the
speaker can hardly, at the end, use death as a threat ('thou shalt die')
without ludicrously betraying himself. He stamps his foot with fine
dramatic conclusiveness, and plummets straight through a trapdoor.
It spoils the act, but improves the poem, for it shows how little its
reasonings have impinged on the speaker's basic fears. Also, it saves
us from having to read the casuistry of the preceding lines as self-
assurance.

The sonnet gives us an inkling of the anxiety from which Donne's
elaborate attempts to discredit and belittle death sprang. But we
should know about the anxiety even without the sonnet, because in
'A Hymne to God the Father' Donne voices it directly:

I have a sinne of feare, that when I have spunne
My last thred, I shall perish on the shore.[5]

The belief that at death you just stop squares so well with the
ascertainable facts that there can be no human being, however
devout, to whom it has not at some time occurred. Probably it has
always been the underlying, unhopeful assumption of the majority
of mankind, despite the exhortations of clerics. Among Classical

proponents of the idea eagerly read by Donne's contemporaries was
Seneca, who relates how he used to comfort himself, during recurrent attacks of asthma, with cheerful and courageous reflections
upon the nothingness of death. Being dead, Seneca told himself,
would be precisely the same as not being born. 'Death is just not
being. What this is like I know already. It will be the same after me as
it was before me.'[6] A person's response to this doctrine will depend
largely on his self-importance, or lack of it. You have to be in a fairly
advanced state of egotism in order to regard the extinction of your
personal identity as an unthinkable, or even a regrettable, occurrence. Donne's ego was, as we have seen, a powerful operative, and
was made more so by the continuous sense of personal dissolution
which it had to combat. Accordingly the prospect of annihilation,
which Seneca regards with equanimity, was highly antipathetic to
Donne. His aim, when he writes about death, is to make it more
active and positive than life, and so negate its deathliness.

One of the things, indeed, which makes the argument of 'Death be
not proud' look bogus is its equation of death with repose ('rest and
sleepe'), for this is a most un-Donnean emphasis. Here, too, he was
singular. The gentle fiction that the dead are sleeping appealed
widely to his contemporaries. It became a deeply ingrained commonplace—a substitute, as it were, for a National Health Service, in
an age of total medical ineptitude. Macbeth, among others, sub-
scribes to it, in suitably world-weary accents:

> Duncan is in his grave;
> After life's fitful fever he sleeps well;
> Treason has done his worst; nor steel, nor poison,
> Malice domestic, foreign levy, nothing,
> Can touch him further.

In fact orthodox Christian teaching was that the souls of the dead did
not stay in the grave but went instantly to commence their eternal
punishment or reward. Christ's story of Dives and Lazarus was
taken as proof of this, for when Lazarus dies he is carried by angels
into Abraham's bosom, and sees Dives already in hell. So there is no
repose in death, and Christian poets could pretend there was only by
wilful amnesia. Not that that stopped them indulging the fancy: its
instinctive seemliness outweighed Christian technicalities.

But it had no charms for Donne. He did not desire a general
anaesthetic. His mind shied away from the idea of slipping peacefully
into oblivion. He told his friend Sir Henry Goodyer as much, in a
letter:

I would not that death should take me asleep. I would not have him merely seize me, and only declare me to be dead, but win me, and overcome me. When I must shipwreck, I would do it in a sea, where mine impotency might have some excuse; not in a sullen weedy lake, where I could not have so much as exercise for my swimming.[7]

Death, so envisaged, becomes a bracing opportunity for athletic exertion. The struggle and drama of a good death-bed attract Donne because they will concentrate his energies. Without them death would hardly be worth dying. He finds death challenging, not mournful—and that, too, distinguishes his image of it from commonplace ideas. Death in Donne is almost never sad, and never simply sad. He was incapable of the funereal note, as evolved by the Victorians and ourselves. Its decorous reticences would have struck him as squeamish, and its snuffling resignation as craven. Preaching to commemorate his friend Lady Danvers, George Herbert's mother, Donne went out of his way to remind his hearers of what was currently happening to Lady Danvers's corpse: 'That body upon which you tread now, That body . . . now, whilst I speake, is mouldring, and crumbling into lesse, and lesse dust, and so hath some motion, though no life.'[8] Donne's witty paradox—that Lady Danvers is moving about during her own memorial service; that she is, indeed, the most mobile member of the congregation, since she is moving with every particle of her person—is not, one imagines, an aspect of the affair her relatives would much wish to contemplate. But Donne does. For him it is more attractive than pretending Lady Danvers is asleep, because it activates death, and rescues it from simple, inert deadness.

In Donne's love poems death intrudes to an extent which, with any other poet, would seem debilitating. Of the fifty-four *Songs and Sonnets*, thirty-two—well over half—find some means of fitting death in. Donne dies, or the girl dies, or they both die. When he says farewell to her, he feels the seas of death, which he had written to Goodyer about, waiting to engulf him. In other poems he is a ghost, or an anatomical specimen, or an exhumed corpse. What is remarkable is how active and influential he remains, although dead. That death actually kills you is the one fact about it he seems not able to grasp. And this is not simply because he is a Christian poet and believes in immortality; because, as we have seen, other Christian poets who believed in immortality could and frequently did write about death as if it were as peaceful as sleeping. With Donne, on the

other hand, the dead walk about and talk. Dying is something they
do frequently, as 'The Legacie' tells us:

> When I dyed last, and Deare, I dye
> As often as from thee I goe . . .

Even when death is not impacted into life, like this, Donne imagines
himself in death still the centre of attention, more important to the
living, and more influential with them, than the living. They will
pray to him, and learn what love really is from him. Alternatively his
dissected corpse will spread noxious influence among them, and
wipe them out like an epidemic, as in 'The Dampe':

> When I am dead, and Doctors know not why,
>   And my friends curiositie
> Will have me cut up to survay each part,
> When they shall finde your Picture in my heart,
>   You thinke a sodaine dampe of love
>   Will thorough all their senses move,
> And worke on them as mee, and so preferre
> Your murder, to the name of Massacre.[9]

The endeavour is, persistently, to treat death as a form of life, or to
vivify it by giving it an active role in poems which are passionately
concerned with living. What we sense, in such poems, is a dread of
yielding to the idea that after death one will simply be forgotten, and
that the life of other people will go on exactly as before. That
generous renunciation is unacceptable because it is self-obliterating,
whereas Donne nurses the egocentric delusion that when he dies it
will be the world, not he, that will perish. 'I'll undo / The world by
dying,' as he put it in 'The Will'.[10]

Death preponderates in Donne's religious poems even more markedly than in his love poems. For Donne to think of God is to think
of death: that alone will bring him to God. To remain cherishingly
sensitive to God as a companion through life, as George Herbert
does, is foreign to Donne. His God lives in death's kingdom, and his
worship of God entails worship of Death. One reason for his death-
craving is that death will put an end to suspense. Dead, he will at last
know whether or not he is saved. Though terrified by the Last
Judgement, he is also impatient for it:

> At the round earths imagin'd corners, blow
> Your trumpets, Angells . . .[11]

Death is definite; life, perplexed. Death also attracts because it is a

crisis. Its insertion into poems, secular or divine, can help to make
them urgent and momentous as the self-dramatizing Donne needs
them to be. Envyingly, and typically, he wants to step into, and take
command of, the most momentous death scene in human history:

> Spit in my face yee Jewes, and pierce my side,
> Buffet, and scoffe, scourge, and crucifie mee . . .[12]

Death is used as an appeal for notice. We are gripped because Donne
is, or says he is, poised on the brink of eternity:

> O my blacke Soule! now thou art summoned
> By sicknesse, deaths herald, and champion . . .

or:

> This is my playes last scene, here heavens appoint
> My pilgrimages last mile; and my race
> Idly, yet quickly runne, hath this last pace,
> My spans last inch, my minutes latest point . . .[13]

The speaker's reiterated announcement that this is our very last
chance of hearing him, blackmails us into attentiveness, like the
words of a man teetering on a tenth-storey window ledge.

Donne refused, then, to think of death as the end of life. It was more
dynamic than life in his version, and more flamboyant. It was also
rich in curiosities, which he loved to dwell on because they made
death seem lively and intriguing, like a chamber of horrors, or some
specially exotic department of knowledge. 'There is scarce anything
that hath not killed somebody,' he remarks relishingly in the *Devotions*, 'a pin, a comb, a hair pulled, hath gangrened and killed.'[14] Men
have even been known to laugh themselves to death, he adds. In an
earlier poem he had fleshed out this little irony with some gruesome
details, imagining a man with an incurable abscess in his chest who
manages to burst it in a fit of hilarity and then, just as he is con-
gratulating himself on his self-administered cure, is caught out by
the flabby coating of the abscess coming up into his throat and
strangling him.[15] The poems, especially the epicedes and obsequies,
invent wonderful adventures for people after they are dead. They
levitate with dizzying speed: they fly straight through the sun; they
turn into gold underground. Death liberates and magically transforms them. Lady Markham, for instance, in the elegy Donne wrote
about her, dramatically improves in physique after her decease:

> . . . as the tide doth wash the slimie beach,
> And leaves embroderd workes upon the sand,
> So is her flesh refin'd by deaths cold hand.[16]

It is one of those occasions when we can see Donne's subtle associative mechanisms knitting up disparate experiences in a daringly undecorous but wholly naïve and shareable way. The touch of a corpse, and the corrugations which you feel under your bare feet walking on the seashore, are alike in their coldly surprising hardness, but so remote in every other respect, that only a mind intent on fitting its piecemeal sensations into a purposeful design, and on finding new faces for death, would catch at the likeness. Even death's ghastliest forms yield to Donne's enlivening treatment. *The Second Anniversarie* incorporates a fascinated account of the convulsive reflex actions observable in the body of a beheaded man immediately after execution. Although the victim's head has been completely severed, and blood is spouting from it and the trunk, Donne observes,

> His eies will twinckle, and his tongue will roll,
> As though he beckned, and cal'd backe his Soul,
> He graspes his hands, and he puls up his feet,
> And seemes to reach, and to step forth to meet
> His soule.[17]

As with Lady Danvers's decomposition, and his own fancied swimming match with death in the Goodyer letter, it is activity, rather than repose, that Donne's imagination drives him to associate death with. The dead and the dying are more spectacularly alive than the living.

The most active death is self-inflicted. It alone allows its victim the glamour and triumph of being a killer. Donne's suicidal tendencies were of long standing. He read and argued keenly about the sociology of suicide, inspecting both case histories and theoretical works. His fifth Paradox puts forward the contention 'That all things kill themselves', and he composed, probably in 1608, the first English defence of suicide to be published (though that was not till after his death), called *Biathanatos. A declaration of that paradoxe, or thesis, that Self-homicide is not so Naturally Sinne, that it may never be otherwise*. Donne's erudite and meticulous survey covers suicide in the animal world as well as in pre- and post-Christian societies. He concludes that its appeal is universal: 'in all ages, in all places, upon all

occasions, men of all conditions have affected it, and inclined to it.'
To illustrate the trivial occasions men will use as an excuse for
suicide, and also the elevated personages who have attempted it, he
cites, in his Preface, the case of the famous contemporary theologian
Theodore Beza, and leads up, from that, to his own confession:

> Beza . . . only for the anguish of a Scurffe, which over-ranne his
> head . . . had once drown'd himselfe from the Millers bridge in
> Paris, if his uncle by chance had not then come that way; I have
> often such a sickely inclination. And, whether it be, because I had
> my first breeding and conversation with men of a suppressed and
> afflicted Religion, accustomed to the despite of death, and hungry
> of imagin'd Martyrdome; Or that the common Enemie find that
> doore worst locked against him in mee, Or that there be a perplex-
> itie and flexibility in the docrine it selfe; Or because my Con-
> science ever assures me, that no rebellious grudging at Gods gifts,
> nor other sinfull concurrence accompanies these thoughts in me,
> or that a brave scorn, or that a faint cowardliness beget it, when-
> soever any affliction assailes me, mee thinkes I have the keyes of
> my prison in mine owne hand, and no remedy presents it selfe so
> soone to my heart, as mine own sword.[18]

Donne's treatise, like Hamlet's 'To be or not to be', was a sign of the
times. Men were starting to question the outright condemnation of
suicide, which traditionalists had for centuries upheld. The right to
cut your own throat may not seem a particularly liberating goal to
contend for, but it was correctly seen as part of the struggle between
authoritarianism and the individual reason which was to convulse
the seventeenth century. If we seek, among the slippery turns of
Donne's thought, for the emotional heart of *Biathanatos*, we find it
in his defiance of law and his assertion of individual autonomy. He
flouts the 'sophisticate inculcatings' of legalists with the insistence
that

> No law is so primary and simple, but it fore-imagines a reason
> upon which it was founded: and scarce any reason is so constant,
> but that circumstances alter it. In which case a private man is
> Emperor of himselfe. . . . And he whose conscience well tempred
> and dispassion'd, assures him that the reason of selfe-preservation
> ceases in him, may also presume that the law ceases too, and may
> doe that which otherwise were against the law.[19]

Decent citizens, in Donne's day as in ours, would be bound to find
this contention appalling. If people are free to pick and choose

which laws they obey, society will collapse in chaos. The anti-suicide case, promulgated by authoritarians, always laid stress on the individual's duty to the state, usually citing Aristotle's opinion, from the *Nicomachean Ethics*, that suicide involves the citizen in neglect of his obligation to the commonwealth. This argument, though satisfying to philosophers, falls short of entire conviction, however. The average suicide is likely to feel that he is more concerned in the matter than the state, and that if he can spare his life, which is the only one he has, then the state, which has many replacements available, may well do without it too.

Since the state's reasoning was not unassailable, legislative measures had to be introduced to render it more persuasive. In Christian Europe, until the nineteenth century, it was common for failed suicides to be executed, and for the bodies of successful suicides to be subjected to various types of public mutilation, and their estates confiscated. English suicides were customarily dragged through the streets, with a stake driven through them, and buried without ceremony at crossroads.[20] Civic anxiety over suicide is understandable, since if the practice became popular it might deplete supplies of labour and revenue. But the Church's antagonism is less easy to account for. Given Christianity's promise of an afterlife freed from the inconveniences of our present existence, suicide might well seem the only reasonable course for the true believer. Early Christians were, in fact, not slow to perceive this, and it was their enthusiasm in doing away with themselves that eventually led the Church to tighten up its regulations. The sect of the Donatists, which had deliberately courted martyrdom, was severely reprehended by St. Augustine. Suicide, he affirmed, was 'an abominable and damnable crime': it was cowardly, it abrogated the sixth commandment, and it showed that you despaired of God's mercy.[21] Aquinas amplified St. Augustine's deterrent arguments and arranged them in a tidy list for the convenience of would-be suicides.[22] For centuries this remained the authoritative statement of the Church's view.

Donne, in *Biathanatos*, attacks these entrenched insensibilities with feverish and sometimes hysterical vigour. His trailing, jumbled sentences, now bafflingly elliptical, now sardonically explicit, retain, among all the jeering and wit, a heated, breathless air, fiercely compassionate. It is the lack of pity, and the bland assumption of superior knowledge, which infuriate him in the Church's doctrine. How can the Church know that suicides despair of God's mercy? How can it presume to say that they are impenitent, and so damned? 'To presume impenitence, because you were not by, and heard it, is an usurpation,' Donne protests.[23] On the surface, his complaint seems reasonable enough, for many suicides have left notes expressing penitence and imploring God's mercy. When Sir Walter Raleigh stabbed himself (unsuccessfully) in the Tower in 1603, he first composed a letter pointing out that it was a 'disputable question' whether suicides died in despair. 'God forgive me' were the last words in Haydon's diary, before he put a bullet through his head.[24] On the other hand the Church might cogently urge that if the suicide were truly penitent he would not proceed to kill himself. Doubt could arise only where the method of self-destruction chosen allowed time for repentance subsequent to the fatal act. Repentant suicide notes must be written after committing suicide in order to qualify. Donne was perfectly aware of these sophistications, but the point he strives to get across is that no one has a right to decide what goes on in someone else's brain. He defends the individual consciousness against the presumption of dictatorial institutions, and that is what we should expect from a poet so attuned to the complexities of the inner self. One thing, he wryly adds, we can be sure of—if the test of true penitence is that we don't keep doing the act we repent of again and again, as St. Clement says, then suicides have a good case for being considered penitent.[25]

Not only, Donne persists, may the suicide's state of mind be blameless, he may kill himself 'by God's insinuation and concurrence'.[26] It was usual for biblical commentators to get round the awkward fact of Samson's suicide by arguing that he was a special case, since he had done it at God's bidding. But if Samson, Donne demands, why not others? If our reason tells us to commit suicide, and if we accept the Church's teaching that reason represents God's voice in man, then God's ultimate responsibility for suicides seems unquestionable. In his sympathy for suicides he subjects the history and traditions of Christendom to a riotous investigation. He displays a Sterne-like taste for ecclesiastical controversies, as, for instance, the great question of whether or not an unborn child could be properly baptized, provided it had a hand or foot protruding from its mother's body to receive the sacrament. With sublime effrontery he treats Christian martyrdom as if it were quite evidently just a manifestation of the death-wish which, before Christianity came along, had to find less illustrious but precisely comparable outlets in pagan rites such as the communal suicide of a man's wives and servants at his funeral. When he embarks on an account of the suicidal excesses of the early martyrs, his fascination with bizarre and spectacular modes of death mingles with excitement at the lavish scale of the killings.

Whole legions offered themselves to the sword; executioners dropped from exhaustion; zealots contended to be the first to die, as if to
kill themselves were 'their daily sport'; 'many were baptized only
because they would be burnt, and children taught to vexe and
provoke Executioners, that they might be thrown into the fire'.[27]
What prompted Donne to launch into this blood-bath was not just
the wish to justify suicide, for the antics of the martyrs were in fact
quite extraneous to that part of his argument. He was drawn to write
about them because, like him, they made death more showy and
purposeful than life, and, at the same time, erased its deadness, since
it became in their eyes life's start not life's end.

To contemporary readers the most extreme claim in *Biathanatos*
must have been its insistence that Christ himself committed suicide,
and the book's most subtle twentieth-century critic Jorge Luis
Borges takes this to be the 'Underlying aim' of the whole work.[28]
Christ's death, Donne argues, was 'an Heroique Act of Fortitude',
because he gave himself up willingly to his killers. He made his
suicidal intention clear in statements like 'I lay down my life for my
sheep'; and on the cross he died with a rapidity which suggests that
his death was an act of will—'many Martyrs', Donne observes, had
'hanged upon Crosses many days alive: And the theeves were yet
alive.' Both Augustine and Aquinas had agreed that Christ's will was
the only cause of his dying, though they did not, of course, call it
suicide. Aquinas notices that, to judge from the biblical accounts of
the crucifixion, Christ cut his life short quite abruptly, while still in
full bodily strength, 'because at the last moment he was able to cry
with a loud voice'. Other commentators remarked that he bowed his
head: it did not fall, as ours do in death. The attractions of the theory
were, for Donne, considerable. God, it appeared, did not only incite
mortals to suicide, but had committed suicide himself. More, Christ's
suicide was of a specially grand and controlled kind, as befitted a
God. He died with superhuman ease. No more was required 'but
that he should wil that his soule should goe out'.[29] Death was for him
not a medical collapse but an exhibition of conscious mastery, like
eclipsing the sun with a wink, and the thought of that was peculiarly
enticing to Donne's ego.

Biathanatos was more important to Donne than to anyone else.
Even after its publication in 1647 it raised relatively little public
interest, and few people seem to have been sufficiently impressed by
its arguments to take their own lives. Anthony Tuckney, the Regius
Professor of Divinity at Cambridge, said in the 1650s that if he
remembered rightly Donne's book had led a condemned man to try

to poison himself. Morhof's *Polyhistor* ascribed 'not a few' suicides
to Donne's influence, but produced no evidence whatsoever.
Thomas Creech, the translator of Lucretius, used to fondle a rope
while reading the first edition of Donne's work in his library, and
eventually hanged himself with it—but Lucretius may have been as
much to blame as Donne.[30] Despite the book's disappointing performance as a persuasive, however, Donne himself was pleased with
it, and pleased that friends he showed it to could not fault its logic.
Scholars in both universities, he reported, had pronounced after
reading it that 'certainly, there was a false thread in it, but not easily
found'. In 1619 Donne sent his manuscript copy to Sir Robert Ker
for safe keeping, urging him to tell any friend to whom he showed it
that it was 'a Book written by Jack Donne, and not by Dr. Donne'.
This bid to pass it off as youthful high jinks does not, though, ring
true. It does not tally with Donne's solicitude about the manuscript's
preservation. He sent it to Ker because he was just off on a foreign
journey, from which he might not return, and if he perished abroad
Biathanatos would be an embarrassing article to turn up among a
clergyman's papers. Obviously the safest measure would have been
to destroy it, but he could not bring himself to do this, and he adjures
Ker not to either: 'Reserve it for me, if I live, and if I die, I only forbid
it the Presse, and the Fire: publishe it not, but yet burn it not; and
between those, do what you will with it.'[31] He wanted it preserved
because it presented a reasoned and (to judge from his experience at
the universities) irrefutable justification of a step which his nature
had always been drawn towards. He owed it to his conscience to
keep *Biathanatos* in existence. Otherwise he might have had to think
of his longing for death as a guilty waywardness rather than—as he
had proved—a common and natural aspiration. The manuscript
constituted a giant suicide note, always ready for use.

We have seen that Donne could not, even when he put his mind to it,
work out why he should be so tempted to do away with himself.
Further, the Preface to *Biathanatos*, where he admits this, seemingly
does not tell the whole truth about the strength of his fixation. He is
tempted, he says there, 'whensoever any affliction assailes me', but in
a letter to Goodyer he reveals that no adversity was needed to bring
on his thoughts of suicide: 'I had the same desires when I went with
the tyde, and enjoyed fairer hopes than now.'[32] To attempt explana-
tions, when Donne himself was baffled, seems presumptuous, but it is
also irresistible, and it happens that the classic work on suicide by the
great French sociologist Emile Durkheim offers some exceptionally

close analogies to Donne's state of mind, in so far as we can determine it.[33]

Durkheim is concerned, of course, to present suicide as a phenomenon explicable by reference to the social structure rather than to the individual psyche. He negates doctrines which ascribe suicide to extra-social causes, and seeks, by the collection and comparison of statistics from various countries and cultural groups, to isolate social factors, such as Protestantism or the legalization of divorce, which can be infallibly shown to generate suicide at a relatively high rate. Since, however, these social factors can produce suicide only through the pressures they exert upon individual minds, the psychological implications of Durkheim's findings are inescapable, and we should not be distracted from them by the impression he sometimes gives of believing that people kill themselves out of respect for sociological laws.

Of the three types of suicide which Durkheim distinguishes, two—egoistic suicide and anomic suicide—seem relevant to Donne's case. Egoistic suicide results from a lack of integration of the individual into society or the family group. The bond attaching man to life relaxes, because that attaching him to society is slack. The egoistic suicide is self-absorbed:

> in revulsion from its surroundings his consciousness becomes self-preoccupied, takes itself as its proper and unique study, and undertakes as its main task self-observation and self-analysis. . . . If he loves, it is not to give himself, to blend in a fecund union with another being, but to meditate on his love.[34]

The applicability of this to Donne's love poetry, and to his insistence that the noblest act of the soul is 'that which reflects upon the soul itself, and considers and meditates it',[35] will need no demonstration. Equally obvious is Donne's abiding sense of ostracism. His apostasy cut him off from the supportive Catholic community in which he had been reared. His failure to make a career for himself left him, he felt, isolated and functionless. The letter to Goodyer, in which he confesses his suicidal tendency, passes immediately, and as if the connection were plain, to his lack of employment and the sense of annihilation it induces: 'I would fain do something; but that I cannot tell what, is no wonder. For to choose, is to do: but to be no part of any body, is to be nothing.'[36] This ties in uncannily with Durkheim's remarks about the suicidal effects of excessive individualism:

When we have no other object than ourselves we cannot avoid the

thought that our efforts will finally end in nothingness, since we
ourselves disappear. But annihilation terrifies us. Under these
conditions one would lose courage to live.[37]

The separateness of Donne and the girl, in the love poems, from the
busy, official world, his recurrent need to boast their self-sufficiency,
and the tendency of his mind, as he broods on this self-sufficiency, to
stray towards death, as in 'The Canonization' or 'The Relique', may
all be seen as ways of coping with the suicidal isolation Durkheim
describes.

Deprived of a niche in society, Durkheim's suicidal solitary is
deprived, too, of social goals. His achievements have no reality to
anyone but himself, and his activities start to feel not just pointless
but illusory. He lives in a dream. This shadowy consciousness is
unmistakable in Donne's writing. The joys of life, he maintains,
don't merely not satisfy, they don't exist. Honour and pleasure, the
Essays in Divinity pronounce, 'are nothing'.[38] The dismissiveness
goes deeper than religious melancholy, and has a metaphysical base.
Place and time, Donne argues in the *Devotions*, have no being. What
we regard as an object's place is 'no more but the next hollow
superficies of the air'. There is only fluid and immeasurable space, in
which we absurdly try to stick fixed points. As for time, we divide it
into past, present and future, but past and future do not exist, and
'that which you call present, is not now the same that it was when
you began to call it so.' So time, like place, is 'an imaginary half-
nothing', and since these are the measures of our happiness, it follows, Donne argues, that our happiness does not exist either.[39] This
doubt about the reality of his experience is a source of Donne's
despair in the religious poems. It must have combined frustratingly
with his ambitious nature. A fervent desire to succeed in life had to
co-exist with the realization that success had no meaning. In these
conditions the hunger for success becomes both insatiable and futile.
Suicide, or madness, are answers. So, in Donne's case, was poetry,
for that was receptive enough to embrace both attitudes. The
ardour of some of the *Songs and Sonnets* is matched, in others, by
disbelief in life's possibilities. Love, Donne decides, is not worth
the effort:

> Our ease, our thrift, our honor, and our day,
> Shall we for this vaine Bubles shadow pay?[40]

'All our joyes are but fantasticall,' as 'Image and Dream' forlornly
puts it—'Alas, true joyes at best are dreame enough.' Even when a

moment of love does seem intense and real, it does so at the cost of all other moments, and shrouds them in a dreamlike mist: 'But this, all pleasures fancies bee.'[41]

The presence in Donne's poetry of this type of disappointment links him with another suicidal category, called by Durkheim the anomic. Suicides of the anomic class are individuals for whom the regulative effect which social organization brings to bear on human goals and aspirations has, for one reason or another, ceased to operate. A simple example is the man who has been overtaken by sudden poverty or sudden wealth, and for whom the normal aims and rewards of life have accordingly disappeared. Another common form of anomic suicide takes place among divorced people. They are more prone to suicide than other sections of the population, and this is because they cannot survive the removal of the regular objects and satisfactions that marriage provides. Anyone who pursues a goal which is by definition unattainable may be in danger of suicidal anomy. Durkheim relates this state particularly to the modern pursuit of unlimited economic aims in commerce, but it has, as he shows, many other kinds of manifestation. What characterizes all anomic suicide is a loss of known and limited goals, and consequently a 'morbid desire for the infinite'. It often, Durkheim observes, assumes a sexual form. The anomic lover, arguing that he has a right to form attachments wherever inclination leads him, aspires to everything and is satisfied with nothing. The closeness of this suicidal type to the state of mind portrayed in, say, 'The Indifferent', or in 'Negative Love', where Donne proclaims that the object of his desire eludes formulation, and is thus endlessly unattainable, will be apparent. But suicidal anomy has much wider relevance to Donne's poetry. As we have seen the aspiration towards infinity is a feature of Donne's thought traceable not just in the love poems but through all his utterances. He exhibits with remarkable fidelity the symptoms of anomic suicide as Durkheim formulates them: 'Beyond experienced pleasures one senses and desires others: if one happens almost to have exhausted the range of what is possible, one dreams of the impossible; one thirsts for the non-existent.'[42]

This correlates with what we have observed about the art of ambition in Donne, and it is tempting to try to ascribe the malady to some particular conditioning feature of his education. We might, of course, say that his restless, dissatisfied temperament was simply a result of his probing intellect. A mind that questions everything risks questioning itself and being engulfed in doubt, which is why, as Durkheim found, suicide is far commoner among the educated and

cultured than the illiterate. But many people in Donne's day underwent education without finding that it brought on a desire to termi-
nate their lives. Some more distinctive factor in Donne's upbringing
must be invoked to account for his peculiar bent, and the zeal for
martyrdom among those who educated him is almost certainly
relevant, particularly as Donne, when casting around for explana-
tions, selects this before anything else: 'I had my first breeding
and conversation with men of a suppressed and afflicted Religion,
accustomed to the despite of death, and hungry for imagin'd
Martyrdome.'

It seems, at first, curious for Donne to proffer this as a reason for
wanting to commit suicide. It might more effectively explain, one
would have thought, a desire to enter the Church, or to undertake
some hazardous missionary enterprise. But Donne's point, though
he does not fully explicate it, appears to be that his upbringing
habituated him to seek life's aims beyond life, and so destroyed his
ultimate satisfaction in anything life could furnish. The only event
which could properly crown his endeavour was that towards which
his preceptors directed his attention—martyrdom. But when he
relinquished his religion the possibility of this vanished, leaving him
with an objectless but insatiable inclination towards the infinite and
the absolute, and with a desire for death which, though robbed of its
Catholic context and rationale, was too deeply etched to eradicate.
The frequent unease about martyrdom, which we have already
noticed in Donne's work from the early poems on, would seem to
justify us in ascribing to it this importance in the generation of his
neurosis. He was a martyr *manqué*, and had to live with a set of basic
psychic configurations which had been oriented towards death by
his educators. This, as much as any other single factor, should help us
to understand the relentless deaths in Donne's love poems. It should
also help us to understand his affection for the theory of universal
flux which, by its constant destruction of human personality, made
life a perpetual dying.

Donne fits so neatly into Durkheim's categories that it seems
almost perverse of him to have remained alive. He was not, though, a
suicide but a suicide-fancier. If we ask what held him back, the
answer, like the others given here, must be conjectural. One deterrent, it seems likely, was his powerful self-assertiveness. True, this
might as easily, had circumstances conspired against him, have
spurred him to take his own life. For suicide is an affirmation of the
self, as well as a destruction of the self. The suicide shrugs off the
inauspicious stars, and grandly chooses his own fate—no longer a

victim, but a conqueror. The Stoic philosophy, popularized among young men of Donne's generation by Seneca, stresses this aspect of self-slaughter. When Donne, in the Preface to *Biathanatos*, speaks loftily of his response to misfortune—'no remedy presents it selfe so soone to my heart, as mine own sword'—it might well be Seneca talking.

Typical of Donne's determination to turn death into a drama of the will was his management of the last days of his life, as described by his biographer Walton. It was his ambition to die in the pulpit, and he very nearly achieved it.[43] On 25 February 1631 he rose from his sickbed to preach his last sermon, the celebrated and macabre 'Death's Duel'. His ghastly appearance caused consternation among his hearers. 'Many that then saw his tears, and heard his faint and hollow voice,' Walton records, opined that 'Dr. Donne had preach't his own Funeral Sermon'.[44] The performance was not, however, fatal, and Donne—if we can believe Walton's account[45]—proceeded to find an alternative way of fashioning his dying into a work of art. He procured a large wooden urn and a plank. Then, when charcoal fires had been lit in his study, he took his clothes off, donned his shroud, with its knots tied at head and foot, and, still wearing the shroud, got up on top of the urn where he balanced looking, one imagines, like a competitor in some grotesque sack race. He remained there while an artist drew his portrait life-size on the wooden plank, and this drawing of himself as a corpse was then hung by his bed, to remind him what the future held, and to exhibit the courage and virtuosity with which he was facing it. Later, when he felt death at last approaching, Donne 'closed his own eyes; and then disposed his hands and body into such a posture as required not the least alteration by those that came to shroud him.'[46] What that gesture, and the acting that had led up to it, testified to was Donne's control. He was stage-managing his own demise. In this way he attained that command of death that the suicide aspires to. He made it appear that, like his 'Heroique' suicidal Christ, he chose how and when to die.

In the poems we can detect the same self-determining attitude—as, for instance, at the start of 'A Valediction: forbidding Mourning':

> As virtuous men pass mildly'away,
>   And whisper to their soules, to goe . . .
>
> So let us melt.[47]

What Donne stresses is that they should part voluntarily: that they should exert power over their own fate, and be their own executioners. Instead of leaving it to circumstances to tear them noisily apart, they should cancel their happiness with dignity, like Christ, or a virtuous man, dispatching his soul. Likewise, the self-reliance of the suicide gives moral strength to 'The Expiration', and makes it entail more than just saying goodbye:

> So, so, breake off this last lamenting kisse,
>   Which sucks two soules, and vapors both away,
> Turne thou ghost that way, and let mee turne this,
>   And let our selves benight our happiest day,
> We ask'd none leave to love; nor will we owe
> Any, so cheape a death, as saying, Goe;
>
> Goe; and if that word have not quite kil'd thee,
>   Ease mee with death, by bidding mee goe too.
> Oh, if it have, let my word worke on mee,
>   And a just office on a murderer doe.
> Except it bee too late, to kill me so,
> Being double dead, going, and bidding, goe.[48]

It reminds us of Romeo and Juliet, in the tomb scene, scrambling joyously into death's clutches. The world-scorning courage of a suicide pact is what the poem nerves itself for. The lovers will not be beholden to anyone else. As in love they were matchless, so in death they will cherish the independence which only the suicide can lay claim to. They will meet death open-eyed as Donne in his letter to Goodyer hoped he would. Donne uses the word 'Goe' like a bullet. He produces it and shows it to the girl at the end of the first stanza. At the start of the second, he fires it. Between, stretches the measureless silence which divides the stanzas, and in which he steels himself to squeeze the trigger. Of course, it is all a game. The gun is from the theatre wardrobe, and the lovers get up none the worse at the end, as Romeo and Juliet also always do. It is the kind of poem which, like romantic tragedy or opera, helps us to live with death by presenting it in resplendent, harmless forms. It is also, we may believe, the kind of poem which helped to keep Donne alive by giving scope to his suicidal fantasies. Suicide drill, like fire drill, reduces the chance of a fatality.

In 'Sweetest Love' Donne is quite explicit about the need to practise dying:

Sweetest love, I do not goe,
For wearinesse of thee,
Nor in hope the world can show
A fitter Love for mee;
But since that I
Must dye at last, 'tis best,
To use my selfe in jest
Thus by fain'd deaths to dye.[49]

This offers as an excuse for leaving the girl no pressing engagement
but simply the explanation that Donne wishes to accustom himself
to death. His departure is a joke, though a practical one. They will
have to part when they die, so it is 'best' to get used to it. His partings
are miniature suicides, and, as the poem goes on, he urges her to take
them in the calm, noble manner that befits a suicide. Her blubbering,
he warns her, merely compounds ill fortune. By a haughty com-
posure, she would defeat fate. This is good Stoic lore, and Donne
could have found it in Seneca, who similarly advises his correspondent to rehearse death: 'To say this is simply to tell a person to
rehearse his freedom. A person who has learned how to die has un-
learned how to be a slave.'[50]

Donne's preparations for his trip to Germany in 1619 also show him
enjoying a mock death. He invested his excursion with the triumph
and deliberation of suicide. This was the occasion which prompted
him to send *Biathanatos* to Ker for safe keeping, lest he should perish
on the journey. He wrote, too, to Lady Montgomery to tell her that
he was 'going out of the kingdom (and perchance out of the
world)'.[51] Preaching a farewell sermon to the Benchers at Lincoln's
Inn, where he was Divinity Reader, he speaks as a man at the portals
of eternity, and fancies himself shepherding his flock of faithful
Benchers through them: 'if I never meet you again till we have all
passed the gate of death, yet in the gates of heaven, I may meet you
all, and there say to my Saviour and your Saviour, that which he said
to his Father and our Father, *Of those whom thou hast given me, have I
not lost one*.'[52] In his imagination Donne arrives at the heavenly
threshold prominent, eloquent, and with a supporting cast.

In fact, his auguries of disaster in 1619 had little basis. True, travel
was hazardous in the seventeenth century, and Donne felt in poor
health. He believed himself, Walton says, to be in a consumption.
But he was going to Germany as official chaplain of the embassy sent
by James I to the German princes. Led by Lord Doncaster, this was a

prodigiously costly affair. The lords, knights and gentlemen accompanying Doncaster were so numerous that, at their ceremonial entry into Brussels, between twenty-five and thirty coaches were needed to carry them. Doncaster's 'vanities of Grandure' on the journey caused grumblings at home, particularly as he received £14,000 from public funds towards his expenses. Donne could hardly have travelled in greater comfort or security. Against this background his doom-laden leave-takings acquire a theatrical appearance. In the poem he wrote to mark his departure, 'A Hymne to Christ, at the Authors last going into Germany', he regards shipwreck and drowning as virtually inevitable, and implies severe misgivings about the seaworthiness of the vessel which is to carry him. These are, it has been said, 'the sick fancies of a troubled mind'.[53] Yet we have only to read the poem to see that Donne's self-dramatizing urge has produced something so fraught with power that it would be absurd to demand, in its stead, a more realistic estimate of the risks involved:

> In what torne ship soever I embarke,
> That ship shall be my embleme of thy Arke;
> What sea soever swallow mee, that flood
> Shall be to mee an embleme of thy blood;
> Though thou with clouds of anger do disguise
> Thy face; yet through that maske I know those eyes,
> Which, though they turn away sometimes,
> They never will despise.

> I sacrifice this Iland unto thee,
> And all whom I lov'd there, and who lov'd mee;
> When I have put our seas twixt them and mee,
> Put thou thy sea betwixt my sinnes and thee.
> As the trees sap doth seeke the root below
> In winter, in my winter now I goe,
> Where none but thee, th'Eternall root
> Of true Love I may know.

> Nor thou nor thy religion dost controule,
> The amorousnesse of an harmonious Soule,
> But thou would'st have that love thy selfe: As thou
> Art jealous, Lord, so I am jealous now,
> Thou lov'st not, till from loving more, thou free
> My soule: Who ever gives, takes libertie:
> O, if thou car'st not whom I love
> Alas, thou lov'st not mee.

Seale then this bill of my Divorce to All,
On whom those fainter beames of love did fall;
Marry those loves, which in youth scattered bee
On Fame, Wit, Hopes (false mistresses) to thee.
Churches are best for Prayer, that have least light:
To see God only, I goe out of sight:
   And to scape stormy dayes, I chuse
   An Everlasting night.[54]

Donne does not so much falsify as master reality, taking one or two fragments as his stage set, and discarding the rest. All the actual circumstances of the embassy are obliterated. The rich coachloads, and the ambassador to whose suite Donne was a relatively minor appendage, vanish without trace. We are left with Donne looming tragic and solitary above a vessel which seems on the point of disappearing as well. 'Torne ship' is strangely belittling—as if Donne were to venture across the Channel in a dilapidated canvas canoe. But as the craft dwindles, Donne grows. He seems more solid by comparison with its flimsiness. His gestures become gigantic. 'I sacrifice this Iland': a sweep of his hand, and Britain is swallowed up.

The struggle between the ambitious careerist and the lofty scorner of the world's rewards is, in this poem, quite naked. Donne acknowledges that fame, wit and hope must be relinquished, but he has to ask God's help in trying to relinquish them. The renunciation which the poem wins through to is triumphant but bitter. By personifying hopes as 'false mistresses' Donne even manages to find a place for his old phobia about the women who have let him down. As in the poems of a modern suicide like Sylvia Plath, resentment against life and its disappointments is readily detectable. The magnificence of the suicidal leap has to compensate Donne for all he has been cheated of. That this is a poem about committing suicide is, by the end, quite patent: 'I chuse / An Everlasting night.' Donne has allowed the circumstances of the Doncaster embassy to be distorted in his mind to such a degree that his decision to participate in it is seen as inevitably fatal. As he plunges into the dark, the memory of his martyred kinsman Sir Thomas More seems, significantly, to have been present. Donne's line about churches with least light being best for prayer is a recollection of the churches in More's *Utopia* which, More says, are designed to exclude light because the Utopians believe darkness intensifies religious faith.[55] By embracing death in order 'To see God only', Donne takes upon himself the glamour of martyrdom. But, typically, the poem contains at this climactic point a powerful and unresolved contradiction. For if Donne is dying in order to see God, then he is not choosing 'An Everlasting night' at all. The everlasting night belongs to the pagan, Senecan tradition of suicide. It is totally un-Christian. What Donne, with sublime inconsistency, manages to do is to arrogate to himself, at the poem's end, both the majestic finality of pagan suicide and the Christian martyr's thirst for union with God. He cannot bear to forgo either kind of grandeur, so the two are asserted side by side in all their urgent discord.

We must turn, finally, to the way Donne, as a theologian, envisaged death. We have seen that the bent of his imagination was towards lively and spectacular renderings of death such as suicide, or the endlessly survivable fatalities of the *Songs and Sonnets*. The aim of this was to negate death by removing its deathliness and turning it into a self-aggrandizing act. Since, as we have argued, theology is ultimately an imaginative expedient, we should expect Donne, as a religious thinker, to opt for those aspects of Christian death which suited his imaginative needs. Speculation about what happens after death is, quite literally, inexhaustible, since nothing can really be known about it at all. Accordingly Donne could take his pick from a vast array of imaginings, and the items he selects (as, indeed, those he leaves out) are inevitably revealing.

The single event in the life after death which Donne recurs to so persistently and in such detail that it virtually eclipses all the rest of eternity is the resurrection of the body. That is no more than we could have predicted from a knowledge of his other portrayals of death. Death, for him, meant activity, and the day of resurrection—'The last busie day', as he calls it in 'The Relique'—would be unprecedentedly active. It would witness the biggest crowd in history. Everyone would get his or her body back, and this would call for a mammoth act of molecular synthesis on the part of God and his angels. It is a subject Donne cannot keep away from, and he imagines it with unflinching and, his more fastidious critics feel, dismaying physicality. What intrigues him are the practical problems. The bodies which have to be reconstructed may have been 'dissolved and liquefied in the Sea, putrified in the Earth, resolv'd to ashes in the fire, macerated in the ayre'. Even before they died they had begun to disintegrate:

Where be all the Atoms of that flesh, which a Corrasive hath eaten away, or a Consumption hath breath'd, and exhal'd away from our arms, and other Limbs? In what wrinkle, in what furrow, in what bowel of the earth, ly all the graines of the ashes of a body burnt a thousand years since? In what corner, in what ventricle of the sea, lies all the jelly of a Body drowned in the generall flood? . . . One humour of our dead body produces worms, and those worms suck and exhaust all other humour, and then all dies, and all dries, and molders into dust, and that dust is blowen into the River, and that puddled water tumbled into the sea, and that ebs and flows in infinite revolutions, and still, still God knows in what Cabinet every seed-Pearle lies, in what part of the world every grain of every mans dust lies; and *sibilat populum suum*, (as his Prophet speaks in another case) he whispers, he hisses, he beckens for the bodies of his Saints, and in the twinckling of an eye, that body that was scattered over all the elements, is sate down at the right hand of God, in a glorious resurrection.[56]

A passage like this makes it clear that Donne's interest in bodily resurrection is not in any distinctive sense religious. It is a corollary of his preoccupation with changing states of matter. The dissolving and recompacting of deceased human bodies provided that part of his imagination which relished material flux with an illimitable field. Necrophilia was, from this viewpoint, even better than alchemy.

Further, the conjuring trick by which God turned dust into instant bodies appealed to Donne because it satisfied in a final and definitive way his desire for integration. As we have seen, he was obsessively worried about being scattered and fragmentary. He felt that he was disconnected from the body of the world, and that his mind was hopelessly centrifugal and diffuse. 'I finde my selfe scattered, melted', as he remarked of his attempts at prayer.[57] God, in the resurrection, would put that right, and fit everything together. The magic of the idea was heightened, for Donne, by consideration of the difficulties God would have to combat. Amputations and haemorrhages would, he reckoned, present the Almighty with special problems, particularly in view of the increase in intercontinental travel. The body to be reconstituted might have lost 'an Arme in the East, and a leg in the West'; an arm in Europe, and a leg 'in Afrique or Asia, scores of yeers between'.[58] It might have lost 'some bloud in the North and some bones in the South'. Then there are the intricate difficulties which arise whenever one creature eats another. Supposing a man is eaten by a fish, and so changes into the fish's body, and then the fish is eaten by a second man. How will God sort out the first man from the second? Donne muses on this pleasing mix-up re-

peatedly.[59] That certain nations practise cannibalism only makes
matters worse—or better—as he points out. Not that anything so
exotic is needed to get you into someone else's stomach. God on the
last day must face the fact that 'mans buried flesh hath brought forth
grasse, and that grasse fed beasts, and those beasts fed men, and those
men fed other men'.[60] God's job will require an intimate knowledge
of every digestive system since the Creation.

When we compare Donne's account of the resurrection with that
found in other Christian commentators known to him, discrepancies
appear which help us to appreciate the personal slant which his
imaginative needs imposed on his theology. First, the problems
raised by cannibals and man-eating fishes, which so intrigue him, are
not, for other writers, a serious part of Christian theology. Both
Augustine and Aquinas emphasize that these questions were originally raised by blasphemous scoffers, who wished to demonstrate
the absurdity of belief in bodily resurrection.[61] But since Donne's
interest lies less in resurrection itself than in reintegration, he gives
these extreme cases of it an unwonted prominence. Secondly, he
does not, as Augustine and Aquinas do, attempt an explanation of
how God will in fact solve such conundrums. His sole intent is to
emphasize the power of the reintegrative act, and the fantastic state
of dispersal that precedes it. Thus he simply asserts that God will
return every particle of flesh to its true proprietor, without considering how ownership will be determined.

Another difficult question, which Donne ignores, concerns the
fact that matter is not permanent in the human body, but in a
perpetual state of flux. As we have seen, he makes much of this point
when stressing the changefulness of life. But it is a factor which raises
dire obstacles to the resurrection of the flesh. For since our physical
tissues are continuously renewing themselves, an immense quantity
of matter will have passed through our bodies by the time we die.
How much of this is going to be resurrected? If God raises the whole
lot, we shall be grotesquely overweight in heaven. If he does not, we
shall not be completely resurrected. Augustine and Aquinas both
struggle with this poser. The aspect of it which most worries Augustine relates to our hair and fingernails, which are constantly being
trimmed in life, and which, if restored to us in bulk, will give us a
most ungainly appearance. After some demur, Augustine decides
that God *will* resurrect hair and nail-clippings, but instead of attaching them in their former positions will use them as padding to fill out
parts of our bodies which could benefit from more rotundity. Aquinas, on the other hand, rejects this neat and economical contrivance

and asserts that, though enough matter will be resurrected to give us human shape, 'the whole will not rise again, if we speak of the totality of matter'.[62]

Donne had no right to remain unconcerned by these difficulties. His belief in total physical resurrection, and his belief in the flux of matter, were simply irreconcilable. But he kept them, it seems, in separate compartments of his mind, and continued to subscribe to both without attempting any rational bridge between them. Augustine's bodies of recycled hair and fingernail evidently did not appeal to him, and Aquinas's denial of complete material reintegration must have been even less acceptable. In fact he never mentions either, nor offers any alternative solution to the problem they confront. He just stuck to his contradictory beliefs because, rational or not, they were what he wanted to imagine. Just in the same way, he had stuck to the pagan plunge into 'Everlasting night' and the Christian martyr's reunion with God because they were both versions of suicide that appealed to him. We should not, of course, assume that he was unaware of his contradictions. It was precisely his sense of the diverse and unco-ordinated nature of his being that gave God's reintegration of scattered persons its allure.

To make the reintegration complete God will not only have to fit the body together, he will have to re-attach it to the soul. Till then, Donne stressed, the soul would be imperfect. The need for bodily existence in heaven obsessed him almost as much as the thought of physical reintegration. He was deeply averse to the prospect of being split up into soul and body, and surviving only in some flimsy form like ectoplasm. His ego demanded that he should be as solidly and completely present in heaven as he was on earth. Accordingly he took issue with the early Christian belief that resurrected bodies would be rarefied—'attenuated, and reduced to a thinnesse, and subtlenesse'. Without proper, solid bodies, he argued, heaven would be deficient, which is why the persons of the Trinity decided to create them. For 'infinite millions of millions of generations' they refrained from doing so. But then they realized that their glory was not so perfect 'but that it might receive an addition from creatures; and therefore they made . . . a materiall world, a corporeall world, they would have bodies'. On the question of the human body's entry into heaven a biblical text which caused Donne some concern was Mark 12:25, where Christ says that those who rise from the dead will be 'as the angels'. Since angels do not have bodies, it was imperative that Donne should reinterpret these words. He returns to them anxiously and often, explaining that though we shall be like the

angels, when resurrected, in the perfection of our spirits, angels 'shall
never attaine to be like us in our glorified bodies', as Christ's words
rather carelessly imply.[63]

So uncongenial did Donne find it to imagine his soul existing apart
from his body that, at the period when he was writing the 'Holy
Sonnets', he adopted the heretical view that the soul would die with
the body and be resurrected at the last day. Hence in 'At the round
earths imagin'd corners' he portrays not merely bodies but 'number-
lesse infinities / Of soules' rising from death.[64] However, this theory
ran counter to Donne's impulse to minimize and enliven death. If the
soul died, even for a while, death would be really deadly. So after
much worry on the point, and after investigating the pros and cons as
set out by early Christian writers,[65] he accepted the orthodox idea
that the soul went straight to heaven (or hell) at death and was later
rejoined by the body. His perplexity over the issue is revealing and
absolutely expectable. For in choosing between the two hypotheses
he had to choose between two imaginative concepts, both of which
profoundly attracted him—the fusion of soul and body, and the
animation of death. Even though he eventually conceded that the
soul would part from the body at death, so was not indivisibly fused,
he did not feel happy about it. He insisted that it was 'contrary to
nature' for the soul to exist in isolation, and that it would feel
dissatisfied and incomplete during its temporary residence in heaven
prior to the resurrection of the body.[66] In one sermon he goes so far
as to maintain, by some exceptionally unconvincing exposition, that
since nothing will really happen to the body in between its death and
its resurrection, resurrection and death may be regarded as simultaneous, so the soul will not have to exist apart from the body after
all.[67] He seems to have the same hope in mind in the 'Hymne to God
my God, in my sicknesse':

> As West and East
> In all flatt Maps (and I am one) are one,
> So death doth touch the Resurrection.[68]

The desperate reasoning shows us an imaginative ideal being
grasped in the teeth of conflicting evidence.

The eagerness with which Donne insists on the body's indissoluble
junction with the soul, even when facts are apparently against him,
naturally reminds us of the poet of 'The Extasie', urging that souls
are incapacitated when apart from bodies. It reminds us, too, of that
feeling for the body's cohesiveness which Donne transmits through

his poetic language, and it reminds us of his delicate perception of the human organism's fused aliveness in the imaginary girl he wrote the *Anniversaries* about—'one might almost say, her bodie thought'. Donne, we can see, created his theology, as he created his poetry, for imaginative ends. To appreciate this fully we have to take stock of the theological questions Donne ignored, as well as those he pursued, for they are equally helpful in determining his individuality. Thus, though it is correct to say that he was abnormally obsessed about the resurrection of the body, it is also true that some aspects of the resurrection, which seemed of paramount importance to other Christians, failed to arouse him at all. The stature and age of resurrected bodies had, for instance, been zealously debated by theologians for several centuries. Whether all resurrected persons would be equally tall and stout and, if so, where God would procure the extra flesh for expanding the undersized, were questions that had occupied many learned heads. But Donne, beyond giving passing assent to the generally accepted idea that all deformities will be straightened out, and that everyone will be extremely beautiful in heaven,[69] simply declined to interest himself in these problems. That, of course, is precisely what we should expect, given the lack of concern about mere visual appearance in his poems.

As for the age at which people would be resurrected, this was an issue of particular and poignant interest to parents who had lost young children. Would they ever see their toddlers again? Or would they be confronted in heaven by strapping strangers who hailed them as mother and father? When Ben Jonson dreamed of his little boy Benjamin, who had died in the plague, 'he appeared to him', he told Drummond, 'of a Manlie shape and of that Grouth that he thinks he shall be at the resurrection.'[70] Henry Vaughan, on the other hand, who had also given the matter much thought, wished, though a grown man, to be resurrected in the shape of a new-born baby, since he felt he would be purer that way:

> Some men a forward motion love,
> But I by backward steps would move,
> And when this dust falls to the urn
> In that state I came return.[71]

A more popular idea, and evidently the one Jonson had in mind, is that we shall all be resurrected at thirty years of age, since this represents the perfection of physical growth, according to Aquinas,[72] and it was also believed to have been Christ's age at death. Augustine, who originated the theory, explains that those who die before they are thirty will be credited with the necessary seniority to bring them into the same age group as everyone else.[73]

Donne was, like Jonson, a bereaved parent, and he was just as capable of being troubled by his own impurity as Vaughan. Yet he shies away from any consideration of the youth and age of the risen dead with a consistency which, in view of his passionate concern about other aspects of resurrection, cannot fail to strike us. It was certainly not because he did not hope to see his lost loved ones again. 'I shall have my dead raised to life againe,' he declares in the sermon he preached shortly after the death of his daughter Lucy, aged eighteen.[74] 'The grave shall restore me my child,' he wrote in a letter comforting his friend Mrs. Cokayne for the death of her eighteen-year-old son.[75] The wording here suggests that he thought Lucy would come back to him no older than she was when she died. But the matter is left indefinite, and in all his discussions of the resurrection Donne studiously refrains from debating it. It seems clear that he wanted to keep his mind blank on this issue because to investigate it would bring him up against possibilities that he did not wish to countenance.

Nor is it hard for us to see why. For if Donne were obliged to decide that the resurrected John Donne would be John Donne at thirty, or at any other definite age, that would exclude from the resurrection all the other John Donnes that he had been. The same urge for integration which made it impossible for him to concede that a single constituent particle of his person would go astray, made it imperative that he should believe that all the selves of his mutable and vacillating self would, at the resurrection, somehow unite. He did not want one stage of his growth to be selected for preservation, and the rest discarded. He wanted to be gathered and concentrated—'contracted', as he put it, 'Like a Lily in Paradise, out of red earth'.[76] Related to this complex is Donne's insistence, in the poems, that anyone who takes him must take all of him. In order to get Donne, God has to promise, in 'A Hymne to God the Father', that he will forgive the sins of every period of Donne's life, from conception to death-bed. Until then, 'thou hast not done.' Nothing less than all Donnes is Donne.[77] Among the love poems, 'The Blossome' presents an alternative form of this egotistical inclusiveness. Donne stands out for a girl who will be 'As glad to have my body, as my minde'[78]—exactly what, when he came to write of the resurrection, he was to demand of heaven. The poet of 'The Canonization' counting his 'five gray haires' shows the same solicitude for each scrap of his person as the theologian or, for that matter, as the poet of 'The

Funerall' who hopes that the girl's love token will keep his limbs
from dissolution until he rises from the dead.[79]

Though the age of the resurrected didn't interest Donne, their
status did. Among the many aspects of heaven celebrated by Christian theorists, none captivated him more than its glory, and he speaks
of this in a curiously challenging and proprietary manner. Even in
the celestial regions he intended to remain competitive:

> . . . as soone as my soule enters into Heaven, I shall be able to say
> to the Angels, I am of the same stuffe as you, spirit, and spirit, and
> therefore let me stand with you, and looke upon the face of your
> God, and my God; so at the Resurrection of this body, I shall be
> able to say to the Angel of the great Councell, the Son of God,
> Christ Jesus himselfe, I am of the same stuffe as you, Body and
> body, Flesh and flesh, and therefore let me sit downe with you, at
> the right hand of the Father.[80]

This vision of the newly arrived Donne trying conclusions with the
other inhabitants of heaven, and drawing their attention to his
meritorious physique, is both ludicrous and wholly in character.
Dead or alive, he was incapable of being either self-effacing or
unambitious. His notion of bliss was deeply and exclusively personal. He does speak of heavenly harmony and the joy of reunion
with the dead, but these are side-shows compared with his personal
advancement. 'I shall be so like God, as that the Devill himselfe shall
not know me from God,' he rejoices.[81]

We are no doubt correct in reading these imaginings as evidence of a
lingering fear—that self-confessed 'sinne of feare' mentioned at the
start of this chapter. Donne exaggerated his assurance so as to
reassure himself. The fear that death might, after all, mean extinction, hovered behind all the resolutely animated and self-assertive
simulations of death that Donne invented. Even if death meant only
the separation of soul and body, it was still repugnant. The thought
of his body helplessly mouldering through its long years of dissolution preyed on his mind. It prompted those relentless harangues
about the putrid and loathsome stuff the human frame breaks down
into, for which his sermons have become notorious. The
psychological motivation behind these tirades seems clearly self-
defensive. He made his fear tolerable by redirecting it at his audience.
What had been a lurking horror in his mind became a resplendent
part of his repertoire for shocking his hearers, and to this extent he
was able to master it. The earliest of his sermons to dwell on the

decay of the body was preached in 1620.[82] By that time he had lost his wife, his son Francis, of whom he was particularly fond, and his daughter Mary. Bodies which he had loved, and watched grow from babyhood, were rotting, and that brought the fear closer.

The pressure of this fear explains Donne's interest in the fate of those human beings who will still be alive at the end of the world. This was the only major theological aspect of death not so far mentioned which absorbed him. He returns to it persistently in the sermons, and his references indicate that he had consulted numerous authorities in order to clarify his opinions. The difficulty arose from an apparent confusion in the Bible itself. St. Paul declares in I Corinthians 15:51, 'We shall not all sleep, but we shall all be changed.' The reading of the verse was much disputed ('I scarce know of a place of Scripture, more diversely read,' Donne remarked),[83] but it was possible to take Paul to mean that those alive at the last day would not die, but would undergo some alternative processing to fit them for glory. Early authorities including St. Chrysostom had interpreted the text in this way, as Donne notes. But if this was St. Paul's meaning it appeared to conflict with his words in Hebrews 9:27 ('It is appointed unto men once to die'), and still more clearly with such biblical passages as Psalm 89:48, 'What man is he that liveth, and shall not see death?' Donne, who cites these texts and others in his extensive discussions of the point, seems to have felt at first that the early commentators might be right, and that not all men would die. Preaching in 1619 he concludes that it is 'a problematicall matter', but that conceivably the people alive on the earth at the time of Christ's second coming would not have to die but would be 'changed', in Paul's sense, instead.[84]

What gives the question more than theoretic interest is that Donne believed he might himself be one of this fortunate few. 'Perchance I shall never die,' he had written to Goodyer in a letter of 1607.[85] For the seventeenth century it was not, of course, an extravagant notion. The end of the world was imminently expected by many, and there was much competition in forecasting its date. The established Church, for its part, frowned on such speculations, and they were increasingly regarded as the preserve of hot-headed sectarians who believed that Doomsday would be followed by a period in which they would enjoy personal rule.[86] As became an orthodox clergyman, Donne is cool, in his sermons, about such apocalyptic dreams. None the less, he clearly cherished the hope that he might indeed be living in the world's final phase, and that the survivors mentioned in I Corinthians might include him. As late as 1627, only four years

before his death, he told his congregation that they and their contemporaries might be destined to lie in the earth many years, or
might 'be chang'd in the Aire in the twinkling of an eye, (God knows
which)'.[87] So far as we can tell, it wasn't until he was practically at his
last gasp that he reconciled himself to the fact that he would have to
go into the ground, and that the neater exit from life adumbrated by
St. Paul was not to be his. In his final sermon, haggard and death-
struck, he reverted to the topic of the last men on earth, and how they
would be 'changed', but added that 'for us that dye now' there would
be no escape from putrefaction.[88]

Meanwhile he had been reconsidering, over the years, just what
the change St. Paul spoke of would entail, and how it could be
reconciled with the biblical texts which predict that everyone will
die. He decided, finally, that St. Paul had not meant that the earth's
last inhabitants would bypass death, but that their death would be
merely technical. Their constituent parts would separate and come
together again instantaneously, and this would count as a genuine
fatality for the purposes of getting into heaven. 'There shall be a
sudden dissolution of body and soul, which is death,' Donne
explains, 'and a sudden re-uniting of both, which is resurrection, in
that instant.'[89] In this way they would escape both the corruption of
the grave and the period between death and resurrection during
which most human souls were obliged to exist in isolation from their
bodies. As we have seen, this period was peculiarly distasteful to
Donne, and it makes his desire to be numbered among the Pauline
escapees the more understandable. In reaching his conclusion about
their instant death and resurrection he was aided by Augustine
and Aquinas, both of whom are, however, significantly more tenta-
tive about it than Donne. Augustine says that our 'weak reason' can't
foresee what will happen to those alive at the last day, but that they
will probably experience momentary death: 'a flash of death while
passing into immortality'.[90] Aquinas observes that the saints are
divided on the question, but that the 'safer and more common
opinion' is that everyone will die and rise from death. Whether these
two operations will be simultaneous for some, he doesn't venture to
judge.[91] But for Donne the idea, once seized on, was far too attractive
to forsake, and he presents it as a virtual certainty. As a version of
death it perfectly met his requirements, since it robbed death of
deathliness, and kept body and soul together. At the same time, since
body and soul would be momentarily distinct and then gloriously
reunited, it retained that integrating and self-healing element which
Donne valued in more conventional accounts of death and resurrection.

It's probably not mere chance that the earliest sermon in which he plumps firmly for this interpretation of Paul's words is that same sermon, preached in 1620, in which for the first time he allows himself to dwell on the corruption of the body in the grave. The ability to confront the subject of dissolution in its full gruesomeness coincided with and depended on a sure perception of his own hoped-for escape from it. Habitually in this and later sermons he talks of those who will survive on the last day as 'we'. 'We that remaine shall bee caught up in the clouds'; 'We shall die, and be alive again, before another could consider that we were dead.'[92] 'We' might, of course, be just a loose locution, equivalent to 'those of us Christians who happen to be alive at that distant time'. But since, as we have seen, Donne believed until almost the end of his life that he and those alive with him could well be the earth's last inhabitants, we can be sure that his 'we' did not sound so vague to him. Of all his imaginative stratagems for enlivening or negating death, this was the most potent, for it held out the hope that he would not, in any normal sense, die at all.

Once we understand this, it explains why Donne should so impatiently request, at the start of 'At the round earths imagin'd corners', that the Last Judgement should take place without more ado. The advantage of the Last Judgement, from his viewpoint, is that it will relieve him of the necessity of dying and rotting, as everyone else in history has had to do. He will be one of those who, as the poem says, will 'never tast deaths woe'. To secure this personal advantage he does not hesitate to order the destruction of the world. In that respect it is a characteristic display of egotism. What eventually deters him, in the second part of the poem, is no thought of the other lives he would be cutting short, or the other souls he would be hastening to judgement, but rather the recollection that an immediate apocalypse might, after all, prove inconvenient for him, in that it might not ensure his salvation.

To conclude: Donne was never more paradoxical than in his preoccupation with death. On the one hand, he felt drawn to suicide, and this morbid inclination shows itself in a number of his poems. On the other hand, he was so repelled by death and its nothingness, that he persistently and ingeniously animates it in his art, and loves to talk in his sermons as if he will be one of the few mortals exempt from dying. These two tendencies might seem to be opposed, but they are not, because they both constitute ways of surmounting and defusing death. The suicide converts death into a part of active life.

He enlivens death, like the artist who portrays death in lurid or dramatic forms, but he does so more splendidly because he is dealing with the real thing and not with imitations. For Donne, the outstanding performer among suicides was Christ, since he had only to tell his life to end for it to end. His command of death was total, requiring none of the usual lethal aids. He was as self-sufficient as Donne, killing himself and his girl with the word 'Goe' in 'The Expiration'. This superiority to death mattered to Donne because death struck him, above all else, as a personal affront. The business of being buried, and decomposing, was, as he observed in his last sermon (when he had finally come to terms with the fact that he was going to rot like everyone else), 'the most inglorious and contemptible vilification'.[93] The question most of us want to ask about death—Is it going to hurt?—never seems to have bothered him. It would have been beneath his dignity to worry about pain. Death was an insult to his ego. It threatened to turn him into an inanimate object. He refused to succumb to it passively, in art as in life. 'I would not that death should take me asleep.' He could tolerate any form of death, so long as it allowed him to remain alive.

The Crisis of Reason

In this chapter I shall consider the way Donne regards reason. This is worth doing, because the force of his reasoning is evidently one thing that makes his poetry distinctive. He is—in J. B. Leishman's phrase—an 'argumentative poet'. But immediately we apply that label we can see how misleading it is. Someone who had never read Donne would get quite the wrong impression from it. An argumentative poet, he would assume, marshals evidence and reaches conclusions. Donne does not. His arguments are frivolous, tenuous or self-contradictory by turns, but they are almost never genuinely argumentative. He treats argument not as an instrument for discovering truth but as a flexible poetic accessory, like rhyme or alliteration. It is an agitated façade through which he projects the desires and inconstancies of his poetic self. We are not at all surprised to find him turning round and disparaging the arguments he has fabricated, as in 'Womans Constancy':

> Vaine lunatique, against these scapes I could
> Dispute, and conquer, if I would.[1]

Argument, he impresses on us, is at the service of the will. Logic is a convenient and adaptable screen for appetite. Given sufficient incentive, he will reason his way in or out of any position.

The precarious and provisional role allotted to reason in Donne's poems is to be ascribed largely to his personal mental development, and that was determined in turn by his retreat from Catholicism and from the logical certitude which it encouraged. However, Donne's private history was in this respect, as I shall try to show, only a more compressed and intense version of a development in European thought. He was fortunate as an artist (though no doubt it caused him considerable distress as a man) to experience within the confines of his own acute sensibility that onrush of scepticism which was to transform, within half a century, the intellectual orientation of the Western world. What is odd about his poems is that they retain a relentless passion for arguing, yet treat argument with patent disrespect. They are, in this sense, fiercely schizoid—and that is what we might well expect from a poet whose early habits of ratiocination, instilled by his educators and intertwined with his most basic beliefs, had met, when he came to manhood, the withering and liberating blasts of limitless doubt.

In Donne's day the great intellectual manifesto of Catholic Europe was still the *Summa Theologica* of Aquinas, a systematic examination of God and his relations with mankind which its author had not quite been able to complete before his death in 1274. Aquinas, like other medieval thinkers, takes it as axiomatic that the human mind is capable of knowing reality. True, he admits that there are certain Christian mysteries, such as the Incarnation and the Atonement, which lie above human reason. But his persistent assumption is that the workings of God's mind and of the creation are humanly comprehensible. The prime author and mover of the universe is, he pronounces at the start of the *Summa*, intelligence. Accordingly man's natural reason does not run contrary to religious faith but supports and illuminates it. Aquinas derives his confident rationalism from Aristotle, who had similarly assumed that the qualities we perceive in objects are truly present in those objects, and that therefore we can build up from them a dependable picture of the universe.

The underlying tenets of Aristotle and Aquinas continued to seem satisfactory even to more revolutionary and unAristotelian spirits at the end of the sixteenth century. Peter Ramus, the *enfant terrible* of the academies, whose death in the 1572 St. Bartholomew's Day massacre (Marlowe's *Massacre at Paris*) greatly enhanced his prestige in Protestant Europe, propounded a system of logic which imposed a simple order and rationality upon the universe, and enabled man to reach absolute truth by dint of tabular diagrams.[2] The same kind of intellectual innocence inspired Donne's friend Lord Herbert of Cherbury to argue, in his *De Veritate*, that man, by the mere exercise of his reason, could discover the universal and unassailable elements of religious belief. Of Donne's own admiration for and attachment to Aquinas there can be no question. He couples him with Augustine as an instrument of God in the *Essays in Divinity*, and in the sermons Aquinas is persistently used as a touchstone.

But in opposition to this devout rationality the Renaissance saw the revival of a more destructive mode of thought stemming from the ancient Greek philosopher Pyrrho of Elis. Pyrrho's philosophy, as recorded by his disciple Sextus Empiricus, entailed a complete suspension of judgement on all issues. Our sense perceptions, Pyrrho pointed out, have no absolute validity. Various animals and birds

demonstrably perceive things differently from ourselves, and are
just as likely to be right. Since the very basis of our knowledge is
uncertain, we can know nothing. We must admit that against every
statement we make, the contrary might be advanced with equal
reason. Henry Estienne's Latin translation of Sextus Empiricus's
Pyrrhonic Sketches in 1562 was a landmark in the growth of the
European mind. But even before Pyrrhonism became popular, sceptical ideas had begun to circulate. The German Nicholas of Cusa, a
busy ecclesiastical diplomatist and Cardinal Bishop of Brixen, completed in 1440 a largely incomprehensible work called *De Docta
Ignorantia* (Of Learned Ignorance), which attempts to come to grips
with the Trinity by imagining infinite geometrical figures, but
which, in one of its more lucid moments, puts forward the principle
that absolute truth is beyond man's grasp, and that that is, in fact, all
we can know about it.[3]

   This idea became the nucleus of a sceptical treatise by another
German, Henry Cornelius Agrippa von Nettesheim, whose *De
Incertitudine et Vanitate Scientiarum et Artium* was published at Ant-
werp in 1531. Agrippa had been a soldier, doctor, magician and spy.
He is not a very serious writer, and probably for that reason his work
proved extremely popular. It was translated into English by James
Sanford in 1568, and into other European languages. Among its
denunciations of intellectual endeavour it manages to fit in lengthy
chapters on prostitution and procuring, and much calumny of the
monastic orders, against whom Agrippa harboured a lifelong
grudge. His major point, constantly reiterated, is that truth can be
apprehended by 'no humane discourse of Reason', and that knowledge of any kind is not only inevitably fallacious but harmful,
inducing pride and contempt of God. He attacks every branch of
learning from agriculture to rhetoric, and is particularly critical of
Scholastic theologians like Aquinas who try to reduce divine matters
to the level of logic and human understanding.

   At bottom Agrippa is not so much an authentic sceptic as an
envious freelance, activated, like most misfits, by hatred of established professions and institutions. In the heat of his indignation he is
apt to forget all about his scepticism. Thus he complains of the
Inquisition that if an accused person tries to justify himself before it
by reason, the inquisitors show him faggots and fire, and retort that
heretics are to be convinced by these and not by arguments. Given
his own onslaught against reason in the rest of the treatise, Agrippa
ought logically to applaud the inquisitors' action. Their insistence on
faith, and dismissal of reason, are precisely his own. Instead he seems

unaware of the tangle he has got himself into, and continues, after his digression on inquisitors, to castigate man's aspiring reason as if nothing had happened.[4]

For all their shortcomings, Nicholas of Cusa and Agrippa were straws in the wind. After the appearance of the 1562 translation of Empiricus, the sceptical movement which they adumbrated was carried forward by clearer and better minds. Montaigne had a medal struck in honour of Sextus Empiricus, and his 'Apology for Raymond Sebond' is the finest summary of Renaissance scepticism. Montaigne's case is Pyrrho's: our reason is worthless because it functions only on sense data, and we have no chance of checking these against reality. Sir Walter Raleigh in 'The Sceptic' offered a condensed version of the first three *Pyrrhonic Sketches*, concluding that, since sense impressions are untrustworthy, we can report only how things appear. 'Whether they are so indeed, I know not.'[5] Sidney's friend Fulke Greville composed his versified 'Treatie of Humane Learning' in order to proclaim that knowledge is impossible, and that all man's intellection amounts to vain deceit. Donne's letters show that he had read Montaigne by 1603 or 1604.[6] It is clear from the concluding lines of *The Progresse of the Soule*, written in 1601, that he had already become, in certain moods at any rate, a convert to scepticism, believing that all values were relative and that man's boasted certainties had no better ground than common prejudice:

> Ther's nothing simply good, nor ill alone,
> Of every quality comparison,
> The onely measure is, and judge, opinion.[7]

Admittedly, this easy dismissiveness was popular among the bright young things round about 1600. Shakespeare makes Hamlet remark, 'there is nothing either good or bad, but thinking makes it so.' 'All that exists', Marston observes in *What You Will*, 'Takes valuation from opinion.'[8] The distrust of received verities was part of the *fin de siècle* fatigue.

But we cannot gloss over Donne's scepticism as if it were merely a fashionable pose, for there is ample evidence that it remained a potent element in his thought throughout his life. 'Except demonstrations', he writes in a letter of 1613, '(and perchance there are very few of them) I find nothing without perplexities.' By 'demonstrations' here Donne means mathematical proofs. His statement shows that, in his search for some department of human thought which might be regarded as trustworthy, he had been driven back upon the abstractions of mathematics. In this respect he anticipates Descartes, who tells us in his *Meditations* how, when he was seeking among the contents of his mind for something dependable, and independent of opinion, it was the idea of a triangle which he finally settled on. A triangle, regarded mathematically,

> possesses a nature, or form, or essence, which is immutable and eternal, which I have not invented, and which in no way depends upon my mind. This follows from the fact that it is possible to demonstrate various properties of the triangle, as that its three angles are equal to two right angles, that the largest angle is subtended by the longest side, and so on, all of which, whether I wish it or not, I recognize to be very clearly and evidently contained in it, even though, when I first imagined a triangle, I had no thought of these properties, which cannot therefore have been invented by me.[9]

Descartes was some twenty-four years Donne's junior, and his *Meditations*, composed in 1628, inaugurated the transformation of European philosophy. Instead of starting with objects and sense impressions, as Aristotle had done, Descartes starts with a disembodied idea, a ghostly triangle, which must, he feels, be eternal and independent of his mind, since it would retain its mathematical properties whether his mind existed or not. Later and more sceptical philosophers than Descartes would argue that this is a comfortable illusion, and that mathematical notions such as triangles are invented by the human mind in order to import meaning into a meaningless universe. The idea of number itself, Nietzsche maintains, is applicable only to a universe we have fabricated: 'To a world which is *not* our idea the laws of numbers are wholly inapplicable: these are valid only in the human world.'[10]

Donne saved himself from the Nietzschean abyss by religious faith—and the struggle in his mind between faith and reason is something we shall discuss. But it is worth pointing out here that his persistent scepticism left its indelible imprint upon his religion, filling it with contempt for human attainment. 'How imperfect is all our knowledge,' he exclaims, typically, in a sermon of 1626:

> What one thing doe we know perfectly? Whether wee consider Arts, or Sciences, the servant knows but according to the proportion of his masters knowledge in that science; Young men mend not their sight by using old mens Spectacles; and yet we looke upon Nature, but with Aristotles Spectacles. . . . Almost all

knowledge is rather like a child that is embalmed to make
Mummy, then that is nursed to make a Man.[11]

The image of the embalmed child conveys the violence with which
Donne is intent on tearing away human pretensions, and that violence (so characteristic of his religion) is a sign of his own anger at the
failure of reason. Because of his indomitable rationality, he is much
more passionately involved in the sceptical debate than Cornelius
Agrippa, from whose treatise—if it were not for that painful
image—Donne's disparagement of arts and sciences might easily
have come.

While we can be sure that Donne's scepticism lasted throughout his
life, it is harder to say when it began. But it is already present in Satire
III, probably written when he was twenty-one, though there it takes
the moderate form, which some of his contemporaries favoured, and
which was more constructive than blank Classical scepticism. Donne
advises a distrust of all established dogma, in the hope that this
wariness may lead to true knowledge: 'Doubt wisely.'[12] Richard
Whitlock, later in the century, quoted this passage from Satire III in
his *Zootomia* when recommending modified scepticism.[13] By 1601,
as we have seen, and still more by 1611, when Donne wrote his
diatribe against human knowledge in *The Second Anniversarie*,[14] his
scepticism had developed into something more extreme and desolate. Or potentially so, for we must remember that scepticism could
be exhilarating as well as mournful, and Donne, who was able to feel
in two minds about almost anything, exploited its gaiety and dazzle
just as keenly as he submerged himself in its inherent gloom. His
Paradoxes expose the slipperiness of reason and logic, and take a
jaunty view of subjects like inconstancy and suicide which, in reality,
deeply concerned him. They allow us to feel the emancipating power
of scepticism, releasing its adherents from conviction and seriousness. Essentially the paradox is a sceptical form (though it often
pretends to be just humorous), and it developed in the Renaissance
alongside scepticism, receiving its initial impulse from the *Paradossi*
of Ortensio Lando, published in 1543, and much imitated. Donne's
formal paradoxes belong to this tradition, and one of their aims is to
bring us up, by dint of their queerly dogged farcicalities, against the
divergence between reasoning and reality. His poetry, of course,
cultivates this irresponsible kind of paradox too, as well as the more
mystical sort which asserts transcendent impossibilities in order to
defeat the reason.[15]

Scepticism also made Donne dubious about the social institutions which reason has evolved. 'Confined Love' criticizes monogamy from the viewpoint of unbridled naturalism.[16] Animals live promiscuously, why shouldn't humans? True, this line of thought, which is found in Ovid, had become, by the time Donne wrote, a rather hackneyed property. In neo-Latin verse, particularly, we find it being imitated by hordes of harmless pedants and clergymen, none of whom had the slightest intention of becoming sexually exorbitant. What gave such naturalistic protests a new force was the writing of Montaigne, who, equipped with the rare gifts of naïveté and systemlessness, surveyed the civilized world in which he found himself and subjected it to a sorrowful indictment. The atrocities recently committed by the Spaniards in their colonization of Mexico had helped to awaken him to civilization's ghastlier aspects, and in his essay 'On Cannibals' he urged the superior claims to human decency of a people whom Western man, in his prejudice, regarded as barbarous. The cannibals of Brazil, Montaigne relates, lack all intellectual accomplishment, being illiterate, innumerate, and without law, money, trade or property. But they enjoy the beauty and innocence of nature. The very words which import lying, falsehood, treason, dissimulation, covetousness, envy and detraction are unknown among them. Their social organization is equitable, and when they are told about the huge gulf between rich and poor which obtains in the civilized world, they are appalled at the injustice of it, and express surprise that the poor do not simply take the rich by the throat and set fire to their houses. As for the cannibals' habit of killing people and roasting them, Europeans are, Montaigne points out, poorly placed to criticize that, since they roast people alive and do it in the name of religion. The healthiness of Montaigne's scepticism could not fail to find disciples, and in France the libertine school of writers, headed by Théophile de Viau, were soon proclaiming the benefits of nature and ignorance. Donne was too complicated an individual to be won over by any single philosophy, but the rebellious side of his love poems and elegies certainly received stimulus from reading Montaigne.

For Renaissance man, however, the question which lay at the centre of the sceptical debate was not whether reason could establish acceptable social norms, but whether it could attain to a knowledge of God. As we have seen, the answer Aquinas had given was broadly yes. It did not take long for his critics to point out the improbability of this reply. In opposition to Aquinas, John Duns Scotus, a brilliant boy from Berwickshire who studied at Merton College, Oxford, and was soon electrifying the University of Paris with his lectures, declared that God was not absolute intelligence but absolute will. Good, Scotus held, is not good because it accords with any rational principle, but simply because God wills that it is good. Accordingly man's reason is, theologically speaking, useless. The nature of God cannot be comprehended, nor can his existence be proved. The followers of Scotus formed the philosophical school of the Nominalists (from the Latin *nomen*, a name), so called because they maintained that the abstract concepts and universals—such as 'truth' or 'humanity'—upon which Aquinas and the 'Realists' built their philosophy, had no reality but were mere names. There is no such thing as 'humanity', the Nominalists argued, there are only individual men.

Scotus's star pupil in Paris was another British product, William of Ockham, who was born in a Surrey village and had a stormy and spectacular career in the Continental academies before dying of the Black Death in 1349. One of his achievements was to popularize Nominalism. His doctrine was pragmatic and reductive. The things which philosophers argue about, he taught, correspond to nothing in actuality, but are just meanings arbitrarily and conventionally attached to words and propositions. All we can hope to know are individual objects: the universal aspects of truth and error lie far beyond our intellectual reach. We cannot even demonstrate by reason that we have a soul; we can only accept it as a matter of faith. The same goes for the existence of God. Like Scotus, Ockham laid great emphasis on God's will. Ockham's God is not subject to reason, and rational assessments of what constitutes good and evil have no relevance to him. What man regards as the greatest sins 'may be performed by God without any sinful circumstance attaching to them'.[17] God's damnation or salvation of particular men and women is, likewise, wholly a matter of will, and it is futile to try to explain it rationally.

It seems obvious, in retrospect, that Nominalism was due for a revival in the late Renaissance. Its distrust of reason was calculated to fit in with the sceptical mood of new thinkers like Montaigne who had themselves been coming to the conclusion that will rather than reason most satisfactorily accounted for the workings of man as well as of God. Its encouragement of the idea that individual things alone enjoy true being was likely to appeal to an age which, with the break-up of Catholic Europe, was increasingly individualistic in its orientation. Further, since Nominalism placed God beyond man's reach, it left the realm of nature as the only legitimate object of investigation, and this was precisely where, in the sixteenth century, the most progressive thought was starting to be done. Though expectable for these reasons, the resurgence of the anti-rational animus upon which Nominalism feeds came, when it did come, in a shattering and dramatic form through the teaching of John Calvin.

Aquinas had based his belief in a reasonable God upon the biblical information that man is made in God's image. He took this to mean that man's mind and the mind of God work in essentially similar ways, and that man's notions of justice and goodness approximate to God's. Calvin totally rejected this as a diminution of God's majesty and mystery. His *Institutes of the Christian Religion*, first issued in 1536, was by far the most momentous book published during the Renaissance, and the God it posits was the most hideous that Christianity had yet evolved. God, Calvin explains, has predestined, before the beginning of time, certain men to salvation and others to eternal damnation. This judicial sentence is an act of pure will, and bears no relation to the merits of the victims, or to any other comprehensible principle. Calvin's God thus creates large numbers of men for the express purpose of torturing them for all eternity, and there is nothing whatsoever they can do to escape this fate. It is true, Calvin acknowledges, that man was made in the image of God with respect to his reason, but the Fall has so corrupted that image 'that whatever remains is frightful deformity'. Hence our reason, though it can give us some knowledge of the natural order, can have no inkling of God or his kingdom. We are left in these matters 'blinder than moles'.[18] Furthermore our nature is, as a result of Adam's fall, totally depraved, and the depravity is diffused through all parts of our being. Infants are born wicked; their whole nature is a seed of sin; and they are consequently hateful and abominable to God.

Calvinism appealed strongly to the feelings of guilt, fear and bewilderment inherent in the human condition. It also drew succour from that widespread sense of our mortal loathsomeness which inspires all kinds of improving activities, from satire to sanitary reform. In common with theories of racial or national superiority, it held out to the elect the prospect of immense and quite undeserved rights and benefits which were to be denied to the majority of mankind. The saved, it was commonly agreed, would be few in number. 'That they are but a small part of mankind is too apparent in Scripture and experience,' remarked Baxter in *The Saints Everlasting Rest*; and Pierre du Moulin the Huguenot calculated that only one person in a hundred thousand stood any chance of salvation.[19] Calvinism has been compared to Marxism, and resembled it in the revolutionary enthusiasm it bred, as well as in its fatalism and the scope it offered to self-righteousness and hate.

Donne, like every other Protestant of his day, was deeply influenced by Calvinism, but he was an admirer of Aquinas too, and this means that he was caught between two irreconcilable estimates of human reason. Each estimate had its advantages and its disadvantages. If one accepted the viewpoint of Aquinas one was able to think more nobly of oneself and one's powers. On the other hand, God suffered. For if God is really subject to reason then he is no longer omnipotent. The more outspoken statements of the rationalist case bring out this danger very clearly. The precocious Dutch genius Hugo Grotius, for example, who, it is said, could compose perfect Latin verses at nine, went to university at twelve, and edited, at fifteen, the encylopedic works of Martianus Capella, required from God a rationality equal to his own. 'God himself cannot make twice two not to be four,' Grotius stipulated, 'and in like manner He cannot make that which, according to reason, is intrinsically bad, not be bad.'[20] Grotius's God is obviously a safer proposition than Calvin's sinister, arbitrary sadist, but he is also a smaller figure, obliged to get his sums right and to obey moral laws. Calvinism had the disadvantage of reducing mankind and his rational notions to footling irrelevance, but it did preserve the untouchable, unthinkable, illimitable majesty of God. Once we separate out the pros and cons of the two systems in this way, we can understand why Donne found it so difficult to choose between them. His egotism, and his intricate, involved rationality, inclined him to the Scholastic view. He wanted a God he could expostulate with and understand. Yet at the same time his need to imagine absolutes and infinites, which surmounted his own fragmented being, forcefully inclined him to the unknowable God of Calvinism.

In his writings we find him teetering backwards and forwards between the two available Gods. Sometimes he asserts that God is decent and reasonable. We must not, he cautions, impute to God 'a sowrer and worse affected nature, then falls into any man', and he quotes St. Augustine approvingly: 'Never propose to thy self such a God, as thou wert not bound to imitate: Thou mistakest God, if thou make him to be any such thing, or make him to do any such thing, as thou in thy proportion shouldst not be, or shouldst not do.'[21] Here God's goodness and man's goodness are evidently the same in kind. Human nature becomes the measure of God's nature. Elsewhere, however, Donne directly contradicts this gratifying belief. 'How poore, how narrow, how impious a measure of God is this,' he exclaims, 'that he must doe, as thou wouldest doe, if thou wert God!'[22] So God's understanding of goodness isn't the same as ours after all, we gather. If we were God we shouldn't behave as he does. He is beyond our reason—a Calvinist monster in the sky.

This inconclusive, internecine struggle over the status of reason continues throughout Donne's work. We can find him deciding both that God is incomprehensible, and that it is wrong to consider God incomprehensible.[23] In his dealings with God he longs to be able to use his understanding: 'I have not the righteousness of Job, but I have the desire of Job: I would speak to the Almighty, and I would reason with God.'[24] But he also feels that his understanding is unequal to the task, and complains to God about this deficiency:

> Reason your viceroy in mee, mee should defend,
> But is captiv'd, and proves weake or untrue.[25]

These lines imply that reason, if only it functioned freely, would bring him close to God, but in other contexts he denounced attempts to make God intelligible to the reason as a 'lamentable perversenesse', and warns his congregation that Scripture will be out of their reach if they believe it only in so far as it concurs with 'Reason' or 'Philosophy' or 'Morality'.[26]

Donne's altercation with himself gets hotter and more muddled as he approaches the question of election and reprobation, since that was the instance of God's reasonableness or otherwise which touched man most nearly. Donne, like most of his countrymen, believed that God, before he made the world or any souls to put in it, chose some souls for salvation and condemned others to eternal damnation. 'God did elect mee, before he did actually create mee,' as Donne explains. This was at 'the first judgement, before all times', when God separated 'those who were his, the elect from the reprobate'.[27] To human reason this seems unfair. Why should God hate some of his creatures so virulently as to damn them even before they have come into being? The answer generally given by religious moderates in Donne's day was that God did it not out of hatred for the individuals but out of hatred for their sins which, being omniscient, he knew they would commit. This answer roused Calvin to contemptuous fury, for he rightly saw it as a feeble compromise. It made God's will dependent on man's future actions, and it did not, in any case, succeed in rescuing God from a charge of injustice. For it left him in the position of one who knowingly creates defective creatures and then punishes them for being defective. Why should God create

sinners at all if he foresees they must be damned? Despite these snags
Donne clung to the moderate view, since the God it proposed did at
least retain some rudiments of rationality, as Calvin's did not. God
predestined the reprobate to damnation before they were created,
Donne affirms, out of hatred 'for their sins, which he foresaw'.[28]
However, on this point, as on others, he evidently felt ambivalent,
for he expressly remarks, in one of the later sermons, that it is an
error to suppose that predestination is attributable to God's fore-
knowledge of man's works, and this presumably means that the
Calvinist alternative of a totally arbitrary God now seems to him
more likely.[29]

In the end Donne's only reply to the old brain-teasers about God's
justice is that we shouldn't ask such questions. 'But who am I, that
dare dispute with thee?',[30] as he puts it in the 'Holy Sonnets', when
interrogating God on the unfairness of damnation. We should simply be extremely grateful if we are among the elect, and leave it at
that. The examples Donne uses in urging this prudent course depict
God's processes of selection as quite haphazard and wilful. If you
were in an army in which one man in ten was to be killed as an
example, you wouldn't, says Donne, grumble about not being one
of the tenth men. If you were a prince's favourite, showered with
'Honours and Fortunes every day', you wouldn't reproach the
prince for not choosing to favour someone else. If you were being led
out to execution, and a king's pardon arrived, you wouldn't question
why it had come.[31] The examples all concede that, to human reason,
God's judgement can never appear other than mere whim. We
cannot understand, and argument is futile. Worse, it is extremely
foolhardy. '*How* or *Why*', warns Donne, quoting Luther, are
'Dangerous and Infectious' monosyllables, 'Execrable and Damnable'.[32] If you argue about going to Hell, you may go there. As for
the estimated number of the damned, Donne took a milder view
than some, declaring that, given God's exceptional clemency, there
were grounds for hope that only one-third of all the Christians who
had ever lived would burn in Hell.[33]

The alternative to argument was faith. Faith meant accepting that
the monster in the sky was unknowable, but being sure that it was a
good and loving sort of monster. Donne keeps assuring himself, in
poems and sermons, that faith, not reason, is the proper faculty to
employ in divine matters. It is 'a presumpteous thing, and a contempt against God, to submit his Decrees to the Examination of
humane reason', he cautions. True, God's punishments seem sav-
agely disproportionate when compared with the offences which

provoke them, but ours is not to reason why.[34] All arguments about God's justice are equivalent in worth to soap bubbles:

> those toys
> Of glassie bubbles, which the gamesome boyes
> Stretch to so nice a thinnes through a quill.

Reasoning is child's play. Worse, Donne darkly intimates, it is 'heretiques game'—playing with fire.[35] This assertion comes in the 1601 *Progresse of the Soule*, and shows us Donne struggling to suppress reason and cling to faith long before the notion of taking Anglican orders occurred to him. The *Essays in Divinity*, written to prepare himself for orders, maintain that men who seek God by reason 'are like Mariners which voyaged before the invention of the Compass'. They hardly get out of sight of land. Reason depends on sense impression—'the crums and fragments of appearances'—and is thus inevitably 'various and perplex'd', whereas faith is 'infallible.'[36] Consequently all argument about God is redundant. This anti-rational strain persists in Donne's sermons. 'We must abstaine', he instructs, 'from enquiring.' The mysteries of Christianity 'are not to be chawed by reason, but to be swallowed by faith'.[37]

Yet Donne never could swallow them without wanting to let his reason go to work, and the persistence of this desire accounts for the vehemence with which reason is denounced. He was eagerly and insatiably a thinking animal, and despised 'stupid and lazy inconsideration'[38]—as he admits in *Essays in Divinity*, even while trying to argue himself into a unquestioning faith. Aware of this contest within himself, he prays in 'A Litanie':

> Let not my minde be blinder by more light
> Nor Faith by Reason added, lose her sight.[39]

Significantly, in view of Donne's chronic indecision on the point, the prayer is ambiguous. For it may mean that he wishes his faith to remain wholly uncontaminated by reason, and this would tally with his fear expressed elsewhere, that 'the common light of reason' might extinguish the light of faith.[40] Or it may mean that he wants reason to be 'added', though only to a degree that will leave his faith clear-sighted. This latter compromise, which professes allegiance to faith but allows reason a supportive role, is one to which Donne, as an impatient reasoner, was naturally drawn. 'Reason is our Soules left hand, Faith her right,'[41] he told the Countess of Bedford. Both must be used. And in the 'Elegie on Prince Henry', after confessing that matters such as God's essence and providence, and the destination of the soul after death, are the province of faith, not reason, Donne enters a plea for reason and urges that, when duly prepared, it can cope with these mysteries almost as ably as faith can:

> Reason, put t'her best extension,
> Almost meetes Faith.[42]

If that is so, then argument need not be 'heretiques game' after all, and one need not leave one's brain outside when going to church.

At the root of the whole problem lay Donne's only too vivid awareness that the claims of Christianity were wildly improbable. He makes this plain to his congregation with characteristic wit and trenchancy:

> He that should come to a Heathen man, a meere naturall man, uncatechized, uninstructed in the rudiments of the Christian religion, and should at first, without any preparation, present him first with this necessitie; Thou shalt burn in fire and brimstone eternally, except thou believe a Trinitie of Persons, in an unitie of one God, Except thou believe the Incarnation of the second Person of the Trinitie, the Sonne of God, Except thou believe that a Virgine had a Sonne, and the same Sonne that God had, and that God was Man too, and being the immortall God, yet died, he should be so farre from working any spirituall cure upon this poore soule, as that he should rather bring Christian Mysteries into scorne, then him to a belief.[43]

The sardonic send-up of Christianity is worthy of Voltaire. But Donne, needless to say, did not intend it irreverently. Nor did he proceed to acknowledge, in the sermon from which this passage is taken, that the matters touched on must be accepted by faith, not reason. On the contrary, he asserts that if one only tackled the hypothetical heathen in the right way, first getting him to admit that the world must have had a creator, and working through from that to the necessary truth of God's revealed word in Scripture, one would end up with a rationally convinced convert. As an imaginary excursion into the mission field this may strike us as optimistic, but it shows the urgency of Donne's desire to believe that belief is rational, as well as his clear recognition of the irrationalities it entails. The Donne who called 'How' and 'Why' execrable and damnable monosyllables was, and knew he was, addicted to using them and he struggled, albeit intermittently, to justify their use.

Donne's estimate of reason in religious matters issues, then, in violent conflict. It remains to ask how he regarded reason as it related

to knowledge of the natural world. One might expect that, given the
difficulty of fathoming God's ways, he would have decided that
reason was best reserved for the mundane sphere, where it had
hopes of operating with some success. Bacon, his contemporary and
friend, realized this, as indeed Ockham had done over two centuries
before. Bacon's *The Advancement of Learning* is an epoch-making
work because it perceives that theologians are obsolete, and directs
human brain power instead towards opening up the secrets of nature
for man's benefit. It makes the customary concessions about the
truth of God's revealed word, and about our duty to believe it
'though we find a reluctation in our reason'. But that very com-
pliance dismissed religion from the realm of what was profitably
discussable, and thus, in effect, refashioned the educational system of
Europe. It was not long before John Amos Comenius, greatest of the
new educators and a fervent disciple of Bacon, was using the old
argument about man being made in the image of God to support his
belief that the whole created world could, through a proper concentration on scientific and practical subjects, such as humanism had
neglected, be brought within man's grasp.[44] Pansophism was born.
Had Donne been a Baconian we should not have his poetry or
sermons. His exceptional argumentativeness would have found
an alternative outlet, and perhaps from the viewpoint of the mass of
mankind a more valuable one, in science.

But in fact Donne's views about science look nowadays perversely
obscurantist. This is to be ascribed partly to his nagging scepticism,
partly to the conservative bent of his Catholic upbringing. Not that
he denied the existence of progress. As we have noted, he regarded
the maritime compass as a discovery separating the modern world
from the ancient, and (like most contemporary commentators) he
cites gunpowder and printing as comparably important break-
throughs. But progress seems to have been for him something that
had already happened. It was virtually synonymous with history.
That it would continue, and subject the world he knew to mighty
transformations, does not appear to have struck him, or rather he did
not care to think about it. Whereas Bacon loves to let his mind drift
forward through the centuries, and to imagine, in a work like the
New Atlantis, what the gradually achieved triumphs of science might
be, the power and tenacity of Donne's ego shrank from conceiving
of a future in which he would have no part. It is a topic in which he
displays severe uninterest. Rather, as we have observed, he nurses
the belief that the world will end with his death. Intellectual enquiry,
as he understands it, is wholly occupied with the past. When he

writes, in the *Essays in Divinity*, about the research projects which
'great wits' engage in, they are all retrospective—deciphering old
marbles and medals, or explaining ancient prophecies.[45] In such
harmless tasks of retrieval, he was prepared to believe that reason
might achieve something. But that it would drastically change the
present or the future, he found unthinkable.

True, he read a number of works, new and old, on biology,
medicine, astronomy and other sciences. He was eager to find out
what had been thought in every field of enquiry. But his passion was
essentially that of a collector. He did not regard the divergent opinions he found in his reading as part of a slow advance towards
certainty. Rather, the fascinating jumble of theories seemed to him
proof that mankind would always be benighted, and that in science,
as in religion, argument was ultimately pointless. How things are is
known only to God; and scientists see everything dimly because
their conclusions are drawn from mere appearances. Hence the wild
disparities in scientific thinking on even the most elementary topics.
'There are marked', Donne scoffs, 'an hundred differences in mens
Writings concerning an Ant.'[46] He was fond of this example: it
occurs again in *The Second Anniversarie*:

> We see in Authors, too stiffe to recant,
> A hundred controversies of an Ant.[47]

Donne's inference is not, as a modern's might be, that ants have a
better chance of being understood because much human attention is
focused upon them. Rather, he takes the present inconclusive state of
knowledge as proof that knowledge will always be inconclusive. To
the same purpose *The Second Anniversarie* triumphantly lists a
number of rudimentary medical and biological subjects on which no
one has been able to shed light: gallstones, mucus, chlorophyl,
corpuscles and the movement of blood in the heart:

> Knowst thou but how the stone doth enter in
> The bladders Cave, and never breake the skin?
> Knowst thou how blood, which to the hart doth flow,
> Doth from one ventricle to th'other go?
> And for the putrid stuffe, which thou dost spit,
> Knowst thou how thy lungs have attracted it? . . .
> Why grasse is greene, or why our blood is red,
> Are mysteries which none have reach'd unto.[48]

The last lines here may owe something to the sceptical Raleigh,
who observes in his *History of the World* that man, being ignorant

even in 'the least things', cannot 'give a true reason for the Grass under his feet, why it should be green rather than red'.[49] Or perhaps Raleigh had been reading Donne. At all events, to a Baconian Donne's list would constitute a programme for future research. Succeeding generations were to address themselves to answering these very questions. Within four years William Harvey had expounded his theory of the circulation of the blood to the College of Physicians, thus disposing of the problem of the connection between the ventricles. An important step on the way to this had already been taken in the first half of the sixteenth century by Gerard Columba, who discovered pulmonary circulation.[50] Donne's failure to mention Columba may be due to ignorance, but in any case his list was not intended to stimulate thought but to discredit it. Science, he wished to convince his readers, was futile. When you died and went to heaven you would have instant knowledge of everything worth knowing. Why bother now? So Donne reasons:

When wilt thou shake off this Pedantery,
Of being taught by sense, and Fantasy?
Thou look'st through spectacles; small things seeme great,
Below; But up unto the watch-towre get,
And see all things despoyld of fallacies . . .
In Heaven thou straight know'st all, concerning it,
And what concerns it not, shalt straight forget.[51]

Whether we shall have a clear view in heaven about the formation of mucus and gallstones and the circulation of the blood, Donne does not say. But if such things matter, we shall, he is sure.

This then is faith's verdict on science: don't waste time with it, you'll know the answer when you're dead. Donne's championship of ignorance was not simple. He found scientific speculation, like theological speculation, compelling as well as pointless. Just as his pronouncement in *The Progresse of the Soule*, that arguing is 'heretiques game', is preceded by a penetrating indictment of God's curious notions of justice as exemplified in the Fall story, so, in the same poem, he conducts a fascinated survey of the conflicting theories about how a fish breathes, only to cut himself short with the declaration that it doesn't matter:

And whether she leape up sometimes to breath
And suck in aire, or finde it underneath,
Or working parts like mills or limbecks hath
To make the water thinne and airelike, faith
Cares not.[52]

Faith might not, but men naturally did. Duverney, the first scientist to investigate in detail the respiratory organs of fishes, was born within twenty years of Donne's death. Two Englishmen, Ray and Willughby, put ichthyology on a modern scientific footing with their classification of fishes according to structure, published in 1686 at Oxford. Plainly, had Donne's attitude prevailed, such projects would never have materialized. He belongs, in this respect, to a dying tradition, not to the brave new Baconian world. A medieval sense of the futility of human endeavour was always at hand, and suited his aloof, sceptical temperament. He regarded scientific enquiry as, at best, an absorbing diversion: it would never solve or change anything.

In astronomy, too, he remained a sceptical conservative. He read a number of the latest books, but could never bring himself to believe that the earth moved or that the sun didn't. Admittedly, the vast majority of his contemporaries could not either. Copernicus's *De Revolutionibus*, which put forward the hypothesis that the earth rotated and, with the planets, revolved round the sun, had been published in 1543, and before the end of the century the English astronomer Thomas Digges had thought of a way (observation of stellar parallax) by which the truth of the theory might be demonstrated. But there were no instruments fine enough to make the necessary readings, and most people felt that, since the sun can be seen revolving round the earth any day of the year, Copernicus's suggestion was crazy. Luther called him a fool, and educationalists continued to dispense to their charges the well-tried earth-centred system of the universe, perfected by the Egyptian astronomer Ptolemy in second-century Alexandria. Besides being highly sophisticated mathematically, this system was the basis of judicial astrology, a branch of learning which plotted the influence of the planetary motions on men's lives. Unlike astronomy, for which no one had yet found any use, astrology was obviously practical and important, and people were unwilling to countenance any ideas that might upset it. Accordingly Manilius's *Astronomicon* (completed shortly after the birth of Christ), which was geocentric and astrological in emphasis, remained the standard textbook in English schools during the seventeenth century, and even an advanced pedagogue like Comenius had no time for Copernican ideas.[53] The usual estimate of the new science can be gauged from its treatment in the popular epic on the Creation by the French Protestant Guillaume du Bartas, which was one of Milton's favourite books. Du Bartas mocks

Those Clarks that think (think how absurd a jest)
That neither Heav'ns nor Stars do turne at all,
Nor dance about this great round Earthly Ball;
But th'Earth itself, this massie Globe of ours
Turns round-about once every twice-twelve hours.[54]

If the earth really revolved on its axis from east to west, du Bartas
explains, a bullet fired towards the east would never leave the gun
barrel, and an arrow shot straight in the air would fall to the west of
the shooter:

Arm'd with these Reasons, 't were superfluous
T'assaile the Reasons of Copernicus.

Donne regards Copernican astronomy as not just ridiculous but
depressing—a melancholy instance of our general human degener-
acy. He morosely associates it, in a verse letter to the Countess of
Bedford, with the way we let our minds grow sluggish and pamper
our bodies:

As new Philosophy arrests the Sunne,
And bids the passive earth about it runne,
So wee have dull'd our minde, it hath no ends;
Onely the bodie's busie, and pretends.[55]

Here the major intellectual breakthrough of the age is, rather
astonishingly, equated with mental torpor.

But we should not imagine that this represents Donne's consistent
attitude, or that he had one. The fact is, he did not care whether the
new theories were true or not, so long as they supplied material for
his speculation. He wanted to feel free to entertain or dismiss them,
and to play them off against his existing patterns of thought, as mood
or occasion prompted. They were grist to his mill, whether he
denounced them or drew on them for images. Writing to Goodyer in
1609 about how man, being earth, should move towards God,
Donne adds that the new astronomy 'is thus appliable well',[56] meaning that it provides a handy illustration, an additional tool for thinking with. In *Ignatius his Conclave*, Donne's Ignatius concedes, when
he addresses Copernicus, the probable correctness of his theories
('Those opinions of yours may very well be true'), and adds that they
are unoriginal anyway since the idea of a heliocentric universe had
been put forward (as indeed it had) by several ancient astronomers.
What's more, Ignatius continues, Copernicus's discoveries simply

don't matter, because they have no significant effect on mankind. Satan, Ignatius's master, gains nothing from them:

> What cares hee whether the earth travell, or stand still? Hath your raising up of the earth into heaven, brought men to that confidence, that they build new towers or threaten God againe? Or do they out of this motion of the earth conclude, that there is no hell, or deny the punishment of sin? Do not men beleeve? do they not live just as they did before?[57]

This nonchalant acceptance of the Copernican theory contrasts strikingly with Donne's glum account, in *The First Anniversarie*, of the universal perplexity and decay to which it has contributed ('new Philosophy cals all in doubt'), though the two passages were written within a few months of each other. We can select neither as Donne's 'real' response. Ideas to him were plastic and, in the end, all equally questionable. He adapted them to suit his mood. His scepticism freed him from the narrow task of making up his mind. Given humankind's imperfect faculties, all science was, on his reckoning, science fiction anyway, and he used it as a bargain basement, picking and choosing among its propositions with complete freedom and inconsistency. Thus, while the theory of the earth's motion had proved attractively 'appliable' in the Goodyer letter, the arguments against its motion became more appealing in the Somerset Epithalamion, when Donne was describing the feasts and revels at the marriage:

> And were the doctrine new
> That the earth mov'd, this day would make it true;
> For every part to dance and revell goes;
> They tread the ayre, and fal not where they rose.[58]

Here the popular, du Bartasian picture of what would happen if the earth revolved—people falling about, and landing, when they jump, to the west of where they took off—is happily adopted by Donne for the sake of its liveliness. Whether he seriously shared these anti-Copernican objections, we can't tell, and it's the wrong sort of question to ask. As with other scientific ideas, he could accommodate them or not as the fancy took him.

Attempts to show the 'development' of Donne's scientific thinking are, as a result, doomed. The assumption that a poem which incorporates ancient or Ptolemaic astronomy must have been written earlier than one which adopts more modern views is unsafe. We can illustrate this from Donne's treatment of new stars. In 1572 the Danish astronomer Tycho Brahe (a man who stuck in the public mind because he had, as a youth, lost his nose in a duel and substituted an artificial one made of copper alloy) observed a new star in the constellation of Cassiopeia. It gradually dimmed, and disappeared in March 1574, and was regarded by many, including Tycho himself, as a miracle. However, Tycho's pupil Kepler identified two other new stars, one in the Swan in 1600, and one in the Serpent in 1604. Kepler published his observations in the *De Stella Nova* of 1606. Then came Galileo with his telescope, and the map of the heavens was revolutionized. In his *Siderius Nuncius* of 1610, Galileo announced that he had discovered innumerable multitudes of stars never suspected before, and also the four satellites of Jupiter. The impact of his findings on an intelligent contemporary can be judged from a letter Donne's friend Sir Henry Wotton wrote to the Earl of Salisbury from Venice on 13 March 1610, enclosing a copy of the *Siderius Nuncius*:

> Now touching the occurrents of the present, I send herewith unto his Majesty the strangest piece of news (as I may justly call it) that he hath ever yet received from any part of the world; which is the annexed book (come abroad this very day) of the Mathematical Professor at Padua, who by the help of an optical instrument (which both enlargeth and approximateth the object) invented first in Flanders, and bettered by himself, hath discovered four new planets rolling about the sphere of Jupiter, besides many other unknown and lastly, that the moon is not spherical but endued with many prominences, and, which is of all the strangest, illuminated with the solar light by reflection from the body of the earth, as he seemeth to say. So as upon the whole subject he hath first overthrown all former astronomy—for we must have a new sphere to save the appearance—and next all astrology. For the virtue of these new planets must needs vary the judicial part, and why may there not be yet more?[59]

It's fair to add that Wotten retains some doubts ('the author', he remarks, 'runneth a fortune to be either exceeding famous or exceeding ridiculous'), and this is only natural, for Galileo's sightings disturbed, as Wotton appreciates, some of the most basic beliefs of the age—beliefs so habitual that they had merged with religious truths. The Aristotelian notion of the perfect geometrical roundness of the heavenly bodies, and of the spheres in which they moved, had become a part, over the centuries, of Christian belief in the metaphysical perfection of the celestial regions. Galileo's discovery of a knobbly moon (together with Kepler's demonstration in the *De*

Motibus Stellae Martis of 1609 that the planets move round the sun in ellipses not circles) irreparably fractured this divine image. Likewise the appearance and disappearance of new stars shook the semi-mystic belief in the supernatural changelessness of the heavens.

Donne's reaction to all this is typically capricious and inconstant. In *Biathanatos* he criticizes Aristotle's followers because they insist on considering the heavens unalterable despite the discovery of new stars which, Donne says, 'utterly defeat' Aristotle. He gives a marginal reference to Kepler's *De Stella Nova*, published only a couple of years before, to show how up-to-date he is. This certainly makes Donne seem like a convinced new thinker, and it has persuaded C. M. Coffin, the most informed commentator on Donne's astronomical interests, that the poem 'A Feaver'[60] must therefore be relatively early, since it refers to the firmament as 'unchangeable'.[61] But in fact Donne can be found alluding to the unchangeable nature of the firmament in a verse letter written some three years after *Biathanatos*,[62] and in a sermon ten years later he again vehemently aligns himself with the traditionalists:

> If another man see, or think he sees more then I; if by the help of his Optick glasses, or perchance but by his imagination, he see a star or two more in any constellation then I do; yet that starre becomes none of the constellation; it adds no limb, no member to the constellation, that was perfect before.[63]

This crusty obscurantism is just what Donne, in *Biathanatos*, blamed the Aristotelians for. But it would be as risky to conclude that he had become durably more conservative by the time he preached the sermon, as to give an early date to 'A Feaver' on astronomical grounds. His scepticism, it's clear, allowed him to bounce back and forth between opposed views as and when he liked.

So, too, with other components of the new scientific thought. One of the structural principles of the medieval world had been the belief that the four elements were arranged in a cosmic stack, so that there was a region of fire, the top element, surrounding the earth at about the same height as the moon. The Italian scientist Jerome Cardan, who adumbrated, among other things, a theory of evolution, natural selection and the origin of species, had denied that there was an elemental region of fire in his *De Subtilitate* of 1551, which Donne had read. Kepler denied it too, arguing that if we really viewed the stars through a barrier of fire their light would appear tremulous, which it doesn't. Donne apparently accepts these modern opinions in *The First Anniversarie* when he announces that 'The Element of fire is quite put out', and Evelyn Simpson offers this statement as an instance of the gradual advance of his scientific thought. In his earlier poems, she notes, he assumes that there is an element of fire, but after reading Kepler he changed his mind.[64] But this is to make Donne's thought too systematic an article. The fact is that we can find him, years after *The First Anniversarie*, asserting quite as a matter of course that there is an element of fire and that it lies out in space beyond the element of air, and equally we can find him asserting, at much the same date, that the whole matter is 'problematicall' and 'disputable'.[65] In each case the view he takes is the one which happens to fit in with his immediate mood and imaginative drift. Against the lament in *The First Anniversarie* that astronomers have destroyed the 'round proportion' of the celestial regions, we may put the defiantly unscientific affirmation from a sermon of 1627 that 'God hath made all things in a Roundnesse', from the 'round superficies' of the earth to the 'round convexity' of the heavens.[66]

Renaissance scepticism was a poetic advantage to Donne, then, because it made all fact infinitely flexible, and so emancipated the imagination. It also forced him to create a new kind of poetry. For the feeling that reason was fallible and, as a way of getting to know God, obsolete, meant that reasonable men had to find some alternative use for it, and one that would take its fallibility into account. The Baconian answer was experimental science, which made no claim to transcendent truth, but worked towards practical ends within reason's acknowledged limits. Donne, unattracted by this futurist programme, engineered instead a wholesale takeover of poetry by reason, but did so in ways which constantly expose reason's insufficiency, arbitrariness and mutability. As we have seen, poems like 'The Apparition' or 'The Sunne Rising' or 'The Anniversarie' reveal, through and by means of their reasoned exterior, the inner conflicts which reason cannot control.

But it would be wrong to end without remarking that the crisis of reason affected Donne's religious and secular selves in different ways. When he writes about love his scepticism has a liberating and deepening effect. It allowed him a wealth of viewpoints to experiment with, and it released him from a rational estimate of the human psyche. But when he thought, or tried to think, about God, the imminent collapse of reason frustrated and alarmed him. The 'Holy Sonnets', as we have noted more than once, owe much of their vividness as human documents to the desperate intellectual straits to which they are reduced as they struggle to approach the divine. Their frantic solecisms and crude stridencies are integral to their success. T. S. Eliot's contention[67] that Donne was more interested in ideas themselves than in the truth of ideas is, insofar as it applies to his thinking about God, quite misleading. It was precisely the impossibility of having true ideas about God which agitated Donne in his religious writing, and it is this above all which accounts for the sense of strain and confusion in the sermons when we compare them with the great love poems.

We may illustrate this divergent effect of the breakdown of reason on the two areas of Donne's work if we compare (I agree it is a remote comparison, but hope to show its relevance) his rational arguments against atheism in the sermons with the rational structure of the poem 'The Prohibition'. Atheism is a subject to which Donne returns, when preaching, frequently. Quite how common it was in his day is hard to tell, since contemporaries tended to brand as atheistic a whole host of political and religious ideas from communism to doubts about the soul's immortality.[68] Donne's brother-in-law William Lyly was known as 'a witty and bold Atheist',[69] but that is no guarantee that he would actually have denied the existence of God. On the other hand, Calvin claims in the *Institutes* that 'not a few' disbelieve in God, and an example of a self-confessed atheist in the England of Donne's day is Robert Greene, whose *Groatsworth of Wit* recalls its author's youthful atheistic depravity and also attributes atheism to Greene's friend Marlowe. It seems probable, though, that Donne was fascinated by the subject less because he suspected there were atheists in his flock than because he recognized that the question of whether God's existence could be rationally proved was crucial in any estimate of reason's utility. In trying to reconcile reason with faith, Donne continually comes up against the unreasonableness of faith's basic tenet, and continually denies that it is unreasonable at all.

On the issue of whether you could prove God's existence, the schools of Aquinas and Scotus had, Donne notes, disagreed, though not much. The Thomists held that the existence of God was self-evident; the Scotists, that it could be denied, though those denying it were failing to use their reason.[70] Donne speaks respectfully of both views, and inclines to that of Aquinas, but neither was really much use to a troubled Renaissance thinker, since they are not arguments but evasions of argument. If your opponent declares that he doesn't believe in God, it will not advance your case on a logical plane to retort that he is lying or not using his head. Donne, however, is repeatedly reduced to this, though he disguises the poverty of his response in rhetorical trappings of great ferocity. You could not even say there was no God, if there were no God, Donne thunders. The atheist cannot seriously think there is no God. He must pull out his eyes before he can say he sees no God.[71] Every worm, every weed, reminds you of God's existence:

> nay lock up all doores and windowes, see nothing but thy selfe; nay let thy selfe be locked up in a close prison, that thou canst not see thy selfe, and doe but feele thy pulse; let thy pulse be intermitted, or stupefied, that thou feele not that, and doe but thinke, and a worme, a weed, thy selfe, thy pulse, thy thought, are all testimonies, that All, this All, and all parts thereof, are *Opus*, a work made, and *opus eius*, his work, made by God.[72]

Insofar as these tirades yield an argumentative kernel, it is the simple proposition that the world, being made, must have had a maker. 'A Clock or an Organ', Donne spells it out, is manufactured by someone, so it follows that the universe was—and it is in this sense that everything the atheist sees ought to remind him of God. This familiar 'proof' is, needless to say, inherently faulty, since it rests on an unproven correspondence between clocks or organs and the universe, and might as plausibly be employed to maintain that the universe ticks or is worked by bellows. As Donne and his hearers were only too well aware, quite other accounts of the universe's origin were available. Aristotle had taught that it was eternal, and had never been created at all (which is no less logical than believing, as Christianity does, that God is eternal and has never been created at all); Lucretius argued that it was created by the fortuitous falling together of atoms. These opinions are, like Donne's, not susceptible of rational proof or disproof, but their presence in his intellectual environment was necessarily a drawback, and the frailty of his own case accounts for the hectic emphasis with which he presents it. The elaborate demonstrations, in the sermons, that God's existence is self-evident sound angry precisely because they would be unnecessary if true.

The difficulty of his position inclined Donne to back up his arguments with terror. When they are in the dark, and alone, he reminds his hearers, they will not dare to deny that there is a God. It is all very well when they are at sermons or at the theatre, hearing the preacher menace them with God's judgements, or watching actors mimic the downfall of the wicked. Such occasions are easily shrugged off:

Bee as confident as thou canst, in company; for company is the Atheists Sanctuary; I respit thee not till the day of Judgement, when I may see thee upon thy knees, upon thy face, begging the hills, that they would fall downe and cover thee from the fierce wrath of God, to aske thee then, Is there a God now? I respit thee not till the day of thine own death, when thou shalt have evidence enough, that there is a God, though no other evidence, but to finde a Devill, and evidence enough, that there is a Heaven, though no other evidence, but to feele Hell; To aske thee then, Is there a God now? I respit thee but a few houres, but six houres, but till midnight. Wake then; and then darke, and alone, Heare God aske thee then, remember that I asked thee now, Is there a God? and if thou darest, say No.[73]

This outburst of intimidation (with its aptly theatrical reminiscence of Marlowe's Faustus imploring the mountains to fall on him and hide him from God's wrath) could not by any stretch of the imagination be called rational. Neither could its inbuilt assumption, that the mind perceives truth more accurately when disturbed by fear, darkness and solitude. Donne's recourse to reason, rather than faith, to prove God's existence has terminated in reason's breakdown. What lies behind the hostile rhetoric of the passage is the realization that reason is a treacherous faculty, which varies according to mood, circumstances and time of day. These are, indeed, the terms on which reason is accepted in the *Songs and Sonnets*. But in the sermons reason's slipperiness fills Donne with rage, whereas in the poems it is accepted as part of a fuller understanding of the human psyche. The sermons register exasperation at the fact that reason cannot be more dependable; the poems do not.

This brings us to the poem, 'The Prohibition', which we are going to compare in its deployment of reason with Donne's anti-atheistical onslaughts:

> Take heed of loving mee,
> At least remember, I forbade it thee;
> Not that I shall repaire my'unthrifty wast
> Of Breath and Blood, upon thy sighes, and teares,
> By being to thee then what to me thou wast;
> But, so great Joy, our life at once outweares,
> Then, least thy love, by my death, frustrate bee,
> If thou love mee, take heed of loving mee.
>
> Take heed of hating mee,

Or too much triumph in the Victorie.
Not that I shall be mine owne officer,
And hate with hate againe retaliate;
But thou wilt lose the stile of conquerour,
If I, thy conquest, perish by thy hate.
Then, least my being nothing lessen thee,
If thou hate mee, take heed of hating mee.

Yet, love and hate mee too,
So, these extreames shall neythers office doe;
Love mee, that I may die the gentler way;
Hate mee, because thy love's too great for mee;
Or let these two, themselves, not me decay;
So shall I live, thy Stage, not Triumph bee;
Then, least thy love, hate and mee thou undoe,
Oh let mee live, yet love and hate mee too.[74]

I have chosen this poem because it illustrates in a fairly patent way Donne's lifelong habit of making the unreasonable appear reasonable. We can feel the two constituent elements of the poem coming unstuck from each other even at first reading, and this allows us to inspect them in isolation more conveniently. On the one hand we have the sombre directives with which the first and second stanzas open. Poised between trepidation and menace, these work at a deeper level than the rest of the poem, and seem more mysteriously alive than anything else it contains. Set against them we have the arguments which make up the rest of the first two stanzas and the whole of the third. These take the form of logical expansions, explaining what the initial warnings mean. But for all their articulateness they seem shallower than the opening lines, and cannot satisfy us that they have fully accounted for them.

Pursuing this discrepancy, we notice that the poem has a rational structure imposed on it. The discourse splits into three equal sections—two preliminaries plus a conclusion—after the fashion of a syllogism or equation. To sustain the rational atmosphere, the first two stanzas also have matching logical patterns ('Not that . . . But . . . Then . . .'). Further, the scheme of two contradictory extremes cancelling each other out, expounded in the third stanza, introduces a principle of quantification into the poem, which is one of the common rationalizing devices of the *Songs and Sonnets*. They are poems which strive to bring emotion within the sphere of the expressible by quantifying the petals on a primrose or the progress of shadows or love's growth.

But when we consider the kinds of feeling out of which the poem's rational framework is actually built, the appearance of reason dissolves. Fear of nothingness ('my being nothing'), familiar in Donne, is strongly present. He is not sure that he can survive being loved. Love is apprehended as a threat to the ego's separate existence (as in 'The Indifferent' where Donne, anxious to stay uninvolved, professes that he can love any girl 'so she be not true'). But he also, irreconcilably, wants to be loved, and in its contorted way the poem is a plea for it. As often, thoughts of death, and unreasoned misgivings about the future, cloud his dream of fulfilled love. Fulfilment itself is a kind of death. Love means 'wast' and 'decay'; it 'outweares' life. This sense of personal impermanence perturbs the poem, and relates to its basic indecisiveness, which in turn reminds us of Donne's often repeated worries about his wayward, inconstant nature. The attitude to the female is extremely complex—guarded and resentful; mistrustful, yet imploring. Like every woman, she is a composite, created by male desires and fears. She is lethal, yet sustaining—cannibal queen and mother rolled into one, and also, as the poem's imperative tone implies, an object which the male must dominate in order to enhance his maleness. The poem, in other words, is a mass of opposed yearnings, over which a shell of rationality has been fixed. The shell does not prevent us from seeing the disturbed interior. On the contrary, the frantic rationalizing of the poem's outside is itself a symptom of its pervasive anxiety, and culminates in the abject, despairing, contradictory cry of the last line, which comes as near as language can to the inarticulate.

The comparison I intend between 'The Prohibition' and Donne's treatment of atheism in the sermons will now, I hope, be clearer. In both sermons and poem, a rational façade is adopted. In both, it proves inadequate to the emotion it contrives to contain. But behind the collapsing façade in the sermons we detect only a simple, indignant wish that reason would stand up to its task better. In the poem, by contrast, reason's failure is the source of all the enlivening complication. Donne's scepticism has allowed him to penetrate reason and show its foundations in obscure, confused passions. As is customary in his poems, he adapts logic—quantitative, universal, toneless—for non-logical purposes which are qualitative, individual and dramatic.

The crisis of reason was a prolonged affair, and debates about the efficacy of reason as against faith persisted throughout the seventeenth century. They eventually provided the intellectual core of its greatest poem, *Paradise Lost*. But as the century wore on and the

Baconian revolution gathered momentum, reason's prestige increased. Disrespect for its claims gradually became no more than an uninteresting eccentricity. The creative scepticism of Donne's poetry happened, and could only have happened, in a brief interval when reason as an instrument for reaching God had been fatally discredited, and reason as the key to nature was still so untried that it could be dismissed out of hand, as Donne dismisses it. In this short period—between, roughly, the ascendancy of Calvin (d. 1564) and of Galileo (b. 1564)—man's reason was to an unusual degree deprived of exterior objects to work on, and it consequently interiorized, exploring the human psyche and producing imaginative and speculative masterpieces such as Shakespeare's plays and Montaigne's *Essays*. Donne's way of conducting this exploration was conditioned by the fact that he had assimilated the tenacious and subtle argumentativeness of the Scholastic theologians. Scepticism robbed this of its original purpose, so Donne modified it to unfold the inconsistencies of his 'riddling, perplexed, labyrinthicall soule'.[75]

Donne's poor opinion of man's reasoning powers never led him, it is worth adding, to think man insignificant. This is hard for us to grasp, because we tend to relate man's predominance directly to his superior intellect: primacy equals brain-weight. But Donne, though he discredited the intellect, had what must seem to us a positively megalomaniacal view of humankind's universal importance. Typically, when he preached on a text from the Psalms which says that man is 'altogether lighter than vanity', he indignantly refuted it. The Bible cannot mean what it says, he argues. Man isn't a vanity at all, but 'the Apple of Gods eye'. Man is 'all; He is not a piece of the world, but the world it selfe; and . . . the reason why there is a world'.[76] 'All the round world, to man is but a pill,' Donne tells Sir Edward Herbert.[77] In the *Devotions*, he launches into a soaring eulogy of man's size, relative to the rest of creation. To call man a microcosm is insulting: he is not a little world, but a huge one, swarming with immense creatures:

Our creatures are our thoughts, creatures that are born giants; that reach from east to west, from earth to heaven; that do not only bestride all the sea and land, but span the sun and firmament all at once; my thoughts reach all, comprehend all. Inexplicable mystery; I their creator am in a close prison, in a sick bed, any where, and any one of my creatures, my thoughts, is with the sun, and beyond the sun, overtakes the sun, and overgoes the sun in one pace, one step, everywhere.[78]

There is, we notice, an apparent contradiction in Donne's thought about thought. On the one hand we have seen him pointing out that the whole collective intellect of mankind cannot even understand an ant. The simplest facts—why grass is green, or blood red—are beyond man's comprehension. Yet here he writes a rhapsody about the limitless extent of human thought. The inconsistency becomes explicable when we observe how Donne conceives of thought in the passage from the *Devotions*. It is not presented as an analytical or cognitive process but as a guided missile, distinguished by its speed and range. The kind of thought necessary for understanding ants could not possibly be characterized in these terms. Nowadays we should call the human faculty Donne applauds not thought but imagination. As the century went on, that is precisely how the matter came to be seen. Cowley asserted that it was 'Fancy' which took the mind on its remote journey:

> Where never foot of man, or hoof of beast
> The passage press'd.

Hobbes, in the 'Answer to Davenant', drily affirmed that when thought 'seemeth to fly from one Indies to the other' it actually remains inside the head. 'Her wonderful celerity consists not so much in motion as in copious Imagery discreetly ordered and perfectly registered in the Memory.'[79] Hobbes belongs to the new rational era which followed the crisis of reason. Intent on understanding, he derides imagination. But for Donne, writing during the crisis, understanding is acknowledged to be impossible, so the kind of thought directed towards it is futile. Imagination becomes, in the passage from the *Devotions*, synonymous with thought, and enables man to conquer the cosmos. That should help us to see why the crisis of reason produced great poets as well as great sceptics.

9

Imagined Corners

These last pages will draw things together, and be about drawing things together. What, we may start by asking, have angels, mummy, mandrakes, coins, maps and shadows in common, apart from the fact that they are among Donne's favourite subjects? The answer seems to be that they are meeting places for opposites. The existence of each involves the proximity of two elements normally antipathetic, so its nature is simultaneously single and double. Also, the listed items are for the most part problematic or technically complicated, surrounded by an outwork of theory. They stand apart, that is to say, from the simple and natural, drawing attention to their singularity. They are conceptual corners: for a corner unites divergent lines or planes, but it also intrusively separates them. This dual function was important to Donne, because though he liked joining things he also liked the joint to show. Division fascinated him as much as union. What pleased his imagination was not a sense of the world's various contents amicably coalescing, but of opposition surviving within union, of paired antagonists locked together (or 'yoked by violence together', as Johnson famously complained).

It is this enjoyment of friction or angularity that is missing from T. S. Eliot's 1921 account of how Donne's mind worked:

A thought to Donne was an experience, it modified his sensibility. When a poet's mind is perfectly equipped for his work, it is constantly amalgamating disparate experience; the ordinary man's experience is chaotic, irregular, fragmentary. The latter falls in love, or reads Spinoza, and these two experiences have nothing to do with each other, or with the noise of the typewriter or the smell of cooking; in the mind of the poet these experiences are always forming new wholes.[1]

The effortless, sensual blending which Eliot depicts here does not, in fact, sound like Donne. It sounds more like Eliot (the Eliot of 'Prufrock'), or Joyce. Eliot himself seems to have come to realize this, and he punished Donne for not living up to his prototype in the

disparaging essay called 'Donne in Our Time' written ten years after
the paragraph just quoted. According to this later account there is in
Donne 'a manifest fissure between thought and sensibility'. Donne
does not, we now learn, unify experience, but manages only 'a
puzzled and humorous shuffling of the pieces'.[2] His experience is, in
other words, chaotic, irregular and fragmentary like that of the
'ordinary man' whom Eliot had, in his earlier piece, contrasted
Donne with. This second version of Donne is as far from the truth as
Eliot's first shot. The puzzled shuffler, shoring fragments against his
ruins, is, like the typewriting Spinoza-reader, a version of Eliot
rather than of Donne—and of an Eliot whom the 1931 Eliot felt he
had outgrown.

But Eliot's two accounts are not just wrong, they are valuably
wrong, because an adequate view of Donne has to take something
from each, contradictory as they are. Donne liked imagining opposites which combined, while remaining opposites. He cultivated
disjunction and junction equally and at the same time. We shall be
able to see this more clearly if we examine the assortment of Donnean enthusiasms listed at the start of the chapter, and how he
handled them. Take, first, angels. The different ways of regarding
angels are practically inexhaustible, since there is no observable
reality to limit one's imaginings. However, when we collect the
many references to angels from Donne's poems and sermons we find
that his interest is repeatedly and narrowly focused on the question
of angelic duality:

> They are Creatures, that have not so much of a Body as flesh is, as
> froth is, as a vapor is, as a sigh is, and yet with a touch they shall
> molder a rocke into lesse Atomes, then the sand that it stands
> upon; and a milstone into smaller flower, then it grinds.[3]

Of course, the dual nature of angels strikes Donne in other ways than
this: they are 'super-elementary meteors', suspended between God's
nature and man's; they are six thousand years old, yet have not 'one
wrinckle of Age in their face, or one sobbe of wearinesse in their
lungs'. But in each case it is the duality of angelhood that he fixes on,
effecting a compromise between elements (youth, age; humanity,
divinity) which are naturally antagonistic. The impossible fusions
angels encompass make them 'the Riddles of Heaven', Donne
appreciatively observes. Single, simple angelic features like beauty
or goodness did not appeal to him.

In deciding what angels were made of he had had to choose
between opposed views. The Scotists believed them composed of

matter (though spiritual matter); Aquinas and his followers denied
that they were material in any way.[4] Donne sided with Aquinas, and
he did so because the Thomist theory preserved the contradictory
nature of angels clean and unblurred, as he wished it to be. Angels, so
conceived, had massive physical powers, yet were not physical at all.
To have attributed body to them, with the Scotists, would have
spoiled them as riddles. For Donne, they were knots of unconnected
worlds, like his own poetic images.

Mummy and mandrakes resemble angels in that there is something unnaturally composite about them. The mandrake is a plant of
the potato family, common in Mediterranean countries, and with a
long history of use as an aphrodisiac and fertility drug. Herbals in
Donne's day showed it with forked roots like legs. It was said to
sprout under gallows where fat or urine dropped from corpses, and
to shriek when pulled up. It was thought that you would die if you
pulled it from the ground, so a dog was generally tied to it to get it
out. Enterprising pedlars perpetuated the belief in its semi-humanity
by carving bryony roots in the shape of men and poking barley or
millet seeds in the scalp and chin, so that the ersatz mandrakes could
be sold complete with growing hair.[5] How far Donne's credulity
stretched, we can't tell. Maybe he left the question unanswered in his
own mind, because the imaginative attraction of mandrakes dis-
inclined him to renounce them on merely intellectual grounds. They
combined human and vegetable, and their uncanny aura drew attention to the unnaturalness of that combination. This made them apt
vehicles for Donne's sense of friction within unity.

The attraction of mummy was similar, but the elements it drew
together were life and death. It was a black substance like pitch,
stocked by apothecaries, and prescribed in the seventeenth century as
a cure for contusions, 'spitting of blood', and other mishaps. The
medical notion behind it was that the bituminous preparations used
by the Egyptian priests in embalming the dead must have had great
preservative power, and could therefore aid the living. The wrap-
pings and flesh of mummies were accordingly imported from the
Near East, and Donne speaks with approval of their pharmaceutical
use. Contemporary medical authorities, it has been noted, did not
share his enthusiasm, and it was reported that in Alexandria mummies for the European trade were manufactured on the spot from the
bodies of beggars and plague victims.[6] Presumably Donne had not
heard these rumours. But even if he had, he would quite probably
have continued to find mummy irresistible. The resurrection of the
body, a bracelet of bright hair about the bone, a sundial in a

grave—to a mind that sustained itself with such imaginings, the actual existence of mummified flesh must have seemed like a dream come true, a poetic image brought down to earth and listed in the pharmacopoeia. What's more, with its reputed life-giving efficacy the dead mummy flesh was a meeting place for logical opposites, a point where light and dark crossed and the poles of the universe folded together.

Maps, though less mystically, gave the same satisfaction, and are, as we have seen, associated with the reconciliation of death and life in the 'Hymne to God my God, in my sicknesse':

> As West and East
> In all flatt Maps (and I am one) are one,
> So death doth touch the Resurrection.[7]

Maps were of great importance to Donne, but not for any geographical purpose. He had no interest in foreign parts and his allusions to them, as a systematic study of his imagery has shown, are 'sparse and surprisingly colourless'.[8] The imaginative potential of maps lay, so far as he was concerned, in the tricks they allowed you to play with space. They were devices for making contraries meet. Through the conventions of cartography, the far points of the compass could be concertinaed:

> In a flat Map, there goes no more, to make West East, though they be distant in an extremity, but to paste that flat Map upon a round body, and then West and East are all one.[9]

Sermons, letters and poems repeatedly come back to this idea.[10] As the maps bent round in Donne's mind, evening blended into dawn, life embraced death, 'that which was nothing' became 'All'. Hurtful contraries healed: 'the farthest West is East, where the West ends, the East begins.'[11]

The peculiar use Donne puts compass points to seems to have struck Gerard Manley Hopkins, and when he wrote a mock-metaphysical poem himself, he copied it:

> The earth and heaven, so little known,
> Are measured outwards from my breast.
> I am the midst of every zone
> And justify the East and West.[12]

The stanza draws attention not only to Donne's imaginative mannerism but also, perceptively, to its motive. The desire to join compass points, like the effort to unify reason and faith, was part of Donne's lifelong concern with the splits in his own nature.

Maps were bound to attract him too, quite apart from their flexibility, because they were concentrated, as he aspired to be himself. They had a compacting power similar to that of love, which could make 'one little roome, an every where' and put the world in your hands. Atlases and girls had, for this reason, always interchanged in Donne's mind. Girls were 'all States'—Americas, New-foundlands, Indias of spice and mine, world maps with meridians and creeks and fair Atlantic navels.[13] Like atlases, they could put you in 'the midst of every zone' without your needing to get out of bed, and could smooth away the world's extremes:

> Where can we finde two better hemispheares
> Without sharpe North, without declining West?[14]

he demands, gazing into the girl's eyes in 'The Good-morrow', and thinking of maps and globes.

Coins and shadows, the other two items on the list we started with, are composites too, or so Donne liked to think. He had a mania about coins, wrote his first extant elegy 'The Bracelet' about them, and continued to dwell on them for the rest of his life. What he persistently stresses is their dual nature.[15] They are minted by the conjunction of a moulded stamp with a piece of bullion, so they exist both as simple discs of metal and also on an abstract plane, as value. Hence they are miniature models of the body and the soul. Their imprint has no physical substance, being merely an indentation in the surface, yet it gives form and worth to the metal upon which it is imposed. What has been purely material becomes 'the soule of trade'.[16] Given this interplay of matter and spirit, it was natural that Donne should associate coins with angels, and the fact that a current English coin was actually called an angel was a lucky coincidence which he exploits in 'The Bracelet' and elsewhere.

Shadows were even more like angels, for they could be seen, yet had no substance. You could regard them as non-existent, just deprivation of light; or you could think of them as thickened air, like that which, in Aquinas and Donne, angels make their faces and wings out of. Their disputable nature suited Donne's temperament, and he takes now one view of them, now another. 'A shadow is nothing,' he pronounces; or alternatively it is 'a thicker light'; or it is 'not no light, but a pallid waterish and diluted one'.[17] Shadows are intermediate, as well as indeterminate, pursuing their existence, or non-existence, between light and darkness; and this too qualified

them for inclusion among the metaphysical half-breeds Donne was
inspired by.

The list we have been looking at is only representative, of course, not
complete. It would be easy to add other items, already touched on in
this book—sponges or jelly, for instance, which mediate between
fluid and solid, or 'specular stone' and the glass houses built from it,
which combine transparency with impenetrability. The principle of
joined opposites which underlies all these interests permeates
Donne's poetry. He works by joining. But before he could be
obsessed by joints he had to be obsessed by division. The mind
which strives to unite east and west must be unusually conscious of
their separation, for it is hardly a matter which troubles most people.
Donne's vision was conjunctive only because it was disjunctive, and
he synthesized only because he was by nature analytic. He created the
fragmentation which he strove to overcome.

The joints which intrigued him most were subtle and complicated
ones: imagined corners where the connection is both intimate and
abstruse. The lovers' hands in 'The Extasie', for instance,

> firmly cimented
> With a fast balme,

are much more intricately stuck together than at first appears, not
only because 'cementing' was an alchemical term for the high-
temperature interpenetration of solids, but also because 'balm' in the
Paracelsian system was a sort of volatile fluid, of great remedial
power, diffused throughout the whole body. Donne's references to
this natural balm (also called 'balsum' and 'balsamus') are frequent.
Its subtle essence amalgamated, for him, the physical and the
spiritual:

> If a man doe but prick a finger, and binde it above that part, so that
> the Spirits, or that which they call the Balsamum of the body,
> cannot descend, by reason of that ligature, to that part, it will
> gangrene.[18]

Medical theory connected balm and mummy, because it was
believed that balm could be extracted from the dead and that
mummy contained it. So the lovers, lying like 'sepulchrall statues',
with clasped hands, are joined by a medico-alchemical life-support
system, transfusing vital balm into each other.

The 'Spirits' which Donne, in the passage just quoted, half-
identifies with Paracelsian balm, are another of the joining agents

which claimed his attention. Their function in the Galenic physiology current in the sixteenth century was intermediate between mind and matter. According to this theory, the blood did not circulate but ebbed and flowed in the veins as a result of the expansion and contraction of the right side of the heart. When food was digested, the liver separated out 'natural spirits', and these passed up with the blood into the heart's right ventricle, and through the central partition, or septum, into the left ventricle, where by mingling with air from the lungs they were refined into 'vital spirits'. Continuing upward through the arteries, these underwent further refinement in the brain, where they became 'animal spirits', virtually indistinguishable in lightness and tenuity from mind. The brain then forced the animal spirits along the nerves to the muscles where, by a process of inflation, they caused muscular contractions, and so operated the limbs.

Viewed in this way the human body was essentially a distilling apparatus, like an alchemical retort, and it had for Donne much the same attraction, appealing to his interest in fumes, sighs, vapours and material diffusion generally. But the spirits were particularly alluring because, like angels, they bridged divided worlds. For Donne, they were the vital human component, as he explained in a sermon:

> In the constitution and making of a natural man, the body is not the man, nor the soul is not the man, but the union of these two makes up the man; the spirits in a man which are the thin and active part of the blood, and so are of a kind of middle nature, between soul and body, those spirits are able to doe, and they doe the office, to unite and apply the faculties of the soul to the organs of the body, and so there is a man.[19]

The imaginative drive towards union is the same, here, as in 'The Extasie', where the desirability of applying the faculties of the soul to the organs of the body in love-making is urged:

> As our blood labours to beget
> Spirits, as like soules as it can,
> Because such fingers need to knit
> That subtile knot, which makes us man:

> So must pure lovers soules descend
> T'affections, and to faculties,
> That sense may reach and apprehend,
> Else a great Prince in prison lies.[20]

But these famous stanzas are not just about fruitful and liberating union. They are also about the effort to overcome an eventually insuperable obstacle. The spirits the blood labours to beget are as 'like' souls as it can possibly manage, but they are not souls. Nor even, being physical ('fingers'), are they much like souls at all. The expression of thwarted strenuousness in the lines keeps alive a sense of division even while urging union; and this, as we have seen, is eminently Donnean.

The spirits were important to Donne because they connected body and soul, and that in turn makes it clearer why (as we have noticed) he was so preoccupied with the nerves. For the nerves functioned as a cohesive network threading through the body, and provided the channels through which the unifying spirits reached the muscles from the brain. Significantly Donne, in his allusions to nerves, does not think of them as making the body move (though that was their ultimate purpose in the Galenic system), not even as making it feel. Rather, they held it together, like strings. The emphasis highlights Donne's worry about personal fragmentation, and his need for something that (as he puts it in 'The Funerall') would 'tye' his 'parts' and make him one.

Allied to this, though the association may not at first be very apparent, are Donne's extraordinarily persistent references to digestion, which of all bodily operations seems to have fascinated him the most. He uses digestive terminology to characterize a wide variety of processes, ranging from education to the Christian's experience of God. We acquire new knowledge, he observes, by rule and example, 'as Assimilation makes that meat, which we have received and digested, like those parts, which are in our bodies before'. Or alternatively, 'as my meat is assimilated to my flesh, and made one flesh with it', so 'my soul is assimilated to my God'. Or again, contemplation of Christ ensures 'a Transfusion, a Transplantation, a Transmigration, A Transmutation into him, (for good digestion brings alwaies assimilation)'.[21] Donne's enthusiasm, when discussing the resurrection of the body, about situations where men have been digested by fishes, and the fishes by other men, belongs to the same imaginative nexus. The key to his digestive obsession lies in his recurrent use of the term 'assimilation'. For the inspiring thing about the stomach, in his view, was that it united food and feeder so closely that one became the other. It was the perfect blender—better, even, than copulation, for though that united people they could come apart afterwards, whereas digestion was irreversible. Presumably this feeling about the stomach's trusty hold explains the cannibalistic tinge which commonly goes with passionate love. 'I could eat you,' we say, meaning that we want total possession. Signs of the same oral craving occur in Donne. He inhales the girl's soul, or drinks her 'sweet salt teares', or crunches her like a nut:

> Chang'd loves are but chang'd sorts of meat,
> And when hee hath the kernell eate,
>   Who doth not fling away the shell?[22]

Behind the adolescent bravado of these lines lurks a desire to possess the external world by consuming it, which corresponds to the infant's first experience of life in separation from its mother. Donne's fondness for the word 'suck' in both poetry and prose is worth noting. Men 'sucke the sweet of the Earth, and the sweat of other Men'; the Commonwealth 'sucks up' money by trade.[23] Like digestion it is fitted into a remarkable range of contexts, secular and divine. God sucks souls, the flea sucks the lovers' blood. Sucking is the primal assimilative act, its end, like that of 'all digestions, and concoctions' being 'that meate may become our body'.[24] Hence its prominence in Donne's universe, where assimilation is one of the aims of being.

The impulse to bind opposites can be seen either in single images or in the planning of whole poems. A characteristic Donne image like that of 'gold to ayery thinnesse beate' reveals a desire to describe something which is material and immaterial at the same time. On a larger scale 'The Extasie' and 'Aire and Angels' and 'A Valediction: forbidding Mourning' and 'The Sunne Rising' and 'The Dreame' all reach towards a compromise or reconciliation of contraries. 'The Extasie' reconciles body with soul; 'Aire and Angels' seeks a compromise between Love which is wholly insubstantial and love which substance overburdens. 'A Valediction: forbidding Mourning' reconciles absence with presence; 'The Sunne Rising' professes that losing the world and having it are the same. In 'The Dreame' waking and sleeping life are not distinguished but superimposed: girl blends into dream, dream into girl: 'My Dreame thou brok'st not, but continued'st it.'[25] It is as if Donne had thought out these poems as variant formulations of a persistent and ultimately insoluble problem, which involved the simultaneous possession of contraries.

As the poet of imagined corners he was also attracted by apparently simple situations which, when examined, split in half, revealing themselves as entailing reciprocity or interaction. Talking of fish in *The Progresse of the Soule*, for instance, he notes how:

> A female fishes sandie Roe
> With the males jelly, newly lev'ned was
> For they had intertouch'd as they did passe.[26]

To most poets 'intertouch' would seem a needlessly fussy verb to invent. Either things touch, or they don't. But for Donne the intimate convergence of male and female, even in fish, involves a two-way touching. Each creature touches, and is touched. The simple collision involves two kinds of contact, and two opposed kinds, for one is active and one is passive. Between the fish, Donne inserts his imagined corner. His eye for such reciprocities made him especially prone to invent verbs with the prefix 'inter-'. 'The main point with which we intercharge one another,' he writes in *Pseudo-Martyr*; and 'The same falsehoods, of which they interaccuse one another'. His lovers are 'inter-assured of the mind'; their love 'Interinanimates two soules'. Tyrants and their subjects 'interwish' curses in 'The Curse'. The 'Blest payre of Swans' in the Somerset Epithalamion are bidden to 'interbring / Daily new joyes'.[27] The mutual action, given and received, is like the balm which passes between the lovers' clasped hands, or like their threaded eyebeams. It bonds by interchange; and in that respect it resembles the returned love which Donne keeps seeking in the poems as a match for his own—'So thy love may be my loves spheare.'[28] The imaginative habit, regulating Donne's choice of prefix and type of coinage, is determined ultimately by emotional need. The subtle embrace of action and passivity within a single verb satisfies him, because it helps to order his world, rescuing it from 'fragmentary rubbidge'[29] (as he called it in *The Second Anniversarie*) and suffusing it with unity and mutuality.

The search for close and subtle bonds seems to have been what attracted him to the subject of two girls making love to each other. 'Sapho to Philaenis' is the first female homosexual love poem in English: a limpid pool of sensuousness, swimming with twinned words and images like a deep mirror:

> Thou art not soft, and cleare, and strait, and faire,
>   As Down, as Stars, Cedars, and Lillies are,
> But thy right hand, and cheek, and eye, only
>   Are like thy other hand, and cheek, and eye. . . .
> My two lips, eyes, thighs, differ from thy two,
>   But so, as thine from one another doe;
> And, oh, no more; the likenesse being such,
>   Why should they not alike in all parts touch?

Hand to strange hand, lippe to lippe none denies;
  Why should they brest to brest, or thighs to thighs?
Likenesse begets such strange selfe flatterie,
  That touching my selfe, all seemes done to thee.
My selfe I'embrace, and mine owne hands I kisse,
  And amorously thanke my self for this.
Me, in my glasse, I call thee; But, alas,
  When I would kisse, teares dimme mine eyes, and glasse.[30]

The union, which Sappho's dreamy accents describe, seals two
bodies which are at once separate and the same—so much the same,
that Sappho does not know whether she is kissing herself or
Philaenis; so separate, that the whole poem is spoken while Sappho
touches herself in front of her glass. Philaenis is not there. Yet she is
there, for Sappho feels her when she feels herself. The two girls are
perfectly united, though apart, for they inhabit a single body—
Sappho's. Making love to herself, Sappho escapes the duality which
ordinary human lovers can never overcome. The beautiful confusion, melting and merging the loved and loving flesh into one
identity, is a physical replica of the union of the interinanimated souls
in 'The Extasie', which also became inextricably fused, so that the
hearer could no longer distinguish their voices, 'Because both meant,
both spake the same.' For that matter, Sappho seeing 'Me' as 'thee' in
her glass inevitably recalls 'A Valediction: of my Name in the
Window', where, in the glass, 'you see me, and I am you.' And
Sappho's expedient for turning absence into presence links her
monologue with the other Donne poems which strive to show that
parted lovers are still together.

The congruence of 'Sapho and Philaenis' with Donne's persistent
concerns is worth remarking, for his modern editor, Dame Helen
Gardner, finds it 'uncharacteristic of Donne in theme, treatment,
and style', and accordingly denies its authenticity, despite its appearance in the first edition of his poems and in various dependable
manuscripts. 'I find it difficult', states Dame Helen, 'to imagine him
wishing to assume the love-sickness of Lesbian Sappho.'[31] To
imagine him, on the other hand, wishing to depict a union of lovers
so complete that the two identities, being identical, sink into one, is
only too easy, and he could not do this unless he wrote about two
precisely similar bodies. Sappho's homosexuality recommended
itself as the answer to an imaginative problem.

The merging instinct, which collapses distinctions and runs east and
west together, lies behind Donne's taste for abstruse comparisons,

and it shows itself, too, in his inclination to enliven inanimate
objects. Take his comparison of lovers with a pair of compasses. This
annoyed Johnson, who 'doubted whether absurdity or ingenuity'
predominated in it.[32] But the singularity does not reside in the
elements compared, though that is what Johnson objected to.
Guarino, it has been pointed out, had likened separated lovers to the
feet of a pair of compasses before Donne. What Donne's unifying
energy contributes is not comparison but assimilation. The compasses come to life, expressing through their stirrings the motions of
the two souls:

> If they be two, they are two so
>   As stiffe twin compasses are two,
> Thy soule the fixt foot, makes no show
>   To move, but doth, if the'other doe.
>
> And though it in the center sit,
>   Yet when the other far doth rome,
> It leanes, and hearkens after it,
>   And growes erect, as it comes home.[33]

The delicacy with which the compasses are imagined, and animated,
is the really remarkable thing. It is achieved by Donne's verbs. The
fixed foot 'leanes, and hearkens', as if bending its ear yearningly to
catch some news of its companion. The moving foot 'far doth
rome'—and the verb makes it sound as if it is travelling trackless
wastes, rather than drawing a circle on a sheet of paper. The dimensions swell; the gestures grow fluid and human. Donne feels with the
compasses, and endues them with feeling. There is nothing of this in
Guarino, or in the other poets who employ the compass image
before Donne.[34] They offer neat, inert comparisons. He interfuses
and animates.

We have already noticed this enlivening tendency in, for example,
the trembling awareness which the 'ragged bony name', scratched in
the pane of glass, acquires, or in the solicitude with which Donne
addresses his jet ring. There were, also, one or two common objects
which almost invariably impressed him by their human look.
Candles and coins come into this category. Through the variation of
their flame and size candles take on, in Donne, distinct expressions
and demeanours. 'Then thy sicke taper will begin to winke,' he tells
the girl in 'The Apparition', and the meagre, flickering thing instantly becomes a responsive participant in the scene. One of the
Problems, too, characterizes Puritan preaching by comparing it to

the unhealthily pious personality which the cheaper type of candle radiates: 'Thin-wretched-sick-watching-Candles, which languish and are in a Divine Consumption from the first minute.'[35] By contrast, the candle in 'Recusancy' sports a sinister, erotic leer:

> the tapers beamie eye
> Amorously twinkling, beckens the giddie flie,
> Yet burnes his wings.[36]

So when Donne in 'The Canonization' proclaims that he and the girl 'are Tapers' the assimilation of people to candles rests upon a well-established habit.

Candles in Donne's day were, of course, much less standardized than the characterless cylinders turned out by modern production methods. For one thing, there was a primary class distinction in candles between those made of wax and those made of tallow. This separation was so rigid that London had two distinct livery companies, the Waxchandlers and the Tallow-chandlers, to control the two branches of the trade. But candle-making was by no means solely commercial. A great deal of more or less makeshift domestic manufacture went on, using strained tallow left over from cooking. Donne evidently found the subject intriguing, and the 'thrifty wench' scraping and barrelling kitchen stuff to sell to the chandlers and help pay for her trousseau earns a place in his second Satire.[37]

Elizabethan coinage was also extremely un-uniform, since it was produced by the primitive technique of hammering. Machined coinage was almost unknown in England until Cromwell introduced it.[38] The sharply embossed, milled-edged, perfectly rounded Cromwellian coins are immediately recognizable as modern currency, and beside them the squashed, irregular products of Elizabeth's Mint look like tribal tokens. But their untidiness made them poetically useful, because they had the endless individuality of people and this, quite apart from their human faces, encouraged Donne's animation of them. So when he remarks in a letter to Goodyer that a coin which has had its stamp removed and been re-struck looks 'awry and squint',[39] or when he calls the coin with which the town crier in 'The Bracelet' is hired a 'lean thred-bare groate', we should recognize that the quick, brilliant metaphors, enduing the external world with human interest, were to some extent the product of the backward, ramshackle technology in which he lived.

However, it's also true that Donne's animating urge was so healthy that it would probably have survived even in modern conditions. He could turn a machine into a human being as naturally as a candle or a coin—witness the highly Dickensian clock in the 'Obsequies to the Lord Harrington' which feels 'mismotion and distemper' in its wheels, gets 'shaking palsies' in its hands, and seizes up amidst a variety of other ailments.[40] Given this imaginative tendency, Donne's choice of subject for his epic poem *The Progresse of the Soule* becomes easy to understand. Whatever he might have made (had he finished it) of its religio-satirical possibilities, the basic attraction of the scheme was that it required him to simulate the consciousness of a host of different vegetables and animals, depicting—as he explains in the Epistle to the reader—what it was like to be a mushroom or a melon or a spider or a post-horse, as if his own soul had inhabited these creatures and could remember the experience.[41]

The subtle knots binding dislocated modes of being, of which Donne's animated coins or candles are one species, can be detected, too, in his observation of time. He is attracted by instantaneousness. The poet who liked to believe that

> Paradise and Calvarie
> Christs Crosse, and Adams tree, stood in one place,[42]

also found 'Upon the Annunciation and Passion falling upon one day'[43] a congenial topic. 'I hate extreames,' he wrote in 'The Autumnall', choosing instead autumn as the time when the contraries of growth and decay meet and are suspended.[44] A similar preference colours, much later, his depiction of the afterlife: 'In paradise, the fruits are ripe, the first minute, and in heaven it is always Autumne.'[45] The notion of instant autumnal fruit, simultaneously pristine and mature, had already been an important aspect of paradise in *The Progresse of the Soule*, where the fatal apple was

> Prince of the orchard, faire as dawning morne,
> Fenc'd with the law, and ripe as soone as borne.[46]

These apples, whether they grow in Eden or heaven, are imagined corners, uniting, like angels, the properties of youth and age.

    Another imagined corner is eternity. It suited Donne, because it collapsed distinctions of time as furled maps collapsed distinctions of space. Eternity has no 'distinctions, no limits, no periods, no seasons, no moneths, no yeares, no dayes', as Donne reminded his congregation. The Creation and the Last Judgement are 'not a minute asunder in respect of eternity, which hath no minutes'.[47] Yet eternity is also, for Donne, duration. He seems to have imagined it as immensely long time, which, for some reason, cannot be subdivided into intervals like ordinary time. Accordingly it satisfied the same cohesive instinct as did mummy or mandrakes, because it impossibly united the idea of extension with the idea of indivisibility. It is the most unimaginable imagined corner of all. Love, in the *Songs and Sonnets*, had served the same purpose:

> Love, all alike, no season knowes, nor clyme,
> Nor houres, dayes, monthes, which are the rags of time.[48]

Love endures, but has no duration; for duration involves time, and love 'no tomorrow hath, nor yesterday'. It melts the poles of past and future, time's east and west.

Simultaneity, and the obliteration of sequence ('houres, dayes, monthes') were goals that appealed, too, to Donne's dramatic taste for paradox and condensation. His impatience for 'The last busie day' when all souls would rise and all the past would magically become the present, was no more than a manifestation in the religious sphere of a connecting and compacting tendency which spreads through all his thought and poetry. The instant eclipse of love, which he warns the girl about in 'A Lecture upon the Shadow', is presented within the fiction of the poem as an undesirable eventuality, but is irresistible to Donne as a poetic event because, like the fruits of paradise, it forces temporal opposites into spectacular alliance:

> Love is a growing, or full constant light;
> And his first minute, after noone, is night.[49]

The paradisal fruit was ripe the first minute; love is dead the first minute. The incidentals vary, and adapt to different contexts, but the fascination of simultaneity persists.

Donne's emphasis on eternity and the Last Judgement is not the only element in his religious sensibility which derives from this fascination. On the crucial theological question of the creation of the soul and its inheritance of original sin he may be observed opting for a doctrine which is transparently a manifestation of the same imaginative interest.

Concerning the soul's creation, two alternative timetables were offered by Christian writers. One view was that God had produced the full complement of human souls at an early stage in his creative process, and that they then remained in a suspended state until they paired up with bodies as their turn for earthly life came round. The other theory, put forward by St. Augustine, was that each soul came into existence separately at the moment of its entrance into a human embryo.[50] The process by which the soul got into the embryo was a further subject of contention. The Western Fathers generally adhered to the belief that it was propagated by the parents. Tertullian, for instance, explained that the reason one experienced faintness and dimness of sight immediately after orgasm was that one had just lost a small portion of one's soul which had been contained in the semen.[51] Milton also favoured this doctrine because the alternative opinion—that God created and infused each new soul individually—struck him as unbecoming. If God had to make new souls every day to go into the bodies spawned by man's libidinous passions it would, Milton argued, be a tiresome occupation and would allow God no rest even on the sabbath.[52] Donne, at the stage when he was formulating his position, saw possible objections to both the propagation and the infusion theories, and he outlines them in a letter to Goodyer.[53]

To complicate the issue more, there was the matter of original sin. The Western Fathers, and Gregory of Nyssa in the East, held that Adam's sin was passed on by the parents and inherent in the propagated soul. But the Eastern Fathers, along with Jerome and Hilary, located original sin in the body, and denied that it affected the soul.[54] There was also disagreement about the corrupting effect of original sin, which some authorities considered quite mild. Faced with this array of conflicting assertions about subjects which were unsusceptible of demonstration or rational argument, Donne followed the example of the previous participants in the debate, and selected the solution most pleasing to his imagination. The soul, he affirms, is infused individually by God, and the very moment the union of soul and body comes about original sin, which is totally corrupting, is present, though it had existed previously neither in the soul nor in the body. To a mind possessed by simultaneity and the convergence of opposites this thesis offered the best of both worlds. The choice of infusion rather than propagation preserved the purity of the soul at its point of entrance into the body, while affording the maximum contrast with the utter blackness which overtakes the soul the instant it is infused. Thus extremes meet, and East and West embrace each other.

The congruence of Donne's standpoint, on this complex topic, with the patterns which his imagination loved to trace, helps us to understand the ebullience with which he puts across the doctrine once he has worked it out. This might otherwise strike us as odd, for Donne is, as it were, calling upon us to applaud the marvellous neatness of an arrangement which has ensured the inexcusable depravity of all mankind:

No man can tell me out of what Quiver, yet here is an arrow comes so swiftly, as that in the very first minute of our life, in our quickning in our mothers womb, wee become guilty of Adams sin done 6000 years before, and subject to all those arrows, Hunger, Labour, Grief, Sicknesse, and Death, which have been shot after it. . . . So swift is this arrow, Originall sin, from which, all arrows of subsequent tentations, are shot, as that God, who comes in my first minute of life, cannot come before death.[55]

Our first minute, after noon, is night. The excitement of simultaneity, fusing opposites, is unmistakable here as Donne staggers his hearers with the unimaginable celerity of the projectile which has destroyed them. The note, despite the subject matter, is of exultation; and that is because Donne has found a way, in and through theology, of freeing himself for imaginative play. Again and again the sermons admire the instantaneousness of our creation and destruction:

The body, being without sinne, and the soule being without sinne, yet in the first minute, that this body and soule meet, and are united, we become, in that instant, guilty of Adams sinne, committed six thousand yeares before.[56]

The subtle knot makes us fallen man. As often in the poems, the mysterious junction of body and soul lies at the heart of Donne's obsession with merging. Further, it is still the act of love, and the intricate conjunction it entails, which occupy his imagination, though he is no longer writing of these matters as a love poet. The womb, the 'centrique part', the growth of the foetus, the blood labouring to beget spirits—his mind still circles about these sensitive areas, as it did in 'The Extasie' or in the account of embryonic development in *The Progresse of the Soule*. The merging he is now intent on takes place, like the merging of lovers, within the mother's body at the moment of conception, and its precise operation, like the operation of love, is unknowable.

The phrase 'the first minute', it will be noticed, keeps recurring in these contexts, as if its victorious resonance were peculiarly satisfying to Donne. He brandishes it, or throws it down like a trump card at the end of a rhetorical period:

Was not God's judgement executed speedily enough upon thy soul, when in the same instant that it was created, and conceiv'd, and infus'd, it was put to a necessity of contracting Original sin, and so submitted to the penalty of Adam's disobedience, the first minute?[57]

Donne is speaking of his own corruption, just as much as of his congregation's. But one would never guess that from the way he talks. Throughout these examples it is his euphoria that impresses us. He has the air of a man expounding a dazzling mathematical proof. His superiority to his hearers is flaunted. He taunts them by harping on their ignorance ('No man can tell me . . . '), and subdues them with gibing questions ('Was not God's judgement executed speedily enough upon thy soul?'). He talks as if he has thought up God's judgement himself (as, of course, he has), and glories in the ingenuity of it. The accents are those of a conqueror, or conjurer, not a fellow sufferer. We sense a mind at home with its subject, and luxuriating in its exposition. It is a sign that Donne's adjustment of his theology to his basic interests has taken place with complete success.

It remains to point out, and this can be done rapidly, that everything else this book has been about has a bearing upon this chapter and comes within its scope. Donne's awareness of the body both as something vital and as an inert anatomical mass ('living walls'), examined in chapter 5, obviously belongs with the habits of mind, simultaneously dualistic and synthesizing, which we have been considering here. So does the extensive array of devices, reviewed in chapter 7, by which Donne demonstrates that it is possible to be alive and dead at the same time. So does his sense of the interpenetration of reason and emotion, illustrated in chapter 8. All these generate the kind of imagined corners to which Donne's mind was drawn.

His preoccupation with change, surveyed in chapter 6, fits the same interest, because it involves things which actually turn the imagined corner and become other things. Besides, in the world view Donne inherited from Aristotle and Aquinas change was inseparable from the conjunction of opposites, because it was believed that only things which combined unequal elements were subject to change.[58] Donne links his own changeability to the discordant elements in his make-up ('Oh, to vex me, contraryes meete in one'), and he felt the 'Contrary repugnancies and adverse fightings of the Elements' in his body as keenly as he did the inconsistencies of his mind.[59]

His impulse to seek conjunction, and his hypersensitivity to division, derive, finally, from his character and circumstances as outlined in the first four chapters, and in particular from his lasting sense of isolation from some greater whole. We may attribute this, in the first instance, to his early experience of persecution as a member of a beleaguered Catholic minority, and later to his disjunction from the

Catholic Church, with its accustomed pieties, as well as to the long-drawn-out failure of his secular career, and his disastrous marriage, which put the kind of employment on which he had set his heart beyond his reach. His desire for a church that would swallow up all existing churches ('Show me deare Christ, thy spouse, so bright and cleare'), and his wish to be united with 'the body of this world', are examples of his synthesizing instinct which obviously relate to these biographical concerns. His insistence that 'no man is an island', taken together with the egotism of his writing, illustrate both his urge to blend and the inescapable selfhood which prompted and frustrated it.

Notes

Works which I refer to frequently are identified by abbreviations, listed below. In addition, I use the customary abbreviations for literary periodicals.

Bald
: R. C. Bald, *John Donne: A Life* (Oxford, 1970)

Biathanatos
: John Donne, *Biathanatos. A declaration of that paradoxe, or thesis, that Self-homicide is not so Naturally Sinne, that it may never be otherwise* (1648)

Devotions
: John Donne, *Devotions upon Emergent Occasions, together with Death's Duel* (Ann Arbor, Mich., 1959)

Divine Poems
: John Donne, *The Divine Poems*, edited with introduction and commentary by Helen Gardner (Oxford, 1952)

Elegies
: John Donne, *The Elegies and The Songs and Sonnets*, edited with introduction and commentary by Helen Gardner (Oxford, 1965)

Epithalamions
: John Donne, *The Epithalamions, Anniversaries and Epicedes*, edited with introduction and commentary by W. Milgate (Oxford, 1978)

Essays in Divinity
: John Donne, *Essays in Divinity*, edited by Evelyn M. Simpson (Oxford, 1952)

Gosse
: Edmund Gosse, *The Life and Letters of John Donne*, 2 vols. (1899)

Grierson
: *The Poems of John Donne*, edited by H. J. C. Grierson, 2 vols. (Oxford, 1912)

Ignatius
: John Donne, *Ignatius His Conclave*, edited with introduction and commentary by T. S. Healy, S. J. (Oxford, 1969)

Jonson
: *Ben Jonson*, edited by C. H. Herford and P. and E. Simpson, 11 vols. (Oxford, 1925–52)

Letters	*Letters to severall persons of honour* (1651)
Paradoxes	John Donne, *Paradoxes, Problemes, Essayes, Characters* (1652)
Pseudo-Martyr	John Donne, *Pseudo-martyr. Wherein out of certaine Propositions and Gradations, This Conclusion is evicted. That those which are of the Romane Religion in this Kingdome, may and ought to take the Oath of Allegeance* (1610)
Ramsay	M. P. Ramsay, *Les Doctrines médiévales chez Donne* (Oxford, 1917)
Satires	John Donne, *The Satires, Epigrams and Verse Letters*, edited with an introduction and commentary by W. Milgate (Oxford, 1967)
Sermons	*The Sermons of John Donne*, edited with introductions and critical apparatus by George R. Potter and Evelyn M. Simpson, 10 vols. (Berkeley and Los Angeles, 1953–62)
Simpson	E. M. Simpson, *A Study of the Prose Works of John Donne* (2nd edn., Oxford, 1948)

INTRODUCTION

1 See W. Milgate, 'The Early
References to John Donne',
N&Q 195 (1950), 229–31, 246–7,
290–2, 381–3, and *N&Q* 198
(1953), 421–4.
2 D. Masson, *Drummond of
Hawthornden* (1873), 357.
3 See Frank J. Warnke, 'Marino
and the English Metaphysicals',
Studies in the Renaissance 2
(1955), 160–75.
4 Jonson i, 135.
5 Gosse i, 219.
6 C. S. Lewis, 'Donne and Love
Poetry in the Seventeenth
Century', in *Seventeenth-Century
Studies Presented to Sir Herbert
Grierson* (Oxford, 1938), 64–84.
7 Browning, 'Too Late', lines
141–4.
8 Barnabe Barnes, *Parthenophil and
Parthenophe*, Sonnet 63.
9 Campion, *Works*, ed. P. Vivian
(Oxford, 1909), 239.
10 Gosse ii, 68.
11 *Satires*, 66.
12 *Satires*, 107.
13 Yeats, 'Who Goes with
Fergus?', line 12.
14 *Paradoxes*, 75.
15 Gosse ii, 124.
16 *Sermons* i, 179.
17 *Sermons* iii, 68, 131; v, 120.
18 *Sermons* iv, 301; vi, 283; vii,
157
19 *Satires*, 13.
20 *Sermons* v, 251.
21 *Elegies*, 24, 19.
22 *Divine Poems*, 30–1.
23 *Elegies*, 17.
24 *Sermons* vi, 231. (The editors
have here, without authority,
emended 'God' to 'Gold': see
Sermons vi, 371.)
25 *Elegies*, 73.
26 *Sermons* i, 236.

27 *Sermons* v, 388; vi, 170; viii, 87,
97; vi, 337, 269.
28 *Sermons* v, 266.
29 Lewis, op. cit., 68.
30 Simpson, 3.
31 T. S. Eliot, 'Rhyme and Reason:
the Poetry of John Donne', *The
Listener* 3 (19 Mar. 1930), 502–3.

I. APOSTASY

1 Bald, 26–34.
2 Baird D. Whitlock, 'The
Heredity and Childhood of John
Donne', *N&Q* 6 (1959), 257–62,
348–53.
3 *Pseudo-Martyr*, 108.
4 Charles Hoole, *A New Discovery
of the Old Art of Teaching
Schoole*, ed. E. T. Campagnac
(1913), 213.
5 For my account of the
persecution of Catholics as seen
by Catholics, see Robert
Southwell, *An Humble
Supplication to her Maiestie*, ed.
R. C. Bald (Cambridge, 1953);
*John Gerard: The Autobiography
of an Elizabethan*, trans. P.
Caraman, with an Introduction
by Graham Greene (2nd edn.,
1956); and *William Weston: The
Autobiography of an Elizabethan*,
trans. P. Caraman, with a
Foreword by Evelyn Waugh
(1955).
6 A. G. Smith, *The Babington Plot*
(1936), 212, 239–42.
7 Richard Challoner, *Memoirs of
Missionary Priests*, ed. J. H.
Pollen, S. J. (1924), 224–5 and
passim.
8 Simpson, 45, 316, 319.
9 *Elegies*, 8–9.
10 *Pseudo-Martyr*, 222.
11 Whitlock, op. cit., 257–62.
12 On Ellis and Jasper Heywood,
see Bald, 25–6 and 39–45.

13 *Pseudo-Martyr*, 46.
14 See, however, Southwell,
  Humble Supplication (see n. 5
  above), 70–80.
15 *Elegies*, 8.
16 *Biathanatos*, 17.
17 *Weston: Autobiography* (see n. 5
  above), 148–50, 178–84.
18 On Donne's travels see Bald,
  50–2; John Sparrow, 'The Date
  of Donne's Travels', in *A
  Garland for John Donne,
  1631–1931*, ed. T. J. Spencer
  (Cambridge, Mass., 1931),
  123–51; and Baird D. Whitlock,
  'Donne's University Years',
  English Studies 43 (1962), 1–20.
19 See Mark H. Curtis, *Oxford and
  Cambridge in Transition,
  1558–1642* (Oxford, 1959), 54–5.
20 William Empson, 'Donne and
  the Rhetorical Tradition',
  Kenyon Review 11 (1949), 585.
21 See Wilfred R. Prest, *The Inns of
  Court under Elizabeth I and the
  Early Stuarts, 1590–1640* (1972).
22 Bald, 58; J. Morris, 'The
  Martyrdom of William
  Harrington', *The Month* 20
  (1874), 411–23.
23 *Sermons* ii, 239.
24 *Sermons* viii, 107.
25 Southwell, *Humble Supplication*
  (see n. 5 above), 27; and *Sermons*
  vii, 368.
26 H. E. G. Rope, 'The Real John
  Donne', *Irish Monthly* 82–3
  (1954), 229–34.
27 *Satires*, 10–14.
28 Peter Alexander, *Shakespeare*
  (1964), 212–20.
29 Bald, 36.
30 *Divine Poems*, 14.
31 *Pseudo-Martyr*, sigs. B2v.–B3r.
32 *Sermons* vi, 163.
33 *Satires*, 12–13.
34 *Divine Poems*, 15 and 121–7.
35 *Sermons* vii, 291, 294.

36 *Sermons* v, 259; viii, 102.
37 *Sermons* vii, 68
38 Bald, 94; *Gerard: Autobiography*
  (see n. 5 above), 66.
39 Bald, 212.
40 *C.S.P. Venetian* (1607–10),
  289–90.
41 John Boys, *Works* (1629), 277,
  cited in Bald, 226.
42 Thomas Fitzherbert, *A
  Supplement to the Discussion of
  M. D. Barlowes Answere* (1613),
  105.
43 *Letters*, 160–4; Gosse i, 221–3.
44 *Pseudo-Martyr*, 168–72 and 207.
45 *Biathanatos*, 36; see also Ramsay,
  148.
46 *Pseudo-Martyr*, 126 and 88.
47 St. Ignatius, *Spiritual Exercises*,
  trans. Fr. John Morris et al., ed.
  Henry Keane, S. J. (5th edn.,
  1952), 132.
48 *Pseudo-Martyr*, 143, 88.
49 *Pseudo-Martyr*, 176.
50 *Ignatius*, 41–2.
51 *Sermons*, ii, 178.
52 Gosse ii, 78; and Itrat Husain,
  *The Dogmatic and Mystical
  Theology of John Donne* (1938),
  144–5.
53 *The Courtier's Library*, ed. E. M.
  Simpson (1930), 74–5.
54 F. A. Yates, 'Paolo Sarpi's
  "History of the Council of
  Trent"', *Journal of the Warburg
  and Courtauld Institutes* 7 (1944),
  123–43; and D. Baker-Smith,
  'John Donne's *Critique of True
  Religion*', in *John Donne: Essays
  in Celebration*, ed. A. J. Smith
  (1972), 404–32.

2. THE ART OF APOSTASY

1 *Elegies*, 38.
2 *Elegies*, 29.
3 *Elegies*, 29.
4 *Elegies*, 19.
5 *Elegies*, 1–4.

6 *Elegies*, 10–11.
7 *Elegies*, 8.
8 *Sermons* ix, 162–3; see also
  Biathanatos, 123.
9 John Mush, *The Life and Death
  of Margaret Clitherow*, ed.
  William Nicholson (1849).
10 *Elegies*, 56, 15, 178, 132.
11 *Divine Poems*, 24.
12 *Elegies*, 75–6.
13 *Elegies*, 73–5.
14 Keith Douglas, *Complete Poems*
   (1978) 74.
15 *Elegies*, 90.
16 *Sermons* iii, 153–4.
17 *Elegies*, 90–1.
18 Wilbur Sanders, *John Donne's
   Poetry* (Cambridge, 1971) 126.
19 *Divine Poems*, 10.
20 *Sermons* vii, 348.
21 *Divine Poems*, 16.
22 *Divine Poems*, 13.
23 *Divine Poems*, 11.
24 *Divine Poems*, 9.
25 *Pseudo-Martyr*, sig. A1r.
26 *Sermons* x, 177; viii, 186; vii, 391.
27 *Divine Poems*, 20.
28 See St. Ignatius, *Spiritual
   Exercises*, trans. Fr. John Morris
   et al., ed. Henry Keane, S. J.
   (5th edn., 1952).
29 *John Gerard: The Autobiography
   of an Elizabethan*, trans. P.
   Caraman (2nd edn., 1956), 27.
30 See Louis Martz, *The Poetry of
   Meditation* (rev. edn., New
   Haven, Conn., 1962); doubts
   about the extent of Ignatius's
   influence are expressed by S.
   Archer, 'Meditation and the
   Structure of Donne's *Holy
   Sonnets*', *ELH* 28 (1961), 137–47,
   and A. Raspa, 'Theology and
   Poetry in Donne's *Conclave*',
   ELH 32 (1965), 478–89.
31 T. S. Eliot, 'Thinking in Verse',
   The Listener 3 (12 Mar. 1930),
   441–3.

32 St. Ignatius, *Spiritual Exercises*,
   ed. cit., 22.
33 *Divine Poems*, 13.
34 St. Ignatius, *Spiritual Exercises*,
   ed. cit., 27.
35 *Divine Poems*, 10.
36 *Divine Poems*, 57, 59, 60; see also
   Itrat Husain, *The Dogmatic and
   Mystical Theology of John Donne*
   (1938), 66–7.
37 *Divine Poems*, 18.
38 *Sermons* i, 200.
39 *Divine Poems*, 2, 60.
40 *Elegies*, 70.
41 Gosse ii, 78.
42 *Sermons* iii, 302–3.
43 *Divine Poems*, 51.
44 *Divine Poems*, 7.
45 Martz, op. cit., 132.
46 *Divine Poems*, 12–13.
47 *Divine Poems*, 11.
48 *Divine Poems*, 6.
49 Keith Thomas, *Religion and the
   Decline of Magic* (1971), 469–77.
50 Henry More, *Historia Provinciae
   Anglicanae Societatis Iesu* (1660),
   iv, 134.
51 On suicide see S. E. Sprott, *The
   English Debate on Suicide from
   Donne to Hume* (La Salle, Ill.,
   1961); A. Alvarez, *The Savage
   God* (1971); R. Wymer, 'Suicide
   and Despair in the Jacobean
   Drama' (Oxford B. Litt. thesis
   1976).
52 Marlowe, *Dr. Faustus* vi, lines
   18–23.
53 *Biathanatos*, 17, 28.
54 *Divine Poems*, 8.
55 Bunyan, *Grace Abounding*,
   sections 84 and 104.
56 *Divine Poems*, 7.
57 For a brief summary of the
   Catholic and Protestant
   positions see T. M. Parker, *The
   English Reformation to 1558*
   (1950), 117–20.
58 *Divine Poems*, 11.

[59] *Divine Poems*, 7, 13, 15.
[60] *Divine Poems*, 14–15.
[61] *Divine Poems*, 79.
[62] *Elegies*, 77–8.

3. AMBITION

[1] *Sermons* viii, 180; see also vi, 299; vii, 149.
[2] *Sermons* iv, 272.
[3] *Sermons* x, 96.
[4] *Sermons* iii, 71.
[5] *Sermons* iv, 149.
[6] *Sermons* iii, 329; and *Pseudo-Martyr*, sig. E1v.
[7] *Sermons* ii, 291.
[8] *Sermons* x, 221.
[9] *Sermons* i, 208; iv, 160; iii, 329; Gosse i, 191.
[10] *Elegies*, 60.
[11] *Devotions*, 109 (Meditation XVII).
[12] Clay Hunt, *Donne's Poetry: Essays in Literary Analysis* (New Haven, Conn., 1954), 147.
[13] *Letters*, 51.
[14] *Satires*, 5.
[15] See e.g. *Divine Poems*, 16.
[16] *Satires*, 14.
[17] See John Wilcox, 'Informal Publication of Late Sixteenth-Century Verse Satire', *HLQ* 13 (1950), 191–200.
[18] *Poems of James VI*, ed. J. Craigie (Edinburgh and London, 1955–8), ii, 185.
[19] J. B. Black, *The Reign of Queen Elizabeth 1558–1603* (2nd edn. Oxford, 1959), 422.
[20] *Satires*, 58.
[21] *Satires*, 55.
[22] *Elegies*, 25.
[23] *Satires*, 51.
[24] *Satires*, 57.
[25] *Satires*, 58.
[26] Arthur Gorges, 'A Larger Relation of the said Iland Voyage', in *Purchas his Pilgrimes* (Glasgow, 1905–7), xx, 66, 83.

[27] Gosse i, 314.
[28] Gorges, op cit., 128.
[29] Fynes Moryson, *Itinerary* (1617), i, 37.
[30] 'To Mr R. W.', lines 18–21, *Satires*, 65.
[31] *Satires*, 22–5.
[32] Simpson, 316.
[33] Gosse i, 171, 197; and *Satires*, 69–70.
[34] Gosse ii, 68.
[35] Gosse ii, 79.
[36] Gosse i, 302.
[37] Bald, 107–8, 114, 116.
[38] L. I. Bredvold, 'Sir Thomas Egerton and Donne', *TLS* (13 Mar. 1924), 160.
[39] *Letters*, 18.
[40] Gosse i, 106.
[41] Bald, 72.
[42] Gosse i, 300.
[43] *Essays in Divinity*, 75.
[44] *Divine Poems*, 10.
[45] Gosse i, 154.
[46] Gosse i, 189.
[47] *Letters*, 147.
[48] Bald, 253.
[49] *Divine Poems*, 15.
[50] *Sermons* ii, 346.
[51] Gosse ii, 48.
[52] Gosse ii, 8.
[53] Gosse ii, 18.
[54] Bald, 191–4.
[55] *Letters*, 59, 48.
[56] Bald, 167–8.
[57] Jonson viii, 55.
[58] *Satires*, 78–9.
[59] *Letters*, 11.
[60] Gosse i, 191.
[61] Gosse i, 200.
[62] Gosse i, 182; for the addressee see R. E. Bennett, 'Donne's "Letters to Several Persons of Honour"', *PMLA* 56 (1941), 137.
[63] Jonson viii, 52.
[64] *Satires*, 90–1.
[65] Gosse i, 217–18.

66 Jonson viii, 60–1.
67 *Elegies*, 83–4.
68 Gosse i, 314.
69 Bald, 275.
70 Bald, 295–7.
71 For Donne's letters to Mrs.
   Herbert see Walton's *Life of
   Herbert*, in Walton, *Works*, ed.
   Geoffrey Keynes (1929), 409–10,
   457–9.
72 *Satires*, 88–90.
73 *Elegies*, 27–8.
74 *Elegies*, 252.
75 Jonson v, 167.
76 Lawrence Stone, *The Crisis of
   the Aristocracy* (1965), 561; Bald,
   432.
77 *A Collection of Letters Made by
   Sir Tobie Mathews* (1660), 334.
78 For Drury and Donne's
   acquaintance with him see R. C.
   Bald, *Donne and the Drurys*
   (Cambridge, 1959).
79 *Satires*, 104.
80 *Satires*, 105–7.
81 *Epithalamions*, 6–10.
82 For Rochester and the Overbury
   scandal see D. H. Willson, *King
   James VI and I* (1956), 336–56;
   and Stone, op. cit., 667.
83 Bald, 272–3.
84 Gosse ii, 23, 41.
85 Gosse ii, 25.
86 *Epithalamions*, 16.
87 Willson, op. cit., 343.
88 Bald, 162.
89 *Divine Poems*, 32.
90 Bald, 327–8.
91 Bald, 413–14.
92 *Sermons* vi, 13.
93 Bald, 372.
94 Bald, 376.
95 Bald, 402.
96 See W. Milgate, 'The Early
   References to John Donne',
   N&Q 195 (1950), 229–31, 246–7,
   290–2, 381–3.
97 See for example John T.

Shawcross, 'Donne's "A
Nocturnall Upon S. Lucies
Day"', *Explicator* 23–4 (1964–6),
56; for the contrary view see
Robert Ellrodt, 'Chronologie
des Poèmes de Donne', *EA*
(1960), 452–63.
98 Jonson i, 136.

4. THE ART OF AMBITION

1 Edward Edwards, *Life of Raleigh*
  (1868), ii, 152–3, quoted in Bald,
  83.
2 *Satires*, 50.
3 *The Collected Works of Isaac
  Rosenberg*, ed. Ian Parsons
  (1979), 183.
4 *Biathanatos*, 137.
5 *Sermons* ii, 266.
6 *Sermons* v, 106.
7 *Sermons* iii, 139; vi, 304; viii,
  278; on the vagabond problem
  see W. K. Jordan, *Philanthropy in
  England, 1480–1660* (1959), i,
  78–95.
8 Gosse i, 128.
9 *Sermons* vii, 370–91.
10 *Sermons* ix, 381.
11 Robert Ellrodt, *L'Inspiration
   personelle et l'esprit de temps chez
   les Poètes métaphysiques anglais*
   (Paris, 1960), I, i, 106–16.
12 *Elegies*, 37.
13 *Elegies*, 87.
14 *Elegies*, 76.
15 Gosse i, 174.
16 *Epithalamions*, 67.
17 Gosse i, 184.
18 *Sermons* viii, 332.
19 Ellrodt, op. cit., I, i, 107.
20 *Elegies*, 61–2.
21 See Helen C. White, 'John
   Donne and the Psychology of
   Spiritual Effort', in *The
   Seventeenth Century*, ed. R. F.
   Jones (Stanford, Calif.,1951),
   357.

[22] *Sermons* viii, 75.
[23] *Epithalamions*, 43, 42, 24, 45.
[24] Jonson i, 133.
[25] William Empson, 'Donne and the Rhetorical Tradition', *Kenyon Review* 11 (1949), 579.
[26] Marius Bewley, 'Religious Cynicism in Donne's Poetry', *Kenyon Review* 14 (1952), 619–46.
[27] D. W. Harding, 'Coherence of Theme in Donne's Poetry', *Kenyon Review* 13 (1951), 427–44.
[28] See Richard E. Hughes, *The Progress of the Soul* (1969).
[29] *The Anniversaries*, ed. Frank Manley (Baltimore, Md., 1963).
[30] B. K. Lewalski, *Donne's 'Anniversaries' and the Poetry of Praise* (Princeton, N. J., 1973).
[31] Gosse i, 302, 306.
[32] R. C. Bald, *Donne and the Drurys* (Cambridge, 1959), 26.
[33] ibid., 88.
[34] See I. A. Shapiro, 'The Date of a Donne Elegy and its Implications', in *English Renaissance Studies Presented to Dame Helen Gardner* (Oxford, 1980), 141–50.
[35] *Elegies*, 14–16.
[36] *Sermons* ix, 79.
[37] Nashe, *Works*, ed R. B. McKerrow (Oxford, 1958), iv, 397–416.
[38] *Elegies*, 72–3.
[39] *Divine Poems*, 33.
[40] *Elegies*, 71–2.
[41] Shakespeare, *Antony and Cleopatra*, IV, xiv.
[42] D. H. Lawrence, *Three Novellas* (Penguin edn., 1970), 79–80.
[43] *Sermons* vii, 128.
[44] *Sermons* ix, 64.
[45] *Sermons* i, 223; v, 85; i, 247; iv, 347.
[46] *Sermons* ix, 129.

[47] *Sermons* iii, 289; iv, 137, 250; iii, 184.
[48] *Sermons* iii, 290.
[49] *Sermons* vi, 245.
[50] *Sermons* vi, 283; vii, 157.
[51] Baird D. Whitlock, 'The Dean and the Yeoman', *N&Q* 199 (1954), 374.
[52] *Sermons* ii, 303.
[53] *Sermons* ii, 290; ix, 328.
[54] *Sermons* ix, 379; vi, 303; iii, 270.
[55] *Sermons* ix, 379; iii, 58.
[56] *Sermons* iv, 329.
[57] *Elegies*, 61.
[58] Milton, *Christian Doctrine*, I, v and vi, in *Complete Prose Works* (New Haven, Conn. 1973), vi.
[59] *Sermons* iv, 28 and 33–4.
[60] *Elegies*, 24.
[61] Coleridge, *Miscellaneous Criticism*, ed. T. M. Raysor (1936), 131.
[62] *Elegies*, 23.
[63] Josephine Miles, 'Ifs, Ands, Buts for the Reader of Donne', in *Just So Much Honour*, ed. Peter A. Fiore (State College, Pa., 1972), 272–91.
[64] *Epithalamions*, 30.
[65] *Elegies*, 52.
[66] Tennyson, *Poems*, ed. Christopher Ricks (1969), 496.
[67] *Epithalamions*, 30.
[68] *Divine Poems*, 28.
[69] *Essays in Divinity*, 36.
[70] *Satires*, 76–7.
[71] *Divine Poems*, 30–1.
[72] *Divine Poems*, 13.
[73] *Elegies*, 63.
[74] *Elegies*, 69.
[75] *Elegies*, 85.
[76] *Sermons* vii, 152; ix, 195; ii, 147, 194; i, 176–7; vii, 80; ii, 86.
[77] *Sermons* viii, 128; vii, 65.
[78] *Sermons* vii, 365–6; iii, 191.
[79] *Sermons* viii, 106.
[80] *Sermons* vii, 396.
[81] *Elegies*, 90.

⁸² *Elegies*, 56.
⁸³ Gosse i, 184.
⁸⁴ *Elegies*, 77–8.
⁸⁵ *Elegies*, 36.
⁸⁶ *Sermons* vii, 78, 138; vi, 278, 363.
⁸⁷ *Sermons* viii, 92.
⁸⁸ *Sermons* x, 243.
⁸⁹ *Sermons* iii, 349; viii, 76; for other examples see ii, 139, 227, 357.
⁹⁰ *Sermons* iii, 339.
⁹¹ See W. K. Jordan, *Philanthropy in England, 1480–1660* (1959), i, 36, 129; John Brinsley, *Ludus Literarius*, ed. E. T. Campagnac (1917), 25; Foster Watson, *The Beginning of the Teaching of Modern Subjects in England* (1909), 254, 277–336.
⁹² *Essays in Divinity*, 72.
⁹³ See Christophori Clavii, *In Sphaeram Ioannis De Sacro Bosco Commentarius* (Lugdini, 1607), 253; also *The Arenarius of Archimedes*, trans. G. Andersen (1784), which contains a translation of Clavius's dissertation; and C. M. Coffin, *John Donne and the New Philosophy* (New York, 1958), 88.
⁹⁴ *Sermons* vii, 368.
⁹⁵ *Elegies*, 40.
⁹⁶ *Elegies*, 57.

5. BODIES

¹ Rupert Brooke, 'John Donne', *Poetry and Drama* 1 (1913), 185–8.
² J. E. V. Crofts, 'John Donne: a Reconsideration', in *John Donne: A Collection of Critical Essays*, ed. Helen Gardner (Englewood Cliffs, N. J., 1962), 84.
³ *Elegies*, 57.
⁴ Traherne, *Centuries, Poems and Thanksgivings*, ed.

H. M. Margoliouth (Oxford, 1958), ii, 4.
⁵ Jonson viii, 41.
⁶ Traherne, ed. cit., i, 111.
⁷ *Sermons* ii, 288; x, 232–3; ii, 83; iii, 169–70, 223; ii, 78; ix, 61; ii, 197.
⁸ *Sermons* vii, 359; vi, 142, 234; vii, 106; iii, 233.
⁹ *Sermons* v, 120.
¹⁰ *Sermons* iv, 227.
¹¹ *Sermons* viii, 174.
¹² *Sermons* iii, 92.
¹³ *Sermons* iii, 113.
¹⁴ *Sermons* iii, 92 and 105.
¹⁵ *Sermons* ii, 84; x, 80; ix, 223, 124.
¹⁶ *Sermons* i, 192.
¹⁷ Winfried Schleiner, *The Imagery of John Donne's Sermons* (Providence, R. I., 1970), 68–85.
¹⁸ See D. C. Allen, 'John Donne's Knowledge of Renaissance Medicine', *JEGP* 42 (1943), 322–42.
¹⁹ Grierson i, 377.
²⁰ Baird D. Whitlock, 'The Heredity and Childhood of John Donne', *N&Q* 6 (1959), 257–62.
²¹ *Sermons* iii, 236.
²² *Devotions*, 23 (Meditation IV).
²³ *Elegies*, 57.
²⁴ A. S. Brandenburg, 'The Dynamic Image in Metaphysical Poetry', *PMLA* 57 (1942), 1039–45.
²⁵ *Elegies*, 43.
²⁶ *Elegies*, 9.
²⁷ *Paradoxes*, 47.
²⁸ D. H. Lawrence, *The Rainbow* (Penguin edn., 1970), 49.
²⁹ *Epithalamions*, 49, 167.
³⁰ *Sermons* v, 353.
³¹ *Elegies*, 90.
³² *Elegies*, 29.
³³ *Sermons* vii, 271.
³⁴ *Divine Poems*, 26 and 94.
³⁵ *Elegies*, 5–6.

36 Wilbur Sanders, *John Donne's Poetry* (Cambridge, 1971), 40.
37 *Sermons* vii, 189; ix, 408.
38 *Epithalamions*, 6.
39 *Epithalamions*, 18.
40 *Satires*, 8.
41 *Elegies*, 91.
42 *Epithalamions*, 47.
43 *Satires*, 58.
44 *Elegies*, 64–6.
45 *Sermons* v, 352.
46 A. Quiller Couch, *Studies in Literature* (Cambridge, 1918), 131.
47 M. Francon, 'Un Motif de la poésie amoureuse au XVIe siècle', *PMLA* (1941), 307–36.
48 *Elegies*, 53.
49 *Sermons* ii, 341; iii, 329; ix, 147.
50 D. H. Lawrence, *Mornings in Mexico and Etruscan Places* (Penguin edn., 1971), 126.
51 *Sermons* vii, 417.
52 *Sermons* viii, 224.
53 Grierson ii, xx.
54 Evelyn Hardy, *Donne: A Spirit in Conflict* (1942), 85; Bald, 123.
55 Simpson, 19.
56 For Browning's and De Quincey's comments see A. J. Smith's essay on Donne's reputation in *John Donne, Essays in Celebration* (1972), 1–27.
57 Jonson i, 136.
58 *Satires*, 33–4.
59 Plato, *Phaedrus*, 251C (from the translation of H. N. Fowler in the Loeb edn.).
60 *Satires*, 45–6.
61 Ted Hughes, *Crow* (1970), 13, 87.
62 *Satires*, 35.
63 *Satires*, 38–9.
64 Milton, *Comus*, lines 115–16.
65 Pope, *Windsor Forest*, lines 141–6.
66 *Satires*, 41.
67 *Satires*, 35.

68 *Satires*, 31.
69 *Divine Poems*, 49.
70 *Elegies*, 77; and *Sermons* iv, 310.
71 *Satires*, 32–3.
72 *Sermons* x, 69.
73 *Elegies*, 28.
74 *Elegies*, 47.
75 *Elegies*, 74–5.
76 *Elegies*, 6.
77 Paracelsus, *The Hermetic and Alchemical Writings*, trans. A. E. Waite (1894), i, 126.
78 ibid., i, 304.
79 ibid., i, 41.
80 ibid., i, 129; ii, 15.
81 *Satires*, 101.
82 Aldous Huxley, *Those Barren Leaves* (1925), Part V, ch. i.
83 ibid., Part I, ch. vi.
84 Aldous Huxley, *After Many a Summer* (1939), Part II, ch. vi.
85 On Pomponazzi see George T. Buckley, *Atheism in the English Renaissance* (Chicago, 1932).
86 *Paradoxes*, 33.
87 *Paradoxes*, 23.
88 Tertullian, *A Treatise on the Soul*, ch. 7 and ch. 18; and *A Treatise on the Resurrection*, ch. 16, in *Ante-Nicene Christian Library*, ed. A. Roberts and J. Donaldson (Edinburgh, 1870), xv.
89 *Divine Poems*, xliii–xlvii.
90 *Sermons* iv, 358.
91 *Epithalamions*, 48.
92 *Satires*, 93, 101–2.
93 *Epithalamions*, 62.
94 D. H. Lawrence, *The Woman Who Rode Away* (Penguin edn. 1968), 76–7.
95 *Elegies*, 58, 30, 54.
96 *Elegies*, 38, 50, 51.
97 *Divine Poems*, 13, 31.

6. CHANGE

1 *Epithalamions* 32; *Sermons* vi, 324.

2 T. E. Terrill, 'A Note on John
Donne's Early Reading', *MLN*
43 (1928), 318–19.
3 *Paradoxes*, 1.
4 *Devotions*, 54 (Expostulation
VIII).
5 *Pseudo-Martyr* Preface.
6 *Divine Poems*, 15.
7 *Sermons* vii, 264–5.
8 *Sermons* x, 56.
9 *Sermons* v, 249.
10 *Sermons* iii, 110.
11 Gosse i, 306.
12 *Sermons* ix, 134.
13 Gosse i, 191.
14 *Satires*, 70.
15 *Elegies*, 56.
16 *Essays in Divinity*, 14.
17 *Sermons* i, 249, 273; iv, 148; vi,
124; viii, 176.
18 *Sermons* iii, 50; also ii, 247.
19 *Sermons* iv, 100; also 85.
20 *Essays in Divinity*, 76.
21 See Arnold Williams, *The
Common Expositor* (Chapel Hill,
N.C., 1948), 80.
22 *Elegies*, 85.
23 *Sermons* iv, 85.
24 Augustine, *The Free Choice of
the Will*, Bk. III, ch. 7.
25 Aquinas, *Summa Theologica*, III,
Q.98, Art. 3.
26 *Devotions*, 72 (Meditation XI).
27 Frank Kermode, *John Donne*
(1961), 23.
28 *Sermons* vii, 271; also iii, 227,
and ix, 305.
29 *Sermons* vii, 259.
30 *Devotions*, 12 (Meditation II).
31 *Sermons* i, 266.
32 *Devotions*, 13 (Meditation II).
33 *Sermons* iv, 70, 159; ix, 154, 177.
34 *Satires*, 45.
35 *Elegies*, 62–3.
36 Allen Tate, 'The Point of
Dying', *Sewanee Review* 61
(1953), 76–81.
37 *Epithalamions*, 14.

38 *Satires*, 58.
39 *Elegies*, 1–4.
40 *Divine Poems*, 15.
41 *Epithalamions*, 42.
42 *Elegies*, 69, 85, 74; *Divine Poems*,
8.
43 *Elegies*, 41; *Satires*, 45.
44 *Sermons* iii, 65.
45 *Sermons* iv, 337.
46 *Sermons* x, 52; viii, 62, etc.; vii,
217.
47 *Elegies*, 11.
48 *Elegies*, 20.
49 *Sermons* i, 230; ii, 306; iii, 127.
50 Walter Pater, *Selected Writings*,
ed. Harold Bloom (New York,
1974), 59–60.
51 ibid., 60–1.
52 See Michael Levey, *The Case of
Walter Pater* (1978), 144, 183.
53 *Elegies* 42, 70, 84; *Divine Poems*
7, 10; see, on this aspect of
Donne's poetry, Robert Ellrodt,
*L'Inspiration personelle et l'esprit
de temps chez les Poètes
métaphysiques anglais* (Paris,
1960), I, i, 82–4.
54 *Elegies*, 36.
55 *Elegies*, 78–9.
56 *Sermons* iii, 133; i, 250.
57 *Sermons* vii, 368–9.
58 *Devotions*, 77 (Meditation XII).
59 *Lyrical Ballads*, ed. G. Sampson
(1903), 26.
60 *Sermons* ix, 176.
61 *Elegies*, 8, 4.
62 *Sermons* v, 314.
63 Milton A. Rugoff, *Donne's
Imagery: A Study in Creative
Sources* (New York, 1962), 61.
64 Paracelsus, *The Hermetic and
Alchemical Writings*, trans. A. E.
Waite (1894), i, 92.
65 *Sermons* i, 163, 272.
66 *Epithalamions*, 12.
67 *Satires*, 95.
68 *Sermons* vii, 410.
69 *Biathanatos*, 155.

[70] Pliny, *Natural History*, xxxiii, 19.

[71] *Sermons* iii, 148; v, 124; vi, 57; vii, 403; viii, 119–20.

[72] *Elegies*, 63.

[73] Tertullian, *A Treatise on the Soul*, ch. 37, in *Ante-Nicene Christian Library*, ed. A. Roberts and J. Donaldson (Edinburgh, 1870), xv.

[74] *Epithalamions*, 52.

[75] Montaigne, *Essays*, trans. Florio, ed. W. H. Henley (1893), ii, 331.

[76] *Epithalamions*, 68.

[77] *Elegies*, 50.

[78] *Elegies*, 64.

[79] *Elegies*, 51.

[80] *Elegies*, 75, 89.

[81] D. L. Peterson, *The English Lyric from Wyatt to Donne* (Princeton, N.J., 1967), 305.

[82] A. J. Smith, 'The Dismissal of Love', in *John Donne, Essays in Celebration* (1972), 89–131.

[83] *Elegies*, 61, 36, 58.

[84] T. S. Eliot, 'John Donne', *Nation and Athenaeum* 33 (1923), 331–2.

[85] Aldous Huxley, 'Ben Jonson', *London Mercury* 1 (1919), 186.

[86] Virginia Woolf, *The Common Reader: Second Series* (1932), 24–39.

[87] Gosse i, 171, 197.

[88] *Sermons* vi, 41.

[89] *Elegies*, 43.

[90] D. L. Guss, 'Donne's Petrarchism', *JEGP* 64 (1963), 17–28.

[91] Hawthorne, *The Scarlet Letter*, ch. 24.

[92] See Leonard Unger, *Donne's Poetry and Modern Criticism* (New York, 1962), 54, 72, etc.

[93] *Elegies*, 42–3.

[94] Wilbur Sanders, *John Donne's Poetry* (Cambridge, 1971), 46.

[95] *Elegies*, 66.

7. DEATH

[1] W. B. Yeats, *Collected Poems* (2nd edn., 1950), 264.

[2] T. S. Eliot, 'Whispers of Immortality', lines 1–16.

[3] Raleigh, *Works* (Oxford, 1829), viii, 900.

[4] *Divine Poems*, 9.

[5] *Divine Poems*, 51.

[6] Seneca, *Epistulae Morales*, liv.

[7] Gosse i, 191.

[8] *Sermons* viii, 92.

[9] *Elegies*, 49.

[10] *Elegies*, 55.

[11] *Divine Poems*, 8.

[12] *Divine Poems*, 9.

[13] *Divine Poems*, 7.

[14] *Devotions*, 44, 79 (Meditations VII and XII).

[15] *Epithalamions*, 55.

[16] *Epithalamions*, 57.

[17] *Epithalamions*, 41.

[18] *Biathanatos*, 17–18.

[19] *Biathanatos*, 47.

[20] See S. E. Sprott, *The English Debate on Suicide from Donne to Hume* (La Salle, Ill., 1961); and A. Alvarez, *The Savage God* (1971).

[21] Augustine, *City of God*, i, 17–27.

[22] Aquinas, *Summa Theologica*, II, ii, Q.65, Art. 5.

[23] *Biathanatos*, 30.

[24] Sprott, op. cit. 17; and B. R. Haydon, *Autobiography and Journals*, ed. M. Elwin (1950), 650.

[25] *Biathanatos*, 32.

[26] *Biathanatos*, 178.

[27] *Biathanatos*, 30, 58, 72, 65.

[28] J. L. Borges, *Other Inquisitions 1937–52*, trans. R. L. Simms (1973), 89–92.

[29] *Biathanatos*, 189–91.

[30] Sprott, op cit., 62–5, 78–9.

[31] Gosse ii, 124.

[32] Gosse i, 191.

[33] Émile Durkheim, *Suicide*, trans.

J. A. Spaulding and George
Simpson (New York, 1951).
[34] ibid., 279.
[35] Gosse i, 174.
[36] Gosse i, 191.
[37] Durkheim, op. cit., 210.
[38] Essays in Divinity, 30.
[39] Devotions, 88–9 (Meditation
XIV).
[40] Elegies, 81.
[41] Elegies, 70.
[42] Durkheim, op. cit., 271.
[43] Simpson, 262.
[44] Bald, 526.
[45] See Helen Gardner, 'Dean
Donne's Monument in St.
Paul's', in Evidence in Literary
Scholarship, ed. R. Wellek and
A. Ribeiro (Oxford, 1979),
29–44, for a sceptical view.
[46] Bald, 530.
[47] Elegies, 62.
[48] Elegies, 36.
[49] Elegies, 31.
[50] Seneca, Epistulae Morales, xxvi.
[51] Gosse ii, 123.
[52] Sermons ii, 248.
[53] Bald, 343–5.
[54] Divine Poems, 48–9.
[55] More, Utopia, trans. P. Turner
(Penguin edn., 1965), 125.
[56] Sermons viii, 98.
[57] Sermons v, 249.
[58] Sermons iii, 109.
[59] Sermons iii, 97; vi, 156, 274.
[60] Sermons vii, 115.
[61] Augustine, City of God, xxii, 19;
Aquinas, Summa Theologica, III,
Q.80, Art. 4.
[62] Augustine, City of God, xxii, 19;
Aquinas, Summa Theologica, III,
Q.80, Art. 5.
[63] Sermons iii, 114; iv, 74; vi, 297.
[64] Divine Poems, 8.
[65] Sermons v, 385.
[66] Sermons iv, 358; v, 274; vi, 75.
[67] Sermons vi, 272.
[68] Divine Poems, 50.

[69] Sermons vii, 273.
[70] Jonson i, 140.
[71] Vaughan, Works, ed. L. C.
Martin (2nd edn., Oxford,
1957), 420.
[72] Aquinas, Summa Theologica, III,
Q.81, Art. 1.
[73] Augustine, City of God, xxii, 15.
[74] Sermons vii, 384.
[75] Gosse ii, 261.
[76] Sermons ii, 211.
[77] Divine Poems, 51.
[78] Elegies, 88.
[79] Elegies, 73, 90.
[80] Sermons iv, 46.
[81] Sermons ix, 89.
[82] Sermons iii, 91.
[83] Sermons iv, 74.
[84] Sermons ii, 198, 204–5; see also i,
232.
[85] Gosse i, 173.
[86] See Keith Thomas, Religion and
the Decline of Magic (1971),
141–3.
[87] Sermons viii, 97.
[88] Sermons x, 238.
[89] Sermons iii, 103.
[90] Augustine, City of God, xx, 20.
[91] Aquinas, Summa Theologica, III,
Q.78, Art. 1.
[92] Sermons iii, 103; iv, 74–5.
[93] Sermons x, 239.

8. THE CRISIS OF REASON

[1] Elegies, 43.
[2] On Ramus see Walter J. Ong,
Ramus, Method and the Decay of
Dialogue (Cambridge, Mass.,
1958).
[3] Nicholas Cusanus, Of Learned
Ignorance, trans. Fr. G. Heron
(1954).
[4] Cornelius Agrippa, The Vanity
of Arts and Sciences (1684), 7,
328–30.
[5] Raleigh, Works (Oxford, 1829),
viii, 556.
[6] See L. I. Bredvold, 'The

Religious Thought of John Donne in Relation to Medieval and Later Traditions', in *Studies in Shakespeare, Milton and Donne by Members of the English Department of the University of Michigan* (New York, 1925), 193–232; and 'The Naturalism of Donne in Relation to some Renaissance Traditions', *JEGP* xxii (1923), 471–502. On scepticism see Margaret L. Wiley, *The Subtle Knot: Creative Scepticism in Seventeenth Century England* (1952); Herschel Baker, *The Wars of Truth*, (New York, 1952); R. H. Popkin, *The History of Scepticism from Erasmus to Descartes* (Assen, 1964).

7 *Satires*, 46.
8 *Satires*, 191.
9 Descartes, *Discourse on Method and Other Writings*, trans. A. Wollaston (Penguin edn, 1960), 145.
10 Nietzsche, *Human, All too Human* (1878), sect. 19.
11 *Sermons* vii, 260.
12 *Satires*, 13.
13 Wiley, op. cit., 78.
14 *Epithalamions*, 48–9.
15 See Michael McCanles, 'Paradox in Donne', *Studies in the Renaissance* 13 (1966), 266–87.
16 *Elegies*, 34, 157.
17 Quoted in Baker, op. cit., 142.
18 Calvin, *Institutes*, II, i and ii.
19 R. Baxter, *The Saints Everlasting Rest*, iv, 2; Baker, op. cit., 211.
20 Grotius, *De Jure Belli ac Pacis*, sect. 16.
21 *Sermons* ix, 390; vii, 360–1.
22 *Sermons* vi, 214.
23 Sermons vi, 184, and iii, 87.
24 *Devotions*, 25 (Expostulation IV).
25 *Divine Poems*, 11.
26 *Sermons* ix, 256; ii, 308.

27 *Sermons* viii, 282; ii, 319, 334.
28 *Sermons* v, 53.
29 *Sermons* ix, 160.
30 *Divine Poems*, 8.
31 *Sermons* ii, 323; *Essays in Divinity*, 87.
32 *Sermons* vi, 188.
33 *Sermons* viii, 370.
34 *Sermons* i, 170, 175.
35 *Satires*, 31.
36 *Essays in Divinity*, 20–2.
37 *Sermons* v, 298, 47.
38 *Essays in Divinity*, 13.
39 *Divine Poems*, 19.
40 *Sermons* iii, 57.
41 *Satires*, 90.
42 *Epithalamions*, 63–4.
43 *Sermons* iii, 359.
44 J. A. Comenius, *The Great Didactic*, trans. M. W. Keatinge (2nd edn., 1910), 41.
45 *Essays in Divinity*, 56.
46 *Essays in Divinity*, 14.
47 *Epithalamions*, 49.
48 *Epithalamions*, 49.
49 Raleigh, *Works* (Oxford, 1829), ii, xlvi.
50 See D. C. Allen, *JEGP* 42 (1943), 322–42.
51 *Epithalamions*, 49.
52 *Epithalamions*, 37.
53 Foster Watson, *The Beginnings of the Teaching of Modern Subjects in England* (1909), 375–83.
54 *Du Bartas His Divine Weekes and Workes*, trans. Joshua Sylvester (1605), Week 1 Day 4, lines 155–9, 182–3.
55 *Satires*, 96.
56 Gosse i, 219.
57 *Ignatius*, 17–19.
58 *Epithalamions*, 17.
59 *The Life and Letters of Sir Henry Wotton*, ed. Logan Pearsall Smith (Oxford, 1907), i, 486–7.
60 *Elegies*, 62.
61 C. M. Coffin, *John Donne and*

the New Philosophy (New York, 1937), 123–4.

[62] *Satires*, 105 (lines 13–14).

[63] *Sermons* iii, 210.

[64] Simpson, 124–5.

[65] *Sermons* ix, 330, 305.

[66] *Sermons* vii, 396.

[67] T. S. Eliot, 'Donne in Our Time', in *A Garland for John Donne*, ed. T. J. Spencer (Cambridge, Mass., 1931), 3–19.

[68] See G. T. Buckley, *Atheism in the English Renaissance* (Chicago, 1932).

[69] Bald, 61.

[70] *Sermons* iv, 168; see Ramsay, 148 f.

[71] *Sermons* ix, 134; viii, 225.

[72] *Sermons* iv, 167.

[73] *Sermons* viii, 332–3; also iii, 257; v, 388.

[74] *Elegies*, 39–40.

[75] *Sermons* viii, 332.

[76] *Sermons* vi, 297–8.

[77] *Satires*, 81.

[78] *Devotions*, 23 (Meditation IV).

[79] See Geoffrey Bullough, *Mirrors of Minds: Changing Psychological Beliefs in English Poetry* (1962), 45–6.

9. IMAGINED CORNERS

[1] T. S. Eliot, *Selected Essays* (1932), 287.

[2] T. S. Eliot, 'Donne in Our Time', in *A Garland for John Donne*, ed. T. J. Spencer (Cambridge, Mass., 1931), 3–19.

[3] *Sermons* viii, 106.

[4] Ramsay, 178–9.

[5] Browne, *Pseudodoxia Epidemica*, ii 6; Gerard, *Herbal*, (1633), 351–2.

[6] See D. C. Allen, *JEGP* 42 (1943), 322–42; and Thomas Blount, *Glossographia*, (5th edn., 1681), under 'Mummy'

[7] *Divine Poems*, 50.

[8] Milton A. Rugoff, *Donne's Imagery: A Study in Creative Sources* (New York, 1962), 143.

[9] *Sermons* vi, 59.

[10] *Sermons* ii, 199; viii, 69; *Elegies*, 69; Gosse ii, 191.

[11] *Sermons* x, 52.

[12] G. M. Hopkins, *Poems*, ed. W. H. Gardner (Oxford, 1956), 147.

[13] *Elegies*, 15, 18, 20, 73.

[14] *Elegies*, 70.

[15] See my 'Donne and Coins' in *English Renaissance Studies in Honour of Dame Helen Gardner* (Oxford, 1980), 151–63.

[16] *Elegies*, 16.

[17] *Sermons* vii, 360; x, 116; Gosse i, 219.

[18] *Sermons* ii, 81; see also v, 347; vi, 116; and Ramsay, 250–1.

[19] *Sermons* ii, 261–2.

[20] *Elegies*, 61.

[21] *Sermons* ix, 274; iii, 112; ii, 212.

[22] *Elegies*, 37, 34.

[23] *Sermons* iii, 65; iv, 190; viii, 62; x, 52.

[24] *Sermons* vii, 280.

[25] *Elegies*, 80.

[26] *Satires*, 35

[27] *Pseudo-Martyr*, 214, 236; *Elegies*, 60, 63, 41; *Epithalamions*, 17.

[28] *Elegies*, 76.

[29] *Epithalamions*, 43.

[30] *Elegies*, 93.

[31] *Elegies*, xlvi.

[32] Johnson, *Life of Cowley*.

[33] *Elegies*, 63.

[34] D. L. Guss, *John Donne, Petrarchist* (Detroit, Mich., 1966), 73–4.

[35] *Paradoxes*, 41.

[36] *Elegies*, 11.

[37] *Satires*, 9.

[38] See Charles Webster, *The Great Instauration* (1975), 403–11.

[39] Gosse ii, 78.

[40] *Epithalamions*, 70–1.

[41] *Satires*, 26.

[42] *Divine Poems*, 50.
[43] *Divine Poems*, 29.
[44] *Elegies*, 28.
[45] *Sermons* vi, 172.
[46] *Satires*, 30.
[47] *Sermons* vi, 331.
[48] *Elegies*, 72.
[49] *Elegies*, 79.
[50] Ramsay, 206.
[51] Tertullian, *A Treatise on the Soul*, ch. 27.
[52] Milton, *Christian Doctrine*, Bk. 1, ch. 7.

[53] Gosse i, 176.
[54] See Itrat Husain, *The Dogmatic and Mystical Theology of John Donne* (1938), 77–9.
[55] *Sermons* ii, 59.
[56] *Sermons* v, 172.
[57] *Sermons* i, 177.
[58] Aquinas, *Summa Theologica*, I, Q.75, Art. 6; see 'The Good Morrow', lines 20–1, and Grierson's note.
[59] *Paradoxes*, 10.

Index